CBT

4th Edition

by Rob Willson, PhD and Rhena Branch, BSc, MSc, Dip CBT

for **dummies**®
A Wiley Brand

CBT For Dummies®, 4th edition

Published by: **John Wiley & Sons, Inc.**, 111 River Street, Hoboken, NJ 07030-5774, www.wiley.com

For general information on our other products and services, please contact our Customer Care Department within the U.S. at 877-762-2974, outside the U.S. at 317-572-3993, or fax 317-572-4002. For technical support, please visit https://hub.wiley.com/community/support/dummies.

Wiley publishes in a variety of print and electronic formats and by print-on-demand. Some material included with standard print versions of this book may not be included in e-books or in print-on-demand. If this book refers to media such as a CD or DVD that is not included in the version you purchased, you may download this material at http://booksupport.wiley.com. For more information about Wiley products, visit www.wiley.com.

Library of Congress Control Number is available from the publisher.

ISBN 978-1-394-33326-4 (pbk); ISBN 978-1-394-33328-8 (ebk); ISBN 978-1-394-33327-1 (ebk)

Printed and bound by CPI Group (UK) Ltd, Croydon, CR0 4YY

C9781394333264_271025

Contents at a Glance

Table of Contents

Introduction

Cognitive behavioral therapy, or CBT, continues to grow in popularity as an efficient and long-lasting treatment for many different types of psychological problems. CBT is the psychological treatment your doctor is most likely to offer you if you consult them about a mental health problem.

Since the COVID-19 global pandemic, the world has become more aware of the importance of mental health, but this awareness is still very far ahead of the availability of good-quality treatment. We sincerely hope that the advice in this book, taken from the leading, most proven form of psychological therapy, will make some small contribution toward offering help and guidance.

If the word *psychological* sends you running from the room screaming, try to consider the term referring to problems that affect your emotional rather than your physical sense of well-being. At some point in your life, something is going to go a bit wrong with your body and seeking help is very natural for most of us. So why on earth do humans assume that their minds and emotions should be above the odd hiccup, upset, or even more serious difficulty? Happily, fewer stigmas about mental health difficulties like anxiety and depression exist now than when this book first published in 2005.

This book offers a comprehensive introduction to the theory and application of CBT techniques. Although we don't have the space to go into nitty-gritty specifics about how to use CBT to overcome every type of emotional or psychological problem, we do try to lead you in a helpful direction by giving an overview of some of the most common problems people encounter. You may not have realized just how common mental health problems can be. We aim to help you see that you aren't alone, that there is help and that you certainly have no need to be embarrassed about seeking support! We believe all the CBT principles and strategies outlined in this book can improve your life and help you to stay healthy, regardless of whether you've worked with or are currently working with a psychiatrist or other psychological professional.

In addition, whether you think your problems are minimal, you're crushing this living thing, you feel mildly depressed, or you've had years of uncomfortable psychological symptoms, CBT can help you. We ask you to be open-minded and to use the stuff in this book to make your life better and fuller.

About This Book

If you're embarking on a journey of self-help or self-improvement, we hope that this book provides a useful introduction to CBT techniques and will be of benefit to you. This book covers the following:

>> The basics of using CBT as a scientifically tested and verified psychotherapeutic method of overcoming common emotional problems.

>> Ways in which you can identify your problems and set specific goals for how you'd rather be living your life.

>> Techniques to identify errors in the way you may be thinking and to adopt more helpful thoughts, attitudes, philosophies, and beliefs.

>> Strategies to help you keep your mental and behavioral activities healthier.

>> Behavioral experiments and strategies you can incorporate into your life to improve your day-to-day functioning.

>> Information that can help you to understand, normalize, and address some common human problems. You may think that you're the only person in the world who feels and thinks the way you do. This book shows you that many problems such as depression, anxiety, anger, and obsessions are in fact very common human experiences, so welcome to the human race! You're not alone.

We hope that the whole experience will be at least a little entertaining in the process. So read on, welcome new concepts, and consider trying some of the ideas we offer in the book.

Note: Depending on the degree of disruption and distress that your personal difficulties are causing you, this book may or may not be enough treatment to help you recover. The book may spur you on to get further help to really knock your emotional demons on the head. See Chapter 24 for tips on finding and working with a professional.

To make your reading experience easier and to alert you to key words or points, we use certain conventions.

>> *Italics* introduce new terms, underscore key differences in meaning between words, and highlight the most important aspects of a sentence or example.

>> We use the pronouns *him* and *her* interchangeably throughout the book to provide balance and promote gender equality.

>> The case studies in the book are illustrative of actual clients we have treated and aren't direct representations of any particular clients.

>> **Bold** text is used to show the action part of numbered lists.

And to make your reading experience even easier, we identify skippable material:

>> **Sidebars and the Technical Stuff icon:** Within most chapters, we include sidebars of shaded text. These sidebars contain interesting nuggets of information or occasionally expand on a topic within the chapter. Read them if they sound interesting to you and skip them if they don't. The same goes for text marked with the Technical Stuff icon.

>> **Our acknowledgments:** Probably pretty boring to the average reader.

Foolish Assumptions

In writing this little tome, we make the following assumptions about you, dear reader:

>> You're human.

>> As a human, you're likely at some stage in your life to experience some sort of emotional problem that you'd like to surmount.

>> You've heard about CBT, or are intrigued by CBT, or have had CBT suggested to you by a doctor, friend, or mental health professional as a possible treatment for your specific difficulties.

>> Even if you don't think you're particularly in need of CBT right now, you want to discover more about some of the principles outlined in this book.

>> You think that your life is absolutely fine right now, but you want to find interesting and useful information in the book that will enhance your life further.

>> You're keen to find out whether CBT may be helpful to someone close to you.

>> You're studying CBT and want to use this book as a hands-on adjunct to your training.

Icons Used in This Book

We use the following icons in this book to alert you to certain types of information that you can choose to read, commit to memory (and possibly pass on to unsuspecting friends and family), or maybe just utterly ignore:

TIP

This icon highlights practical advice for putting CBT into practice.

REMEMBER

This icon is a cheerful, if sometimes urgent, reminder of important points to take notice of.

WARNING

This icon marks out specific things to avoid or possible traps to keep your eye open for in your quest for better emotional health.

TECHNICAL STUFF

This icon highlights information that may be interesting but isn't essential for understanding the topic at hand. You can skip these bits if you like.

Beyond the Book

We made a "cheat sheet" that sums up the key points in this book; you can use it as a handy reminder or give it to anyone who might benefit from its tips.

Go to www.dummies.com and search for "Cognitive Behavioral Therapy For Dummies Cheat Sheet" and commence cheating!

Where to Go from Here

This book is written in a rough order to help you progress from the basics of CBT on to more complex techniques and ideas. However, you can read the chapters in any order you like or just hit on the ones that cover subjects you think you want to know more about.

We'd really like you to read everything in this book and then post positive reviews all over the Internet, get t-shirts printed with the title (and maybe design yourself a *CBT For Dummies* tattoo), make the cover your profile pic on social media, and scream about its virtues to random people you meet on the street. Too much? Well, failing that, just use this book as your reference guide to CBT, dipping in and out of it as and when you need to.

Have a browse through the table of contents and turn to the chapters that look as if they may offer something helpful to you and your current difficulties.

When you've used the book in one way or another, you may decide that you want to get stuck into CBT treatment with a therapist. If so, consult Chapter 24 for more advice on getting treatment.

1

Introducing CBT Basics

Chapter **1**

Discovering How Thinking and Behavior Affect Emotions

C ognitive behavioral therapy — more commonly referred to as *CBT* — focuses on the way people think and act to help them with their emotional and behavioral problems.

Many of the effective CBT practices discussed in this book should seem like common sense. In our opinion, CBT does have some straightforward and clear principles and is a largely sensible and practical approach to helping people overcome problems. However, human beings don't always act according to sensible principles, and most people find that simple solutions can be difficult to put into practice. CBT can harness your reason and good sense, helping you consistently think and act in a healthy and self-enhancing way.

In this chapter, we take you through the basic principles of CBT and show you how to use these principles to better understand yourself and your problems.

Understanding CBT

Cognitive behavioral therapy is a school of psychotherapy that aims to help people overcome their emotional problems.

>> **Cognitive** means mental processes like thinking. The word *cognitive* refers to everything that goes on in your mind, including dreams, memories, images, thoughts, and attention.

>> **Behavior** refers to everything that you do. This includes what you say, how you try to solve problems, how you act, and what you try to avoid. *Behavior* refers to both action and inaction. As an example, biting your tongue instead of speaking your mind is still a behavior even though you're trying *not* to do something.

>> **Therapy**, in this context, is a word used to describe a systematic psychological approach to combating a problem, illness, or irregular condition.

A central concept in CBT is that you feel the way you think. Therefore, CBT works on the principle that you can live more happily and productively if you're thinking in healthy ways. This principle is a simple way of summing up CBT. We have many more details to share with you later in the book.

Combining science, philosophy, and behavior

CBT is a powerful treatment because it combines scientific, philosophical, and behavioral aspects into one comprehensive approach to understanding and over-coming common psychological problems.

>> **Getting scientific.** CBT is scientific not only in the sense that it has been tested and developed through numerous scientific studies but also in the sense that it encourages clients to become more like scientists. For example, during CBT, you may develop the ability to treat your thoughts as theories and hunches about reality to be tested (what scientists call *hypotheses*) rather than as facts.

>> **Getting philosophical.** CBT recognizes that people hold values and beliefs about themselves, the world, and other people. One of the aims of CBT is to help people develop flexible, nonextreme, and self-helping beliefs that support them in adapting to reality and pursuing their goals.

Your problems aren't all just in your mind. Although CBT places great emphasis on thoughts and behavior as powerful areas to target for change and development, it also places your thoughts and behaviors within a context. CBT recognizes that you're influenced by what's going on around you and that your environment contributes toward the way you think, feel, and act. However, CBT maintains that you can make a difference in the way you feel by changing unhelpful ways of thinking and behaving — even if you can't change your environment. Incidentally, your environment in the context of CBT includes other people and the way they behave toward you. Your living situation, culture, workplace dynamics, and financial concerns are all features of your larger environment.

>> **Getting active.** As the name suggests, CBT also strongly emphasizes behavior. Many CBT techniques involve changing the way you think and feel by modifying the way you behave. Examples include gradually becoming more active if you're depressed and lethargic, or facing your fears step by step if you're anxious. CBT also emphasizes where you focus your attention. *Mental behaviors,* such as worrying and chewing over negative events, can be helped by learning to focus your attention in a more helpful direction.

Progressing from problems to goals

A defining characteristic of CBT is that it gives you the tools to develop a *focused* approach. It aims to help you move from defined emotional and behavioral problems toward your goals of how you'd like to feel and behave. Thus, CBT is a goal-directed, systematic, problem-solving approach to emotional problems.

Using Scientifically Tested Methods

The effectiveness of CBT for various psychological problems has been researched more extensively than any other psychotherapeutic approach. CBT's reputation as a highly effective treatment is based on continued research. Several studies reveal that it's more effective than medication alone for the treatment of anxiety and depression. As a result of research like this, briefer and more intense treatment methods have been developed for particular anxiety disorders such as panic, anxiety in social settings, or feeling worried all the time.

As scientific research of CBT continues, more is being discovered about which aspects of the treatment are most useful for different types of people and which therapeutic interventions work best with different types of problems.

Research shows that people who have CBT for various types of problems — in particular, for anxiety and depression — stay well for longer. This means that people who have CBT relapse less often than those who have other forms of psychotherapy or take medication only. This positive result is likely due in part to the educational aspects of CBT: People who have CBT receive a lot of information that they can use to become their own therapists.

More and more physicians and psychiatrists refer their patients for CBT to help them overcome a wide range of problems with good results. These problems include the following:

>> Addiction

>> Anger problems

>> Anxiety

>> Body dysmorphic disorder

>> Body image problems

>> Chronic fatigue syndrome

>> Chronic pain

>> Depression

>> Eating disorders

>> Gender identity and sexuality issues

>> Obsessive-compulsive disorder

>> Panic disorder

>> Personality disorders

>> Phobias

>> Post-traumatic stress disorder

>> Psychotic disorders

>> Relationship problems

>> Social anxiety

We discuss many of the disorders in the preceding list in more depth throughout this book, but it's difficult to cover them all. Fortunately, you can apply the CBT skills and techniques in this book to most types of psychological difficulties, so give them a try whether or not your particular problem is specifically discussed.

Making the Thought–Feeling Link

Like many people, you may assume that if something happens to you, the event *makes* you feel a certain way. For example, if your partner treats you inconsiderately, you may conclude that they *make* you angry. You may further deduce that their inconsiderate behavior *makes* you behave in a particular manner, such as sulking or refusing to speak to them for hours — possibly even days; people can sulk for a very long time! We illustrate this common (but incorrect) causal relationship with the idea that "A causes C." In this equation, *A* stands for a real or *actual* event, such as being rejected or losing your job. It also stands for an *activating* event that may or may not have happened. It could be a prediction about the future, such as "I'm going to get fired," or a memory of a past rejection, such as "Hilary will dump me just like Judith did ten years ago." *C* stands for *consequence*, which means the way you feel and behave in response to an actual or activating event.

> A (*actual* or *activating* event) causes C (emotional and behavioral *consequence*)

CBT encourages you to understand that your thinking or beliefs lie between the event and your ultimate feelings and actions. Your thoughts, your beliefs, and the meanings that you give to an event produce your emotional and behavioral responses.

So in CBT terms, your partner doesn't *make* you angry and sulky. Rather, your partner behaves inconsiderately, and you assign a meaning to their behavior such as "They're doing this deliberately to upset me, and they absolutely should not do this," thus *making yourself* angry and sulky. In the next formula, A × B = C, *B* stands for your *beliefs* about the event and the *meanings* you give to it.

> A (*actual* or *activating* event) × B (*beliefs* and *meanings* about the event) = C (emotional and behavioral *consequence*)

This is the formula or equation that CBT uses to make sense of your emotional problems.

Emphasizing the meanings you attach to events

The *meaning* you attach to any sort of event influences the emotional responses you have to that event. Positive events normally lead to positive feelings of happiness or excitement, whereas negative events typically lead to negative feelings like sadness or anxiety.

However, the meanings you attach to certain types of negative events may not be wholly accurate, realistic, or helpful. Sometimes your thinking may lead you to assign extreme meanings to events, leaving you feeling disturbed.

For instance, Tilda meets up with a nice man that she met on a dating app. She likes him on their first date and hopes he'll contact her for a second meeting. Unfortunately, he doesn't. After two weeks of eagerly checking her phone, Tilda gives up and becomes depressed. The fact that the man failed to ask Tilda out again *contributes* to her feeling bad. But what really leads to her acute depressed feelings is the meaning she's derived from his apparent rejection, namely, "This proves I'm old, unattractive, past it, and unwanted. I'll be sad and single for the rest of my life."

As Tilda's example shows, drawing extreme conclusions about yourself (and others and the world at large) based on singular experiences can turn a bad, distressing situation into a deeply disturbing one.

TECHNICAL
STUFF

Psychologists use the word *disturbed* to describe emotional responses that are unhelpful and cause significant discomfort to you. In CBT terminology, *disturbed* means that an emotional or behavioral response is hindering rather than helping you to adapt and cope with a negative event.

For example, if a potential girlfriend rejects you after the first date (event), you may think, "This proves I'm unlikeable and undesirable" (meaning) and feel depressed (emotion).

CBT involves identifying thoughts, beliefs, and meanings that are activated when you're feeling emotionally disturbed. If you assign less extreme, more helpful, more *accurate* meanings to negative events, you're likely to experience less extreme, less disturbing emotional and behavioral responses.

Thus, on being rejected after the first date (event), you could think, "I guess that person didn't like me that much; oh well — they're not the one for me" (meaning) and feel disappointment (emotion).

TIP

You can help yourself figure out whether the meanings you're giving to a specific negative event are causing you disturbance by answering the following questions:

>> **Is the meaning I'm giving to this event unduly extreme?** Am I taking a simple event and drawing harsh conclusions about myself (or others or the future) from it?

>> **Am I drawing global conclusions from this singular event?** Am I deciding that this one event defines me totally? Or that this specific situation indicates the course of my entire future?

>> **Is the meaning I'm assigning to this event loaded against me?** Does this meaning lead me to feel better or worse about myself? Is it spurring me on to further goal-directed action or leading me to give in and curl up?

If your answer to these questions is largely "yes," you probably are disturbing yourself needlessly about a negative event. The situation may well be negative, but your thinking is making it even worse. In Chapters 2 and 4, we guide you toward correcting disturbance–creating thinking and help you feel appropriate distress instead.

Acting out

The ways you think and feel also largely determine the way you act. If you feel depressed, you're likely to withdraw and isolate yourself. If you're anxious, you may avoid situations that you find threatening or dangerous. Your behaviors can be problematic for you in many ways, such as the following:

>> **Self-destructive behaviors,** such as excessive drinking or using drugs to quell anxiety, can cause direct physical harm.

>> **Isolating and mood-depressing behaviors,** such as staying in bed all day or not seeing your friends, increase your sense of isolation and maintain your low mood.

>> **Avoidance behaviors,** such as avoiding situations you perceive as threatening (attending a social outing, using an elevator, speaking in public), deprive you of the opportunity to confront and overcome your fears.

CONSIDER THE REACTIONS OF TEN PEOPLE

People can attach different meanings to a specific situation, resulting in the potential for a vast array of emotional reactions to one situation. For example, consider ten basically similar people who experience the same event, which is having their partner treat them inconsiderately. Potentially, they can have ten or more different emotional responses to precisely the same event, depending on how they think about the event:

● **Person 1** attaches the meaning, "That idiot has no right to treat me badly — who do they think they are?" and feels angry.

● **Person 2** thinks, "This lack of consideration means that my partner doesn't love me" and feels depressed.

(continued)

(continued)

- **Person 3** believes that "This inconsideration must mean that my partner is cheating on me with someone else" and feels jealous.

- **Person 4** thinks, "I don't deserve to be treated poorly because I always do my best to be considerate to my partner" and feels hurt.

- **Person 5** reckons the event means that "I must have done something serious to upset my partner for them to treat me like this" and feels guilty.

- **Person 6** believes that "This inconsideration is a sign that my partner is losing interest in me" and feels anxious.

- **Person 7** thinks, "Aha! Now I have a good enough reason to break up with my partner, which I've been wanting to do for ages!" and feels happy.

- **Person 8** decides the event means that "My partner has done a bad thing by treating me in this way, and I'm not prepared to put up with it" and feels annoyed.

- **Person 9** thinks, "I really wish my partner had been more considerate because we're usually highly considerate of each other" and feels disappointed.

- **Person 10** believes that "My partner must have found out something despicable about me to treat me in this way" and feels ashamed.

You can see from this example that people can assign different meanings to the same event and in turn produce different emotional responses. Some emotional responses are healthier than others; we discuss this matter in depth in Chapter 7.

Learning Your ABCs

When you start to get an understanding of your emotional difficulties, CBT encourages you to break down a specific problem you have using the *ABC format*, in which

TECHNICAL STUFF

» **A** is the *activating event*. An activating event means a real *external* event that has occurred, a future event that you anticipate occurring, or an *internal* event in your mind, such as an image, memory, or dream.

The *A* is often referred to as your *trigger*.

» **B** is your *beliefs*. Your beliefs include your thoughts; your personal rules; the demands you make on yourself, the world, and other people; and the meanings you attach to external and internal events.

>> **C** is the *consequences*. Consequences include your emotions, behaviors, and physical sensations that accompany different emotions.

Figure 1-1 shows the ABC parts of a problem in picture form.

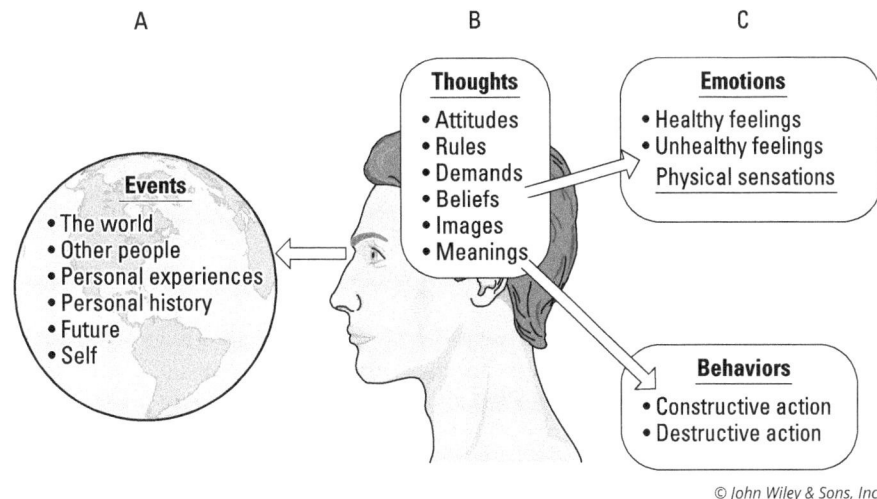

FIGURE 1-1: **A** is the activating event, **B** is your beliefs and thoughts, and **C** is the consequences, such as the emotions you feel after the event and your subsequent behavior.

Writing down your problem in *ABC form*, a central CBT self-help technique, helps you differentiate among your thoughts, feelings, and behaviors and the *trigger* event. We give more information about the ABC form in Chapter 4, and you can find a blank ABC form in Appendix B.

Consider the ABC formulations of two common emotional problems: anxiety and depression.

The ABC of anxiety may look like this:

>> **A:** You imagine failing a job interview.

>> **B:** You believe, "I've got to make sure that I don't mess up this interview; otherwise, I'll prove that I'm a failure."

>> **C:** You experience anxiety (emotion), butterflies in your stomach (physical sensation), and drinking to calm your nerves (behavior).

The ABC of depression may look like this:

>> **A:** You fail a job interview.

>> **B:** You believe, "I should've done better. This means I'm a failure!"

>> **C:** You experience depression (emotion), loss of appetite (physical sensation), staying in bed and avoiding the outside world, and drinking to quell your depressed feelings (behavior).

You can use these examples to guide you when you're filling in an ABC form on your own problems. Doing so helps ensure that you record the actual facts of the event under A, your thoughts about the event under B, and how you feel and act under C. Developing a clear ABC of your problem can make it much easier for you to realize how your thoughts at B lead to your emotional/behavioral responses at C. (Chapter 4 describes the ABC form more fully.)

Characterizing CBT

We give a much fuller description of the principles and practical applications of CBT in the rest of this book. However, here's a quick reference list of key characteristics of CBT. CBT

>> Emphasizes the role of the personal meanings you give to events in determining your emotional responses.

>> Was developed through extensive scientific evaluation.

>> Focuses more on how your problems are being maintained rather than on searching for a single root cause of the problem.

>> Offers practical advice and tools for overcoming common emotional problems. (See Chapters 10 through 18.)

>> Holds the view that you can change and develop by thinking things through and trying out new ideas and strategies. (Head to Chapter 5.)

>> Can address material from your past if doing so can help you understand and change the way you're thinking and acting now. (Chapter 19 covers this in depth.)

>> Shows you that some of the strategies you're using to cope with your emotional problems are maintaining those problems. (Chapter 8 is all about this.)

>> Strives to normalize your emotions, physical sensations, and thoughts rather than to persuade you that they're clues to "hidden" problems.

>> Recognizes that you may develop emotional problems *about* your emotional problems, such as feeling ashamed about being depressed. (See Chapter 7 for more on this concept.)

>> Highlights learning techniques and maximizes self-help so that, ultimately, you can become your own therapist. (Head to Chapter 23.)

GETTING COMPLEX

Sticking to the simple ABC formulation in which A × B = C can serve you well. But if that seems a little simplistic, you can consider the more complex formulations shown here:

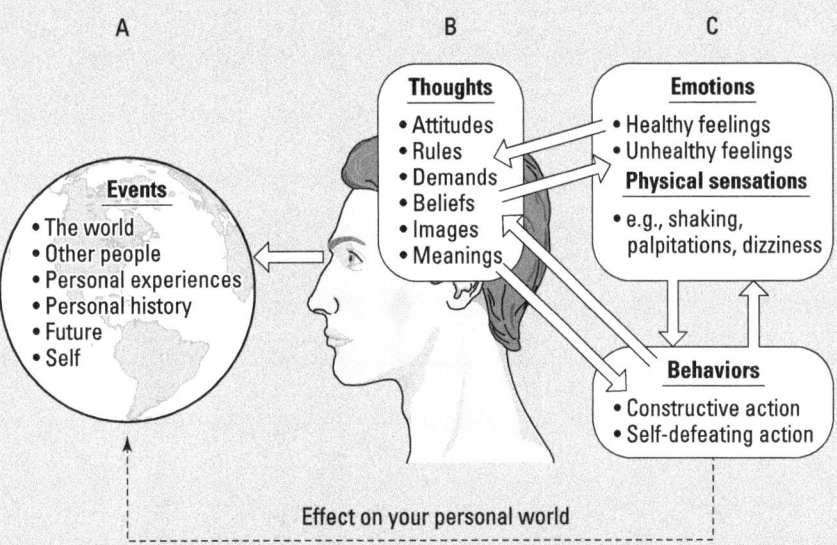

This diagram shows the complex interaction among your thoughts, feelings, and behaviors. Although your thoughts affect how you feel, your feelings also affect your thinking. So, if you're having depressed thoughts, your mood is likely to be low. The lower your mood, the more likely you are to act in a depressed manner and to think pessimistically. The combination of feeling depressed, thinking pessimistically, and acting in a depressed manner can, ultimately, influence the way you see your personal world. You may focus on negative events in your life and the world in general and therefore accumulate more negative As. This interaction among A, B, and C can become a vicious circle.

CBT pays a lot of attention to changing both unhealthy thinking patterns and unhealthy patterns of behavior.

Chapter **2**

Spotting Errors in Your Thinking

You probably don't spend a lot of time mulling over the pros and cons of the way you think. Most people don't. But to be frank, most people ought to.

One of the central messages of CBT is that your thoughts, your attitudes, and your beliefs affect the way you experience yourself, other people, and the world around you. So, if you're feeling excessively bad, chances are that you're thinking badly — or, at least, in an unhelpful way. Of course, you probably don't *intend* to think in an unhelpful way, and no doubt you're largely unaware that you do.

Thinking errors are slips in thinking that everyone makes from time to time. Just as a poor signal stops your phone from functioning effectively, thinking errors prevent you from making accurate assessments of your experiences. Thinking errors lead you to get the wrong end of the stick, jump to conclusions, and assume the worst. They get in the way of, or cause you to distort, the facts. They can act as a bias in the way you process information and end up sustaining beliefs that you hold that may not be the best for your emotional health. The good news is that you can step back and take another look at the way you're thinking and set yourself straight. In this chapter we show you how to do just that.

Months or years after the event, you've probably recalled a painful or embarrassing experience and been struck by how differently you feel about it at this later stage. Perhaps you can even laugh about the situation now. Why didn't you laugh back then? Because of the way you were thinking at the time.

To err is most definitely human. Or, as the famous American psychologist Albert Ellis is quoted as saying, "If the Martians ever find out how human beings think, they'll kill themselves laughing." Ellis made that observation back in the '60s, but not a lot has changed about our tendency to "think unhelpfully" since. By understanding the thinking errors we outline in this chapter, you can spot your unhelpful thoughts and put them straight more quickly. Get ready to identify and respond in healthier ways to some of the most common faulty and unhelpful ways of thinking that researchers and clinicians have identified.

TIP

Albert Ellis was one of the founders of what we now know as CBT. He developed a treatment for emotional disorders called *Rational Emotive Behavior Therapy*, or REBT. A long-winded name, no doubt, but it basically involves much of what's in this book. Alongside Aaron Beck, who developed cognitive therapy for the treatment of depression and later further popularized CBT, Ellis developed many of the underlying philosophical foundations that still comprise CBT today. So if you're keen on learning more about how CBT developed, look for books by Ellis and early work by Beck.

Catastrophizing: Turning Mountains Back into Molehills

Catastrophizing is taking a relatively minor negative event and imagining all sorts of disasters resulting from that one small event, as we sum up in Figure 2-1.

Consider these examples of catastrophizing:

>> You're at a party and you accidentally stumble headlong into the ice sculpture. After you slide your way across the floor and to the bathroom to clean up, you scurry home and conclude that everyone at the party witnessed your little trip and laughed at you.

>> You're waiting for your daughter to return home after an evening at the movies with friends. The clock strikes 10 p.m., and you hear no reassuring rattle of a key in the door. By 10:05 p.m., you start imagining her accepting a lift home from a friend who drives recklessly. At 10:10 p.m., you're convinced she's been involved in a head-on collision and paramedics are at the scene. By 10:15 p.m., you're weeping over her grave in your mind.

FIGURE 2-1:
Catastrophizing.

© John Wiley & Sons, Inc.

>> Your new partner declines an invitation to have dinner with your parents. Before giving them a chance to explain their reasons, you put down the phone and decide that this is just their way of telling you the relationship's over. Furthermore, you imagine them phoning friends and telling them what a mistake it was dating you. You decide you're never going to find another partner and will die old and lonely.

Catastrophizing leads many an unfortunate soul to misinterpret a social faux pas as a social disaster, a late arrival as a car accident, and a minor disagreement as total rejection.

Nip catastrophic thinking in the bud by recognizing it for what it is — just thoughts. When you find yourself thinking of the worst possible scenario, try the following strategies:

>> **Put your thoughts in perspective.** Even if everyone at the party did see your ice-scapade, are you sure no one was sympathetic? Surely you aren't the only person in the world to have tripped in public. Chances are, people are far less interested in your embarrassing moment than you think. Falling at a party isn't great, but in the grand scheme of things it's hardly newsworthy.

>> **Consider less terrifying explanations.** What other reasons are there for your daughter being late? Isn't being late for curfew a common feature of adolescence? Perhaps the film ran over or she got caught up chatting and forgot the time. Don't get so absorbed in extreme emotions that you're startled to find your daughter in the doorway apologizing about missing the bus.

>> **Weigh the evidence.** Do you have enough information to conclude that your partner wants to leave you? Has he given you any reason to think this before? Look for evidence that contradicts your catastrophic assumption. For example, have you had more enjoyable times together than not? Isn't dinner with the parents something a lot of partners may want to avoid due to nerves or something else?

>> **Focus on what you can do to cope with the situation and the people or resources that can come to your aid.** Engaging in a few more social encounters can help you put your party faux pas behind you. You can repair a damaged relationship — or find another. Even an injury following an accident can be fixed with medical care.

REMEMBER

No matter how great a calamity you create in your mind, the world's unlikely to end even if your catastrophic fear comes to pass. You're probably far more capable of surviving embarrassing and painful events than you give yourself credit for. Human beings are resilient. Often people say that they can't imagine dealing with a tragedy like losing a loved one or perhaps developing a terminal illness even when they know other people just like them who are dealing with those tragedies. You don't always need to be able to imagine coping with a negative event to be able to do so if the time comes. Sometimes you just need to have faith that your coping resources will be there when you need them.

All-or-Nothing Thinking: Finding Somewhere in Between

All-or-nothing or *black-or-white thinking* (see Figure 2-2) is extreme thinking that can lead to extreme emotions and behaviors. People either love you or hate you, right? Something's either perfect or a disaster. You're either responsibility-free or totally to blame. Sound sensible? We hope not!

Unfortunately, humans fall into the all-or-nothing trap all too easily:

>> Imagine you're trying to eat healthily, and you cave in to the temptation of a donut. All-or-nothing thinking may lead you to conclude that your plan is in ruins and convince you to eat the other 11 donuts in the pack.

>> You're in a degree program and you fail one test. All-or-nothing thinking makes you decide that the whole endeavor is pointless. Either you get the course totally right or it's just a write-off.

FIGURE 2-2:
All-or-nothing
thinking.

© John Wiley & Sons, Inc.

>> You're trying to overcome a degree of social anxiety or shyness and notice that you tend to worry a lot about people judging you negatively. You try to overcome this by following the (often given, far too all-or-nothing) advice to "not care what people think."

TIP

Consider the humble thermometer as your guide to overcoming the tendency of all-or-nothing thinking. A thermometer reads degrees of temperature, not just hot and cold. Think like a thermometer — in degrees, not extremes. You can use the following pointers to help you change your thinking:

>> **Be realistic.** You can't possibly get through life without making mistakes. One donut doesn't ruin a healthy diet. Remind yourself of your goal, forgive yourself for the minor slip, and resume your diet.

>> **Develop both–and reasoning skills.** An alternative to all-or-nothing thinking is *both–and reasoning*. You need to mentally allow two seeming opposites to exist together. You can *both* succeed in your overall educational goals *and* fail a test or two. Life isn't a case of being either a success or a failure. You can *both* assume that you're an okay person as you are *and* strive to change.

>> **Draw out a continuum.** If you notice that you tend to think in an all-or-nothing fashion about something and this causes you significant trouble, it's worth drawing out a continuum as a scale (literally a line drawn across a piece of paper) that plots out the concept 0 to 100. For example, seeing where your success truly lies on a scale of 0 to 100 success rather than binary "If I don't succeed at this, then I'm a failure" can be significantly more helpful. You can do the same for love, intelligence, likability, singing ability — you name it!

All-or-nothing thinking can sabotage goal-directed behavior. You're far more likely to throw in the towel at the first sign of something blocking your goal when you refuse to allow a margin for error. Beware of either-or statements and global labels such as "good" and "bad" or "success" and "failure." Neither people nor life situations are often that cut and dried.

Fortune-Telling: Stepping Away from the Crystal Ball

Often, clients tell us after they've done something they were anxious about that the actual event wasn't half as bad as they'd predicted. Predictions are the problem here. You probably don't possess extrasensory perceptions that allow you to see into the future. You probably can't see into the future even with the aid of a crystal ball like the one in Figure 2-3. And yet, you may try to predict future events. Unfortunately, the predictions you make may be unduly negative:

>> You've been feeling a bit depressed lately and you aren't enjoying yourself like you used to. Someone from work invites you to a party, but you decide that if you go you won't have a good time. The food will be unpalatable, the music will be irksome, and the other guests are sure to find you boring. So, you opt to stay in and bemoan the state of your social life.

>> You have a thing for the person who sells you coffee every morning on the way to the office, and you'd like to go out with them on a date. You predict that if you ask, you'll be so anxious that you'll say something stupid. Anyway, they're bound to say "no thanks" — someone that attractive must surely be in a relationship.

>> You've been thinking that pickleball would be fun, but you have an anxious disposition. If you try the sport, you're sure to lose your nerve at a crucial moment and just end up with a bruised ego and a physical injury.

You're better off letting the future unfold without trying to guess how it may turn out. Put the dustcover back on the crystal ball, flog the Ouija board on eBay, leave the tarot cards alone, and try the following strategies instead:

>> **Test out your predictions.** You really never know how much fun you might have at a party until you get there — and the food could be amazing. Maybe the guy at the coffee shop has a partner, but you won't be sure until you ask. To find out more about testing your predictions, read Chapter 5.

FIGURE 2-3: Fortune-telling.

>> **Be prepared to take risks.** Isn't it worth possibly sustaining a few bruises for the opportunity to try a sport you've been eyeing? And can't you bear the possibility of appearing a trifle nervous for the chance to get to know someone you really like? There's a saying that "a ship is safe in a harbor, but that's not what ships are built for." Learning to live experimentally and taking calculated risks is a recipe for keeping life interesting and rewarding.

>> **Understand that your past experiences don't determine your future experiences.** Just because the last party you went to turned out to be a dreary homage to the seventies, the last person you asked out went a bit green, and that scuba-diving venture resulted in a severe case of the bends doesn't mean that you'll never have better luck again.

REMEMBER

Often, fortune-telling stops you from acting. It can also become a bit of a self-fulfilling prophecy. If you keep telling yourself that you won't enjoy that party, you're liable to make that prediction come true. Same goes for meeting new people and trying new things. So, get your party on, ask the coffee guy out for a drink, and turn up at your local pickleball court!

Mind Reading: Taking Your Guesses with a Pinch of Salt

So, you think you know what other people are thinking, do you? With *mind reading* (see Figure 2-4), the tendency is to assume that others are thinking negative things about you or have negative motives and intentions.

FIGURE 2-4:
Mind reading.

© *John Wiley & Sons, Inc.*

Here are some examples of mind-reading tendencies:

>> You're chatting with someone, and they look over your shoulder as you're speaking, break eye contact, and (perish the thought) yawn. You conclude immediately that the other person thinks your conversation is mind-numbing and that they'd rather be talking to someone else.

>> Your boss advises that you book some time off to use up your vacation time. You decide that they're saying this because they think your work is rubbish and want the opportunity to interview for your replacement while you're away.

>> You pass a neighbor on the street. They say a quick hello but don't look very friendly or pleased to see you. You think that they must be annoyed with you about your dog howling at the last full moon and are making plans to report you to the city.

You can never know for certain what another person is thinking, so you're wise to ignore your negative assumptions. Stand back and look at all the evidence on hand. Take control of your tendency to mind read by trying the following:

>> **Generate some alternative reasons for what you see.** The person you're chatting with may be tired, be preoccupied with their own thoughts, or have just spotted someone they know.

>> **Consider that your guesses may be wrong.** Are your fears really about your boss's motives, or do they concern your own insecurity about your abilities at work? Do you have enough information or hard evidence to conclude that your boss thinks your work is substandard? Does it follow logically that "consider booking time off" means "you're getting canned"?

>> **Get more information (if appropriate).** Ask your neighbor whether your dog kept them up all night, and talk to your vet about ways to calm your pet the next time the moon waxes.

>> **Become familiar with your own mind-reading bias and learn to correct for it.** The conclusions to which you tend to leap about what other people are thinking will often form an unhelpful habit. If you know that you're prone to assuming people are judging you negatively, it can help to practice assuming people are judging you favorably.

REMEMBER

You tend to mind read what you fear most. What you project or imagine is going on in other people's minds is based on what's already in yours.

Emotional Reasoning: Reminding Yourself That Feelings Aren't Facts

Surely we're wrong about this one and your feelings are hard evidence of the way things are. You've heard that it's good to trust your instincts. Well, that depends. Sometimes using your feelings as a guide leads you off the healthy path. Here are some examples of emotional reasoning:

>> Your partner has been spending long nights at the office with a coworker for the past month. You feel jealous and suspicious of your partner. Based on these feelings, you conclude that your partner's having an affair with their coworker.

>> You feel guilty out of the blue, so you conclude that you must have done something wrong.

>> You wake up feeling anxious, with a vague sense of dread. You assume that there must be something seriously wrong in your life and search your mind frantically for the source of your ill feeling.

Often your feelings are simply due to a thought or memory that you may not be aware of having. Other times they can be symptoms of a condition such as depression or anxiety problems. (See Chapter 10 for information about anxiety disorders and Chapter 11 for more on depression.) Some of the feelings you experience on waking are left over from dreams that you may or may not remember. As a rule of thumb, it pays to be somewhat skeptical about the validity of your feelings in the first instance. Your feelings can be misleading, so it's worth being aware of your tendencies so you can counter them.

When you spot emotional reasoning taking over your thoughts, take a step back and try the following:

1. **Take notice of your thoughts.**

   Take notice of thoughts such as, "I'm feeling nervous; something must be wrong" and, "I'm so angry, and that really shows how badly you've behaved." Recognize that feelings aren't always the best measure of reality, especially when you're not in the best emotional shape.

2. **Ask yourself how you'd view the situation if you were feeling calmer.**

   Look to see if any concrete evidence supports your interpretation of your feelings. For example, is there really any evidence that something bad is going to happen?

3. **Give yourself time to allow your feelings to subside.**

   When you're feeling calmer, review your conclusions and remember that it's possible that your feelings are the consequence of your present emotional state (or even just fatigue) rather than reliable indicators of the state of reality.

4. **If you can't find any obvious and immediate source of your unpleasant feelings, overlook them.**

   Get into the shower despite your sense of dread, for example. If a concrete reason to be anxious does exist, it won't be dissolved in the shower. If your anxiety is all smoke and mirrors, you may well find it washes down the drain.

REMEMBER

The problem with viewing your feelings as factual is that you stop looking for contradictory information — or for any additional information at all. Balance your emotional reasoning with a little more looking at the facts that support and contradict your views, as we show in Figure 2-5.

FIGURE 2-5: Emotional reasoning.

© John Wiley & Sons, Inc.

Overgeneralizing: Avoiding the Part/Whole Error

Overgeneralizing is the error of drawing global conclusions from one or more events. When you find yourself thinking "always," "never," "people are . . .," or "the world's . . .," you may well be overgeneralizing. Check out Figure 2-6. Here, our stick man sees one sheep in a flock and instantly assumes the whole flock of sheep is black. However, his overgeneralization is inaccurate because the rest of the flock are white sheep.

FIGURE 2-6:
Overgeneralizing.

© *John Wiley & Sons, Inc.*

You might recognize overgeneralizing in the following examples:

» You feel down. When you get into your car to go to work, it doesn't start. You think to yourself, "Things like this are always happening to me. Nothing ever goes right," which makes you feel even more gloomy.

» You become angry easily. Traveling to see a friend, you're delayed by a fellow passenger who can't find the money to pay her train fare. You think, "This is typical! Other people are so stupid," and you become tense and angry.

» You tend to feel guilty easily. You yell at your child for not understanding his homework and then decide that you're a thoroughly rotten parent.

Situations are rarely so stark or extreme that they merit terms like "always" and "never." Rather than overgeneralizing, consider the following:

>> **Get a little perspective.** How true is the thought that nothing *ever* goes right for you? How many other people in the world may be having car trouble at this precise moment?

>> **Suspend judgment.** When you judge all people as stupid, including the poor creature waiting in line for the train, you make yourself more outraged and are less able to deal effectively with a relatively minor hiccup.

>> **Be specific.** Would you be a *totally* rotten parent for losing patience with your child? Can you legitimately conclude that one incident of poor parenting cancels out all the good things you do for your little one? Perhaps your impatience is simply an area you need to target for improvement.

REMEMBER

Shouting at your child in a moment of stress no more makes you a rotten parent than singing them a favorite lullaby makes you a perfect parent. Condemning yourself based on making a mistake does nothing to solve the problem, so be specific and steer clear of global conclusions. Change what you think you *can* and *need* to, but also forgive yourself and others for singular errors or misdeeds.

Labeling: Developing Self-Acceptance

Labels, and the process of labeling people and events, are everywhere. For example, people who have low self-esteem may label themselves as "worthless," "inferior," or "inadequate" (see Figure 2-7).

FIGURE 2-7:
Labeling.

© *John Wiley & Sons, Inc.*

If you label other people as "no good" or "useless," you're likely to become angry with them. Or perhaps you label the world as "unsafe" or "totally unfair." The error here is that you're globally rating things that are too complex for a definitive label. The following are examples of labeling:

>> You read a distressing article in the newspaper about a rise in crime in your city. The article activates your belief that you live in a thoroughly dangerous place, which contributes to your feelings of anxiety about going out.

>> You receive a bad grade for an essay. You start to feel low and label yourself as a failure.

>> You become angry when someone cuts in front of you on the highway. You label the other driver as a total loser for his bad driving.

Strive to avoid labeling yourself, other people, and the world around you. Accept that they're complex and ever-changing. (See Chapter 12 for more on this.) Recognize evidence that doesn't fit your labels to help you weaken your conviction in your global rating. For example,

>> **Allow for varying degrees.** Think about it: The world isn't a dangerous place but rather a place that has many different aspects with varying degrees of safety and risk.

>> **Celebrate complexities.** All human beings — you included — are unique, multifaceted, and ever-changing. Labeling yourself as a failure on the strength of one failing is an extreme form of overgeneralizing. Likewise, other people are just as complex and unique as you. One bad action doesn't equal a bad person.

When you label a person or aspect of the world in a global way, you exclude potential for change and improvement. Accepting yourself as you are is a powerful first step toward self-improvement.

Making Demands: Thinking Flexibly

Albert Ellis, founder of rational emotive behavior therapy, one of the first cognitive-behavioral therapies, places demands at the heart of emotional problems. Thoughts and beliefs that contain words like "must," "should," "need," "ought," "got to," and "have to" are often problematic because they're extreme and rigid (see Figure 2-8).

FIGURE 2-8:
Demands.

© John Wiley & Sons, Inc.

The inflexibility of the demands you place on yourself, the world around you, and other people often means you don't adapt to reality as well as you could. Consider these possible examples:

>> You believe that you *must* have the approval of your friends and colleagues. This leads you to feel anxious in many social situations and drives you to try to win everyone's approval — possibly at great personal cost.

>> You think that because you try hard to be kind and considerate to others, they really *ought* to be just as kind and considerate in return. Because your demand isn't realistic — sadly, other people are governed by their own priorities — you often feel hurt about your friends (or even strangers) not acting the way you do yourself.

>> You believe that you *absolutely should* never let people down. Therefore, you rarely put your own welfare first. At work, you do more than your fair share because you don't assert yourself, and you often end up feeling stressed and depressed.

Holding *flexible preferences* about yourself, other people, and the world in general is the healthy alternative to inflexible rules and demands. Rather than making demands on yourself, the world, and others, try the following techniques:

>> **Pay attention to language.** Replace words like "must," "need," and "should" with "prefer," "wish," and "want."

>> **Limit approval seeking.** Can you manage to have a satisfying life even if you don't get the approval of everyone you seek it from? Specifically, you'll feel more confident in social situations if you recognize your *preference* for approval rather than viewing approval as a dire need.

>> **Understand that the world doesn't play to your rules.** In fact, other people tend to have their own rulebooks. So, no matter how much you value considerate behavior, your friends may not give it the same value. If you can give others the right to not live up to your standards, you'll feel less hurt when they fail to do so.

>> **Retain your standards, ideals, and preferences and ditch your rigid demands about how you, others, and the world "have to" be.** So keep acting consistently with how you *would like* things to be rather than becoming depressed or irate about things not being the way you believe they *must* be.

REMEMBER

When you hold rigid demands about the way things "must be," you have no margin for deviation or error. You leave yourself vulnerable to experiencing exaggerated emotional disturbance when things in life just don't go your way. Being flexible doesn't mean becoming a pushover. It's part of maintaining good psychological health. In nature, trees that bend a little survive a storm better than those that are rigid.

Mental Filtering: Keeping an Open Mind

Mental filtering is a bias in the way you process information, in which you acknowledge only information that fits with a belief you hold. The process is much like a filter on a camera lens that allows in only certain kinds of light. Information that doesn't fit tends to be ignored. If you think any of the following, you're making the "mental filtering" thinking error:

>> You believe you're a failure, so you tend to focus on your mistakes at work and overlook successes and achievements. At the end of the week, you often feel disappointed about your lack of achievement — but this is probably largely the result of you not paying attention to your successes.

>> You believe you're unlikeable and really notice each time your friend is late to call back or seems too busy to see you. You tend to disregard the ways in which people act warmly toward you, thus sustaining your view that you're unlikeable.

To combat mental filtering, look more closely at situations you feel down about. Deliberately collecting evidence that contradicts your negative thoughts can help you correct your information-processing bias. Try the following:

>> **Examine your filters closely.** For example, are you sifting your achievements through an "I'm a failure" filter? If so, then only failure-related information gets

through. If you look for a *friend's* achievements over the same week *without* a filter, you're likely to find him in far greater possession of success. So drop the filter when assessing yourself in the same way you do when looking at your friends' achievements.

>> **Gather evidence.** Imagine you're collecting evidence for a court case to prove that your negative thought isn't true. What evidence do you cite? Would, for example, an assertion that you're unlikeable stand up in court against the proof of your friends behaving warmly toward you?

REMEMBER

If you only ever take in information that fits with your negative thinking, you can easily end up reinforcing undesirable thinking habits. The fact that you don't see the positive stuff about yourself, or your experiences, doesn't mean it isn't there. (Just bear in mind Figure 2-9!)

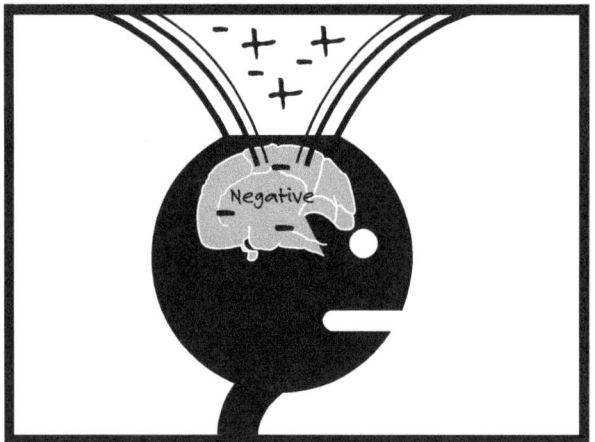

FIGURE 2-9:
Mental filtering.

© *John Wiley & Sons, Inc.*

Disqualifying the Positive: Keeping the Baby and Throwing Out the Bathwater

Disqualifying the positive (see Figure 2-10) is related to the biased way that people can process information. Disqualifying the positive is a mental response to a positive event that transforms it into a neutral or negative event.

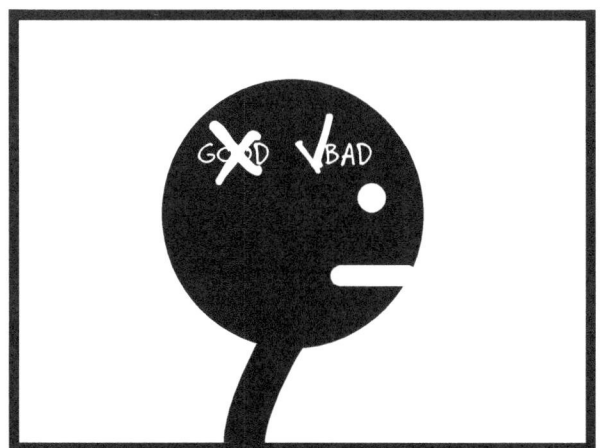

FIGURE 2-10:
Disqualifying the
positive.

© John Wiley & Sons, Inc.

The following are examples of disqualifying the positive:

>> You believe that you're worthless and unlovable. You respond to a work promotion by thinking, "This doesn't count because anyone could get this sort of thing." The result: Instead of feeling pleased, you feel quite disappointed.

>> You think you're pathetic and feel low. A friend tells you you're a very good friend, but you disqualify this in your mind by thinking, "They're only saying that because they feel sorry for me. I really am pathetic."

Hone your skills for accepting compliments and acknowledging your good points. You can try the following strategies to improve your skills:

>> **Become aware of your responses to positive "data."** Practice acknowledging and accepting positive feedback and acknowledging good points about yourself, others, and the world. For example, you could override your workplace disappointment by recognizing that *you're* the one who got the promotion. You can even consider that the promotion may well have been a result of your hard work. Use a notebook (or a suitable app) to log the positive data that you tend to overlook, and get into the habit of deliberately looking out for that data!

>> **Practice accepting a compliment graciously with a simple thank-you.** Rejecting a sincerely delivered compliment is rather like turning down a gift. Steer your thinking toward taking in positive experiences. When others point out attributes you have, start deliberately making a note of those good points. Even if your current thinking bias leads you to doubt the validity of a compliment or good experience, try considering that you may well be wrong to do so. Trust what others say for a change!

REMEMBER

If you frequently disqualify or distort your positive attributes or experiences, you can easily sustain a negative belief, even in the face of overwhelming positive evidence.

Low Frustration Tolerance: Choosing to Tolerate Discomfort When It's Good for You

Low frustration tolerance refers to the error of rating something that's difficult to tolerate as "intolerable." This thinking error means magnifying discomfort and not tolerating temporary discomfort when it's in your interest to do so for longer-term benefit, as we show in Figure 2-11.

FIGURE 2-11: Low frustration tolerance.

© *John Wiley & Sons, Inc.*

The following are examples of low frustration tolerance:

>> You often procrastinate on college assignments, thinking, "It's just too much hassle. I'll do it later when I feel more in the mood." You tend to wait until the assignment is nearly due and it becomes too uncomfortable to put off any longer. Unfortunately, waiting until the last moment means that you can rarely put as much time and effort into your coursework as you need to in order to reach your potential.

>> You want to overcome your anxiety of traveling away from home by facing your fear directly. And yet, each time you try to travel farther on the bus, you become anxious, and think, "This is so horrible; I can't stand it," and quickly return home, which reinforces your fear rather than helping you experience travel as less threatening.

>> You feel angry with someone. You fear that if you don't get it off your chest it will just keep building up, so you let them have it! The problem is that not tolerating that emotional discomfort long enough for it to lose its sharp edge can mean communicating in a way you might regret.

The best way to overcome low frustration tolerance is to foster an alternative attitude of *high frustration tolerance*. You can achieve this way of thinking by trying the following:

>> **Pushing yourself to do things that are uncomfortable or unpleasant.** For example, you can train yourself to work on assignments even if you aren't in a good mood. Finishing work in good time, and to a good standard, outweighs the hassle of doing something you find tedious.

>> **Giving yourself messages that emphasize your ability to withstand pain.** To combat a fear of travel, you can remind yourself that feeling anxious is unpleasant, but you can stand it. Ask yourself whether, in the past, you've ever withstood the feelings you're saying you presently "can't stand."

>> **Experiment with tolerating your frustration to see if it can help you gain more control over your emotions.** Your emotional system is an amazing thing, but sometimes it needs a bit of guidance and regulation.

REMEMBER

Telling yourself you can't stand something has two effects. First, it leads you to focus more on the discomfort you're experiencing. Second, it leads you to underestimate your ability to cope with discomfort. Many things can be difficult to tolerate, but rating them as "intolerable" often makes situations seem more daunting than they really are.

Personalizing: Removing Yourself from the Center of the Universe

Personalizing involves interpreting events as being related to you personally and overlooking other factors. This can lead to emotional difficulties, such as feeling hurt easily or feeling unnecessarily guilty (see Figure 2-12).

FIGURE 2-12:
Personalizing.

© John Wiley & Sons, Inc.

Here are some examples of personalizing:

>> You may tend to feel guilty if you know a friend is upset and you can't make them better. You think, "If I was really a good friend, I'd be able to cheer them up. I'm obviously letting them down."

>> You feel hurt when a friend you meet in a shop leaves quickly after saying only a hurried "hello." You think, "They were obviously trying to avoid talking to me. I must have offended them somehow."

You can tackle personalizing by considering alternative explanations that don't revolve around you. Think about the following examples:

>> **Imagine what else may contribute to the outcome you're assuming personal responsibility for.** Your friend may have lost their job or be suffering from depression. Despite your best efforts to cheer them up, these factors are outside your control.

>> **Consider why people may be responding to you in a certain way.** Don't jump to the conclusion that someone's response relates directly to you. For example, your friend may be having a difficult day or be in a big hurry. They may even feel sorry for not stopping to talk to you.

REMEMBER

We tend to greatly underestimate how much other people have going on, making it all too easy to assume things are happening because of us. Because you really aren't the center of the universe, look for explanations of events that have little or nothing to do with you.

GETTING INTIMATE WITH YOUR THINKING

Figuring out which thinking errors you tend to make the most can be a useful way of making your CBT self-help more efficient and effective. The simplest way of doing this is to record your thoughts whenever you feel upset and note what was happening at the time. Remember the maxim: When you feel bad, put your thoughts on the pad! See Chapter 4 for more on managing unhelpful thoughts by writing them down or recording them on your phone or tablet.

You can then review your thoughts against the list of thinking errors in this chapter. Write down beside each unhelpful thought the specific thinking error you're probably making. With practice you can get better at spotting your thinking errors and challenging them. You may notice that you're more prone to making some errors than others, which can let you know which alternative styles of thinking to develop.

You may also become aware of patterns or themes in the kinds of situations or events that trigger your negative thoughts. These can help you focus on the areas in which your thoughts, beliefs, and attitudes need the most work.

Chapter **3**

Observing Overthinking

This chapter is all about the processes of overworking your mind and getting stuck with your worries or regrets going around and around in your mind. Chapter 2 covers many of the key ways we think that can bias the way we process experiences. This chapter focuses on the common processes of thinking associated with common mental health problems.

Some problems have obvious overthinking placed at the heart of the problem, with obsessive-compulsive disorder (OCD) being perhaps the most obvious example. *Health anxiety* (or illness anxiety disorder) is a preoccupation with a fear that one is or may become ill. Similarly, *body dysmorphic disorder* (BDD) is a preoccupation with perceived flaws in one's appearance. In fact, one indicator that preoccupation with appearance has become excessive is that it's on the person's mind for more than an hour a day.

With other problems, overthinking may not be so immediately obvious, but its role is hugely important. Worrying about life situations like school or work is at the core of *generalized anxiety disorder* (GAD). GAD is one of the most common mental health problems. It causes anxiety (obviously), fatigue, muscle tension, sleep problems, and irritability. The field has benefited hugely from the work of researchers like Adrian Wells and Mark Freeston to really sharpen our understanding of worry.

When people become depressed, they often *ruminate* — chewing things over again and again in their minds. They dwell on events and regrets, as well as their depression itself, forming a negative cycle that can keep low mood going and even worsen it. The work of Ed Watkins has been hugely helpful in furthering our understanding and treatment of rumination.

What's interesting about helping people with their mental activities is that they often report one of three things:

>> I thought I was the only one who did this.

>> I assumed everyone did this as much as I do.

>> I know I shouldn't do this so much, but I really don't think I can control it.

The reality is that the mental activities presented here are common, can have a surprisingly harmful effect on your mood, and, thankfully, are very much possible to change.

Have you ever noticed that the more time you spend overthinking, worrying about a problem, the harder it is to keep things in perspective? Deloading your mind can be an important step in allowing your nervous system to restore its calm and help you think more realistically and constructively.

TIP

Try to spot when and where you tend to overthink. This will help you avoid the rabbit hole by deliberately choosing to redirect your mind.

Worrying: Managing Mental Preparation and Living with Uncertainty

Human beings worry when two psychological factors interact. The first factor is our brain's remarkable ability to think beyond what we can see, to consider "what if . . . ." This is incredible in terms of creativity and planning. It may also have helped human beings stay safe by enabling them to think about possible threats and consider potential responses. The second factor is planning, analyzing, trying to work out solutions, and attempting to figure out answers.

The snag is that we live in a complex and uncertain world, and it's often not possible to plan, prepare, and find a solution or answer. Frequently, as soon as we think we've planned for how to deal with a future situation, another possibility, twist, or turn will occur to our creative mind. So when a creative, imaginative, safety-seeking mind interacts with intolerance of uncertainty, worry and anxiety can result.

To break free from worry, it's important to learn to live with (and even embrace) uncertainty and to avoid trying to remove it by overthinking. It can also help to try to solve a problem only when you're in the right time and place. For example, aim to solve work problems at your desk during work hours rather than when you're lying in bed and really wanting to sleep.

TIP

You can't help but have concerns and problems crossing your mind; that's completely normal. However, you can limit the extent to which you follow the concern and start working on solving it. Another classic strategy for managing worry, often employed by students preparing for exams, is to take a *worry break*, which involves setting aside a few minutes each day to focus on worry and then moving on.

REMEMBER

Worrying is a normal and natural process, but it's also one that you don't want to become excessive. That said, it's important not to worry about your worry. Some people end up fearing that all their worrying will make them ill or drive them crazy. Keep worry in perspective and try not to catastrophize about it since that only serves to increase your anxiety. With steady patience and practice, there's every chance that you will break free from excessive worry.

Ruminating and Dwelling: Freeing Yourself from Unanswerable Questions and Toxic Regret

Ruminating can really fuel feelings of hopelessness and helplessness, thus powerfully maintaining depression. Here are some examples of ruminative thinking:

>> Why did this happen to me?

>> Why can't I just pull myself together?

>> Why does this keep happening?

>> Why can't I just stop it?

>> What does this mean about my life, my future?

>> What does this say about me?

>> What's wrong with me?

>> Why can't I cope like other people seem to?

>> If only things had turned out differently.

>> If only I/they had done X rather than Y.

TIP

Breaking out of rumination can be tough and is, at least in part, driven by the emotional state of feeling depressed. If you're feeling persistently low in mood, consider gradually "activating" yourself by using a timetable to restore regular eating and sleeping patterns, as well as counteracting any patterns of avoidance or inactivity. See Chapter 11 for more on defeating depression.

Beyond planning and preparing for your rumination hotspots across the day and having activities planned to help you interrupt your ruminating (more on this below), it can help to practice anti-rumination, action-focused thinking, like:

>> What was the sequence of events that led to this problem?

>> What resources can I use to help me tackle this?

>> What might someone else do to cope or improve the situation?

>> How can I solve this?

>> What would the first steps be?

>> How can I get started on tackling this problem?

>> What can I do right now to start solving the problem?

TIP

Like most things in life, you'll find that you'll get better at switching from one mode of thinking to the other with practice. A tip is to look back at past moments when you've ruminated and practice switching from "why?" or "if only" to "how can I?" and "what's the first step?"

REMEMBER

One of the traps of ruminating when your mood is low is that it can feel legitimate and authentic. This is because the style of thinking flows naturally from your mood. Keep in mind that this is part of emotional reasoning and that, in this case, the fact that it "feels right" is misleading.

Mental Reviewing: Keeping Your Focus on the Here-and-Now

In Chapter 18, we introduced some of the key elements of social and performance anxiety. Mental reviewing is an important activity in this problem area, which is sometimes called a *postmortem*. This means reviewing a conversation, a presentation, a meeting, a date, or even your dancing at a party. The list could go on. You don't have to have full-blown social anxiety for this to be a problem. It can be common even when people feel a bit out of their social or work comfort zone.

The problem is that your review will likely be negatively biased by embarrassment, self-criticism, and concerns about how others perceive you. This, in turn, will fuel your negative view of yourself as a "social entity" and then prime the pump for you to feel anxious in the next similar situation. And that means you're likely to be self-conscious again, which will mean you're likely to feel compelled to review again. We could go on.

Try to pay attention to your reviewing after a social, work, or academic encounter. Can you think of a time when it has really helped you? Even if you answer no, it's well worth doing a cost-benefit analysis on the pros and cons to give your mind a boost to not fall into the trap.

Thought Suppression: Letting Thoughts and Images Take Care of Themselves

"Try not to think about it" can be particularly tricky advice. Taking your mind off a problem for a while by refocusing or using a distraction might be just what your mind needs. However, trying hard *not* to think about something — an unwanted thought, image, or memory, for example — can sometimes backfire. Experiments have shown that this rebound effect can increase the frequency and intrusiveness of unwanted and suppressed thoughts. Consider what it's like when you have an *earworm* — an annoying tune that you can't get out of your head. The harder you try, the less able you are to push it out of your mind.

REMEMBER

Observations about suppression are nothing new. Famous Russian novelist Fyodor Mikhailovich Dostoevsky (1821-1881) described his brother being perplexed for some time over the challenge not to think of a white bear.

The answer is to take a leaf out of the book(s) on mindfulness meditation and practice detached observation and redirecting your attention. This allows your mind to take care of the thought or image as you allow it to be in your mind and then gently fade away of its own accord.

Comparing: Being the One Unique You

The quote "comparison is the thief of joy," attributed to the 26th president of the United States, Theodore Roosevelt, captures the idea that repeatedly comparing yourself to others can lead to unhappiness and dissatisfaction. The problem here is that your brain very often tends to notice the gap between you and another, and you come off worse. Your focus on what you lack or perceive as a shortcoming leads to feelings of inadequacy and envy. You might get a temporary boost from what's called *downward comparing* (where you see yourself as better off in some way), but even that keeps you in the toxic rating and comparing game. Comparing doesn't only steal your joy, but delivers anxiety, depression, and low self-esteem.

We've had evidence of the impact of comparing in body dysmorphic disorder (BDD) for many years. We've also known for a long time that it can be corrosive for self-esteem and life satisfaction. However, it's relatively less well described in the literature on therapy and coaching, which is an oversight. Human beings have always compared themselves to one another, but social media makes it alarmingly too easy, especially against filtered and curated images. So if you struggle to believe you're good enough, consider whether comparing might be a problem for you.

Alongside the mental activity management plan outlined below, here are some thoughts on combating comparing:

>> Focus on accepting yourself, and value your own unique blend of strengths, qualities, values, and preferences. To quote Judy Garland, "Always be a first-rate version of yourself instead of a second-rate version of somebody else." Let's face it: She knew the right road to follow.

>> Practice gratitude for what you have and the positive aspects of your life.

>> Focus on your own growth over time.

>> Treat yourself with the same kindness and understanding you'd offer a friend.

>> Manage (and very likely, limit) your use of social media so you're not using it for comparing.

REMEMBER

There may be times when comparing can be helpful. Comparing the way you hit a tennis ball to the way a really good player hits it might help you learn from them. Sometimes finding an inspirational role model in growth and development can help you generate ideas on how to think and act more constructively. However, be guided by the effect of any comparing you do. How much is it helping you?

Managing Your Mental Acts

Hopefully, we've helped you clarify some of the activities you might be engaging in that are hindering, rather than supporting, your mental health. To reduce the frequency, duration, and intensity of those activities, below are some steps to work through.

Making sense of your mind's motivations

The thoughts and beliefs you hold about your mental activities are referred to in the literature as *metacognition*, which is cognition about cognition. There's even a variant of CBT called metacognitive therapy that places significant emphasis on mental processes like those listed here. One simple way to identify this is to think about in what way you think your mind believes it's helping or protecting you.

This chart can help you analyze your mental activity.

Mental Activity	Intended Consequence	Unintended Consequence	Alternative to Try Out

Tracking your overthinking

Learning when, where, and with whom you might overthink is one of the keys to significant improvement. You can then plan and prepare to interrupt your overthinking and test some strategies to keep you out of the rabbit hole.

You can use this table to track any moments of unhelpful overthinking to aid in your plan of attack.

	Mon	Tues	Wed	Thurs	Fri	Sat	Sun
Waking							
Morning							
Morning							
Afternoon							
Afternoon							
Evening							
Night							
Bedtime							

Swapping to help you stop

The more you can plan alternatives to any mental activities you find unhelpful, the better your odds of staying on a healthier path. Have a handful of options to try so that, with experience and practice, you'll be able to find those that work well. We've included some examples, but dozens of alternatives will be worth attempting.

>> Play a game on your phone.

>> Listen to music, a podcast, or an audiobook.

>> Direct your attention to the part of your body where you may experience a distressing emotion, such as a knot in your stomach.

>> Watch a movie, TV show, or video clip.

>> Do some exercise.

>> Call a friend or family member.

>> Finish a household chore, such as rearranging your sock drawer.

>> Dance.

The aim is to help you redirect the focus of your attention and disrupt any unhelpful mental processes. The key is persistence, as breaking a mental habit is much the same as breaking a behavioral one. It takes practice, practice, and more practice. Your brain will truly thank you in the long term for not overworking it via reduced stress and increased mental clarity.

REMEMBER

Gaining control over the focus of your attention can take practice, especially when you're trying to train your brain out of old and unhelpful habits. So persistence is key, as is switching your attention in situations you find less stressful. Refer to Chapter 6 for more on taming your attention.

Chapter **4**

Transforming Troublesome Thoughts

I n your endeavors to become your own cognitive behavioral therapist, one of the key techniques you can use is a tool known as an *ABC form*, which provides a structure for identifying, questioning, and replacing unhelpful thoughts.

Many practitioners who utilize CBT modalities use similar tools to the ABC form that we offer in this chapter. All these tools can help patients identify and replace negative thoughts. Different therapists may refer to these forms as *thought records, mood logs, thought diaries, daily records of dysfunctional thoughts,* or *dysfunctional thought records (DTRs).* Fret not. In general, all these forms are simply different ways of saying the same thing: Your thinking affects your feelings and actions.

REMEMBER

The way you think powerfully affects the way you feel. Therefore, changing your unhelpful thoughts is a key to feeling better.

In this chapter, we give you two versions of the ABC form: one to get you started with identifying your triggers, thoughts, and feelings, and another that takes you right through to developing alternative thoughts so you can feel and act differently in the future.

Catching NATs

Getting the hang of the ABC form is often easier if you break down the process into two steps. The first step is to fill out the first three columns (*Activating* event, *Beliefs* and thoughts, *Consequences*) of the form, which you can find in the later section "Stepping Through the ABC Form I." This gives you a chance to focus on catching your *negative automatic thoughts* (NATs) on paper and to see the connection between your thoughts and emotions.

TIP

Using the ABC form is great, but if you don't have one on hand when you feel an upsetting emotion, grab anything you can write on to scribble down your thoughts and feelings. Smartphones are a great method of recording thoughts when you're out and about. You can always transfer your thoughts to a form later. The key thing is to record your thoughts quickly because people sometimes either forget them or tend to censor them later when their emotions have dulled.

Making the thought–feeling link

A crucial step in CBT is to make the *thought–feeling link* or *B-to-C connection*. That means seeing clearly for yourself the connection between what goes through your mind and your resulting emotions. When you see this connection, you can make much more sense of why to challenge and change your thoughts.

Becoming more objective about your thoughts

One of the biggest advantages of writing down your thoughts is that the process can help you regard these thoughts simply as hunches, theories, and ideas rather than as absolute facts. Add to this "spotting your thinking errors," and you have a great tool to help you become more detached from troubling thoughts and reducing their impact.

REMEMBER

The more negative or extreme the meaning you give to an event, the stronger your emotional reaction, and the more likely you'll act in a way that supports that feeling. Crucially, when you feel negative, you're more likely to generate negative thoughts. See how easily you can get caught in a vicious circle? It's just one of the reasons to take your negative thoughts with a bucket of salt!

Stepping Through the ABC Form I

So, it's time to embark on this major CBT self-help technique using Figure 4-1. The basic process for completing the ABC form is as follows:

1. **In the Consequences box, point 1, write down the emotion you're feeling.**

   Therapy is about becoming emotionally healthier and acting in a more self-helping or productive way. So, when you're filling out the ABC form, the most important place to start is with the emotion you're feeling.

   REMEMBER

   Emotions and behaviors are *consequences* (C) of the interaction between the *activating event or trigger* (A) and the *beliefs or meanings* (B) in the ABC model of emotion.

   Examples of emotions you may choose to list in the Consequences box include the following:

   - Anger
   - Anxiety
   - Depression
   - Envy
   - Guilt
   - Hurt
   - Jealousy
   - Shame

   REMEMBER

   Fill out an ABC form when you feel emotionally upset, when you've acted in a way that you want to change, or when you feel like acting in a way that you want to change. We give you more information on how to help you understand and identify emotions in Chapter 7.

2. **In the Consequences box, point 2, write down how you acted or what you felt like doing.**

   Write down how your behavior changed when you felt your uncomfortable emotion. Examples of the behavior that people often identify as their actions in this box include these:

   - Avoiding something
   - Becoming withdrawn, isolated, or inactive
   - Being aggressive

- Participating in binge-eating or comfort eating or restricting food intake

- Escaping from a situation

- Putting off something (procrastination)

- Seeking reassurance

- Taking alcohol or drugs

- Mentally escaping, such as by scrolling social media on your phone

- Using safety-seeking behaviors, such as holding on to something if you feel faint

3. **In the Activating Event box, write down what triggered your feelings.**

As we discuss in Chapter 1, the *A* in ABC stands for *activating event or trigger,* which is the thing or things that triggered your unhelpful thoughts and feelings. Activating events or triggers to put in this box can include the following:

- Something happening right now

- Something that occurred in the past that you've been reminded of

- Something that you're anticipating happening in the future

- Something in the external world (an object, place, or person)

- Something in your mind (an image or memory)

- A physical sensation (increased heart rate, headache, feeling tired)

- Your own emotions or behavior

An activating event can be anything. Use your feelings — rather than whether you think the event is important — as a guide to when you should fill out a form.

TIP

To keep your ABC form brief and accurate, focus on the specific aspect of the activating event that you're upset about. Use the table of emotions in Chapter 7 to help you detect the themes to look out for if you're unsure about what may have triggered your thoughts and feelings.

4. **In the Beliefs box, write down your thoughts, attitudes, and beliefs.**

Describe what the event you listed in the Activating Event box meant to you when you felt the emotion (what you've written under point 1 in the Consequences box).

- What's the meaning being triggered that's behind how you feel?

- What went through your mind?

The thoughts, attitudes, and beliefs you put in the Beliefs box often pop up on reflex. They may be extreme, distorted, and unhelpful — but they may *seem* like facts to you. These NATs may include the following:

- Here I go again, proving that I'm useless.

- I'm letting everyone down.

- I should've known better!

- Now everyone knows what an idiot I am!

- Why can't I cope like normal people do?

- They clearly don't care about me.

- Why can't I just stop feeling this way?

Thoughts are what count, so think of yourself as a detective and set out to capture suspect thoughts. If your thoughts are in the form of a picture, describe the image or what the image means to you. Then write them down in the Beliefs box.

REMEMBER

We think not only in words but in pictures. People who are feeling anxious frequently describe that they see catastrophic images going through their mind. For example, if you fear fainting in a restaurant, you may imagine yourself on the restaurant floor with staff fussing over you.

5. **In the Thinking Error box, consider what your thinking errors may be.**

One of the key ways to become more objective about your thoughts is to identify the thinking errors that may be represented in the thoughts you list in this box. (See Chapter 2 for more details on common thinking errors.)

Questions that you might ask yourself to identify your thinking errors include the following:

- Am I jumping to the worst possible conclusion? (Catastrophizing)

- Am I thinking in extreme — all-or-nothing — terms? (Black-and-white thinking)

- Am I using words like "always" and "never," reflecting that I've drawn generalized conclusions from a specific event? (Overgeneralizing)

- Am I predicting the future instead of waiting to see what happens? (Fortune-telling)

- Am I jumping to conclusions about what other people are thinking of me? (Mind reading)

- Am I focusing on the negative and overlooking the positive? (Mental filtering)

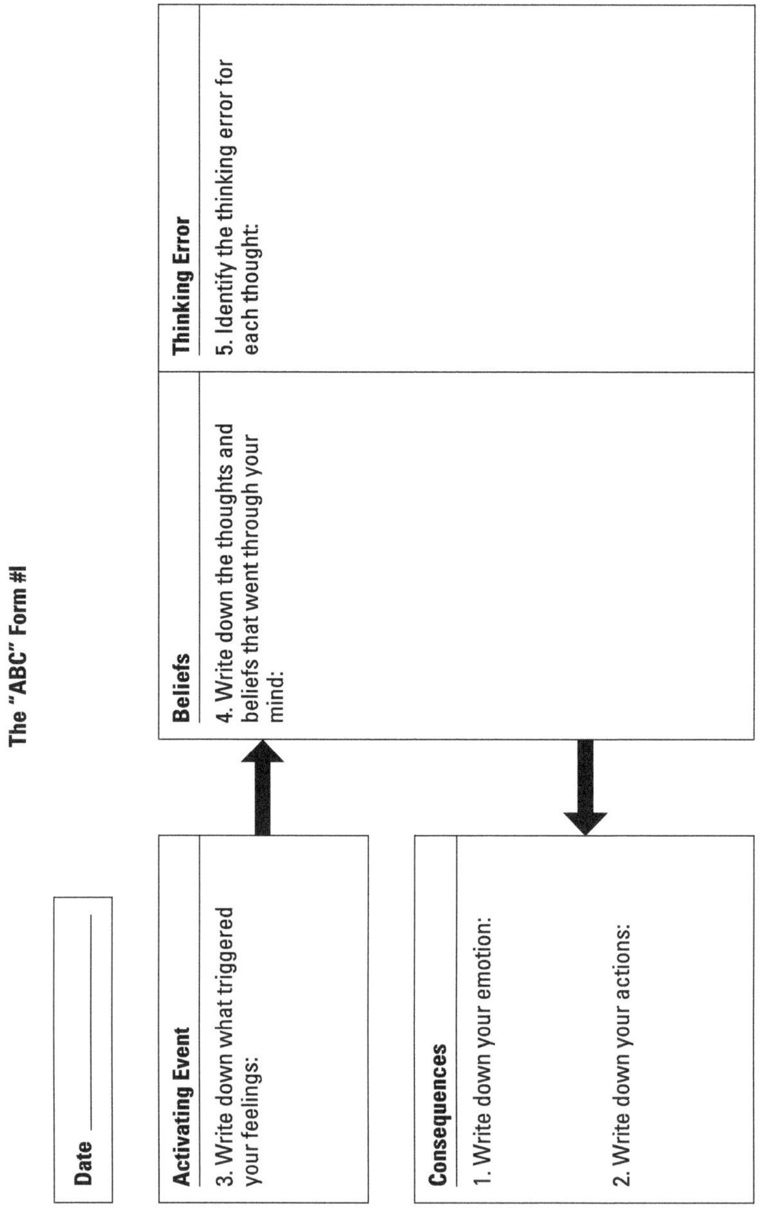

The "ABC" Form #1

Date _____	

Activating Event

3. Write down what triggered your feelings:

Beliefs

4. Write down the thoughts and beliefs that went through your mind:

Thinking Error

5. Identify the thinking error for each thought:

Consequences

1. Write down your emotion:

2. Write down your actions:

© John Wiley & Sons, Inc.

FIGURE 4-1:
The ABC form I.

- Am I discounting positive information or twisting a positive into a negative? (Disqualifying the positive)

- Am I globally putting myself down as a failure, worthless, or useless? (Labeling)

- Am I listening too much to my negative gut feelings instead of looking at the objective facts? (Emotional reasoning)

- Am I taking an event or someone's behavior too personally or blaming myself and overlooking other factors? (Personalizing)

- Am I using words like "should," "must," "ought," and "have to" to make rigid rules about myself, the world, or other people? (Demanding)

- Am I telling myself that something is too difficult or unbearable or that "I can't stand it" when it's hard to bear but *is* bearable and worth tolerating? (Having a low frustration tolerance)

Creating Constructive Alternatives: Completing the ABCDE

When you feel more confident about identifying your As, Bs, Cs, and thinking errors, you can move on to the ABCDE form. This second form helps you question your unhelpful thoughts so you can reduce their intensity, generate and rate the effects of alternative thoughts, and focus on acting differently.

The first five steps for completing the ABCDE (see Figure 4-2) are the same as those for the ABC form I. Then come five more steps. You can find a blank version of the ABCDE form in Appendix B. In the ABCDE form, Column A is the Activating Event, Column B is Beliefs, Column C is Consequences, Column D is Dispute, and Column E is Effect.

6. **Examine your negative thoughts more closely.**

   Ask yourself the following questions to examine and weaken your unhelpful thoughts:

   - Can I prove that my thought is 100 percent true?

   - What are the effects of thinking this way?

   - Is my thought wholly logical or sensible?

   - Would people whose opinions I respect agree that this thought's realistic?

   - What evidence exists against this thought?

   - Is my thought balanced or extreme?

- How will I view this situation a year from now?

- Would I encourage someone I deeply care about to see the situation this way?

- Is my thought rigid or flexible?

- Am I thinking objectively and realistically, or are my thoughts being biased by how I feel?

TIP

Consider long and hard your negative or unhelpful thoughts in light of the preceding questions. Don't simply give glib "yes" or "no" answers. Instead, think things through and perhaps write down your challenges to your unhelpful thoughts in Column D. See the list of questions and prompters at the bottom of the ABC form II, which can help you further with this.

7. **Generate alternatives for each of your unhelpful thoughts, attitudes, and beliefs.**

This step is critical because it's your alternative thoughts that will help you feel better. In Column D, write down a flexible, non-extreme, realistic, and helpful alternative for each thought, attitude, or belief that appears in Column B. The following questions may help you generate some alternatives:

- What's a more helpful way of looking at the situation?

- What would I encourage a good friend to think in this situation?

- When I'm feeling okay, how do I think differently?

- Have any past experiences shown me that another possibility exists?

- What's a more flexible or less extreme way of thinking?

- What's a more realistic or balanced way of thinking that considers the evidence that *doesn't* support my thought?

- With warmth and kindness as my motivation, how might I think?

- What do I need to think to feel and act in a healthier way?

Some thoughts are more stubborn than others, and you won't turn your thinking around completely in one go. Wrestling with NATs for a while before they weaken is typical and appropriate. Think of yourself as *training* your mind to think more flexibly and constructively over time.

WARNING

Some intrusive thoughts, images, and doubts can worsen if you engage with them. If you have obsessive-compulsive disorder (OCD), health anxiety, body dysmorphic disorder (BDD), worry, or jealousy, be sure to develop the capability to live with doubt, and allow catastrophic thoughts to pass through your mind rather than challenging them. We explain this in more depth in Chapters 12 and 14. So if you think you need to learn to live with doubt or to tolerate upsetting, intrusive thoughts in general, we suggest steering clear of using ABC forms for these problems.

8. **In Column E, rate the effects of your alternatives on your feelings.**

Rate your original feelings from 0 to 100 percent. Also note whether you experience any alternative, healthier emotions such as these:

- Concern

- Annoyance

- Sadness

- Remorse

- Disappointment

- Sorrow

REMEMBER

Just like any other skill, learning to transform your thinking takes a bit of practice. You won't always notice a great deal of change in how you feel at first, but keep persevering. Changes in the way you behave and think tend to precede improved emotional responses. Keep thinking and acting in line with how you want to ultimately feel.

9. **Develop a plan to move forward.**

The final step on the ABC form II is to develop a plan to move forward. Your plan may be to conduct a behavioral experiment to help you gather more information about whether your thoughts are true or realistic or to behave differently in a specific situation. Go to Chapters 5 and 6 for more ideas.

10. **Give yourself homework.**

When you've completed several ABC forms, you may begin to notice recurring themes, thoughts, attitudes, or beliefs. Such repetitions may suggest that you need to add other CBT techniques, such as the following, to overcome certain emotions or behaviors:

- Facing a fear until it reduces (Chapter 10)

- Conducting a behavioral experiment to test a thought (Chapter 5)

- Acting repeatedly as if you believe an alternative thought, attitude, or belief (Chapter 18)

- Completing a Zig-Zag form to strengthen an alternative thought, attitude, or belief (Chapter 18)

Read on and set yourself additional therapy assignments using the CBT principles in this book.

Date March 18th

The "ABC" Form #II

Activating Event (Trigger).	Beliefs, thoughts, and attitudes about A.	Consequences of A+B on your emotions and behaviors.	Dispute (question and examine) B and generate alternatives. The questions at the bottom of the form will help you with this.	Effect of alternative thoughts and beliefs (D).
2. Briefly write down what triggered your emotions. (e.g. event, situation, sensation, memory, image)	3. Write down what went through your mind, or what A meant to you. B's can be about you, others, the world, the past, or the future.	1. Write down what emotion you felt and how you felt this emotion.	4. Write an alternative for each B, using supporting arguments and evidence.	5. Write down how you feel and wish to act as consequence of your alternatives at D.
Returning to work for the first time after being off sick.	*Things will have changed and I won't know what to do* (Fortune Telling). *People will ask me awkward questions about why I've been off sick and I won't know what to say* (Catastrophising). *They'll think I'm crazy if they find out I've had depression* (Catastrophising, Mind Reading).	**Emotions** e.g. Depression, guilt, hurt, anger, shame, jealousy, envy, anxiety. Rate intensity 0–100. *Anxiety 70%*	*I don't know whether things have changed. Even if they have I've coped with changes many times before. I'm sure my colleagues will help.* *Possibly one or two people will ask, and I can just keep my answers short.* *Mostly everyone will be glad to have me back.*	**Emotions** Re-rate 0–100. List any healthy alternative emotion e.g. Sadness, regret, concern. *Anxiety 40%*
		Behaviour e.g. Avoidance, withdrawing, escape, using alcohol or drugs, seeking reassurance, procrastination *Running over in my mind what I'll say to everyone.*	*I've no reason to think they'll think I'm crazy. When Peter was off with stress people were mostly supportive and understanding. When Helen called last week she seemed to treat me just the same as normal.*	**Alternative Behaviour or Experiment** e.g. Facing situation, increased activity, assertion *Wait and deal with things when I get there, and stop trying to work it out in advance.*

© John Wiley & Sons, Inc.

Disputing (Questioning and Examining) and Generating Alternative Thoughts, Attitudes, and Beliefs: 1. Identify your 'thinking errors' at **B** (e.g. Mind Reading, Catastrophising, Labelling, Demands, etc.). Write them next to the appropriate 'B'. 2. Examine whether the evidence at hand supports that your thought at **B** is 100% true. Consider whether someone whose opinions you respect would totally agree with your conclusions. 3. Evaluate the helpfulness of each **B**. Write down what you think might be a more helpful, balanced and flexible way of looking at **A**. Consider what you would advise a friend to think, what a role model of yours might think, or how you might look at **A** if you were feeling OK. 4. Add evidence and arguments that support your alternative thoughts, attitudes and beliefs. Write as if you were trying to persuade someone you cared about.

FIGURE 4-2: An example of a filled-in ABC form II.

AN ABC A DAY KEEPS THE DOCTOR AT BAY!

If you want to develop any skill, remember these three words: *Practice, practice, practice!* You may not need to fill out an ABC form every day. Other days, you may need to complete more than one form. The point is that practicing ABCDE forms regularly is worthwhile because

- Practice helps change disturbing feelings and the thoughts that underpin them.

- Sinking a new thought into your head and heart takes repetition.

- By completing forms on paper, you can become increasingly able to challenge unhelpful thoughts in your head — although you may still need to do it on paper sometimes.

As you progress in your ability to overcome difficulties and develop your CBT self-help skills, you may still find the ABCDE form useful when you're hit with a biggie. And remember: If you can't work out your unhelpful thinking on the fly, sit down and bash it out on paper.

TIP

Keeping your old ABC forms can be a rewarding record of your progress and a useful reminder of how to fill them in if you need to use one again in the future. Many of our clients look back over their ABC forms after they feel better and tell us: "I can't believe I used to feel and think like that!"

Chapter **5**

Testing Things Out with Behavioral Experiments

E ven in a "talking treatment" like CBT, actions speak louder than words. Aaron Beck, founder of cognitive therapy, described the approach as client and therapist being "scientific together." Beck emphasizes that testing your thoughts, rather than simply talking about them, underpins effective therapy.

CBT is very much a "doing" approach to better emotional health. At the heart of the approach is the spirit of inquiry: How does the world (including us) work? If you want to know whether your hunch about reality is accurate or your way of responding is optimally helpful, put it to the test. It's a particularly powerful key to moving a new thought, belief, or perspective from an intellectual understanding to something you really believe.

This chapter is an introduction to behavioral experiments, a key CBT strategy. We include in this chapter an overview of several behavioral experiments that you can try for yourself. We also give you examples of these experiments in action. As with the other examples we use in this book, try to look for *anything* useful you can draw from them. Try not to home in too much on how the examples differ from your specific problem. Instead, focus on what you have in common with the examples and work from there to apply the techniques to your own problems.

REMEMBER

This book is all about helping you develop your emotional health and live more effectively. Some of your thoughts, such as ideas about what might happen in the distant future, you can't fully "test." However, you *can* test how your mental and behavioral strategies work. Do they make things better, worse, or no different? Tolerance of uncertainty, for example, has been the subject of research attention in recent years. Several studies indicate that boosting your tolerance of doubt and ambiguity can seriously improve the mental health of people who are intolerant of uncertainty. Running your own behavioral experiment can help you see if this is true for you too.

Seeing for Yourself: Reasons for Doing Behavioral Experiments

The proof of the pudding's in the eating. The same can be said of your assumptions, behaviors, beliefs, and predictions about yourself and the world around you. Use experiments to test the truth about your beliefs and to assess the usefulness of your behaviors.

You can use behavioral experiments in the following ways:

>> To test the validity of a thought or belief that you hold about yourself, other people, or the world

>> To test the validity of an alternative thought or belief

>> To discover the effects that mental or behavioral activities have on your emotions, health, and relationships

>> To gather evidence to clarify the nature of your problem

Living according to a set of beliefs because you think they're true and helpful is both easy and common. You can also easily stick to familiar ways of behaving because you *think* they keep you safe from feared events or help you achieve certain goals. An example of this may be holding a belief that other people are out to find fault with you. With this thought in mind, you then work hard to hide your mistakes and shortcomings.

The beauty of a behavioral experiment is that you may well find that your worst imagined scenarios don't happen or that you deal with such situations effectively when, or even if, they do occur.

We may be stating the obvious, but change can be less daunting if you keep in mind that you can always return to your old ways of thinking about things if the new ways don't seem any better. If your old ways are the best option, nothing's stopping you from going back to them. The trick is to prepare yourself to try new strategies and give them a chance before returning to your former ways. Find out what works best for you and your situation.

Testing Predictions

When testing your predictions, strive to get unambiguous disconfirmation if you can. *Unambiguous disconfirmation* means coming to the conclusion that your fears *don't* come true, even if you do something to prevent them from occuring. An example of unambiguous disconfirmation may be finding out that your dizziness is caused by anxiety and that you won't collapse even if you don't sit down or hold on to something.

Go through the following four steps to devise a behavioral experiment:

1. **Describe your problem.**

   Write down the nature of your problem and include your *safety behaviors* (things you do to try to prevent your feared catastrophe; head to Chapter 8 for loads more on safety behavior). Phrase the problem in your own words and make a note of how the problem negatively affects your life.

2. **Formulate your prediction.**

   Decide what you think will happen if you try out a new way of thinking or behaving in real life.

3. **Execute an experiment.**

   Think of a way of putting a new belief or behavior to the test in a real-life situation. Try to devise more than one way to test your prediction.

4. **Examine the results.**

   Look to see whether your prediction came true. If it didn't, check out what you've learned from the results of the experiment.

You can rate the degree to which you believe a prediction will come true on a percentage between 0 and 100 at the start of your experiment. After you've done the experiment and processed your results, rerate your conviction in the original prediction.

TIP

Take care not to use subtle ways of keeping your feared catastrophe at bay, such as doing experiments only when you feel "right," are with "safe" people, have *safety signals* at hand (such as a mobile phone or a bottle of water), or are using safety behaviors (such as trying to control your anxiety with distraction or by gripping tightly to your steering wheel). Using these subtle safety measures during your exposure to a fear can leave you with the impression that you've had a narrow escape rather than highlighting that your predicted fear didn't come true.

For example, consider the following experiment, which Nadine initiates to examine her fear of rejection and social anxiety:

» **Describe the problem.** Nadine's afraid of people thinking negatively of her and of being rejected by her friends. In social situations, Nadine monitors her body language and censors what she says, taking great care not to express any strong opinions in case others disagree with her. She often plans what she's going to say.

» **Formulate a prediction.** Nadine predicts, "If I express an opinion or disagree with my friends, they'll like me less." She rates her conviction in this idea as 90 percent.

» **Execute an experiment.** For the next six social gatherings Nadine attends, she decides that she'll speak up and try to offer an opinion. If possible, she'll find a point on which to disagree with someone.

» **Examine the results.** Nadine discovers that no one took exception to her saying more. In fact, two friends commented that it was nice to hear more about what she thought about things. Nadine rerates her conviction in her original prediction as 40 percent.

By conducting a behavioral experiment, Nadine observed that her feared prediction — "Others will like me less if I express my opinions" — didn't happen. This result gives Nadine the opportunity to change her behavior according to the results of her experiment and speak up more often. It also helps to reduce how much she believes the original prediction. Nadine can now adjust her thinking based on evidence gathered through the experiment.

Nigel used a behavioral experiment to test his prediction that he wouldn't enjoy engaging in social activities. Since self-isolating and disengaging from previously enjoyed activities promotes depression, Nigel really needs to understand the benefits of becoming more active. Nigel worked through an experiment as follows:

» **Describe the problem.** Nigel's depression typically leads to him having gloomy and pessimistic thoughts. He tends to avoid going out with his friends or doing any of his regular hobbies because he's not in the mood these days.

He believes that he won't enjoy himself; therefore, there's no point in trying any of these activities. (As we note in Chapter 11, self-isolating behavior is one of the key ways in which depression is maintained.)

» **Formulate a prediction.** Nigel chooses to experiment with the prediction "Even if I do go out, I won't enjoy myself and I'll end up feeling even worse once I get home." He rates his strength of conviction in this thought as 80 percent.

» **Execute an experiment.** Nigel structures his week and schedules two occasions to see friends. He also plans to spend two half-hour sessions riding his bike, which he used to enjoy. He rates each day over the next seven days in terms of his mood and of how much he enjoys his activities.

» **Examine the results.** Nigel notices that he gets some enjoyment from seeing his friends, although less than he usually would. Although he doesn't particularly enjoy his cycling and feels more tired than usual, he notes that he at least felt glad he'd done something. He rerates his conviction in his original prediction as 40 percent and decides to conduct further experiments to see whether his mood and energy levels improve over the next two weeks if he continues to be more active.

This experiment helped Nigel see that he felt better for doing *something*, even if he didn't enjoy cycling or socializing as much as he would when he wasn't depressed. Noting these results can help Nigel stick to a schedule of activity and ultimately help him to overcome his depression.

Seeking Evidence to See Which Theory Best Fits the Facts

The scientific principle known as *Occam's razor* states that, all things considered, the simplest theory is usually the best. Whichever theory explains a phenomenon most simply is the one a scientist adopts. When you want to test a theory or idea you hold about yourself, others, or the world, developing an alternative theory is a good idea. This gives you the chance to disprove your original theory and to endorse the healthier alternative.

Some emotional problems don't respond well to attempts to disprove a negative prediction. In such cases, you may be better off developing competing theories about what the problem is. You then devise experiments to gather more evidence and see which theory reflects reality most accurately.

For example, imagine that your boss never says a cheerful "good morning" to you. You develop the following two theories:

>> Theory A: "My boss doesn't like me at all."

>> Theory B: "My boss isn't friendly in the mornings and is a bit rude, but he's like this to a lot of employees, not just me."

You're now able to gather evidence for whether Theory A or Theory B best explains the phenomenon of your boss failing to be cheerful toward you in the mornings.

A *theory* is just an idea or assumption that you hold, which, to your mind, explains why something happens. *Theory* is a technical word for a simple concept.

Often, developing one additional theory to compete with your original theory is enough. However, you can develop more alternative theories if you think they may help you get to the bottom of what you're experiencing. Taking the previous example, you may have a third theory, such as, "My boss is cheerful only with employees that he knows very well," or even a fourth theory, such as, "My boss is cheerful only with employees of the same rank or above him."

Developing competing theories can be particularly helpful in the following situations:

>> **Dealing with predictions that may be months or years away from being proven:** If you fear hellfire and damnation for having an intrusive thought about causing harm to someone, you'll probably be waiting a while to see if that happens. Similarly, if you have *illness anxiety* and spend hours each day preoccupied with the idea that physical sensations in your body may be signs that you'll become ill and die, you're unlikely to know straightaway whether this will actually happen. With this kind of catastrophizing (see Chapter 2), you need to design experiments to help you gather evidence that supports the theory that you have a worry or anxiety problem, rather than a damnation ticket or a terminal illness.

>> **Dealing with beliefs that are impossible to prove or disprove conclusively:** Perhaps you're anxious about others having negative opinions of you. You can't know for sure what other people think. And even if someone tells you that your fears are unfounded, you can't know with certainty what they're thinking. Similarly, if you feel jealous that your partner might desire someone else, but they reassure you otherwise, you may remain uncertain of their true feelings.

For both these situations, you can employ the Theory A or Theory B Strategy:

>> Design an experiment to gather evidence to support the idea that your jealous feelings are based on your jealous thoughts (Theory B) rather than on reality (Theory A).

>> Similarly, devise an experiment to test whether your original Theory A, that "People don't like me," or alternative Theory B, that "I often think that people don't like me because I'm so worried about others' opinions that I end up seeing a lot of their behavior as signs of dislike," best explains your experiences in social situations.

Here is an example of how Alex used the competing theories approach to get a better understanding of his physical sensations. Originally, Alex assumed his theory that uncomfortable bodily sensations signaled the onset of a heart attack was correct. By testing this in practice, Alex was able to consider that an alternative theory — uncomfortable bodily sensations are a by-product of anxiety — may be more accurate.

>> **Describe the problem.** Alex suffers from panic attacks. He feels hot and his heart races, sometimes unexpectedly. When he feels these sensations, he fears he's having a heart attack. Alex sits down to try to reduce the strain on his heart, which is an example of a safety behavior. He goes out of his way to avoid situations in which he has experienced these symptoms.

>> **Develop competing theories.** Alex devises two theories about his raised heart rate:

  ● Theory A: "My heart beating quickly means I'm vulnerable to having a heart attack."

  ● Theory B: "My heart beating quickly is a consequence of anxiety."

>> **Execute an experiment.** Alex decides to deliberately confront situations that tend to trigger his raised heart rate and to stay in them, without sitting down, until his anxiety reduces. He predicts that if Theory B is correct, his heart rate will reduce after his anxiety subsides and he can leave the situation without having come to any harm.

>> **Examine the results.** Alex finds that his heart rate does indeed reduce when he stays with his anxiety. He's struck by what a difference this knowledge makes to his confidence and the realization that he's not going to come to any harm from his raised heart rate when he resists the urge to sit down. He concludes that he can have about 70 percent confidence in his new theory that his raised heart rate is a benign consequence of anxiety.

TIP

You can't always prove conclusively that something isn't so. However, you can experiment to see whether certain emotional states, and mental or behavioral activities, have a beneficial or detrimental effect on the kinds of thoughts that play on your mind.

Conducting Surveys

You can use the clipboard and pen of the survey-taker in your endeavors to tackle your problems by designing and conducting your own survey. Surveys can help you get more information about what the average person thinks, feels, or does.

We suggest you have more than one type of behavioral experiment in your repertoire. Surveys are useful if you believe that your thoughts, physical sensations, or behaviors are out of the ordinary. If you have upsetting, intrusive thoughts and images or experience urges to say socially unacceptable things (symptoms typical of obsessive-compulsive disorder, OCD), feel pulled to the edge of high places (as in vertigo), or get a sense of impending doom when you're in an unfamiliar place (symptoms associated with agoraphobia), you may think that you're the only person who ever feels this way. Use surveys to see whether other people have the same thoughts and urges. You'll probably discover that other people experience the same things as you do. You may also discover that the symptoms you experience are less of a problem than the way you currently deal with them.

Henry suffers from OCD. His obsessional problem is related to frequent intrusive images of harm coming to his family. He's convinced that he's the only person in the world who gets such unpleasant and unwanted images entering his mind. Henry concludes that there's something different and wrong about him because he has such images. He tests his theory about his abnormality by conducting the following survey:

>> **Describe the problem.** Henry's convinced that his intrusive thoughts about his family being hurt in a car accident are unusual and mean that he must protect his family by changing the image in his mind to them being happy at a party.

>> **Formulate a prediction.** Henry produces the prediction, "No one will admit to having the kind of thoughts I have." He rates his strength of belief as 70 percent.

>> **Execute an experiment.** Henry tests his perception that his images are abnormal by devising a checklist of intrusive thoughts and asking his friends and family members to check any that they experience.

>> **Examine the results.** Henry's surprised at the variety of thoughts that people report entering their minds. Henry concludes that his images aren't so abnormal after all. He rerates his conviction in his original prediction as 15 percent. Henry also learns that other people simply discount their unpleasant images and don't worry that they mean anything sinister.

Charlotte worries a lot about her health and the possibility of developing a life-threatening illness. Sometimes she notices funny sensations in her body and instantly interprets them as signs of an undiagnosed disease. Charlotte assumes that no one else experiences unusual bodily sensations from time to time.

>> **Describe the problem.** Charlotte worries that the bodily sensations she experiences are a sign of disease. She's unsatisfied by frequent reassurance from her family doctor and husband. Charlotte's problems are based partly on two ideas:

- Physical sensations must have a clear medical explanation.

- Any sensible person would seek an immediate explanation for the physical sensations she's currently experiencing.

>> **Formulate a prediction.** Charlotte makes the following prediction: "Most people won't have many physical sensations, and if they do they go immediately to see their doctor." She rates her strength of conviction in this idea as 80 percent.

>> **Execute an experiment.** Charlotte devises a list of physical sensations, including many of those that she worries about herself. Her checklist requires people to check whether they've ever experienced the sensation and to indicate how long they might ignore it before consulting their doctor about such sensations. She asks ten people to fill out her questionnaire.

>> **Examine the results.** Charlotte's shocked that many reported experiencing the bodily sensations she described and stated that they'd wait to visit their doctor for several days or even weeks. Some people reported that they probably wouldn't bother seeing their doctor at all for certain sensations. Charlotte concludes that perhaps she's worrying too much about her health and plans to delay consulting her doctor when she next has unexplained physical sensations. Her strength of belief in her original prediction reduces to 30 percent.

Making Observations

Observations can be an easier way of getting started with experiments to test the validity of your thoughts. Observations usually involve collecting evidence related to a specific thought by watching other people in action.

You may assume, for example, that no one in their right mind would admit to confusion about an important point in a work procedure. If they did, they'd no doubt be ridiculed and promptly fired based on highlighting their incompetence.

Test this assumption by observing what other people actually do. Behave like a scientist and gather evidence of others admitting lack of understanding, asking for clarification, or owning up to mistakes. Observe whether your prediction that they'll be ridiculed or fired is accurate. Making observations to gather evidence both for and against your assumptions is another way of behaving like a scientist.

Ensuring Successful Behavioral Experiments

To get the most benefit when designing and carrying out behavioral experiments, keep the following in mind:

>> Ensure that the type of experiment you choose is appropriate. Make your experiments challenging enough for you to gain a sense of accomplishment from conducting them. Equally, take care to devise experiments that won't overwhelm you.

>> Have a clear plan about how, when, and where (and with whom, if relevant) you plan to carry out your experiment.

>> Be clear and specific about what you want to find out from your experiment. "To see what happens" is too vague.

>> Decide in advance how you'll know whether your prediction comes true. For example, what are the clues that someone's thinking critically of you?

>> Plan what you'll do if your prediction comes true. For example, how do you respond assertively if someone is critical of you?

>> Use the behavioral experiments record sheet in the following section to plan and record your experiment.

>> Consider what obstacles may interrupt your experiment and how you can overcome them.

>> When evaluating the outcome of your experiment, check that you're not being biased (for example, discounting the positive or mind-reading, thinking errors we describe in Chapter 2) in the way you process your results.

>> Consider whether you rely on any (including subtle) safety behaviors. Safety behaviors can affect the results of your experiment or determine how confident you feel about the outcome — for example, thinking that you avoided collapsing by concentrating rather than discovering conclusively that your feelings of dizziness are a result of anxiety, not imminent fainting.

>> Plan ways to consolidate what you discover from your experiment. For example, should you repeat the experiment, devise a new experiment, change your daily activities, or take some other action?

Treating your negative and unhelpful thoughts with skepticism is a key to reducing their emotional impact. Experiments can help you realize that many of your negative thoughts and predictions aren't accurate. Therefore, we suggest you take many of your negative thoughts with a pinch or more of salt.

TIP

Think about making changes to your thoughts and behaviors as an experiment rather than a lifelong commitment, especially at the beginning. By thinking in this manner, you can feel less under pressure and more able to approach therapy with an open mind. If your problems seem big and complicated, a key principle is to start small. Change can be tough. Taking a small step and building up often works so much better than going for substantial change that turns out to be unrealistic and keeps you stuck.

Keeping Records of Your Experiments

All good scientists keep records of their experiments. If you do the same, you can look back over your results to do the following:

>> Draw conclusions

>> Decide what kind of experiment you may want to conduct next to gather more information

>> Remind yourself that many of your negative predictions won't come true

To help you keep records of your experiments, photocopy Figure 5-1, and use it as often as you like, following the instructions in the figure.

Behavioural Experiment Record Sheet

Date: _____

Prediction or Theory	Experiment	Results	Conclusion/Comments
Outline the thought, belief, or theory you are testing. Rate your strength of conviction 1–100%.	Plan what you will do (including where, when, how, with whom), being as specific as you can.	Record what actually happened including relevant thoughts, emotions, physical sensations, and other people's behaviour.	Write down what you have learned about your prediction or theory in light of the results. Re-rate your strength of conviction 0–100%.

Guidance on carrying out a behavioural experiment: 1. Be clear and specific about the negative and alternative predictions you are testing. Rate your strength of conviction in the prediction or theory you are testing or evaluating. 2 Decide upon your experiment, and be as clear as you can be as to how you will measure your results. 3. Record the results of your experiment, emphasizing clear, observable outcomes. 4. Evaluate the results of your experiment. Write down what these results suggest in terms of the accuracy of your predictions, or which theory the evidence supports. 5. Consider whether a further behavioural experiment might be helpful.

© *John Wiley & Sons, Inc.*

FIGURE 5-1: Photocopy and fill in your own Behavioral Experiment Record Sheet.

Try to have a no-lose perspective on your experiments. If you do one experiment and it goes well, that's great! However, if you plan an experiment but avoid doing it, you can at least identify the thoughts that blocked you. Even if your negative predictions turn out to be accurate, you have an opportunity to see how well you cope — it probably isn't the end of the world — and then decide whether you need to take further action. The point is that you can always gather information to make into a useful experience.

DON'T TAKE OUR WORD FOR IT . . .

This book is full of suggestions on how to reduce and overcome emotional problems. If you're skeptical about whether CBT can work for you, you're in good company. However, loads of scientific evidence show that CBT is more effective than all other psychotherapies.

So, CBT may well work for you, but how can you tell? Consider applying a specific tool or technique for a while as an experiment to see how the technique works for you. Depending on the outcome, you can then choose to do more, modify your approach, or try something different.

Chapter **6**

Pay Attention! Refocusing and Retraining Your Awareness

Traditionally, CBT has tended to focus many of its techniques on helping people change the *content* of their thinking — from a negative to a more realistic thought, for example. However, modern CBT has begun to tackle another area of human psychology: how we focus our attention, and the way we relate to our mental processes.

This chapter doesn't discuss *what* you think but does discuss *how* you manage your thoughts and attention. We introduce task concentration training and mindfulness, two techniques for managing problematic thoughts and exerting some power over your attention. This chapter has two main messages:

>> For the most part, your random thoughts, no matter how distressing and negative, aren't the real problem. Rather, the importance or meaning you attach to those thoughts is. If you view the notion "I'm a hopeless case" as a thought rather than a fact, you can greatly lessen its impact. Similarly, if you experience an unpleasant intrusive thought, you can see it as a normal human phenomenon and not fall into the trap of taking it too seriously. As we see in Chapter 12, it's the meaning assigned to an intrusive thought that underpins many individuals' OCD.

>> When you have an emotional problem, your mind tends to attach unhelpful meanings to aspects of yourself, the world around you, and other people. You can also tend to *overfocus* on particular aspects of these unhelpful meanings. Fortunately, you can develop the ability to steer your attention toward, and away from, any features of your experience you choose, which can improve your mood and reduce anxiety.

Training in Task Concentration

Becoming adept at redirecting attention away from yourself — your bodily sensations, thoughts, and mental images — in certain situations is the essence of *task concentration*. Rather than thinking about yourself, focus your attention on your external environment and what you're doing.

REMEMBER

Task concentration involves paying less attention to what's going on inside of you and more attention to what's happening outside of you. It involves focusing less on *how well* you're doing — for example, when giving a speech — and more on *what* you're doing. The task gets the bulk of your attention.

Task concentration can be particularly useful in situations that trigger your anxiety. Task concentration can help you counterbalance your tendency to focus on threats and on yourself when you feel anxious.

As you begin to practice task concentration, break down the process into two rehearsal arenas — just as when learning to drive you begin on quiet roads and eventually advance to busier roads.

The two rehearsal arenas are as follows:

>> **Nonthreatening situations:** Here, you typically experience little or no anxiety. For example, if you have social phobia, you may feel a little anxious

walking through a park, traveling on a quiet train, or socializing with family members and close friends.

>> **More challenging situations:** Here, you may experience moderate to severe anxiety. More challenging situations may include shopping in a busy grocery store, traveling on a train during rush hour, or attending a party with many guests you may not know.

Typically, you gradually progress from nonthreatening situations to more challenging situations as you practice and develop greater skill.

REMEMBER

After you've practiced redirecting your attention in situations you regard as relatively nonthreatening, you can move on to using the techniques in increasingly challenging situations.

Choosing to concentrate

The point of task-concentration exercises is not to lessen your overall concentration but to concentrate harder on different aspects of the external environment. Some tasks require you to focus your attention on certain behaviors, such as listening to what another person is saying during a conversation or attempting to balance a tray of drinks as you walk through a crowded room.

In other situations, you may feel anxious but not have a specific task to attend to. In such a situation (for example, while sitting in a crowded waiting room), you can still focus externally. You can direct your attention to your surroundings, noticing other people, the features of the room, sounds, and smells.

REMEMBER

With practice, you can be both task- and environment-focused rather than self-focused, even in situations that you regard as highly threatening.

The following exercises aim to increase your understanding of how paying attention to sensations and images limits your ability to process information around you. The exercises will also help you realize that you can attend to external task-related behaviors. In other words, you can master *choosing* what you pay attention to in situations when your anxiety is triggered.

WARNING

Intentionally directing your attention away from yourself doesn't mean trying to avoid noticing your sensations or suppressing your thoughts. Sometimes people try to use thought suppression as a means of alleviating uncomfortable sensations and anxiety. However, suppression usually works only briefly, if at all. External focus is really about controlling your focus of attention even while feeling uncomfortable.

Concentration exercise: Listening

For this exercise, sit back-to-back with someone else, perhaps a friend or your therapist. Ask the person to tell you a story for about two minutes. Concentrate on it. Then summarize the story. Note how much of your attention you direct toward the task of listening to the other person, toward yourself, and toward your environment. Try using percentages to do this. Your partner can give you feedback on your summary to give you some idea of how you did.

Now do the exercise again, but this time around sit face-to-face with the storyteller and make eye contact. Ask the person to tell you a story, but consciously distract yourself by focusing on your thoughts and sensations, and then redirect your attention toward the storyteller. Summarize the story, and note (using percentages again) how you divide your attention between yourself, listening to the other person, and your environment.

Repeat the storytelling activities, sitting back-to-back and then face-to-face, several times until you become readily able to redirect your attention to the task of listening after deliberate distraction through self-focusing. Doing so helps you develop your ability to control where you focus your attention. Use a new story each time so that you don't end up just memorizing the details.

Concentration exercise: Speaking

Follow the same steps for this speaking exercise as you do for the listening exercise, as we describe in the preceding section. Starting with your back to the back of the other person, tell a two-minute story, focusing your attention on making your story clear to the listener.

Next, position yourself face-to-face with the listener, making eye contact. Deliberately distract yourself from the task of storytelling by focusing on your feelings, sensations, and thoughts. Then refocus your attention on what you're saying and toward the listener, being aware of their reactions and whether they understand you.

Again, using percentages, monitor how you divide your attention among yourself, the task, and your environment.

Concentration exercise: Graded practice

For this exercise, prepare two lists of situations. For your first list, write down five or so examples of situations you find nonthreatening. As you write down the situations, practice distracting yourself by focusing on your internal sensations and thoughts. Now read back through the list of these situations, but this time try refocusing your attention outward. For your second list, write down ten or so examples of situations you find threatening. Arrange the situations in a hierarchy, starting from the least anxiety-provoking and graduating up to the most anxiety-provoking. Now you can work through your hierarchy by deliberately entering the situations while practicing task concentration until you reach the top of your list. This means you can start to practice mastering your anxiety in real-life situations.

Concentration exercise: Taking a walk

For this exercise, walk through a park, paying attention to what you hear, see, feel, and smell. Focus your attention for a few minutes on different aspects of the world around you. First, focus your attention mainly to what you can hear. Then shift your attention to focus on smells, and then on to the feel of your feet on the ground, and so on. You can move your attention around to different sensations, which can help you tune your attention onto the outside world. Switching between your five senses can also help you realize that you can direct your attention as you choose.

After you've practiced directing most of your attention to individual senses, try to integrate your attention to include all aspects of the park. Do this for at least 20 minutes. Really let yourself drink in the detail of your surroundings. Discover what hooks your attention. You may be drawn to water or have a keen interest in birds, plants, or perhaps even woodland smells. Notice how you feel much more relaxed and less self-conscious as you train your attention on the world around you.

Tuning in to tasks and the world around you

If you're suffering from anxiety, you're probably self-focused in many situations and fail to notice the rest of the world. On top of feeling unnecessarily uncomfortable, your self-focus means that you're likely to miss out on a lot of interesting stuff. Luckily, you can change your attention bias and overcome much of your anxiety.

TIP

You can also use retraining your attention onto the outside world to interrupt yourself from engaging with the stream of negative thoughts that accompanies depression, which will help you lift your mood.

Here's an example of how you can use task-concentration techniques to overcome anxiety, specifically social phobia. (See Chapter 10 for more on social phobia.)

Harold was particularly worried that people would notice that he blushed and sweated in social situations. He believed that people would think he was odd or a nervous wreck. Harold constantly self-monitored for blushing and sweating and tried hard to mask these symptoms of his anxiety.

Here's Harold's list of situations, with each one becoming gradually more challenging:

1. Having dinner with his parents and brother
2. Socializing with his three closest friends at a local bar
3. Using public transportation during quiet periods
4. Eating lunch with colleagues at work
5. Going to the cinema with a friend
6. Walking alone down a busy street
7. Socializing with strangers at a party
8. Going to the grocery store alone
9. Going to the gym alone
10. Initiating conversation with strangers
11. Using public transportation during busy periods
12. Eating alone in a restaurant
13. Going on an interview
14. Offering his opinion during work meetings
15. Giving a presentation at work

Harold used the principles of task concentration to increase his ability to focus deliberately on chosen external factors in nonthreatening situations. When Harold was at the bar with his friends, he focused his attention on what his friends were saying, other people in the pub, the music, and the general surroundings. Harold also deliberately distracted himself by focusing on whether he was blushing and sweating, and then he refocused his attention again.

Harold then used the same techniques in more threatening situations. In the grocery store, Harold found that the more he focused on his blushing and sweating, the more anxious he felt and the less able he was to pack up his shopping. When he paid attention to the task of packing his groceries, made eye contact with the cashier, and even made a bit of small talk, his anxiety symptoms reduced, and he became more aware of what he was doing and what was going on around him.

Harold worked diligently through his hierarchy of feared situations and now feels much more confident and relaxed in social situations.

Imagine that you're going to be called on by the police to act as an eyewitness. For a few minutes, try to take in as much information as you can about the environment and the people around you. What are people doing? What do they look like?

Could you give a reliable description of someone an hour from now? Notice how much more detail you can recount when you choose to focus outward, compared with when you're concentrating on your thoughts and physical sensations.

Tackling the task-concentration record sheet

You can keep an account of your task-concentration practice, and note the results, by using a task-concentration record sheet; the one in Table 6-1 uses Harold's example from the preceding section. The brief instructions at the top of the sheet are there to remind you how to do your concentration exercises. You can find a blank copy of the form in Appendix B.

TABLE 6-1   **Harold's Task-Concentration Record Sheet**

Who were you with? Where were you? What were you doing?	Record your focus of attention. Note what you focused on most. 1. Self % 2. Task % 3. Environment and other people % (Total = 100%)	Use task concentration to direct your attention outward. Remember to focus on your task or environment. Note what you did.	Record how you felt.	Record anything you learned from the exercise. Note how the situation turned out, how your anxiety level changed, and your ability to complete the task.
Eating by myself in restaurant at lunchtime.	*1. Self 40%* *2. Task 35%* *3. Environment and other people 25%*	*Took my time to eat rather than rushing.* *Made eye contact with waiter.* *Tried to eat my meal mindfully and enjoy it.* *Observed other diners.* *Kept my head up and didn't hide away at a corner table.*	*Anxious.* *Scared at first.*	*My anxiety lessened as I ate.* *No one seemed to think I was odd for eating alone.* *I felt less awkward than I expected to feel.* *It took a lot of effort at first to keep my attention on the task of eating, but it got easier.*

Becoming More Mindful

Mindfulness meditation, commonly associated with Zen Buddhism, has become popular in the past few years as a technique for dealing with depression and managing stress and chronic pain. Evidence shows that mindfulness meditation can reduce the chance of problems such as depression returning for people with recurrent depression, and it adds another string to your bow against emotional problems.

Being present in the moment

Mindfulness is the art of being present in the moment, without passing judgment about your experience. The mindfulness process is so simple, yet so challenging. Keep your attention focused on the moment that you're experiencing *right now*. Suspend your judgment about what you're feeling, thinking, and absorbing through your senses. Simply observe what's going on around you, in your mind, and in your body without doing anything. Just allow yourself to be aware of what's happening.

Mindfulness literature talks about the way your mind almost mechanically forms judgments about each of your experiences, labeling them as good, bad, or neutral depending on how you value them. Things that generate good and bad feelings within you get most of your attention, but you may ignore neutral things or deem them to be boring. Mindfulness meditation encourages awareness of the present moment with an uncluttered mind, observing even the seemingly mundane without judgment. The whole experience is a bit like looking at the world for the first time.

When you meet someone you know, try to see them through fresh eyes. Suspend your prior knowledge, thoughts, experiences, and opinions. You can try this with acquaintances or people you know very well, such as family members and close friends.

Try mindfulness exercises when you're in the countryside or walking down the street. Whether the surroundings are familiar to you or not, aim to see the details of the world around you through fresh eyes.

Letting your thoughts pass by

You can develop your mindfulness skills and use them to help you deal with unpleasant thoughts or physical symptoms. If you have anxiety, for example, you can develop the ability to *focus away* from your anxious thoughts.

Watching the train pass by

Imagine a train passing through a station. The train represents your thoughts and sensations (your "train of thought"). Each train car may represent one or more specific thoughts or feelings. Visualize yourself watching the train pass by without hopping into any specific car. Accept your fears about what other people may be thinking about you without trying to suppress them or engaging with them. Simply watch them pass by like a train through a station.

Standing by the side of the road

Another version of the exercise is to imagine that you're standing on the side of a reasonably busy road. Each passing vehicle represents your thoughts and sensations. Just watch the cars go by. Observe and accept them passing. Don't try to hitchhike, redirect the flow of traffic, or influence the cars in any way.

Discerning when not to listen to yourself

One of the real benefits of understanding the way your emotions influence the way you think is knowing when what you're thinking isn't likely to be helpful or realistic. Being mindful means learning to experience your thoughts without passing judgment as to whether they're true.

Given that many of the negative thoughts you experience when you're emotionally distressed are distorted and unhelpful, you're much better off letting some thoughts pass you by, recognizing them as *symptoms* or *output* of a given emotional state or psychological problem. Chapter 7 covers the *cognitive consequences* of emotions, giving you an idea of the types of thoughts that can occur because of how you're feeling.

TIP

Becoming more familiar with the thoughts that tend to pop into your head when you feel down, anxious, or guilty makes it easier for you to recognize them as thoughts and let them come and go rather than treating them as facts. This familiarity gives you another skill to help manage your negative thoughts in addition to challenging or testing them in reality.

Incorporating mindful daily tasks

Becoming more mindful about little, everyday tasks can help you strengthen your attention muscles. Essentially, everything you do throughout the day can be done with increased awareness. For example, think about the following:

>> Showering mindfully can help you experience the process more fully. Notice the smell of the soap, the temperature of the water, and the movement of your hands.

>> Eating mindfully can give you a more enjoyable eating experience. Slow down the speed at which you eat, and pay attention to the texture of the food, the subtlety of the flavors, and the appearance of the dish.

Tolerating upsetting images and unpleasant ideas

Certain psychological problems such as depression and anxiety disorders like OCD are frequently accompanied by unwelcome, unsettling images or thoughts. Depressed people can have ideas about harming themselves or get strong visual images of doing so — even when they have no real intention of taking suicidal action. These thoughts are understandably distressing, and people may worry that they indicate a real risk. Happily, this isn't often the case; most of these thoughts are merely an unpleasant by-product of depressed mood. It's easy to misinterpret these images and thoughts as dangerous or portentous, but learning to see them as what they really are — just unpleasant symptoms of depression or anxiety — can render them less frightening.

WARNING

Not all suicidal ideas are to be ignored. If you find yourself becoming increasingly preoccupied with ideas of harming yourself or ending your life, seek help immediately. This advice is especially important if you've begun to develop a plan and find your suicidal thoughts comforting. Talk to your doctor, a family member, or a friend or take yourself to the psychiatric emergency unit at your nearest hospital. Chapter 11 deals with depression. You can also read Chapter 24 for valuable information about seeking professional help.

People with OCD (more on this disorder in Chapter 12) often experience intrusive thoughts and images. The content of these thoughts and mental pictures can vary widely, but they're frequently about harming people you love or acting in a way that dramatically violates your moral code. Other emotional or anxiety problems can also give rise to a host of nightmarish ideas and images. Some classics may include the following:

>> Losing control of your bladder or bowels in public

>> Blurting out something offensive

>> Behaving in a sexually inappropriate manner

>> Jumping onto a train track

>> Driving your car recklessly

>> Harming an animal

>> Harming yourself or another person

>> Having a panic attack in a public place

>> Making a bad decision that results in irreparable consequences

>> Being harshly rejected or humiliated

>> Experiencing thoughts and images about death or violence to self and others

When you have such unsolicited ghoulish mental activity, it's understandable that you want to get rid of it. Typically, however, the harder you try to rid yourself of such thoughts and images, the more they take hold. This is because your attempts to eliminate, avoid, or neutralize unwelcome thoughts are driven by the fundamental rule:

> "I must not have such thoughts; they're unacceptable and mean something dreadful."

When you put effort into preventing or eliminating a certain thought, you're inadvertently focusing more attention on it. If you regard certain kinds of mental activity as taboo, you increase your fears of it occurring. Paradoxically, you may end up increasing the frequency of intrusive images and thoughts plus elevating your disturbance in response to them. Everyone has intrusive thoughts and images from time to time. Even if you're not in any form of psychological or emotional distress, you're not immune to the occasional gruesome mental image. People without anxiety or depression, however, are more readily able to dismiss the thought or image as unpleasant (or even shocking) but of ultimately no real importance. You can begin to tolerate unpleasant thoughts by adopting the following attitude:

> "I don't like these thoughts, but they aren't abnormal or important. They don't mean something bad about me."

Knowing a thought is just a thought

Because the content of these types of thoughts is so abhorrent to you, they can *feel* terribly important. You might assume that they mean you're more likely to do some horrendous deed or that something awful is now going to happen to a loved one because you thought them. More accurately, these types of thoughts are merely a reflection of what you hold dear and value. Rather cruelly, you tend to be afflicted by the kind of thoughts that run counter to your true character and value system.

TIP

You can try to think of intrusive thoughts and images as "waking nightmares." When you have a nasty dream, you probably shake it off quickly because you realize it was just a dream. You likely don't give the content of your dreams much credence. Do the same with unpleasant images that come when you're awake. Just because you're awake doesn't make these thoughts any more valid or important.

REMEMBER

Even though some thoughts and images are uncomfortable, you *can* tolerate them. As you increase your tolerance for unwelcome mental images, you simultaneously reduce your fear of them. Disliking specific kinds of thought is okay, but remind yourself that thoughts are *all* they are.

Letting unwelcome thoughts extinguish themselves

Worrying and upsetting thoughts and images don't last forever. If you do nothing, they eventually fade away. As we've already mentioned, trying to control unwelcome thoughts rarely works for long. The key is treating these thoughts as though they're of no importance. When something is of little or no importance, you tend to ignore it or give it little attention. Instead of fighting against these trivial, though tormenting, thoughts, do nothing. Remove the boxing gloves and just let your mind move onto other more neutral images and thoughts naturally. Doing so sounds simple and straightforward, but letting go can be hard to master. Your feelings of anxiety, disgust, or horror about intrusive thoughts can compel you to action. Resist the pull of your feelings.

TIP

Try these tips:

>> Let unwelcome thoughts play out in the background as though they were just noise. Think of these thoughts like static on the radio or street noise outside your office window. You can filter them out and refocus your attention onto a task.

>> Busy your mind doing something else more interesting or compelling. Pick up the phone and make some important calls, do a crossword puzzle, or go for a walk.

>> Raise your heart rate. Going for a run, playing a sport, or vacuuming vigorously can relieve anxiety and clear your mind.

As you pay less attention to unwelcome thoughts, you'll probably find that your adverse feelings about them become less intense. Eventually, just allowing your thoughts to extinguish will become much easier because you'll have reduced their emotional impact.

WARNING

It may be tempting to ask for reassurance from friends or your CBT therapist that your thoughts aren't dangerous. This can be a slippery slope since you unwittingly reinforce fear and intolerance of unwanted thought content. Instead of repeatedly seeking reassurance, remember to treat thoughts of this ilk as unimportant. You probably don't dwell on or talk incessantly about unimportant things, so practice the same policy in this instance.

2

Charting the Course: Defining Problems

Chapter **7**

Exploring Emotions

This chapter is all about emotions. If your first instinct is to immediately skip over this messy subject, we aim to introduce you to some of the key differences between the unhealthy negative emotions you may experience and their healthy counterparts. The information we offer also helps you discover ways to identify whether you're experiencing a healthy or an unhealthy emotional response.

You may be wondering why we're focusing on negative emotions in this chapter and neglecting positive feelings such as happiness. You may be thinking, "They've missed the point; I want relief from discomfort and to find happiness." The reason for dealing with the negative is that few people sign up for therapy because they're having problems with positive emotions. Not a lot of people come to us looking for a way to overcome their relentless feelings of contentment. The emotions that give people trouble typically include guilt, anger, depression, and shame.

Although feeling bad when bad things happen is natural, you don't need to make things worse for yourself by giving yourself unhealthy negative emotions. Healthy negative emotions are generally less profoundly uncomfortable and less problematic than their unhealthy counterparts. For example, feeling intensely sad (a healthy negative emotion) is less uncomfortable than feeling intensely depressed (an unhealthy emotion). Likewise, feeling intense sadness can prompt you to do things to improve your situation, but depression's more likely to lead to your inaction and resignation.

Fortunately, you can think what to feel, to a greater or lesser extent, which can reduce your emotional discomfort. By choosing to think in healthy and helpful ways, you're more likely to experience healthy emotions.

Naming Your Feelings

One of the key benefits of learning more about your emotions is learning to "read" and label them. The psychological literature offers solid evidence that *alexithymia*, difficulty in reading one's emotions, makes people significantly more vulnerable to emotional problems.

If someone asks you how you feel, you may have difficulty describing exactly which emotion you're feeling. You may not be sure what name to give to your internal experience, or perhaps you're feeling more than one emotion at the same time.

WARNING

Don't get caught up on words. When you start to distinguish between healthy and unhealthy feelings, what you call them isn't terribly important. The main point is to be able to analyze your thoughts and behaviors and to notice where your attention is focused. (CBT refers to this as *attention focus*.) These three areas are your most reliable guides as to which type of emotion you're experiencing.

For the sake of clarity, therapists can often encourage people to use different words for unhealthy and healthy alternatives to common feelings. For example, you could use the word *anger* to describe an unhealthy emotion and *annoyance* to describe a healthy counterpart.

Some people find it simpler to choose a descriptive word for their emotion and to add the term *healthy* or *unhealthy* to that word. Whatever way you prefer to describe your emotions is okay. The important bit is understanding the category each emotion falls into. People have different ways of describing things. Think about how you'd describe an oil painting compared with the way a friend or art critic may talk about it. Similarly, people describe emotional states in diverse ways. You, a friend, and a psychotherapist (someone highly skilled in discussing emotions) may all use unique words to describe the same type of feeling.

If you're not used to talking about the way you feel, you may have difficulty finding the words to reflect your feelings.

The following is a reference list of common human emotions and their synonyms, which you can use to increase your vocabulary of *emotive* (relating to emotions) terminology. This list is not broken down into healthy and unhealthy emotions.

» **Angry:** Aggressive, annoyed, bad-tempered, complaining, confounded, cross, displeased, enraged, fractious, fuming, furious, hostile, ill-tempered, incensed, irritate, livid, miffed, peevish, prickly, resentful, testy, touchy, truculent

» **Anxious:** Agitated, apprehensive, bothered, concerned, edgy, fearful, fretful, frightened, jumpy, nervous, nervy, panicky, restless, tense, troubled, uneasy, vexed, worried

» **Ashamed:** Belittled, debased, defamed, degraded, discredited, disgraced, dishonored, humiliated, mortified, scorned, smeared, sullied, tarnished, undignified, vilified

» **Disappointed:** Crestfallen, deflated, dejected, discouraged, disenchanted, disheartened, disillusioned, dismayed, gutted, let down, thwarted

» **Disgusted:** Abominated, appalled, baulked at, cloyed at, disturbed, filled with loathing, gagging, grossed out, horrified, made to shudder, morally outraged, nauseated, repelled, repulsed, revolted, sickened, squicked, stomach-turned

» **Embarrassed:** Awkward, diminished, discomfited, humiliated, ill at ease, insecure, self-conscious, small, timid, uncomfortable, unconfident, unsure of oneself

» **Envious:** Geen with envy, malevolent, malicious, Schadenfreude, sour, spiteful

» **Guilty:** Answerable, at fault, blameworthy, condemned, culpable, deplorable, indefensible, inexcusable, in the wrong, liable, reprehensible, unforgivable, unpardonable

» **Hurt:** Aggrieved, broken-hearted, cut to the quick, cut up, damaged, devastated, gutted, hard done by, harmed, horrified, injured, marred, offended, pained, wounded

» **Jealous:** Bitter and twisted, distrustful, doubtful, green-eyed, skeptical, suspicious, wary

» **LOVE (we threw this one in just to lighten the mood):** Admiring, adoring, affectionate, blissful, crazed, devoted, enamored, esteemed, fond, head over heels, infatuated, keen, loved-up, love-struck, mad about, on cloud nine, smitten, struck by Cupid's arrow, worshipping

» **Sad:** bereft, blue, depressed, distraught, distressed, down, downcast, downhearted, grief-stricken, heartsick, inconsolable, melancholic, mournful, shattered, sorrowful, tearful

Thinking What to Feel

One benefit of understanding the difference between healthy and unhealthy emotions is that you give yourself a better chance to check out what you're thinking. If you recognize that you're experiencing an unhealthy emotion, you're in a position to challenge any faulty thinking that may be leading to your unhealthy emotional response. Disputing and correcting thinking errors can help you experience a healthy, negative emotion instead of an unhealthy feeling. (See Chapter 2 for more on thinking errors and how to correct them.)

REMEMBER

A common axiom is "I think; therefore I am." A CBT version is "I think; therefore, I feel."

Feelings aren't as one-dimensional as they may seem. How you feel is more than just the emotion itself because feelings don't just come out of thin air. They have a context. When you begin to make a distinction between your healthy and unhealthy emotions, look at the *interaction* among your thinking, your actions, your attention focus, your memory, your themes or triggers, and the way you feel. Table 7-1 gives a clear breakdown of the characteristics of healthy and unhealthy emotions.

TABLE 7-1 **Healthy and Unhealthy Emotions**

Emotion	Theme	Thoughts	Attention Focus	Behavior/Action Tendencies
Anxiety (unhealthy)	Threat or danger	Has rigid or extreme attitudes	Monitors threat or danger excessively	Withdraws physically and mentally from threats
		Overestimates degree of threat		Uses superstitious behavior to ward off threat
		Underestimates ability to cope with threat		Numbs anxiety with drugs or alcohol
		Increases threat-related thoughts		Seeks reassurance
Concern (healthy)	Threat or danger	Has flexible and preferential attitudes	Doesn't see threat where no threat exists	Faces up to threat
		Views threat realistically		Deals with threat constructively

Emotion	Theme	Thoughts	Attention Focus	Behavior/Action Tendencies
		Realistically assesses ability to cope with threat		Doesn't seek unneeded reassurance
		Doesn't increase threat-related thoughts		
Depression (unhealthy)	Loss or failure	Has rigid and extreme attitudes	Dwells on past loss/failure; assumes failures in the past have implications for the future	Withdraws from others
		Sees only negative aspects of loss/failure		
	Ruminates on unsolvable problems	Neglects self and living environment		
		Feels helpless	Focuses on personal flaws and failings	Attempts to end feelings of depression in self-destructive ways
		Thinks future is bleak and hopeless	Focuses on negative world events	
Sadness (healthy)	Loss or failure	Has flexible and preferential attitudes	Doesn't dwell on past loss/failure; assumes failures can be overcome	Talks to significant others about feelings of loss/failure
		Sees both negative and positive aspects of loss/failure	Focuses on problems that one can change	Continues to care for self and living environment
		Can help self	Focuses on personal strengths and skills	Avoids self-destructive behaviors
		Can think about future with hope	Balances focus between positive and negative world events	
Anger (unhealthy)	Personal rule is broken or self-esteem is threatened	Has rigid and extreme attitudes	Looks for evidence of malicious intent in other person	Seeks revenge

(continued)

TABLE 7-1 *(continued)*

Emotion	Theme	Thoughts	Attention Focus	Behavior/Action Tendencies
		Assumes other person acted deliberately	Looks for evidence of offensive behavior being repeated by other people	Attacks other person physically or verbally
		Thinks of self as right and other person as wrong		Takes anger out on innocent person, animal, or object
		Can't see other person's point of view		Withdraws aggressively/sulks
				Recruits allies against other person
Annoyance (healthy)	Personal rule is broken or self-esteem is threatened	Has flexible and preferential attitudes	Looks for evidence that other person may not have malicious intent	Doesn't seek revenge
		Considers other person may not have acted deliberately	Doesn't see further offense where it may not exist	Asserts self without physical/verbal violence
		Considers that both self and other person may be right to some degree		Doesn't take out feelings on innocent parties
		Can see other person's point of view		Remains in situation, striving for resolution (doesn't sulk)
				Requests other person to change their offensive behavior
Shame (unhealthy)	Shameful personal information has been publicly revealed by self or others	Overestimates shamefulness of information revealed	Sees disapproval from others where it doesn't exist	Hides from others to avoid disapproval
		Overestimates degree of disapproval from others		May attack others who have shamed self, in attempt to save face

Emotion	Theme	Thoughts	Attention Focus	Behavior/Action Tendencies
		Overestimates how long disapproval will last		May try to repair self-esteem in self-destructive ways
				Ignores attempts from social group to return to normal
Regret (healthy)	Shameful personal information has been publicly revealed by self or others	Is compassionately self-accepting about information revealed	Focuses on evidence that self is accepted by social group despite information revealed	Continues to participate in social interaction
		Is realistic about degree of disapproval from others		Responds to attempts from social group to return to normal
		Is realistic about how long disapproval will last		
Hurt (unhealthy)	Other person treats one badly (self is undeserving)	Has rigid and extreme attitudes	Looks for evidence of other person not caring or being indifferent	Stops communicating with other person/sulks
		Overestimates unfairness of other's behavior		Punishes other person through silence or criticism, without stating what one feels hurt about
		Thinks other person doesn't care		
		Thinks of self as alone and uncared for		
		Dwells on past hurts		
		Thinks other person must make first move toward resolution		
Disappointment (healthy)	Other person treats one badly (self is undeserving)	Has flexible and preferential attitudes	Focuses on evidence that other person does care and isn't indifferent	Communicates with other person about feelings

(continued)

TABLE 7-1 *(continued)*

Emotion	Theme	Thoughts	Attention Focus	Behavior/Action Tendencies
		Is realistic about degree of unfairness of other's behavior		Tries to influence other person to act in fairer manner
		Thinks other person acted badly but doesn't think that they don't care		
		Doesn't think of self as alone or uncared for		
		Doesn't dwell on past hurts		
		Doesn't wait for other person to make first move		
Jealousy (unhealthy)	Threat to relationship with partner, friend or family member, or another significant relationship from another person	Has rigid and extreme attitudes	Looks for sexual/romantic connotations in partner's conversations with others Looks for signs that best friend prefers a new friend Looking for evidence that a parent favors one's sibling	Seeks constant reassurance that partner is faithful and loving
		Overestimates threat to the relationship	Creates visual images of partner being unfaithful	Monitors or restricts partner's movements and actions
		Thinks partner is always on verge of leaving for another	Looks for evidence that partner is having an affair	Retaliates for partner's imagined infidelity
		Thinks partner will leave for another person whom they have admitted to finding attractive		Sets tests/traps for partner
				Sulks

Emotion	Theme	Thoughts	Attention Focus	Behavior/Action Tendencies
Concern for relationship (healthy)	Threat to relationship with partner, friend, or family member from another person	Has flexible and preferential attitudes	Doesn't look for evidence that partner is having an affair	Allows partner to express love without needing excessive reassurance
		Is realistic about degree of threat to relationship	Doesn't create images of partner being unfaithful	Allows partner freedom without monitoring them
		Thinks partner finding others attractive is normal	Views partner's conversation with others as normal	Allows partner to express natural interest in opposite sex without imagining infidelity
Unhealthy envy (unhealthy)	Another person possesses something desirable (self lacks desired possession or condition)	Has rigid and extreme attitudes	Focuses on how to get the desired possession or condition without regard for any consequences	Criticizes the person with desired possession or condition
		Thinks about the desired possession or condition in a negative way to try to reduce its desirability	Focuses on how to deprive other person of the desired possession or condition	Criticizes the desired possession or condition
		Pretends to be happy without desired possession even though this is untrue		Attempts to steal/destroy the desired possession to deprive others
Healthy envy (healthy)	Another person possesses something desirable (self lacks desired possession or condition)	Has flexible and preferential attitudes	Considers how to acquire the desired possession or condition without detriment to self or others	Is fair about the person who has the desired possession or condition

(continued)

TABLE 7-1 *(continued)*

Emotion	Theme	Thoughts	Attention Focus	Behavior/Action Tendencies
		Thinks positively about the desired possession or condition	Focuses on allowing other person to enjoy the possession or condition	
		Accepts some degree of unhappiness without the desired possession or condition	Acknowledges the desirability of the possession or condition	Hopes the other person will enjoy the possession or condition and does not attempt to deprive the other person
Guilt (unhealthy)	Broken moral code (by failing to do something or by committing a sin), hurting, or offending significant other	Has rigid and extreme attitudes	Looks for evidence of others blaming one for the sin	Desires to escape from guilt feelings in self-defeating ways
		Thinks one has definitely sinned	Looks for evidence of punishment or retribution	Begs for forgiveness
		Thinks that one deserves punishment		Promises that a sin will never be committed again
		Ignores mitigating factors		Punishes self either physically or through deprivation
		Ignores other people's potential responsibility for sin		Attempts to disclaim any legitimate responsibility for the wrongdoing as an attempt to alleviate feelings of guilt
Remorse (healthy)	Broken moral code (by failing to do something or by committing a sin), hurting or offending significant other	Has flexible and preferential attitudes	Doesn't look for evidence of others blaming oneself for the sin	Faces up to healthy pain that comes with knowing that one has sinned

Emotion	Theme	Thoughts	Attention Focus	Behavior/Action Tendencies
		Considers actions in context and with understanding before making a judgment about whether one has sinned	Doesn't look for evidence of punishment or retribution	Asks for forgiveness
		Takes appropriate level of responsibility for the sin		Atones for the sin by taking a penalty or making appropriate amends
		Considers mitigating factors		Doesn't have tendency to be defensive or to make excuses for the poor behavior
		Doesn't believe that punishment is deserved or imminent		
Unhealthy disgust (unhealthy)	Something physically noxious or morally offensive is experienced or witnessed	Has rigid and extreme attitudes	Sees further toxicity or offense where none exists	Withdraws physically and mentally from the experience
		Overestimates the degree of disgust appropriate to the experience	Focuses on the discomfort of the experience and discounts coping behaviors	Repeatedly seeks reassurance that the experience won't happen again soon
		Underestimates ability to cope with the toxicity or offense and take corrective action	Selectively notices reactions of others that seem to justify extreme disgust response	
		Amplifies probability of the noxious or offensive experience happening again		Dwells on the noxious or offensive experience

(continued)

TABLE 7-1 *(continued)*

Emotion	Theme	Thoughts	Attention Focus	Behavior/Action Tendencies
				Develops elaborate avoidance strategies and ritualistic behaviors to prevent future similar experiences
				Vilifies the offensive person(s) or noxious event
Distaste/ healthy disgust (healthy)	Something physically noxious or morally offensive is experienced or witnessed	Has flexible and preferential attitudes	Doesn't see further toxicity or offense where none exists	Confronts the experience both physically and mentally
		Estimates a degree of distaste proportionate to the experience	Focuses on coping behaviors rather than on the discomfort of the experience	Accepts reassurance that the experience won't happen again soon
		Recognizes ability to cope with the toxicity or offense and take corrective action if appropriate	Notices reactions of others that seem to justify moderate disgust response	Doesn't dwell on the noxious or offensive experience
		Is realistic about the probability of the noxious or offensive experience happening again		Develops functional strategies to prevent future similar experiences if possible
				Fairly and accurately judges the offensive person(s) or noxious event

Understanding the Anatomy of Emotions

Figure 7-1 shows the complex processes involved in human emotion. Whenever you feel a certain emotion, a whole system is activated. This system includes the thoughts and images that enter your mind, the memories you access, the aspects of yourself or the surrounding world that you focus on, the bodily and mental sensations you experience, physical changes such as appetite, your behavior, and the things you *feel like* doing.

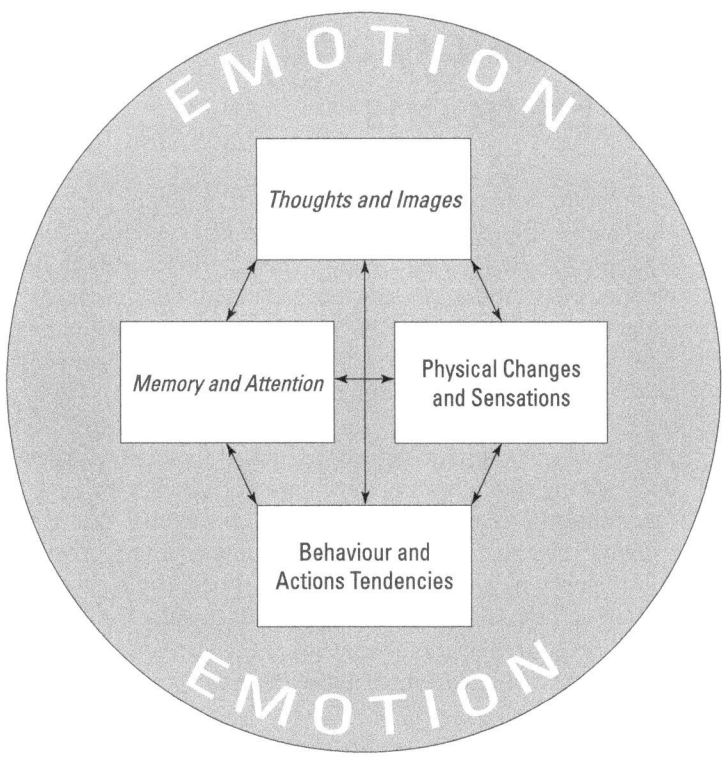

FIGURE 7-1:
The anatomy
of emotion.

As the figure shows, these dimensions interact in complex ways. For example, training your attention on possible threats is likely to increase the chance of anxious thoughts popping into your mind, and vice versa. Not sleeping well may increase the chances of your being inactive; continued inactivity can further disrupt your usual sleeping pattern. The advantage of understanding this system of emotion as presented in Figure 7-1 is that it gives you plenty of opportunity to make changes. Changing even one aspect of the system can make changing other parts easier.

An example of change is becoming more active if you've been inactive, which may alleviate your feelings of depression and make it easier for you to challenge your depressive, pessimistic thinking. Being prescribed antidepressant medication, which works by affecting brain chemistry, can take the edge off your depression. Use of antidepressants can make it easier for you to train your attention *away* from your negative thoughts and uncomfortable symptoms and *toward* possible solutions to some of your practical problems. (See Chapter 11 for more about over-coming depression.)

Comparing Healthy and Unhealthy Emotions

Deciphering between healthy and unhealthy versions of negative emotions can be challenging, especially when the process is new to you. Think of Table 7-1 as your emotional ready reckoner for the characteristics of both healthy and unhealthy emotions. Everything you may need to identify the emotion you're experiencing is in this table. Plus, if you do identify that an emotion you're experiencing is unhealthy, you can implement the thoughts, attention focuses, and behaviors of the healthy version to aid you in feeling better.

Themes refer to situational aspects linked to emotion. Themes are the same for both healthy and unhealthy negative emotions. For example, when you feel guilty (an unhealthy negative emotion), the theme for that emotion is that you've "sinned" by either doing or failing to do something. Another way of saying that you're guilty is that you've transgressed or failed to live up to your moral code. Remorse, the healthy alternative to guilt, results from the same theme as guilt. However, your thoughts, behaviors, and focus of attention are different when you're remorseful and when you're guilty.

Themes can be useful in helping you put your finger on the nature of the emotion you're experiencing. However, they're not enough to help you decide whether your emotion is a healthy or unhealthy one. Consider the following situation:

> Imagine that you have an elderly aunt who needs your help to continue living independently. You usually visit her on the weekends and do jobs that she's too frail to do for herself, like changing light bulbs and cleaning windows. Last weekend you went skiing with friends instead of checking in on your aunt. She became impatient waiting for the light bulb in her hallway to be changed and tried to do it herself. Unfortunately, she fell off the chair she was standing on and broke her hip.

Thematically, this situation is one in which you broke or failed to fulfill a personal moral code, resulting in hurting or offending someone else.

If you feel guilty (an unhealthy negative emotion), you're likely to experience the following:

>> **Type of thinking:** Your thinking becomes rigid and demand-based. You conclude that you've done a bad thing (sinned). You assume more personal responsibility than may be legitimate, discounting or not considering mitigating factors. You may believe that some form of punishment is deserved or imminent.

- » **Focus of attention:** You look for more evidence that you've sinned, or you look for evidence that others hold you responsible for the sin.

- » **Behavior (action tendency):** You may desire to escape from guilty feelings in self-defeating ways, such as begging for forgiveness, promising that you'll never commit a sin again, punishing yourself either physically or through deprivation, or attempting to disclaim any legitimate responsibility for the wrongdoing.

REMEMBER

Action tendency refers to an urge to behave in a certain way that you may or may not actually act upon. Different emotions produce an urge within you to do certain things. In some cases, you may actually do or say something, and in others you may just be aware that you *want* to do or say something. An example of action tendency might be *wanting* to run out of a room and hide when feeling ashamed or feeling unhealthily angry and *wanting* to punch someone's lights out without actually doing so. By contrast, you can think about the situation differently and feel remorse (a healthy negative emotion). Although the same theme (a broken or failed moral code, causing hurt or offence to a significant other) still applies, you experience the following:

- » **Type of thinking:** Your thinking is more flexible and preference-based. You look at actions in context and with understanding before making a judgment about whether you sinned. You consider mitigating factors of the situation and don't believe that punishment is deserved or imminent.

- » **Focus of attention:** You don't look for further evidence that you sinned. Neither do you look for evidence that others hold you responsible for the sin.

- » **Behavior (action tendency):** You face up to the healthy pain that comes with knowing you've sinned. You may ask for, but not beg for, forgiveness. You understand the reasons for your wrongdoing and act on that understanding. You may atone for the sin by taking a penalty or making appropriate amends. You avoid defensiveness and excuse-making.

REMEMBER

The theme involving both guilt and remorse is the same, but your thinking, action tendencies, and focus of attention are different. This point is true for all the healthy and unhealthy emotion pairs.

Spotting the difference in thinking

As the example in the preceding section illustrates, unhealthy emotions can spring from rigid, demand-based thinking. Thoughts or beliefs like "other people must behave respectfully toward me at all times" and "I should always get what I want without hassle" can lead to unhealthy anger when other people and the world don't meet these demands.

Healthy emotions spring from flexible, *preference-based thinking.* So, thoughts and beliefs like "I prefer others to treat me respectfully, but they're not bound to do so" and "I prefer to get what I want without hassle, but no reason exists that this should always be the case" can lead to healthy annoyance when other people and the world don't meet your preferences.

TIP

Rigid thinking is a reliable indicator that you're having an unhealthy feeling. When you think rigidly, you're more likely to underestimate your ability to cope with and overcome the negative event in question. The more adept you become at identifying your thoughts, beliefs, and attitudes as either rigid and demanding or flexible and preferential, the easier you can work out whether your feelings are healthy or unhealthy.

When you feel *guilty,* you think in an unhealthy, rigid, demand-based manner and may say things like the following:

>> "I absolutely shouldn't have left my aunt alone."

>> "Leaving my aunt alone was a bad thing and means I'm a bad person."

>> "I can't bear the pain of knowing that I've done this bad thing of leaving my aunt alone."

You may then continue to think in the following guilt-enhancing ways:

>> You fail to acknowledge that your aunt ultimately chose to try to change the light bulb herself. You fail to acknowledge that other members of your family can also check in on your aunt.

>> You ignore the fact that you had no way of knowing that the light bulb needed changing and that you hadn't foreseen your aunt taking such a risk.

>> You expect that your aunt will blame you entirely. You think about the punishment that you believe you deserve.

By contrast, if you feel *remorseful,* you think in a healthy, flexible, preference-based manner and may say things such as these:

>> "I wish I hadn't left my aunt alone, but regrettably I did."

>> "Leaving my aunt alone may mean that I've done a bad thing but not that I'm a bad person."

>> "I can bear the pain of knowing that I've done this bad thing of leaving my aunt alone."

You can then continue to think in helpful ways:

>> You can acknowledge your part in the accident's occurrence, but you can also consider that other members of the family failed to check in on your aunt.

>> You can acknowledge that you didn't foresee your aunt taking the risk of changing a light bulb. Nor did you know that the bulb would burn out.

>> You can expect that your aunt may be upset with you, but you believe that you don't deserve a severe punishment.

Taking legitimate responsibility for what happens in a situation enables you to think about the event in a holistic way. You don't need to prolong uncomfortable feelings of remorse beyond what's reasonable and appropriate to the situation. Your ability to solve problems isn't impeded by feelings of guilt.

Spotting the difference in behaving, and ways you want to behave

Another way of figuring out whether your emotion is in the healthy or unhealthy camp is to look at your actual behavior or the way in which you feel inclined to behave.

Healthy negative emotions are accompanied by largely constructive behaviors, whereas unhealthy feelings usually go hand-in-hand with self-defeating behaviors. Problem-solving is still possible when you're healthily sad, annoyed, remorseful, or regretful, but you have much greater difficulty planning clear ways to surmount your problems when you're unhealthily depressed, enraged, guilty, or ashamed.

For example, if you respond to your aunt's falling over with *guilt-based action tendencies*, you may do one or more of the following:

>> Go out and get drunk, trying to block out your guilty feelings.

>> Visit your aunt in the hospital and plead for her forgiveness.

>> Promise that you'll never again let down your aunt, or anyone else dear to you, for as long as you live.

>> Decide that you won't go on any other trips while your aunt is alive.

The preceding behaviors are problematic because they're extreme and unrealistic. These actions focus on self-punishment rather than look at the reality of the situation and how you can, in this example, best meet your aunt's needs.

On the other hand, if you're feeling healthy remorse, your *action tendencies* may include some of the following:

>> Endure the discomfort of knowing that your aunt has been hurt (rather than getting drunk to avoid it).

>> Visit your aunt in the hospital regularly and apologize for having left her alone.

>> Understand that your aunt needs continuous support but that you have the right to go out with friends.

>> Plan to stay with your aunt for a week or so after she's discharged from hospital.

>> Resolve to plan your trips away more carefully and to arrange for nursing staff to be with your aunt when you're unavailable.

The preceding behaviors are geared toward making sure that your aunt doesn't hurt herself again during your absence. By taking an appropriate amount of responsibility for the accident, you can still look for ways to provide comfort for your aunt rather than concentrate on punishing yourself.

Spotting the difference in what you focus on

In addition to differences in types of thinking and behaving, you can distinguish healthy from unhealthy emotions by checking out the focus of your attention. If you're having an unhealthy emotion, your mind is likely to focus on catastrophic possibilities in the future based on the primary event.

If you're responding to the injured auntie situation from a place of guilt, you may focus your attention on the following:

>> Blaming yourself for abandoning your aunt and for the accident happening

>> Feeling the pain of your guilt while neglecting to consider potential solutions to the problem of your aunt needing continuous care

>> Looking for evidence that your aunt blames you entirely for the accident

>> Looking for blame from other people, such as hospital staff and family members

You continue to give yourself an unduly rough ride, thereby prolonging your distressing guilt feelings by focusing on the bleakest possible aspects of your aunt's accident.

If you respond to the situation from a place of remorse, you're likely to focus your attention on the following:

>> Accepting that leaving your aunt alone may have been a bad decision but that you had no intention of putting her at risk

>> Feeling the pain of remorse over the accident but also trying to find ways to improve the situation

>> Not seeking out evidence of blame from your aunt

>> Accepting evidence that hospital staff or family members don't blame you for the accident

Thus, your attention focus when you respond from a place of remorse enables you to take some responsibility for your aunt's broken hip but avoid dwelling on the potential for blame and punishment.

Seeing Similarities in Your Physical Sensations

Butterflies in your stomach, blood racing through your veins, light-headedness, sweaty palms, heart pounding. Sound familiar? We expect so. If someone described these physical symptoms to you, you may try to guess what emotion they were experiencing. However, it would be difficult to confidently determine the specific emotion because these sensations can accompany several positive and negative emotional states. For example, you may get butterflies in your stomach when you're excited, angry, anxious, or in love, as illustrated in Figure 7-2.

The sensations that you feel in your body also tend to overlap in both healthy and unhealthy negative emotions. For example, you may get butterflies in your stomach when you're unhealthily anxious *and* when you're healthily concerned. Therefore, using your physical symptoms as a guide to judging the healthiness of your negative feelings isn't reliable.

© John Wiley & Sons, Inc.

FIGURE 7-2:
Notice the
similarities in
your physical
sensations.

The main way in which your physical responses are likely to vary between the healthy and unhealthy categories is in their intensity. You probably find that sensations are more intense, uncomfortable and debilitating when you're having unhealthy emotions, such as anxiety and anger. You may also notice that uncomfortable physical sensations last longer when you're experiencing unhealthy negative emotions.

Identifying Feelings About Feelings

Getting two emotions for the price of one isn't such a great deal when two unhealthy negative emotions are on offer.

TECHNICAL STUFF

CBT professionals call feelings about feelings *meta-emotions.* The prefix *meta* comes from Greek and means "beside" or "after."

Sometimes you can give yourself a second helping of unhealthy emotion by holding rigid demands about which emotions you believe are acceptable for you to experience in the first place.

A common example of feelings about feelings is found in depression. Many people have guilty feelings about their depression. This guilt often comes from the demands people make of themselves. An example might be that they mustn't let other people down or put undue strain on loved ones. Here are some typical guilt-producing thoughts that are common in depressed people:

>> "I should be contributing more to the running of the home."

>> "I must be able to demonstrate love and care to my children."

>> "My partner and children are worried about me, and I'm making them suffer."

>> "I shouldn't be neglecting my friends in this way."

Recognizing your meta-emotions is important because meta-emotions can prevent you from dealing with your primary emotional problems. For example, you may be feeling guilty about having depression. If you can stop feeling guilty, you'll almost certainly find that you can work on overcoming your depression more effectively.

If you find that the concept of feeling guilty about being depressed really strikes a chord with you, go to Chapter 11, where we discuss it in more detail.

TIP

HANDY EMOTIONAL HEALTH CHECKLIST

The following is an abbreviated list of ways that can help you find out the nature of a feeling and give it a name. The list can also help you assess whether an emotion is of the healthy or unhealthy negative variety.

- Have you identified a word to describe how you feel inside?

- Can you identify the theme of your emotion?

- How does your emotion lead you to behave? Are your actions or urges to act helpful or unhelpful?

- Are you thinking in a flexible way, or are you thinking in a rigid and demanding way?

- What are you paying attention to? Are you looking at the event from all angles?

- Is another emotion getting in the way of your being able to identify your first emotion? For example, are you feeling guilty or ashamed about your anger, depression, or other emotion?

Defining Your Emotional Problems

The aim of CBT is to help you overcome your emotional problems and move you toward your goals. As with all kinds of problem-solving, *defining* your emotional problems is the first step in solving those problems.

Making a statement

Writing down a problem statement has three main components — the emotion, the theme or event (what you feel your emotion about), and what you do in response to that emotion. You can effectively describe an emotional problem by filling in the blanks of the following statement:

Feeling ____ (emotion) about _____ (theme or event), leading me to _____ (response).

For example:

Feeling *anxious* about *my face turning red in social situations,* leading me to *avoid going out to bars and clubs and to splash my face with water if I feel hot.*

Feeling *depressed* about *the end of my relationship with my girlfriend,* leading me to *spend too much time in bed, avoid seeing people, and take less care of myself.*

Rating your emotional problem

Human nature leads you to focus on how bad you feel rather than how much better you feel. As you reduce the intensity of any emotional disturbance, you can find motivation in being able to see a difference. After you describe a problematic emotion, rate it on a scale of 0 to 10, based on how much distress the emotion causes you and how much it interferes with your life.

As you work on resolving your emotional problem by making changes to your thinking and behavior, continue to rate the distress and interference it's causing you. Your ratings are likely to decrease over time as you make efforts to overcome your unhealthy negative emotions. Review your ratings once a week or so. Doing this review reminds you of your progress and replenishes your motivation to keep up the good work.

TIP

Share your ratings with your CBT therapist if you have one. Your therapist can haul out your rating records and show you the progress you've made if your motivation begins to flag.

PONDERING POSITIVE EMOTION

We've deliberately focused on the idea that the better psychological well-being is related to moving from unhealthy negative emotions to healthy negative emotions. This isn't because we're negative-nellies only interested in the negative stuff. It's because some sort of negative emotion is a natural and healthy response, at least for a while, when we experience adversity. As we've already noted, being able to label your emotions is a positive input to your mental health, whereas avoidance of negative emotion predicts poorer mental health. However, all of that said, research shows that positive emotion can be good for you and even enhance your results from CBT. Emotions like love, curiosity, joy, gratitude, and contentment support living life to the fullest and may help you be more creative and connected. So alongside your healthy negative emotions when they're appropriate, positive emotions should be on the menu too.

Chapter **8**

Identifying the Solutions That Maintain Your Problems

A potentially unhelpful way of thinking about CBT is as a "treatment" like, say, taking a pill. It probably has more in common with physical therapy, in fact. Correcting your cognitive biases might be like correcting your posture. You can think of strengthening more helpful beliefs, facing your fears, and systematically breaking free from old or unhelpful patterns as psychological exercises. This chapter is about identifying areas to work on so that you can experiment with change and see its effect.

Often, the problematic behaviors that maintain or worsen emotional problems in the long term are the very ones that people use to help themselves cope in the short term — hence, the common CBT expression, "Your solution becomes the problem."

The reality is that you probably weren't taught how to best tackle emotional problems such as anxiety, depression, and obsessions. We confess that even though we've been trained in the art of emotional problem-solving, when it comes to dealing with our own emotions, we can still manage to get it wrong.

In this chapter, I guide you toward identifying how your coping strategies may make you feel better in the moment but how they're actually counterproductive — and can make things worse in the long run.

When Feeling Better Can Make Your Problems Worse

Aaron Beck, founder of CBT, and Dennis Greenberger, a well-known CBT therapist, note that, if you can turn a counterproductive strategy on its head, you're well on the way to a real solution. This concept basically means that by doing the opposite of your established coping strategies, you can recover from your problems.

Exposing yourself to feared situations rather than avoiding them is a good example of turning a counterproductive strategy on its head. The more you avoid situations that you fear, the more afraid you become of ever encountering feared situations. Avoidance also undermines your sense of being able to cope with unpleasant or uncomfortable feelings. For example, never using an elevator may temporarily stop your anxious feelings about being in an enclosed space, but avoiding elevators doesn't help you overcome your fear of enclosed spaces once and for all.

Windy Dryden, one of the key people who trained me in CBT, coined the phrase "Feel better, get worse; feel worse, get better" when referring to people overcoming emotional problems. Many of the things that you may be doing — but in so doing maintaining your current problems — are driven by a highly understandable goal to reduce your distress. However, when you aim to get short-term relief, you may well be reinforcing the very beliefs and behaviors that underpin your problems.

REMEMBER

One of the most powerful ways of changing your emotions in a lasting way is to act against your unhelpful beliefs and to act on your alternative helpful beliefs. (Chapters 4 and 19 contain more information about forming alternative healthy beliefs.)

Problem-maintaining solutions can show up in the following ways:

>> **Avoiding situations that you fear or that provoke anxiety:** Avoidance tends to erode rather than boost your confidence. You remain afraid of the situations you avoid, so you don't give yourself a chance to confront and overcome your fears.

>> **Drinking alcohol or taking drugs to block out uncomfortable feelings:** Often, those bad feelings persist in the long term, and you end up with the added effect of the alcohol or drugs (hangover, comedown). Also, you have the potential to develop a new problem: substance dependence. (Have a look at Chapter 11 for more information about addiction.)

>> **Concealing aspects of yourself that cause you shame:** Hiding things about yourself — such as imperfections in your appearance, childhood experiences, mistakes from the past, or current psychological difficulties — can make you feel chronically insecure that someone may "find you out." Hiding shameful aspects of your experiences also denies you the opportunity to find out that other people have similar experiences, and they won't think any less of you for revealing your secrets.

>> **Putting off dealing with problems or tasks until you're in the mood:** If you wait to act until "the right time," until you "feel like it," or when you feel sufficiently inspired, you may wait a long time. Putting off essential tasks may save you some discomfort in the short term, but undone tasks also tend to weigh heavily on your mind.

The following sections deal with common counterproductive strategies for coping with common psychological problems. We explain that doing what makes you feel briefly better may be perpetuating your problem.

Getting Over Depression Without Getting Yourself Down

If you're feeling depressed, you're likely to be less active and may withdraw from social contact. Inactivity and social withdrawal are often attempts to cope with depressed feelings, but they can reduce the positive reinforcement you get from life, increase isolation, increase fatigue, lead to the build-up of problems or chores, and leave you feeling guilty.

For example, if you've been feeling depressed for some time, you may use any of these ultimately negative strategies to relieve your depression:

>> To avoid feeling ashamed about being depressed, you may avoid seeing friends. This coping strategy leaves you feeling more isolated and means you don't get the support you need.

>> To avoid being irritable around your partner or children, you may try to minimize contact with them. Your children may become unruly, your

relationship with your partner may suffer, and you may end up feeling guilty about not spending time with any of them.

>> To avoid the embarrassment of finding it hard to keep on top of deadlines at work, you may stop going to work on a regular basis.

>> To try to pull yourself together, you may ruminate on why you feel the way you do.

>> To mentally escape from the pain that you're in, you might ruminate on wishing "if only" you had made a different choice in your life.

>> To cope with feeling tired and to find some relief from your depression, you may take naps during the day. Unfortunately, napping can disrupt your sleeping pattern, leading to even more fatigue.

TIP

To see how your depression is affecting your activity levels, record a typical week on the *activity schedule* in Chapter 13 (and Appendix B). Then, as we explain in Chapter 13, combat depression by scheduling your activities and rest periods for each day, and gradually build up your activity levels over time.

Loosening Your Grip on Control

Letting go of control is an especially relevant skill if you have any sort of anxiety problems, including obsessive-compulsive disorder (OCD), panic disorder, and post-traumatic stress disorder (PTSD). But it also applies to other types of emotional problems, such as anger and jealousy, and to eating disorders like anorexia and bulimia.

Following are some common examples of how you may be gripping the controls too hard:

>> Trying to limit your body's physical sensations because you believe that certain bodily symptoms will result in harm to yourself. For example, "If I don't stop feeling dizzy, I'll pass out."

>> Trying to control and monitor your thoughts because you think that if they get out of control, you'll go crazy.

>> Being very controlling about the types of food you eat, when you eat and how much you eat.

>> Trying to control your appetite and diminish your need for food.

>> Suppressing upsetting thoughts, doubts, or images because you believe that allowing them to enter your mind will cause harm to yourself or others. (This characteristic is typical of OCD. Check out Chapter 15 for more info.)

>> Trying to control your body's physical reactions to anxiety, such as trembling hands, blushing, or sweating, because you think that others will judge you harshly if they notice your symptoms.

Trying to control the uncontrollable is destined to leave you feeling powerless and ineffective. Instead of striving for control, look to change your attitude about needing control by accepting the discomfort of certain types of thoughts or bodily sensations. (Head to Chapter 10 for more information.)

If you try too hard to gain immediate control, you often end up doing some of these:

>> Focusing more on feeling out of control, thus making yourself feel even more powerless than you did at the beginning

>> Trying to control things that go against biology, like the need for food, leading to preoccupation and a further diminished sense of control

>> Putting pressure on yourself to control symptoms and thoughts that aren't within your control, thus making yourself feel more anxious

>> Concluding that something must be deeply wrong with you because you can't keep symptoms under control, thus making you feel more anxious, and experiencing more racing thoughts and unpleasant physical sensations

The next time you feel anxious in a public place or find yourself blushing, sweating, or having disturbing thoughts, put the concepts in this section to the test by trying harder to stop yourself from having those thoughts, blushing, or sweating. Chances are that you'll find your efforts produce even more of the thoughts and sensations you're trying so hard to control. Sometimes it's easier to see for yourself that the 'solution is the problem' by boosting the unhelpful strategy temporarily as an experiment.

Feeling Secure in an Uncertain World

Intolerance of uncertainty is a common contributing factor in anxiety, worry, PTSD, obsessional problems, and jealousy. Since the COVID-19 pandemic, this has become a particular focus in research. Taking a deeper dive into this literature reveals some interesting things about the way some of us relate to uncertainty. Some people have an almost philosophical objection to uncertainty, even seeing it as unfair and something to eliminate. Our ability to reach into our pocket and grab a device that can provide instant answers to any question we can think of can further erode our tolerance.

The universe we live in always has and always will include uncertainty. Regardless of our attitude toward uncertainty about the future and our health, we were hit by a global pandemic in the early 2020s. And an intolerance of uncertainty hurt substantially more people than it helped. Some people are intolerant of uncertainty (and its twin *ambiguity*) in quite a general way and others about quite a specific sort of threat. In any case, the key questions that CBT brings are these: "Is this helping you the best?" and "Might there be an attitude that is more helpful to you?"

As the saying goes, the only things you can be 100 percent sure of are death and taxes. Over and above that, humans live in a pretty uncertain universe. Of course, many things are predictable and pretty sure bets, like the sun rising in the morning and setting in the evening. However, other things in life are much more uncertain. "Will I be pretty?" "Will I be rich?" "Will I live to a ripe old age surrounded by grandchildren and a few cats?" *Qué será, será*. Whatever will be, will be . . .

Trying to get rid of doubt by seeking certainty is like trying to put out a fire by throwing more wood on it. If you're intolerant of uncertainty, have you ever noticed that as soon as you quell one doubt, another one's sure to pop up? The trick is to find ways to tolerate and even embrace ambiguity, doubt, and uncertainty — they exist whether you like it or not.

Your demands for certainty may be reflected in your behavior in these ways:

>> **Frequent requests for reassurance:** Constantly asking yourself and other people questions, such as, "Is it safe to touch the door handle without washing my hands?," "Do you find that person more attractive than me?," "Are you sure I haven't gained weight?," "Do you think I'll pass the exam?," and "Are you sure I won't get mugged if I go out?" are efforts to find some reassurance in an uncertain world. Unfortunately, excessive reassurance-seeking can reduce your confidence in your own judgment.

>> **Repeated checking behaviors:** *Checking behaviors* are actions you perform to create more certainty in your world. Such actions include checking several times that your doors and windows are locked, frequently asking your partner where they've been, seeing lots of different doctors to ensure that a physical sensation isn't a sign of serious illness, checking that you can still feel your hip bones and not fat, and going over conversations in your mind to be sure that you haven't said anything offensive. The irony is that the more you check, the

more uncertain you feel. You may feel temporarily better immediately following your checks, but it's not long before you feel compelled to carry them out again. Excessive checking can be time-consuming and tiring, and it can lower your mood.

>> **Superstitious rituals:** *Superstitious rituals* are things that you do to try to keep yourself safe or to prevent bad things from happening. Typically, superstitious rituals aren't directly related to whatever it is that you fear most. Examples of rituals include touching wood, repeating phrases in your mind, wearing lucky clothes or jewelry, and avoiding unlucky numbers out of a faulty belief that these rituals will stop unfortunate or tragic events befalling you or your loved ones. Engaging in superstitious behaviors can lead you to conclude that the ritual has prevented bad things from happening rather than help you understand that many bad events are unlikely to occur regardless of whether you perform a ritual.

Superstitious thinking also involves making faulty links between your subtle behaviors or thoughts (and even *dreams*) and reality. If you think about a loved one coming to harm (due to acute anxiety about their safety), you may assume, falsely, that you caused a subsequent accident by imagining it. If you have a vivid image (or dream) of a young child being abducted, you may conclude, "If it happens, maybe I made it happen by imagining it." Pretty disturbing stuff. What I point out to many of my clients is that people don't make superstitious links anywhere near as readily about good stuff. When was the last time you thought, "It's a beautiful day because I thought about the weather being amazing this week" or "My aunt's tumor is benign because I imagined it would be" or "I've won the lottery because I willed it to happen?" If your superstitious thinking makes any real sense at all (and it really *doesn't*), it has to hold true for both good and bad events.

>> **Avoiding risk:** Risks — such as global pandemics, becoming ill, having an accident, making poor decisions, or committing a social gaffe — are unavoidable and ever-present. You may be trying to eliminate risk by staying home or in "safe" places, eating only certain foods, never deviating from set routines, overplanning for trips away, or overpreparing for unlikely events such as war, plague, or famine. In fact, risk is a part of life and can only be avoided to a limited extent. The more you try to eliminate all risk from your life, the more you're likely to focus on all the possible things that could go wrong. You're fighting a losing battle and are likely to undermine your sense of security even further. Focusing too much on the risks inherent in everyday life will leave you chronically worried and cause you to overestimate the probability of bad things happening to you.

>> **Trying to influence others:** Examples of influencing others' behavior include encouraging your partner to socialize only with members of the sex that isn't their romantic preference, persuading your children to stay at home rather than go out with their friends, coercing family members into excessive washing and cleaning, feeding others in lieu of you yourself eating, and asking your doctor to send you for yet another test. Demanding that other people act in ways to minimize your intolerance of uncertainty and risk can seriously damage your relationships. People close to you are likely to perceive you as controlling, suffocating, or suspicious.

TIP

Try to understand that uncertainty has always been a major feature of the world, and people still manage to keep themselves safe and secure. You don't need to change the world to feel secure. The answer is to accept uncertainty and even try to make friends with it. You *can* happily coexist with uncertainty — it's always been that way. Remind yourself that ordinary people cope with bad events every day and that you're likely to cope as well as others do if something wicked this way comes.

The next section deals with accepting uncertainty and letting go of unhelpful coping strategies.

Surmounting the Side Effects of Excessive Safety-Seeking

One of the main ways in which you maintain emotional problems is by rescuing yourself from your imagined catastrophes. Often, these anticipated disasters are products of your worried mind, rather than real or probable events. People with specific anxiety problems, such as the ones listed in this section, often take measures to reduce their anxiety and increase their sense of safety but in effect make themselves even more intolerant of the inevitable uncertainty of everyday life.

The actions that people take to prevent their feared catastrophes from occurring are called *safety behaviors.*

Avoiding, escaping, or trying too hard to stop a feared catastrophe prevents you from realizing three key things:

>> Your feared event may never happen even if you didn't use a safety-seeking behavior.

>> If your feared event *does* happen, most likely you'll find ways to cope. For example, other people or organizations may be available to help you.

>> The feared event may well be inconvenient, uncomfortable, upsetting, and deeply unpleasant, but you discover ways to cope with it.

REMEMBER

Anxiety affects your thinking. It leads you to overestimate the probability and gravity of danger and to underestimate your ability to cope. In more extreme forms of anxiety, problems avoidance and safety-seeking can have severe impacts on work, family, education, and other important areas of life. Recovery is about making sure your mind hasn't become caught up in overfocusing or avoiding certain threats at the expense of living your life to the fullest.

Using ultimately unhelpful strategies to avoid feared outcomes is prevalent in anxiety disorders. You might be using some counterproductive safety behaviors to cope with specific anxiety problems:

>> **Panic attacks:** Michael's panic attacks are maintained by his fear that feeling dizzy will make him collapse. Whenever he feels dizzy, he takes a sip of water, sits down, or holds on to something. In this way, he prevents himself from finding out that he probably won't collapse simply because he feels dizzy. Alternatively, he might find out that if he does collapse, that people come to his aid.

>> **Social anxiety:** Sally tends to overprepare what she's going to say before she says it, for fear of making a fool of herself. She monitors her speech and body language and reviews in her mind what she did and said when she gets home. In this way, she maintains her excessive self-consciousness.

>> **Post-traumatic stress:** Since she had a car accident, Nina avoids highways, grips tightly on to the steering wheel when driving in her car, repeatedly checks the rearview mirror, and avoids being a car passenger. Because she's being so careful, her anxiety about having another accident remains at the forefront of her mind.

>> **Agoraphobia:** Georgina's afraid of traveling far from her home or familiar places for fear of getting into a panic and ultimately losing control of her bowels and soiling herself. She has become almost housebound, and she relies heavily on her husband to drive her around. This means that she doesn't go out on her own and never discovers that her fears are likely to be (?)KD unfounded.

>> **Fear of heights:** James is afraid of heights because he believes that the "pulling" sensation he experiences in high places means that he's at risk of unintentionally throwing himself to his death. To cope with this sensation, he digs his heels firmly into the ground and leans slightly backward to resist his feelings. He also tries to avoid high places as much as he can. These behaviors fuel his fear and leave him believing that somehow he's more at risk than other people in high places.

After you've drawn up a list of your avoidance and safety behaviors, you can better understand what areas you need to target for change. In essence, the real solution to your problem lies in deliberately facing feared situations without using safety behaviors. You can then see that you're able to cope with anxiety-provoking events and that you need not rely on distractions or spurious attempts to keep yourself safe. Give yourself the chance to see that your anxiety isn't harmful in itself and that anxious feelings diminish if you let them do so of their own accord. (Chapter 10 contains more information about dealing with safety behaviors and devising exposures.)

Wending Your Way Out of Worry

One of the dilemmas faced by people who worry too much is how to reduce that worry. Some degree of worry is entirely normal — of course, problems and responsibilities will cross your mind from time to time. Yet you may be someone who worries all the time. Being a true worrywart is intensely uncomfortable. Understandably, you may want to stop worrying quite so much.

Three reasons may account for your excessive worrying:

>> You may think that by worrying about unpleasant events, you can prevent those events from happening. Or you may believe that your worry can give you clues as to how to prevent negative events from coming to fruition.

>> You may think that worry protects you by preparing you for negative events. Perhaps you believe that if you worry about bad things enough, they won't catch you off guard and you'll be better able to deal with them.

>> You believe that it's safer to assume the worst for fear that the universe might punish you for being arrogant enough to relax into assuming that things will work out.

If you can convince yourself that excessive worry really doesn't prevent feared events from happening or prepare you for dealing with bad things, you may be in a better position to interrupt your repetitive cycle of worries.

Ironically, many people worry about things in a vain attempt to get all possible worries out of the way so they can then relax. Of course, this never happens. Worry's a movable feast, and something else always comes along for you to worry about.

If you worry excessively about everyday events, you may try to solve every possible upcoming problem in advance of it happening. You may hope that your worry will solve potential problems so that you won't have to worry about them anymore.

Unfortunately, trying too hard to put your mind at rest can lead to increased mental activity and yet more worry. All too often, people then worry that worrying so much is harmful, and they end up worrying about worrying!

TIP

Try to see your worrying as a habit you can train yourself to manage. Instead of focusing on the content of your worries, try to interrupt the worry process by engaging your mind and body in activities outside of yourself. Chapter 6 has some helpful hints on refocusing your attention away from worries.

Preventing the Perpetuation of Your Problems

Sometimes the things you do to cope with your problems can bring about the very things you're trying to avoid. An example of this is when you try to push upsetting thoughts out of your mind. Pushing away unpleasant thoughts is called *thought suppression* and can generally make unwanted thoughts intrude more often. Research shows that when people try to suppress an unwanted thought, it can intrude into their minds twice as often as if they accepted the thought and let it pass.

By way of experiment, close your eyes and try not to think of a pink elephant. Just for a minute, really push any images of pink elephants out of your mind. What happened? Most people notice that all they can think of are pink elephants. This demonstrates that trying to get rid of thoughts by pushing them out of your mind usually results in them hanging around more persistently.

Trying too hard not to do, feel, or think specific things, and attempting to prevent certain events, can bring about what you most fear and want to avoid:

>> Trying too hard not to make a fool of yourself in social situations can make you seem aloof and uninterested.

>> Trying too hard to make sure a piece of work is perfect can lead you to miss a deadline or become so nervous that you produce poor work.

>> Insisting that you must succeed at a task, like passing an exam or learning a skill, makes you concentrate too much on *how well* you're doing and not

enough on *what* you're doing. This misplaced attention focus can lead to poor results.

» Feeling jealous and repeatedly checking up on your partner, testing them or demanding reassurance that they're not about to leave you, can drive your partner away.

» Lying in bed, trying to deal with fatigue when you're depressed, can lower your mood further and lead to feelings of shame and guilt about your inactivity.

Helping Yourself: Putting the Petals on Your Vicious Flower

The *vicious flower exercise* is a way of putting together different elements of your problem to aid your understanding of how your problem is maintained. Look at the example in Figure 8-1 and turn to Appendix B for a blank flower to photocopy and fill in. Follow these steps to fill in your own vicious flower:

1. **In the Trigger box, write down the trigger that makes you feel anxious or upset.**

2. **In the central circle, write down the key thoughts and meanings you attach to the trigger.**

3. **In the flower petals, write down the emotions, behaviors, and sensations you experience when your uncomfortable feeling is triggered; in the top petal, write down what you tend to focus on.**

Key negative thoughts, attitudes, or beliefs are at the heart of your vicious flower. The petals are your attentional, emotional, physical, and behavioral responses to the meaning you've attached to the trigger.

One of the most important aspects of building a vicious flower is to think through how the petals affect the thought or "meaning" that underpins your emotional problem. For example, the effect of anxiety on your thinking is to make you more likely to interpret experiences as more dangerous than they really are. The effect of depression is to make your thinking more gloomy and negative. (See Chapter 7 for more on these and other emotions.)

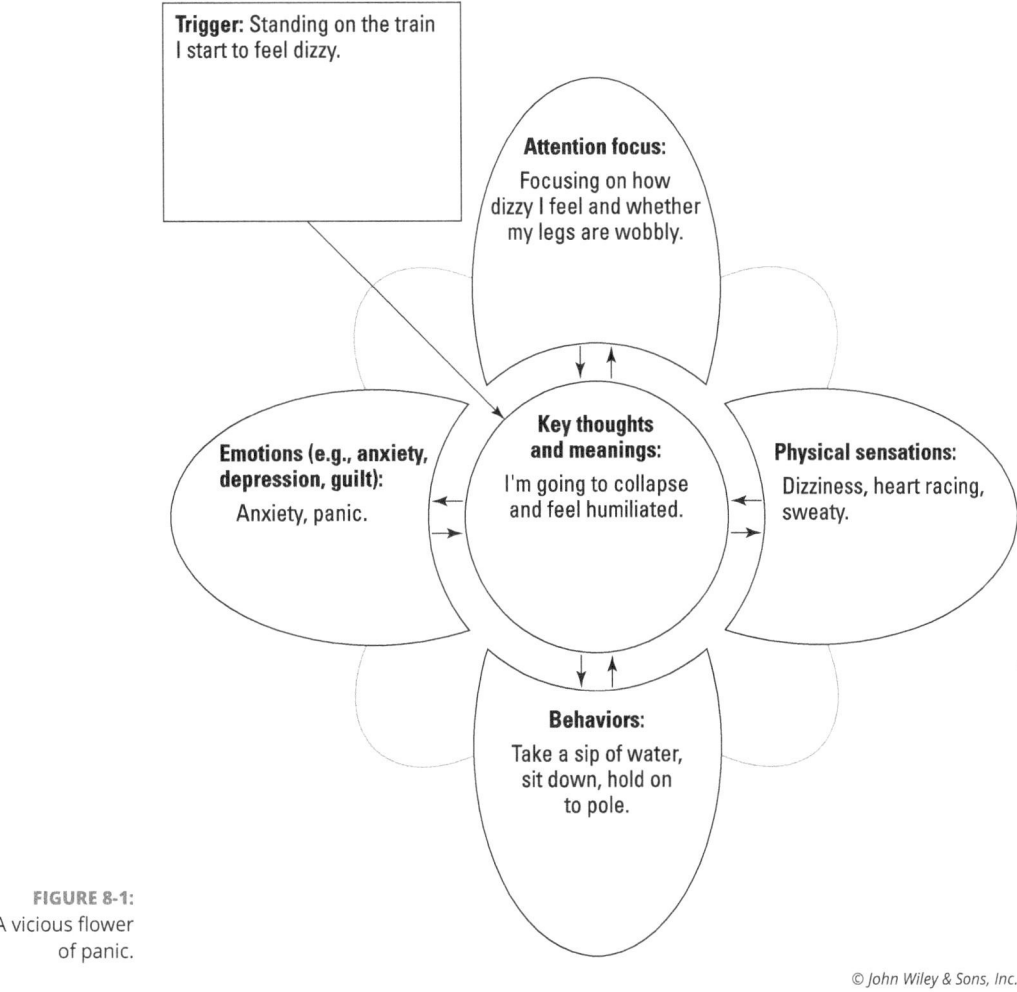

FIGURE 8-1:
A vicious flower
of panic.

© John Wiley & Sons, Inc.

Focusing your attention on a sensation usually makes that sensation feel more intense. Acting upon an unhelpful thought or meaning usually makes that meaning seem more true than they are. Unpleasant physical sensations accompanying your reaction can make upsetting thoughts feel more real. You can design behavioral experiments to test the effect of increasing or reducing a behavior on your problems. (Refer to Chapter 5.)

When you understand the mechanisms that maintain your problems, it will seem far more practical and sensible to target your petals for change.

REMEMBER

The Physical Sensations petal is the aspect of your problem that you're least able to change directly because physical sensations are outside your immediate conscious control. However, you can minimize the impact of physical sensations by learning to tolerate them while you overcome your problem and to interpret them as no more dangerous than they really are.

PUT DOWN THAT SHOVEL AND EMPTY YOUR POCKETS!

One of the best metaphors for the kinds of behavior we discuss in this chapter is the idea that some of your coping strategies may be like unwittingly trying to dig your way out of a hole. Naturally, the first step to overcoming your problems is to put down the shovel — to stop your self-defeating strategies and gradually work out more productive ways of overcoming your emotional problems.

Over time, you may seek out bigger and better shovels in the guise of bigger and better avoidance and safety behaviors. I regularly invite those clients who suffer from agoraphobia, panic attacks, obsessive-compulsive disorder, and body dysmorphic disorder to share with me the contents of their pockets or handbags, which is often illuminating. Examples of *safety props* that people carry "just in case" include over-the-counter drugs, packets of tissues, antiseptic wipes, candy or gum, handheld fans, make-up, plastic bags, paper bags, deodorant sprays, laxatives, and alcohol.

To help clients eliminate safety behaviors, we often encourage them to throw out or hand over these seemingly innocent everyday items in the spirit of getting rid of problematic solutions. Go through your pockets and handbag and collect all your safety props. Throw them in the bin or hand them over to someone who knows about your problems and has an interest in helping you. (This person can be anyone in your life if you aren't currently seeing a CBT therapist.) Be wary of purchasing or accumulating items to replace what you've already handed over or tossed away. Work on the basis that you only need essentials in your purse and pockets, such as money, keys, and bank cards.

Chapter 9

Setting Your Sights on Goals

I f we had to define the purpose of therapy, its purpose would *not* be to make you a straighter-thinking, more rational person. The purpose of therapy is really to help you achieve greater emotional and behavioral health. Exactly how that looks from one person to the next varies greatly. Thinking differently and behaving in ways that support your new thinking is a powerful way of achieving those goals. This chapter helps you define your goals and suggests some sources of inspiration for change.

Aaron Beck, founder of cognitive therapy, says that CBT is whatever helps you move from your problems to your goals. This definition emphasizes the pragmatic and flexible nature of CBT and encourages clients and therapists to select from a wide range of psychological techniques to help achieve goals in therapy. The crucial message, though, is that effective therapy is a constructive process, helping you achieve your goals.

Putting SPORT into Your Goals

Many people struggle to overcome their problems because their goals are too vague. To help you develop goals that are clearer and easier to set your sights on, we developed the acronym SPORT, which stands for the following:

>> **Specific:** Be precise about where, when, or with whom you want to feel or behave differently. For example, you may want to feel concerned rather than anxious about making a presentation at work, and during the presentation you may want to concentrate on the content rather than on yourself.

>> **Positive:** State your goals in positive terms, encouraging yourself to develop more, rather than less, of something. For example, you may want to gain more social confidence (rather than become less anxious) or to hone a skill (rather than make fewer mistakes).

TIP

Think of therapy as a journey. You're more likely to end up where you want to be if you focus on getting to your destination rather than on what you're trying to get away from.

>> **Observable:** Try to include in your goal a description of a behavioral change that you can observe. Then you can tell when you've achieved your goal because you can see a specific change.

TIP

If you're finding it hard to describe an observable change, think to yourself, "How would someone who knows me well be able to observe a positive change in my mood — just by looking at what I do?"

>> **Realistic:** Make your goals clear, concrete, realistic, and achievable. Focus on ones that are within your reach and that depend on change from you rather than from other people or the world. Try to visualize yourself achieving your goals. Realistic goals help you stay motivated and focused.

>> **Time:** Set a timeframe to keep you focused and efficient in your pursuit of a goal. For example, if you've been avoiding something for a while, decide when you plan to tackle it. Specify how long and how often you want to carry out a new behavior, such as going to the gym three times a week for an hour at a time.

WARNING

Some goals, such as recovering from severe depression, can vary a lot in terms of how long they take to achieve. Setting schedules too rigidly can lead you to become depressed or angry at your lack of progress. Also, many changes work best when you integrate them into your routines, so they ultimately become automatic, a new habit. So use "time" and "timing" flexibly to really support your growth and well-being. Accept yourself if you don't achieve them on time, and persevere!

Homing in on How You Want to Be Different

Defining your goals and writing them down on paper forms the foundation of your CBT program. This section helps you identify how you may want to feel and act differently.

Setting goals in relation to your current problems

To set a goal concerned with overcoming an emotional problem, you first need to define the problem. We talk about that in Chapter 7, where I explore unhealthy emotions and behaviors and their healthy counterparts. Also refer to Chapter 8, where I explore how attempts to make yourself feel better can sometimes make problems worse.

A *problem statement* contains the following components:

>> Feelings/emotions

>> A situation or theme that triggered your emotion

>> The way you tend to act in the situation when you feel your problem emotion

Defining how you want to feel as an alternative

CBT can help you attain changes in the way you feel emotionally. For example, you may decide that you want to feel sad and disappointed, rather than depressed and hurt, about the end of your marriage.

WARNING

Aiming to feel "okay," "fine," or "relaxed" may not fit the bill if you're dealing with a tough situation. Feeling negative emotions about negative events is realistic and appropriate. Keep your goals realistic and helpful by aiming to have healthy emotions, and try to maintain an appropriate level of intensity of your emotions when you're faced with difficult events. (Take a look at Chapter 7 for more on healthy emotions.)

Defining how you want to act

The second area of change that CBT can help you with is your behavior. For example, after going through a divorce, you may decide that you want to begin seeing your friends and return to work, instead of staying in bed and watching TV all day.

TIP

You can also include changes to your mental activities within your goal, such as refocusing your attention on the outside world or allowing *catastrophic* (upsetting or worst-case scenario) thoughts to pass through your mind.

Making a statement

A *goal statement* is similar to a problem statement. They have the same components, but the emotions and behaviors are different. A good goal statement involves the following:

To feel _____ (emotion) about _____
(theme or situation) and to _____ (behavior).

So, for example, you may want to feel *concerned* (emotion) about *saying something foolish at a dinner party* (situation) and to *stay at the table to make further conversation* (behavior).

Maximizing Your Motivation

Motivation has a funny way of waxing and waning, just like the moon. Luckily, you don't necessarily have to feel motivated about changing before you can take steps forward. Motivation often follows rather than precedes positive action. Often people find they "get into" something once they've started. This section suggests some ways to generate motivation and encourages you to carry on working toward goals in the temporary absence of motivation.

Identifying inspiration for change

Lots of people find change difficult. Your motivation may flag sometimes, or you may never be able to imagine overcoming your difficulties. If either of these situations sounds familiar to you, you're in good company. Many people draw on sources of inspiration when starting with, and persevering through, the process of overcoming emotional problems. Sources of encouragement worth considering include the following:

>> **Role models who have characteristics you aspire to adopt yourself:** For example, you may know someone who stays calm, expresses feelings to

others, is open-minded to new experiences, or is assertive and determined. Whether real-life or fictional, alive or dead, known to you or someone you've never met, choose someone who inspires you and can give you a model for a new way of being.

>> **Inspirational stories of people overcoming adversity:** Ordinary people regularly survive the most extraordinary experiences. Stories of their personal experiences can inspire you to make powerful personal changes.

WARNING

When it comes to inspirational role models, focus on taking a leaf out of an inspirational individual's book, not on comparing yourself negatively with someone's "superior" coping skills.

>> **Images and metaphors:** Think of yourself as, for example, a sturdy tree withstanding a strong wind blowing against you, which can be an inspiring metaphor to represent you withstanding unreasonable criticism.

>> **Proverbs, quotes, and icons:** Use ideas you've heard expressed in novels, religious literature, films, songs, or quotes from well-respected people to keep you reaching for your goals.

>> **You 2.0:** Imagine flashing forward a year from now, and you've significantly improved your emotional and behavioral health. What are you like? How are you living? What's your daily and weekly routine like? Life may still have its challenges, but how do you rise to them? How do you look after your mind and body so you're ready to deal with challenges, pursue your hopes and dreams, and maintain connections with others?

Focusing on the benefits of change

People often maintain apparently unhelpful patterns of behavior (such as consistently arriving late for work) because they focus on the short-term benefit (in this case, avoiding the anxiety of being on a crowded bus or train) at the time of carrying out that behavior. However, away from the immediate discomfort, these same people may focus on wishing they were free from the restrictions of their emotional problem (able to travel carefree on public transport).

REMEMBER

Choose change because you know it's worth it. People often don't take steps to solve a problem until the problem is significantly more uncomfortable than the remedy. Record the reasons that suffering short-term effort, possible deprivation, or tedium and discomfort is worth it. Refer to them often.

Completing a cost–benefit analysis

Carrying out a *cost–benefit analysis* (CBA) to examine the pros and cons of something can galvanize your commitment to change. You can use a CBA to examine the advantages and disadvantages of things such as these:

>> **Behaviors:** How helpful is this action to you? Does it bring short-term or long-term benefits?

>> **Emotions:** How helpful is this feeling? For example, does feeling guilty or angry really help you?

>> **Thoughts, attitudes, or beliefs:** Where does thinking this way get you? How does this belief help you?

>> **Options for solving a practical problem:** How can this solution work out? Is this really the best possible answer to the problem?

When using a CBA form similar to the one shown in Table 8-1, remember to evaluate the pros and cons:

>> In the short term

>> In the long term

>> For yourself

>> For other people

TABLE 8-1

The Cost-Benefit Analysis Form

Costs and Benefits of: Costs (Disadvantages)	Benefits (Advantages)

Try to write CBA statements in pairs, particularly when you're considering changing the way you feel, act, or think. What are the advantages of feeling anxiety? And the disadvantages? Write down pairs of statements for what you feel, do, or think currently, and for other, healthier alternatives. Tables 8-2 and 8-3 show a completed CBA form. You can find a larger, blank cost–benefit analysis form in Appendix B, which you can photocopy and fill in.

TABLE 8-2 Cost–Benefit Analysis: Costs and Benefits of Saying What Comes into My Mind and Paying Attention to the Conversation

Costs	Benefits
I may end up saying something stupid.	I won't have to think so much, and I might be able to relax.
I may not come up with the best thing to say.	I can be more spontaneous.
I may end up running off at the mouth, and people might not like me.	I'll be able to concentrate on what's being said, and I won't seem so distracted.

TABLE 8-3 Second Cost–Benefit Analysis: Costs and Benefits of Preparing in My Head What I'm Going to Say Before Speaking

Costs	Benefits
I end up feeling tired after going out.	I can make sure I don't say something foolish.
I can't relax into the conversation.	I may think of something funny or entertaining to say.
Sometimes I feel like the conversation moves on before I've had the chance to think of the right thing to say.	I can take more care not to offend people.

After you've done a CBA, review it with a critical eye on the "benefits" of staying the same and the "costs" of change. You may decide that these costs and benefits aren't strictly accurate. The more you can boost your sense that change can benefit you, the more motivated you can feel in working toward your goals.

TIP

Write out a motivational flashcard that states the *benefits of change* and the *costs of staying the same,* drawn from your cost–benefit analysis. You can then refer to this card to give yourself a motivational boost when you need it.

A large aspect of achieving a goal, whether learning to play the guitar or building up a business, is accepting temporary discomfort to bring long-term benefit.

Recording your progress

Keeping records of your progress can help you stay motivated. If your motivation flags, spur yourself on toward your goal by reviewing how far you've come. Use a problem-and-goal sheet like that in Figure 9-1 to specify your problem and rate its intensity. Then define your goal and rate your progress toward achieving it. Do this at regular intervals, such as every one or two weeks.

1. **Identify the problem you're tackling.**

    Include information about the emotions and behaviors related to a specific event. Remember, you're feeling an emotion about a situation, leading you to behave in a certain way.

2. **At regular intervals, evaluate the intensity of your emotional problem and how much it interferes with your life.**

    A 0 equals no emotional distress and no interference in your life, and a 10 equals maximum possible emotional distress, at great frequency, with great interference in your life.

3. **Fill in the goal section, keeping the theme or situation the same but specifying how you want to feel and act differently.**

4. **Rate how close you are to achieving your goal.**

    A 0 equals no progress whatsoever, at any time, and a 10 means that the change in your emotion and behavior is completely and consistently achieved.

REMEMBER

Change doesn't happen overnight, so don't rate your progress any more frequently than weekly. Look for overall changes in the frequency, intensity, and duration of your problematic feelings and behaviors.

MERCURIAL DESIRES

People often find that they want to change their goals on a whim or a fancy. For example, you may have a goal of being more productive and advancing your position at work. Then after going to a Summer Solstice festival, you decide that really your goal is to be free and to travel the world, communing with the essence of life. What you choose as your definitive goal is up to you. But be wary of being influenced too easily by whatever's foremost in your mind. Constantly abandoning former goals and adopting new ones can be a mask for avoidance and procrastination. Use the SPORT acronym, as described in the earlier section titled "Putting SPORT into Your Goals," to assess the durability and functionality of each of your chosen goals.

Using the form below, identify one of the main problems you wish to work on in therapy. A problem statement includes information about the emotions and behavior related to a specific situation or event. For example: *'Feeling depressed about the end of my marriage leading me to become withdrawn and spend until around 6pm each day in bed'* or *'Feeling anxious about social situations leading me to avoid going to pubs, restaurants, and meetings, or to be extremely careful about what I say if I do socialise'*. Think of writing your problem statement as filling in blanks: *Feeling _____ (emotion) about _____ (situation), leading me to _____ (behavior)*. Use the same format to identify the goal you would like to achieve, but this time specify how you would like things to be different in terms of your emotions and behavior.

PROBLEM No. ☐	DATE:	DATE:	DATE:	DATE:
	RATING:	RATING:	RATING:	RATING:
	DATE:	DATE:	DATE:	DATE:
	RATING:	RATING:	RATING:	RATING:

Rate the severity of your emotional problem 0 - 10. **0 = No distress/No impairment in ability to function 10 = Extreme distress/Virtuality unable to function in any area of life**

GOAL RELATED TO PROBLEM	DATE:	DATE:	DATE:	DATE:
	RATING:	RATING:	RATING:	RATING:
	DATE:	DATE:	DATE:	DATE:
	RATING:	RATING:	RATING:	RATING:

Rate how close you are to achieving your goal. **0 = No progress whatsoever 10 = Goal achieved and sustained consistently**

FIGURE 9-1:
The Problem-and-Goal Sheet.

3

Putting CBT into Action

IN THIS PART . . .

Demolishing depression

Building a better body image

Overcoming low self-esteem

Chapter **10**

Standing Up to Anxiety and Facing Fear

To understand anxiety and fear well, it helps to get to know your nervous system. We all have a "threat system," which is part of our sympathetic nervous system. This is the part of our brain and body that has evolved over thousands of years to keep us safe. And it has become very good at it. Thankfully, we also have a "calm down" system called the parasympathetic nervous system. The challenge can be that our modern lives are complex and nuanced, and we're exposed to vast amounts of information. It's all too easy to "switch on" our threat system, and our brain may need a little help to calm itself down again. In producing anxiety and fear, our mind and body are trying to help us. What it may not be able to register is when that attempt to keep us safe actually causes its own set of troubles.

Acquiring Anti-anxiety Attitudes

Your thoughts are what count because your feelings are influenced greatly by how you think. Feeling anxious increases the chance of you experiencing anxiety-provoking thoughts. (Refer to Chapter 7.) Anxious thoughts can increase anxious feelings, so a vicious cycle can develop. You can face your fears by adopting the attitudes we outline in this section.

Thinking realistically about the probability of bad events

If you have any kind of anxiety problem, you probably spend a lot of time worrying about bad things that *may* happen to you or your loved ones. The more you focus your attention on negative events and worry about bad things being just around the corner, the more likely you're going to believe that they'll actually happen.

Proving for sure that bad events won't happen isn't that easy, with or without a crystal ball, but you can acknowledge that you tend to overestimate the probability of bad things happening. Adjust your thinking appropriately to counterbalance for this tendency. Counterbalancing your attitude is a lot like riding a bike with the handlebars offset to the left. To steer straight, you need to pull the handlebars to the right; otherwise, you keep veering to the left. If you tend to always imagine the worst, straighten out your thinking by deliberately assuming that things are likely to be okay.

Avoiding extreme thinking

Telling yourself that things are "awful," "horrible," "terrible," or "the end of the world" only turns up the anxiety heat. Remind yourself that few things are really that dreadful, and instead rate events more accurately as "bad," "unfortunate," "inconvenient," or "unpleasant" but not "the end of the world."

Extreme thinking leads to extreme emotional reactions. When you mislabel a negative event as "horrible," you make yourself overly anxious about unpleasant but relatively non-extreme events, such as minor public embarrassment.

Taking the fear out of fear

When people say things like, "Don't worry, it's *just* anxiety," they're implying — wrongly — that anxiety's a mild experience. Anxiety can, in fact, be a profound experience, with strong bodily and mental sensations. Some anxious people misinterpret these intense physical symptoms as dangerous or as signs of impending peril. You might assume that a nauseous feeling means you're about to be sick, or you might think you're going crazy because your surroundings feel "unreal."

REMEMBER

If you have concerns about your physical sensations, you may consider seeing your family doctor prior to deliberately confronting your fears. Your doctor may then be able to advise you as to whether deliberately increasing your anxiety in the short term, to be free of it in the long term, is safe enough for you. It's rare for people to be advised against facing their fears.

Understanding and accepting common sensations of anxiety can help you stop adding to your anxiety by misinterpreting normal sensations as dangerous. Figure 10-1 outlines some of the more common physical aspects of anxiety.

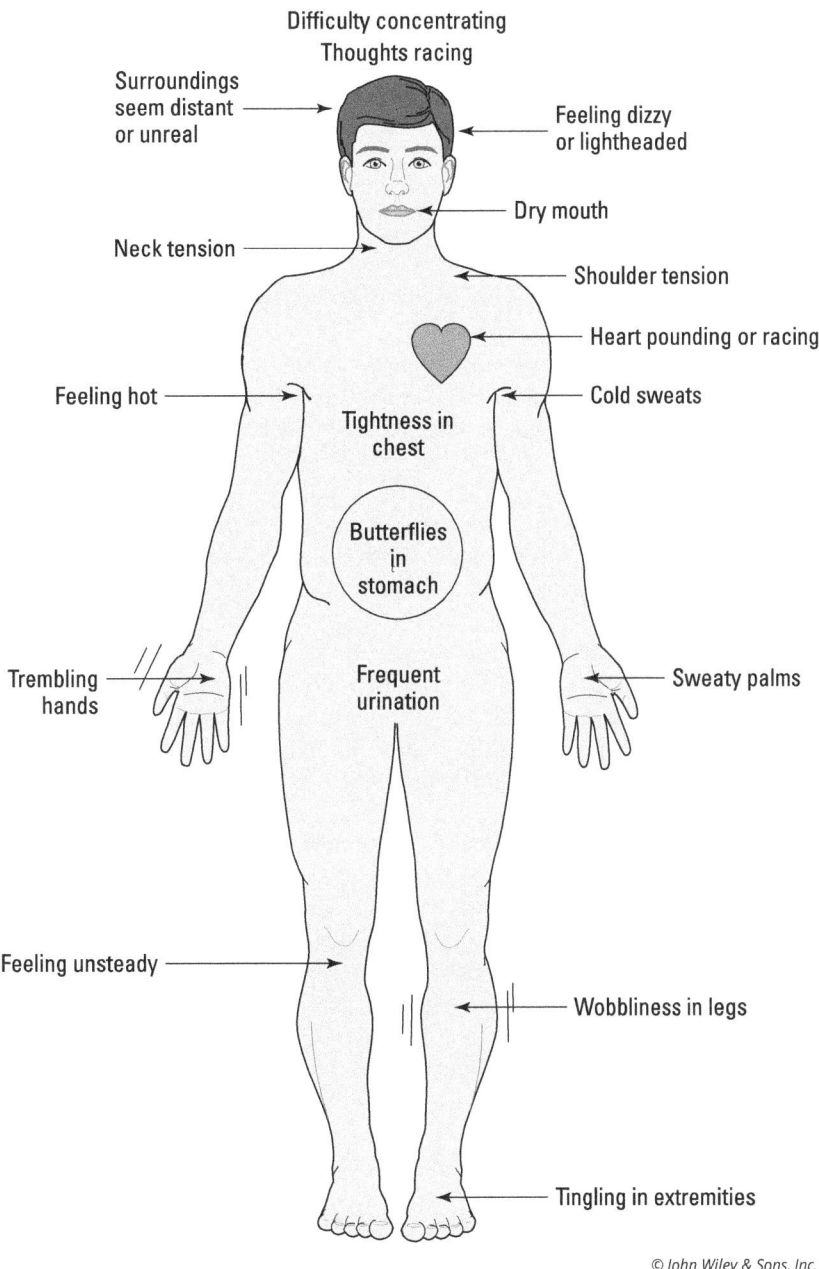

FIGURE 10-1: Common physical sensations of anxiety.

Undoubtedly, anxiety is an unpleasant, sometimes extremely disturbing experience. However, evaluating your anxiety as "unbearable" or saying "I can't stand it" only ramps up the emotional impact. Remind yourself that taking an attitude of tolerance will actually help improve your anxiety and the less you avoid it, the weaker it will become.

Attacking Anxiety

The following are some key principles for targeting and destroying anxiety.

Winning by not fighting

Trying to control your anxiety can lead you to feeling more intensely anxious for longer. (For more on this, read through Chapter 8.) Many of my clients say to me, "Facing my fears makes sense, but what am I supposed to do while I'm feeling anxious?"

The answer is . . . nothing. Well, sort of. Accepting and tolerating your anxiety when you're deliberately confronting your fears is usually the most effective way of making sure that your anxiety passes quickly.

TIP

If your anxiety is more generalized, try to relegate it to the back burner of your mind. Carry on with mundane everyday tasks and let the anxiety burn itself out. Try taking the attitude "I can still function and do what needs to be done in the day even with feelings of anxiety." The less you focus upon it, the less your brain feels like it has another problem to solve, meaning it's less stressed.

If you're convinced that your anxiety won't diminish by itself, even when you do nothing, test it out. Pick one anxiety-provoking situation that you normally withdraw from — examples include using a lift, travelling on a busy bus, standing in a crowded room, and eating alone in a cafe. Make yourself stay in the situation and just let your anxiety do its thing. Don't do anything to try to stop the anxiety. Just stay where you are and *do nothing* other than feel anxious. Imagine the anxiety like waves crashing onto a beach and let the waves get smaller and smaller until they're only a gentle ripple. Eventually, your anxiety will begin to ebb away.

Defeating fear with FEAR

Perhaps the most reliable way of overcoming anxiety is the following maxim: FEAR — Face Everything And Recover. Supported by numerous clinical trials and used daily all over the world, the principle of facing your fears until your anxiety reduces is one of the cornerstones of CBT.

The process of deliberately confronting your fear and staying within the feared situation until your anxiety subsides is known as *exposure* or *desensitization*. The process of getting used to something, like cold water in a swimming pool, is called *habituation*. The principle involves waiting until your anxiety reduces noticeably before ending your session of exposure — usually between twenty minutes and one hour, but sometimes more. However, don't get too bogged down with how much your anxiety is reducing in a given session. The main thing is to overcome the avoidance and safety-seeking behaviors that are maintaining your problem.

Repeatedly confronting your fears

As Figure 10-2 shows, if you deliberately confront your fears, your anxiety becomes less severe and reduces more quickly with each exposure. The more exposures you experience, the better. When you first confront your fears, aim to repeat your exposures at least daily.

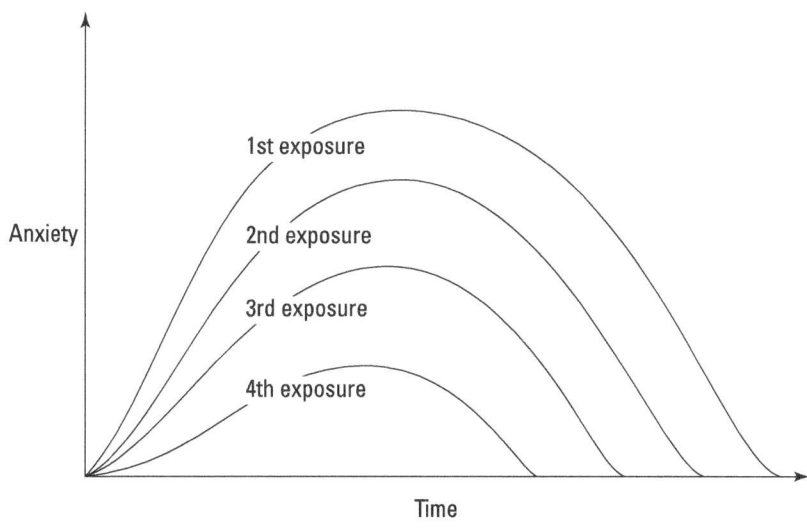

FIGURE 10-2:
Your anxiety reduces with each exposure to a feared trigger.

© John Wiley & Sons, Inc.

Keeping your exposure challenging but not overwhelming

When confronting your fears, aim for manageable exposure so that you can successfully experience facing your fears and mastering them. If your exposures are overwhelming, you may end up resorting to escape, avoidance, or safety behaviors. The flipside of choosing overwhelming exposures is taking things too gently, which can make your progress slow and demoralizing. Strive to strike a balance between the two extremes.

WARNING

If you set yourself only easy, gentle exposures, you risk reinforcing the erroneous idea that anxiety is unbearable and must be avoided. The point of exposure work is to prove to yourself that you *can* bear the discomfort associated with anxious feelings.

Taking it step by step

Avoid overwhelming or underchallenging yourself by using a graded hierarchy of feared or avoided situations. A *graded hierarchy* is a way of listing your fears from the mildest to the most severe.

REMEMBER

If you want to kill your fear, let it die of its own accord.

You can use Table 10-1 to list people, places, situations, objects, animals, sensations, or whatever triggers your fear. Be sure to include situations that you tend to avoid. Rank these triggers in rough order of difficulty. Alongside each trigger, rate your anticipated level of anxiety on the good old 0–10 scale. *Voila!* You have a graded hierarchy.

TABLE 10-1

Graded Hierarchy of Anxiety

Feared or Avoided Trigger	Anticipated Anxiety or Discomfort 0–10	Actual Anxiety or Discomfort 0–10

TIP

After you've confronted your fear, rate the *actual* level of anxiety or discomfort you experienced. Then tailor your next exposure session accordingly. Most situations aren't as bad as you expect them to be. In the unlikely event that the reality is worse than your expectations, you may need to devise more manageable exposures for the next few steps and work your way up the hierarchy more gradually. Alternatively, you might recognize that even though it was worse than you imagined you still cope better than you expected.

Jumping in at the deep end

Although we caution about striking a balance between under- and overchallenging yourself, jumping in with both feet does have its benefits. The sooner you can face your biggest fears, the sooner you can master them. Consider whether you can climb to the top of your hierarchy straight away.

REMEMBER

Graded exposure is a means to an end. Going straight to your worst-feared situation without resorting to safety behaviors (which we talk about in the next section) can help you get rapid results as long as you stick with the exposure long enough to discover that nothing terrible happens.

Shedding safety behaviors

You can overcome anxiety by turning your anxiety upside down. The best way to make your anxiety go away is to invite it to do its own thing. As we explain in a bit more detail in Chapter 8, the things you do to reduce your fear in the short term are often the very things that start you feeling anxious in the first place. (Check out Chapter 8 for some common examples of safety behaviors.)

Recording your fear-fighting

Keep a record of your work against fear so you can check out your progress and make further plans. Your record can include the following:

>> The length of your exposure session

>> Ratings of your anxiety at the beginning, middle, and end of your exposure session

A record helps you see whether you're sticking with your program long enough for your fear to subside. If your fear doesn't seem to be reducing, it's worth checking you've dropped those safety-seeking behaviors and your exposure sessions are long enough, with regular repetition.

TIP

You can use the behavioral experiment record sheet in Chapter 5 to record your exposure and to compare your predicted outcome of confronting your fears with the actual outcome.

Overriding Common Anxieties

The following sections outline the application of CBT for some common anxiety problems. A full discussion of all the specific types of anxiety problems lies outside the scope of this book. However, the CBT principles that we introduce here are the best bet for overcoming most anxiety problems.

First, define what you're doing to keep your anxiety alive in your thinking (see Chapters 3 and 7) and alive in your behavior (see Chapters 7 and 8). Then start to catch your unhelpful thoughts, generate alternatives (Chapter 4), and test them in reality (Chapter 5). Understanding where you focus your attention, and retraining your attention, can also be hugely helpful (see Chapter 5). We discuss anxiety about OCD in Chapter 14, fears of being ugly in Chapter 13, and anxiety about illness in Chapter 18.

Socking it to social anxiety

Attack *social anxiety* (excessive fear of negative evaluation by other people) by drawing up a list of your feared and avoided social situations and the safety behaviors you tend to carry out. (Check out Chapter 8 for more on safety behaviors.)

Hang on to the idea that you can accept yourself even if other people don't like you. Be more flexible about how witty, novel, and entertaining you "have" to be. Systematically test out your predictions about people thinking negatively about you. How do people act when you don't try so hard to perform? Refocus your attention on the world around you and the people you interact with, rather than on yourself. For more help on retraining your attention, refer to Chapter 6. Once you've left the social situation, resist the tendency to replay your social encounters in your mind.

Waging war on worry

To wage war on your excessive worry, resist the temptation to try to solve every problem in advance of it happening. Try to live with doubt and realize that the most important thing is not what you specifically worry about but *how* you manage your worrying thoughts. Overcoming worry is the art of allowing thoughts to enter your mind without trying to "sort them out" or push them away.

Pounding on panic

Panic attacks are intense bursts of anxiety in the absence of real danger and can often seem to come out of the blue. Panic attacks often have very strong physical sensations such as nausea, heart palpitations, a feeling of shortness of breath, choking, dizziness, and hot sweats. Panic sets in when people mistake these physical sensations as dangerous and get into a vicious cycle because these mis-interpretations lead to more anxiety, leading to more physical sensations.

Break free from panic attacks by deliberately triggering panic sensations. Enter situations you've been avoiding and resist using safety behaviors. Realize, for example, that feeling dizzy doesn't cause you to collapse, so you don't need to sit down, and other uncomfortable sensations of anxiety will pass without harming you. Carry out a behavioral experiment (see Chapter 5) to specifically test whether your own feared catastrophes come true as a consequence of a panic attack.

Assaulting agoraphobia

Georgina was afraid to travel far from her home or from familiar places she felt safe in, which are common characteristics of *agoraphobia*. She feared losing con-trol of her bowels and soiling herself. She'd become virtually housebound and relied heavily on her husband to drive her around. She learned about the nature of anxiety and developed the theory that, although she may *feel* like she's going to soil herself, her sensations are due largely to anxiety and she will be able to "hold on."

To gain confidence and overcome agoraphobia, develop a hierarchy of your avoided situations. Begin to face them, and stay in them until your anxiety reduces. This may include driving progressively longer distances alone, using public transpor-tation, and walking around in unfamiliar places. At the same time, work hard to drop your safety behaviors so you can discover that nothing terrible happens if you do become anxious or panicky, and ride it out.

Dealing with post-traumatic stress disorder

Post-traumatic stress disorder (PTSD) can develop after being involved in (or wit-nessing) an accident, assault, or other extremely threatening or distressing event. The symptoms of PTSD include being easily startled, feeling irritable and anxious, having memories of the event intruding into your waking day, experiencing nightmares about the event, or feeling emotionally numb. If you have PTSD, you may be sustaining your distress by misunderstanding your normal feelings of dis-tress in response to the event, trying to avoid triggers that activate memories of the event, or trying too hard to keep yourself safe.

To combat PTSD, remind yourself that memories of a traumatic event intruding into your mind and feelings of distress are normal reactions to trauma. Allowing memories to enter your mind and spending time thinking about them is part of processing traumatic events and a crucial part of recovery. Many people find that deliberately confronting triggers or writing out a detailed first-person account can be helpful. At the same time it's important to reduce any excessive safety precautions you may have begun to take.

REMEMBER

Depending on the nature of your trauma and the severity of your symptoms, your best bet may be to seek a CBT therapist with expertise in treating PTSD. A trained therapist can help you ground yourself after exposures and be alongside you as you confront disturbing memories. Don't hesitate to get professional help with what may now feel overwhelming.

Hitting back at fear of heights

Begin to attack a fear of heights by carrying out a survey among your friends about the kind of feelings they have when standing at the edge of a cliff or at the top of a tall building. (See Chapter 5 for more on conducting surveys.) You'll probably discover that your sensation of being unwillingly drawn over the edge is common. Most people, however, just interpret this feeling as a normal reaction.

Put this new understanding into action to gain more confidence about being in high places. Work through a hierarchy of entering increasingly tall buildings, looking over bridges, and climbing to the top of high cliffs.

FASCINATING PHOBIAS

One of the interesting things about anxiety problems is the variety of things that human beings fear. In our practice, we still encounter people with fears we've never heard of before. Crucially, what matters isn't what you're afraid of but how negatively your fear is affecting your life.

Sometimes people are embarrassed by their phobias because they think others may find them silly or trivial. But extreme fear is never trivial. Terror and fear can be disabling, even if your fear is of something as simple as buttons. We suggest you seek out health professionals who take you seriously so you can get help for your phobia.

Common phobias include these:

- **Acrophobia:** fear of heights or high levels

- **Agoraphobia:** fear of open spaces, crowded public places, or being away from a place of safety

- **Aichmophobia:** fear of pins, needles, and pointed objects

- **Arachnophobia:** fear of spiders

- **Claustrophobia:** fear of confined or small spaces

- **Emetophobia:** fear of vomiting

- **Hemophobia:** fear of blood and blood injury

- **Lockiophobia:** fear of childbirth

- **Noctiphobia:** fear of the night and the dark

- **Trypanophobia:** fear of injections

Less common phobias include these:

- **Arachibutyrophobia:** fear of peanut butter sticking to the roof of one's mouth

- **Automatonophobia:** fear of ventriloquists' dummies, dolls, animatronic creatures, or wax statues

- **Barophobia:** fear of gravity

- **Bibliophobia:** fear of books (if you've got this one, stick with us — you're doing well!)

- **Blennophobia:** fear of slime

- **Lutraphobia:** fear of otters

- **Lyssophobia:** fear of going insane

- **Necrophobia:** fear of death or dead things

- **Ombrophobia:** fear of rain or being rained on

- **Soceraphobia:** fear of parents-in-law

- **Trypophobia:** fear of irregular patterns or small holes

Chapter **11**

Deconstructing and Demolishing Depression

S tatistics show that as many as one in two people are estimated to experience depression at some point. Luckily, the problem is well recognized and treatable.

If, for the past month, you've felt down, lacked energy, been pessimistic or hopeless about the future, and lost interest or enjoyment in doing things, you may be suffering from depression. If you've also had difficulty concentrating, had a poor appetite, been waking early and experienced a low mood, anxious thoughts, or feelings of dread, you're even more likely to be depressed. If you have three or more of these symptoms, your symptoms have been present for two weeks or more, and they're intense enough to interrupt your usual day-to-day activities, we recommend that you visit your doctor and investigate the possibility that you're suffering from depression.

CBT for the treatment of depression is well researched, and the results show that it produces good outcomes. CBT and antidepressant medication may be used in conjunction to treat depression, especially if it's more severe.

This chapter provides you with a guide for self-assessment of depression and offers classic CBT strategies for defeating it.

Understanding the Nature of Depression

The sort of depression we're talking about in this chapter is different from feeling down or blue for a few days in response to a bad event. We're talking about an illness now ranked as one of the most common reasons for people having to take time off work.

Specifically, depression has the following symptoms, usually lasting for at least two weeks:

>> Appetite variation, such as eating far less or more ("comfort eating") than usual

>> Sleep disturbance, including having difficulty sleeping, wanting to sleep too much, or experiencing early-morning wakefulness

>> Lack of concentration and poor memory

>> Irritability

>> Loss of libido

>> Loss of interest in activities previously enjoyed

>> Social isolation and withdrawal from others

>> Self-neglect with respect to feeding (especially eating junk food) or grooming

>> Neglecting to take care of your living environment

>> Decreased motivation and activity levels, often described as a feeling of lethargy

>> Hopelessness about the future and thinking bleak thoughts, such as "What's the point?"

>> Strong and enduring negative thoughts about yourself

>> Feelings of guilt and shame

>> Inability to experience feelings of love, often described as a flattening of emotions or feeling numb

>> Suicidal thoughts, such as thinking that you no longer care whether you live or die

Looking at What Fuels Depression

The good news is that our minds and bodies are good at regulating themselves and will naturally restore our moods, especially if given good conditions for healing. As we'll see, the tricky thing about depression is that it can lead us to get stuck in patterns of thinking and behavior that lower our mood.

In fact, some things that you do to alleviate your feelings of depression may be making your symptoms worse. CBT helps depressed individuals learn to override their depressed mood and do the opposite of what their depression makes them feel like doing. Here are actions and thoughts that can fuel depression:

>> **Rumination:** Getting hooked into a repetitive, cyclical process of negative thinking, repeatedly going over problems in the past or asking yourself unanswerable questions. (We discuss rumination in detail in the next section.)

>> **Negative thinking:** In depression, your negative thoughts are often based on beliefs that you're helpless and worthless. Thoughts about the world being an unsafe and undesirable place to live in are also common features of depression.

>> **Inactivity:** Feeling that you can't be bothered to do day-to-day tasks or finding simple tasks overwhelming, not participating in activities that previously you enjoyed, and staying in bed because you don't believe you can face the day.

>> **Social withdrawal:** Avoiding seeing other people and not interacting with the people around you.

>> **Procrastination:** Avoiding specific tasks, such as paying bills, booking appointments, and making phone calls because you think they're too difficult or scary to confront.

>> **Shame:** Feeling ashamed about your depression and telling yourself that other people would judge you harshly if they knew how much your effectiveness and productivity had decreased.

>> **Guilt:** Feeling guilty about your depression and overestimating the degree to which your low mood causes inconvenience and suffering for your loved ones.

>> **Hopelessness:** Thinking that you'll never feel better or that your situation will never improve.

TIP

Doing only what you want to do when you're depressed is likely to maintain or worsen your symptoms. Instead, try doing the opposite of what your depression seems to be directing you to do. For example, if you feel depressed and want to stay in bed all day avoiding phone calls and seeing friends, try to do the opposite to a degree. Try to make the colossal effort (and it can really feel colossal!) of getting up and dressed, answering the phone, and going out of the house to meet friends. Doing so limits you ruminating on your bad feelings and thoughts and forces your attention onto external things, such as other people and your environment.

Most people find that they feel better for having done *something,* even if they don't experience enjoyment from social interaction like they did before they became depressed.

REMEMBER

Depression typically dulls your ability to glean enjoyment from previously enjoyed activities. Be patient with yourself and trust that your feelings of enjoyment can return over time. In the first instance, it's enough to simply do the things that you've been avoiding for the sake of it. Doing something is better than doing nothing. Don't put pressure on yourself to have a good time at this early stage in your recovery. The key phrase here is to follow your plan, not how you feel. However, make sure your plan is sympathetic to your body and mind so that you can steadily progress.

Going Round and Round in Your Head: Ruminative Thinking

Rumination is an integral process in maintaining your depression. Most people with depression are likely to engage in it to some degree, even if they're not aware that they do.

Rumination is a circular thought process in which you go over the same things repeatedly. Often, the focus is on how bad you feel or doubting that you can ever feel differently or better. Your rumination may also focus on trying to work out the root cause of your depression or on the events that have contributed to your depression. You may have thoughts like the following, over and over again:

>> Why is this happening to me?

>> Why can't I just pull myself together?

>> What could I have done to stop this from happening?

>> If only *x, y,* or *z* hadn't happened, I'd be okay.

Depression makes people feel compelled to ruminate. In a sense, rumination is like a faulty attempt to solve problems. Rumination is compelling because your depressed mood tells you that you must try to get to the bottom of why you feel bad. But rumination simply doesn't work: You end up trying to solve your depression by going over the same old ground and looking for answers inside the problem. You focus your attention on how depressed you feel, which leads to feeling more depressed.

Fortunately, you can catch yourself going into a ruminative state by using the techniques we discuss in the following sections to interrupt the process.

Catching yourself in the act

Rumination is all-consuming. It typically absorbs you completely. You may look like you're simply staring blankly into space, but in your head your thoughts are firing at rapid speed. The key is to know when you're going *into* rumination so you can take steps toward getting out of it.

Early warning signs of rumination taking hold include the following:

>> **Getting stuck:** You may be in the middle of doing something and find that you've stopped moving and are deep in thought. For example, you may be perching on the side of the bed for several minutes or longer when you intended to take a shower.

>> **Feeling low:** Beware of times when your mood's at its lowest ebb. This is when you're most likely to engage in rumination. Most people ruminate at particular times of the day, although rumination can happen at any time.

>> **Slowing down:** You may be doing something and then start to move more slowly, like pausing in the aisle at the supermarket. You start to slow down because your concentration is heading elsewhere.

>> **Thinking repetitive thoughts:** The same old thoughts and questions drift into your head. You get a familiar niggling feeling that you must answer these vague questions.

REMEMBER

The content of your ruminations isn't the problem; the process of rumination is. You don't need to do anything with your thoughts other than disengage from them, as we explain in the following section.

Arresting ruminations before they arrest you

Several tricks can help you stop the rumination process:

>> **Get to know your rumination.** Track your pattern of rumination for a few days so you can learn when and where you tend to ruminate. This can help you side-step the rumination trap by seeing it coming and implementing some of the ideas below.

>> **Get busy.** Perhaps one of the most effective strategies you can adopt is to busy your body and mind with something outside yourself. If you're absorbed in an activity, you may find it harder to engage in rumination. These types of activities may include doing the housework while listening to the radio, making a phone call, surfing the internet, running errands, and taking the dogs for a walk.

>> **Work out.** Hard aerobic exercise can exorcise those toxic thought processes. Be sure to exercise during the day or in the early morning; exercising too near bedtime can disturb your sleep.

>> **Get up and out.** Rumination is more difficult when you're outside of your home or in the company of others. If you know that you're most vulnerable to ruminating at certain hours of the day, schedule activities for those times.

>> **Let your thoughts go.** Practice letting your negative thoughts pass by and simply observe them like pictures across a television screen. Don't engage with your negative thoughts, judge them, or try to answer any questions. Just accept their existence and let them slip by. (Check out Chapter 6 for more on this technique.)

>> **Get good at redirecting your attention.** You can strengthen your attention muscles and deliberately focus on less depressing things. Try using *task concentration training,* a method of attending to external aspects of your environment, because it can successfully interrupt rumination. (See Chapter 6 for more on task concentration training.) Some people find that briefly bringing their attention to their bodies, such as where they feel their bodily feelings of sadness, can help to refocus.

>> **Be skeptical.** Your depressed thoughts are a symptom of your depression, so try to take them with a sizable pinch of salt. You can resist the urge to ruminate about your depressed thoughts by deciding that they're neither true nor important. Even though they *feel* important and worthy of scrutiny, they aren't. You won't learn anything new about your depression by focusing on negative, repetitive thoughts.

WARNING

Keeping busy is a great technique for interrupting ruminative thinking. However, you can still end up ruminating while you're engaged in an activity. Pay attention to whatever you're doing. Be mindful of your actions when you're ironing, cleaning, stringing beads, and weeding the garden. Rumination can take hold during activities if you're acting *mindlessly* rather than *mindfully*. (Refer to Chapter 6 for more on this distinction.)

Activating Yourself as an Antidepressant

Withdrawal and inactivity are the two most fundamental *maintaining factors* in depression. They keep you in a vicious cycle of isolation and low mood. For example, to counteract feelings of fatigue, you may be tempted to spend more time in bed. Unfortunately, remaining in bed means more inactivity and less energy.

If you feel ashamed of being "flat" about having nothing to say or feel guilty about burdening your friends, keeping to yourself may seem sensible. The problem is that the less you do and the fewer people you see, the less pleasure and satisfaction you'll get out of life, the less support you'll receive, and the more your problems will pile up and weigh heavy on your mind. Staying away from others may seem like the right thing to do when your mood is low. You may believe that you have nothing to offer others. You may even have thoughts about being undeserving of friendship or love. However, the more you act on these destructive ideas, the more you reinforce them and convince yourself that they're true. Following your depressive tendency to isolate yourself can lead to true loneliness.

TIP

You don't have to talk about feeling down when you see friends; in fact, it's often good not to. Talking about superficial things and listening to what others have been up to can give you a break from your own thoughts. Moreover, noticing that others treat you normally can help you to feel a bit more normal rather than afflicted. Try not to worry about making interesting conversation and just allow yourself to absorb the company of those you're with.

REMEMBER

A good rule of thumb for recovery from many psychological problems is this: If you want to *feel* normal again, you need to start *acting* as you would normally.

WARNING

Because depression puts such a negative bias in your thinking, you may end up making negative self-comparisons when in the company of others. Be wary of letting stealthy depressed thoughts such as "I should be getting on with my life like my friends are" or "Why can't I be happy like so and so?" take hold. The worst time to self-evaluate is when you're depressed. So resist making comparisons and instead gently encourage yourself to engage in social interaction.

Tackling inactivity

One of the best ways of breaking free from depression is to gradually become more active. Your brain substantially benefits from the natural antidepressants of rewarding activities and satisfaction of completing a chore.

TIP

Use the activity schedule in Table 11-1 to start to plan each day with a realistic balance of activities and rest. Build up your activities gradually. If you've been in bed for days, getting out of the bedroom and sitting in a chair is a big move in the right direction. Remember: Take it step by step. Start small and gradually build up. Using the activity schedule is simple. It merely involves allocating a specific time to do a specific activity. You can copy the blank schedule in Table 11-1 and fill it in.

TABLE 11-1   **Activity Schedule**

	Monday	Tuesday	Wednesday	Thursday	Friday	Saturday	Sunday
6–8 a.m.							
8–10							
10–12							
12–2 p.m.							
2–4							
4–6							
6–8							
8–10							

WARNING

Don't overload your activity schedule; otherwise, you may feel overwhelmed, sink back into inactivity, and berate yourself for being ineffective. It's crucial to *realistically* plan a gradual increase in activities, starting from where you are now, not from where you think you should be.

Dealing with the here and now: Solving problems

As with other aspects of your daily or weekly activities, you need to be steady and systematic in your attempts to deal with practical problems, such as paying bills, writing letters, and completing other tasks that can pile up when you're less active.

To get started, set aside a specific amount of time each day for dealing with neglected chores. Allocating your time can help things seem more manageable. Try the following problem-solving process:

1. **Define your problem.**

   At the top of a sheet of paper, write down the problems you're struggling with. For example, you might consider problems with the following:

   - Relationships

   - Isolation

   - Interests and hobbies

   - Employment and education

   - Finances

   - Legal issues

   - Housing

   - Health

   Apply the following steps to each of your identified problems. You may need to do Steps 2 to 5 on each of your different problems.

2. **Brainstorm solutions to your problem.**

   Write down all the possibilities you can think of. Consider the following questions to help you generate solutions:

   - How did you deal with similar problems in the past?

   - How have other people coped with similar problems?

   - How do you imagine you'd tackle the problem if you weren't feeling depressed?

   - How do you think someone else would approach the problem?

   - What resources (such as professionals and voluntary services) can you access for help with your problems?

3. **Evaluate your solutions.**

   Review your brainstormed list. Select some of your most realistic solutions, and list the pros and cons of each.

4. **Try out a solution.**

   Based on your evaluation of pros and cons, choose a solution to try out.

WARNING

You can easily feel overwhelmed when your mood is low. Even the best of solutions can seem too difficult. To deal with this, break down your solution into a series of smaller, more manageable steps. For example, if you're dealing with financial problems, your first step may be to ask friends to recommend an accountant or to visit a financial consultant in your area. A second step may be to get your tax returns or proof of income together. A third step may be selecting an accountant and contacting them for information about their fees and the services they provide.

5. **Review.**

   After trying out a solution, review how much it has helped you resolve your problem. Consider whether you need to take further steps, try another solution, or move on to tackling another problem.

Taking care of yourself and your environment

One of the hallmarks of depression is neglecting yourself and your living environment, which in turn leaves you feeling more depressed.

Instead of allowing your depression to be mirrored in your appearance and your home, make greater effort to spruce things up. Your environment can have an astounding effect on your mood, both positive and negative.

TIP

Include bathing, laundry, tidying, and cleaning as part of your weekly activity schedule.

ACTing Against Depression

Acceptance and commitment therapy (ACT), founded by Stephen Hayes, is one of the third-wave developments in cognitive therapy. It's a newer approach to treating depression but still largely based on core cognitive therapy principles. ACT differs in pertinent ways from standard CBT. The chief difference is that instead of challenging your negative thoughts directly, you observe them without judgement and let them pass naturally. We touch on this concept in the earlier section "Arresting ruminations before they arrest you." (Also see Chapter 6 for more on allowing thoughts to pass.)

In addition to tolerating and nonjudgmentally observing negative thoughts, ACT focuses on commitment to personal values. According to ACT, people who recognize their values and pursue action to reflect those values avoid depression. (We look at value-based living in Chapter 21.)

The following three sections expand on basic principles involved in recovery from depression found in both CBT and ACT.

Practicing acceptance

The feeling of depression, and the thoughts that go with it, is deeply unpleasant and unwelcome. We've never met anyone who said they elected to become depressed. You may conclude that you're miserable or fundamentally negative based on your depression. We find that this is rarely the case. Being depressed isn't the same as holding a cynical and pervasively negative view of the world. In fact, the opposite is typically the case. If you're depressed, one of the things you may find hardest to accept is the change from being a person who enjoys life to one who feels utterly defeated and devoid of enjoyment. People who are depressed sometimes express feeling that they no longer recognize themselves.

Because symptoms of depression frequently run so counter to your understanding of your natural temperament, they can be uniquely difficult to accept. We're not suggesting that you learn to *like* being depressed. That would be crazy. But it can help to accept your depression for what it is: an illness. Thankfully, depression is usually temporary (even if it does last for a long while) and isn't a change of personality. Your personality is still intact; your depression is merely masking it. Unwittingly, you may be putting extra pressure on yourself by issuing demands such as "I must not feel this way," "this is intolerable," and "I have to get better *now!*" Such demands, though understandable, just reinforce your bad feelings and build bigger obstacles to recovery. They're like banging your head against a wall. Try practicing these accepting attitudes instead:

>> I hate being depressed but unfortunately I'm not immune to depression.

>> Depression is hard to bear but I *am* tolerating these unpleasant feelings.

>> I want to get better now, but I can't bully myself out of depression, so I'll be patient but determined.

Give yourself credit for coping even though you may feel like you're not. You *are* coping; it's just not easy.

Considering compassion

You can't bully yourself out of depression. If that strategy worked, we'd have far fewer clients. Giving yourself a hard time for being low is kicking yourself when you're down. So many depressed people both berate and refuse to look after themselves because doing so's part of an insidious cycle. See Figure 11-1.

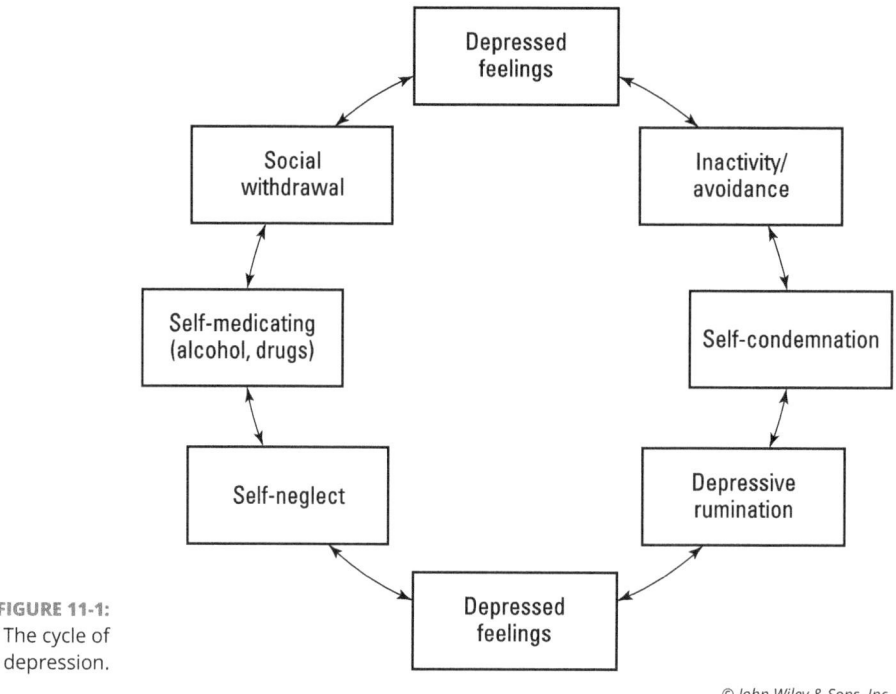

FIGURE 11-1:
The cycle of depression.

When you're ill, you want to be well again. That involves looking after yourself, both mentally and physically. When you have the flu or some other physical illness, you probably don't tell yourself that you should never have become ill in the first place or that you're weak and pathetic because you've done so. Depression is a different ball game, as Figure 11-1 illustrates. An essential part of recovery is offering yourself compassion instead of criticism. (We talk more about compassionate mind training in Chapter 18.) Try these tips for being kind to yourself:

>> **Give yourself credit for your efforts to act against depression.** Instead of telling yourself that you should be doing more, start from where you are now. If yesterday you didn't get out of bed and today you did, that's significant progress. The next step may be going shopping or answering your telephone. Focus on your small daily improvements instead of benchmarking yourself against where you ultimately want to be.

>> **Compliment and kindly cajole yourself.** Depression invites you to think of yourself in negative ways and call yourself bad names. Stop yourself from verbalizing or mentally constructing self-directed insults. Instead, deliberately call to mind your good points and encourage yourself to do more through praise. Be nice!

>> **Be wary of false friends.** Using illicit drugs, alcohol, or food to alleviate your feelings and thoughts can grant you a brief respite, but at a high cost. You're likely to feel far worse when you come down from drugs and alcohol or after an eating binge. You may end up with a dependency that prolongs a period of depression, which may otherwise shortly relent. Alcohol and drug use can also interfere with the effectiveness of antidepressant medication.

Obtaining a new outlook

A depressed outlook is typically bleak. The future feels impossible to contemplate because everything seems tinged with gray. Even as you make steps toward recovery, your outlook may remain stubbornly negative for a while. Constructing a new optimistic outlook and practicing it daily — even several times each day — can be useful. You may not feel as though you believe it at first but, with time, this bright outlook will begin to ring true. Try adopting these new outlooks:

>> I look forward to feeling better soon.

>> I may not see the light at the end of the tunnel, but I know it's there.

>> This will pass.

>> I'll deal with the future when it comes; I don't need to worry about it now.

>> Hanging on is worth it because things will get better.

WARNING

The road to recovery from depression is rarely a steady uphill climb. Setbacks and difficult days are part of a normal recovery. Don't be too disappointed if, after a series of good days, you have a hard one. This difficult day isn't a return to square one or a sign that you're not improving. Just saddle up and get back on the horse.

Managing Suicidal Thoughts

The most dangerous element of depression is that the feelings of hopelessness, or sense that you're defeated, may become so strong that you try to take your own life. Don't panic about having suicidal thoughts if you're depressed. Such thoughts are common, and having them doesn't necessarily mean that you'll act on them.

WARNING

If you've been feeling hopeless or defeated about the future and started to make plans about how to kill yourself, immediately seek medical assistance. Make an appointment with your regular doctor as a first point of call, or call 988 or 911 if it feels like an emergency.

Follow these tips for managing suicidal thoughts:

>> Recognize your feelings of hopelessness about the future as a symptom of depression, not a fact.

>> Remember that depression is a temporary state, and you can treat it in several ways. Decide to tackle your depression for, say, six weeks, as an experiment to see whether things can improve.

>> Tell a friend or family member how you're feeling.

>> See a doctor or therapist, or join a support group for further help and support if you're finding it difficult to overcome your depression on your own.

>> Try instigating the problem-solving process we outlined in the earlier section "Dealing with the here and now: Solving problems" for any problem you currently see as hopeless.

Contemplating Complex Forms of Depression

Although the most well-known type of depression is major depressive disorder (MDD) or unipolar depression (the kind we've focused on thus far), other more complicated forms of depression exist. Unfortunately, they're more life limiting and require additional professional care. We explain a bit about them in this section.

If the conditions in the following sections are distressing, take heart: Help is out there. CBT can help with these complex forms of depression, and, with the correct medication, you can lead a fulfilling life. Complex depression is every bit as debilitating as many physical long-term conditions, no question. Be patient and compassionate with yourself, and don't give up until you find the right CBT therapist and mental health professional for you. You can use this book to accompany your therapy and help your mood. You can also find support groups for complex depression. Talking to others who understand how it feels to live with your type of depression can be helpful.

Bipolar disorder

Formerly called *manic depression*, *bipolar disorder* is defined by sustained periods of severe depression alternating with sustained periods of mania or *hypomania* (feelings of euphoria accompanied by impulsive and often risky behavior). These periods aren't mood swings like most people can have within a given day or a few hours. The up or down mood lasts weeks, not days or hours.

Bipolar depression is a complicated and disabling condition that the public doesn't understand very well, and the media often misrepresent it as schizophrenia (a different but still serious mental health problem) or dissociative identity disorder, previously referred to as either split or multiple personality disorder. People who suffer with bipolar don't have alternate personalities, aren't a risk to others, and don't typically hear voices or lose touch with reality.

REMEMBER

Bipolar is a lifelong condition that needs appropriate medication to be managed; you can't manage it just by using the techniques covered in this chapter for overcoming MDD (depression that's not accompanied by periods of mania or hypomania). To stabilize your mood and keep you well, the right combination of psychiatric medications is essential. We advise you to seek an assessment from a psychiatrist, who can diagnose you and prescribe appropriate medications that are outside the remit of your family doctor. A psychiatrist can also refer you to a CBT therapist who has experience working with bipolar sufferers.

However, you can use the techniques in this chapter, such as solving problems, scheduling your activities, and interrupting rumination, to keep your mood stable. Maintaining a day-to-day level of activity is one of the main CBT strategies for managing bipolar disorder, as is healthy sleep behavior, which we discuss in Chapter 15.

If you think that you have bipolar disorder, someone else in your family tree likely has it, too, as genetics play a large role in its development.

Cyclothymic disorder

Cyclothymia has more similarities with bipolar than differences. Think of it as a milder form of bipolar with less frequent or severe highs and lows. Even psychiatrists can have difficulty deciding whether a person better fits a diagnosis for bipolar or cyclothymic disorder, so you and your family doctor are unlikely to be able to make the distinction. If you have cyclothymia, you need medications like those used to treat bipolar, but you may not need such high dosages, and you may not need to take them as consistently.

REMEMBER

For both bipolar and cyclothymia, you need regular medication reviews and blood tests to make sure you're on the right dosage and that the drugs are having the desired effect. If you're not seeing your doctor and psychiatrist at least every six weeks, request regular appointments.

Dysthymic disorder

Dysthymia or *persistent depressive disorder (PDD)* consists of the same symptoms of uni polar depression (MDD) that we've discussed throughout this chapter. The difference is that the symptoms can be milder but last much longer, rarely disappearing for more than two months at a time. People with PDD often report not being sure how it feels to be undepressed. They seem to have always felt low. If this assessment describes how you feel, make sure you explain your persistent symptoms to your doctor and psychiatrist. PDD requires medication, but not the same combination as for bipolar or cyclothymia.

FAMOUS AND DEPRESSED

One of the most crucial aspects of recovering from depression is shedding any feelings of shame you may have about the problem. Realizing that no one is immune from depression can help here. Depression has affected people from every walk of life and all creeds, colors, and levels of intelligence.

Dozens of famous people have publicly reported or discussed their battles with depression. Celebrities are now coming out about their depression or bipolar disorder. We hope that their actions can remove the stigma of mental health problems and enable others to identify and seek help for depression.

A sampling of those who've suffered from depression or bipolar disorder follows:

- Buzz Aldrin (astronaut)
- Ludwig van Beethoven (composer)
- Kristen Bell (actor, comedian)
- William Blake (poet)
- Winston Churchill (British prime minister)
- John Cleese (comedian, actor, and writer)
- Charles Dickens (writer)
- Eminem (rapper)
- Stephen Fry (comedian, actor, writer, and presenter)
- Professor Green (rapper)
- Germaine Greer (writer and journalist)
- Dwayne "The Rock" Johnson (former wrestler, actor)
- Demi Lovato (singer)
- Spike Milligan (comedian, actor, and writer)
- Isaac Newton (physicist)
- Joanna Scanlan (writer, actor, comedian)
- Mary Shelley (writer)
- Vincent Van Gogh (artist)
- Lewis Wolpert (embryologist and broadcaster)

In our clinical practice we often treat doctors, psychiatrists, and other mental health professionals for depression. So even those who earn a living treating psychological illness can suffer from it.

Chapter **12**

Overcoming Obsessions

This chapter introduces you to common obsessional problems and shows how to tackle them using CBT. Specifically, in this chapter we focus on obsessive–compulsive disorder (OCD) and using a strategy for tackling OCD called exposure and response prevention (ERP).

OCD can cause significant levels of distress and interference in daily living. However, you can use the CBT principles outlined in this chapter to reduce your obsessions and compulsions. If you have a more severe form of OCD, consider adding some professional help. The core principles can still be useful.

Many people have some degree of compulsive behavior, such as checking, cleaning, or ordering, that doesn't particularly interfere with their lives. This level of problem is usually regarded as *subclinical.* However, problems like OCD are disruptive and distressing when they reach more severe levels. People suffering from severe OCD can have difficulties maintaining relationships and jobs and leaving the house; their physical health can suffer, and they frequently develop secondary depression.

Fortunately, obsessional problems are being diagnosed more accurately than ever before. OCD is now ranked among the most common psychiatric disorders. This change is probably due to increased awareness among health professionals and to more accurate assessment measures. CBT is well recognized as the psychological treatment of choice for obsessional problems and has far superior relapse rates compared to medication alone.

A second OCD-related disorder includes body dysmorphic disorder (BDD), which involves being preoccupied and dissatisfied with one or more aspects of your physical appearance. Health anxiety, also known as *illness anxiety disorder* (IAD), is a third OCD-related disorder. It's a preoccupation with the chance of either having or getting a serious, life-limiting illness. See Chapters 13 and 14 for more on IAD and BDD.

Identifying and Understanding Obsessional Problems

Obsessional problems are among the most disabling of common emotional-behavioral problems. People with *obsessional problems* can spend hours every day plagued by upsetting thoughts and feel driven to repeatedly carry out rituals or fervidly avoid certain situations.

REMEMBER

Some degree of obsession is entirely normal. For example, around half of all people have a particular thing that they check more than they think is necessary, such as whether the gas stove has been switched off or the door's been bolted. Obsessional problems have their roots in normal experiences, but the rituals and avoidance behaviors serve to make the frequency, severity, and duration of obsessions worse. The more you try to rid yourself of doubts, the greater they tend to play on your mind.

We define the terms related to obsessions in this list:

>> An *obsession* is a persistent, unwanted thought, image, doubt, or urge that intrudes into your mind and triggers distress. Obsessions are said to have reached a *psychiatric problem* level when they cause significant levels of distress, interfere with your life, and are present for more than an hour a day.

>> *Preoccupation* means being absorbed with something troubling that won't leave your mind. You feel compelled to give it your attention. Preoccupations are fueled by self-doubt that reaches proportions outside of typical everyday human experience. They're similar to obsessions in that they're regarded as problematic when they cause significant distress, interfere with your life, and last for more than an hour per day.

In this chapter, we focus on obsessions common to OCD, like the prevalence of germs or poisons or the content of an unwanted or intrusive thought such as "Do I want to harm my loved one?" or a doubt such as "Did I turn off the stove?"

>> *Compulsions,* also called *rituals,* are the actions you may take in response to your obsessions or preoccupations but that do not particularly help you in your life. Compulsions can be observable behaviors (such as checking or washing your hands) or thoughts (such as repeating a phrase in your head or counting). Compulsions are usually attempts to get rid of a thought, image, urge, or doubt; an attempt to reduce danger; or an attempt to reduce discomfort. They may provide immediate relief, but the relief doesn't last, and you have to repeat the rituals over and over.

>> *Avoidance behaviors* are things you do to avoid triggering your obsession or preoccupation. Your avoidance behavior may be avoiding driving in areas of heavy pedestrian traffic; avoiding holding sharp objects when around other people; or avoiding discarding empty cleaning products for fear of inadvertently poisoning someone.

Rituals and avoidance behaviors are the lifeblood of obsessional problems. Add to these catastrophic thinking and emotional reasoning (see Chapter 2), regarding negative emotions as facts (see Chapter 7), and attention bias (see Chapter 6), and you have the basic anatomy of obsessional problems.

Understanding obsessive–compulsive disorder (OCD)

According to the American Psychiatric Association:

Obsessions are: Recurrent and persistent thoughts, urges, or images that are experienced, at some time during the disturbance, as intrusive, unwanted, and that in most individuals cause marked anxiety or distress. The individual attempts to ignore or suppress such thoughts, urges, or images, or to neutralize them with some thought or action (i.e., by performing a compulsion).

Compulsions are: Repetitive behaviors (e.g., hand washing, ordering checking) or mental acts (e.g., praying, counting, repeating words silently) that the person feels driven to perform in response to an obsession, or according to the rules that must be applied rigidly. The behaviors or mental acts are aimed at preventing or reducing distress or preventing some dreaded event or situation. However, these behaviors or mental acts either are not connected in a realistic way with what they are designed to neutralize or prevent or are clearly excessive.

The obsessions or compulsions are time-consuming (e.g., take more than 1 hour per day) or cause clinically significant distress or impairment in social, occupational, or other areas of functioning.

Common obsessions in OCD include the following:

>> Fear of contamination (to yourself or others) via germs, bodily fluids, or toxins

>> Fear of accidentally or deliberately causing harm to yourself or others (jumping off a bridge or poking a needle into someone's eye) or of acting impulsively and becoming uncontrollably violent or aggressive

>> Dire need for order, symmetry, or strict routines, including the need to carry out activities in a particular sequence

>> Religious obsession, such as fear of offending God, committing a mortal sin, or inadvertently acting in allegiance with the devil

>> Sexual obsession, such as fear of being a pedophile or doubt as to whether you've viewed illegal pornography or behaved in a sexually inappropriate manner

>> Ritual driven by superstitions to prevent harm coming to yourself or others, like deciding only even numbers are "safe" or having to recite a specific phrase before bed to protect your family until morning

>> Fear of losing something physically important (such as a possession, paperwork, or ideas) or your *autobiographical memory* (memory of personal events)

>> Fear of behaving irresponsibly and causing a fire, flood, or other type of accident

>> Fear of acting out an intrusive thought/image in a way that violates your moral code

>> Need to perform an action until it feels "right," like locking a door until it feels "properly locked," kissing your children goodnight until it feels like you've given them your love, or taking a shower until you feel "clean"

REMEMBER

This list includes some of the more common ways that OCD manifests. It's an idiosyncratic disorder, so don't be surprised if your experience is a little different from those here.

Compulsions frequently associated with OCD include the following:

>> Checking (for example, if a light is switched off or the front door is locked)

>> Cleaning or washing (such as yourself, others, your home, car, or possessions that you take outside)

>> Counting, ordering, and doing things in a sequence

>> Repeating actions or special words, images, or numbers in your mind to stave off a vaguely defined danger

- ❯❯ Organizing and making things "just so"

- ❯❯ Having difficulty discarding possessions that have no real value, interest, or function but may have once had sentimental worth

- ❯❯ Making excessive numbers of lists before taking any action or doing too much research before making a decision

- ❯❯ Replaying or repeating scenes, images, or actions in your mind (mentally retracing your steps)

The severity and impact of OCD varies greatly, and in its most extreme form individuals can become housebound, even bedridden. While the severity of symptoms can wax and wane, most people with mild to moderate OCD do function, have relationships, hold down jobs, and complete education, but they are under considerable extra strain.

You can think of OCD as a stress response. We sometimes refer to it as "mental eczema" because it tends to flare up when you're at a low ebb due to stress, illness, fatigue, or hormonal changes or even in response to positive changes like moving into a new house or embarking on an adventurous holiday. Clearly, many people may recognize some degree of the excessive worries and rituals outlined here. What determines whether you meet criteria for a diagnosis of OCD is how much choice you feel to stop a ritual without debilitating distress and how much interference OCD is causing in your daily life.

Identifying Unhelpful Behaviors

As we note in Chapter 8, the things humans do to reduce their distress in the short term often maintain problems in the long run, so the solution becomes the problem. In the case of OCD, behaviors such as avoidance, checking, washing, seeking reassurance, comparing, readjusting, and repeating (to name but a few) are the maintaining mechanisms.

Most clients we work with on their obsessional problems agree *intellectually* that their behaviors perpetuate and aggravate their problems, but they often say, "Now I really see what you mean!" after they experiment with them. Check out Chapter 5 for more information on designing CBT experiments to challenge your thinking.

The first step is to understand the concept of problem maintenance. The next step is to really experience how your behaviors affect your obsessions and preoccupation — by doing experiments.

In the broadest sense, you can try two kinds of experiments with your obsessional thinking:

>> *Reduce* (or stop) a particular ritual and see how this affects the frequency, intensity, and duration of your upsetting thoughts.

>> *Increase* a ritual or avoidance for a day and see what effect this has on the frequency, intensity, and duration of your upsetting thoughts.

Increasing a ritual or avoidance is often easier to do in the short term and yields more results more rapidly.

Say you worry frequently about your house being burgled, so you repeatedly check your doors and windows before leaving the house or going to bed. To find out whether your checking is part of the problem rather than the solution, record the frequency, duration, and intensity of your worry about burglary on a usual day of checking. Then spend another day trying as hard as you can to double your checking, and record the results. If you note a clear increase in your worry on the day of extra checking, the ritual behavior is clearly part of your problem.

Acquiring Anti-obsessional Attitudes

Research and clinical observation shows that numerous thinking styles are related to the development of obsessional problems. Fortunately, you can also use thinking to combat obsessional problems. The following sections offer alternative ways of thinking that can help you in your fight against your obsessional problem.

Tolerating doubt and uncertainty

In our own and other therapists' experience, one of the main protestations that clients make about stopping rituals or avoidance behaviors is this: "How can you guarantee that what I'm afraid of won't happen?"

The truth is, of course, that we can't. But no one without obsessional problems gets those kinds of guarantees, either, so clearly the problem *isn't* a lack of certainty. We can offer a different kind of guarantee, however: If you continue to demand a guarantee or certainty that your fears won't come true, you're likely to keep your obsessional problem.

Instead, practice *consistently* and *repeatedly* tolerating doubt and uncertainty without resorting to checking, washing, reassurance-seeking, or whatever you do compulsively. Your rituals only fuel your belief that you need certainty. Initially, staying with doubt may feel uncomfortable, but if you stick with it your anxiety can reduce. Deliberately seek out triggers for your doubt and practice resisting the urge to carry out rituals, seek reassurance, or work things out in your mind.

Trusting your judgment

To explain why individuals with obsessional problems check so much more than those without these problems, scientists explored the hypothesis that people with OCD have poorer memories. The rationale here was, perhaps, that people with OCD check or seek reassurance because they can't remember properly. The scientists did make an important discovery: People with obsessional problems have no memory deficiency. What they do have, however, is poor confidence in their memory.

Poor confidence in one's memory may be related to unrealistic demands for certainty. (See the preceding section on how to tolerate doubt and uncertainty.) No amount of checking removes that grain of doubt from your recall.

The best thing you can do to boost your confidence in your memory is to act more confident and cut back on rituals. Doing so consistently and repeatedly gradually builds your confidence.

Treating your thoughts as nothing more than thoughts

One of the main thinking errors in obsessional problems is overestimating the importance of the intrusive doubts, thoughts, and images that occur naturally in your mind. Experts in OCD have shown that the following three key misinterpretations contribute to obsessional problems:

>> **The probability misinterpretation:** The idea that having a thought about an event in your mind affects the probability of that event occurring. For example, "If I allow myself to picture myself hurting someone, it's more likely I'll do it."

>> **The moral misinterpretation:** The idea that an unpleasant thought entering your mind reveals something unpleasant about yourself. For example, "Having thoughts of causing harm means I'm a bad and dangerous person."

>> **The responsibility misinterpretation:** The idea that having a thought about an event means that you have responsibility for it happening or for preventing it from happening. For example, "Having an image of myself jumping from a tall building means that I need to be more vigilant than the average person when confronting heights."

Intrusive thoughts, images, doubts, and impulses are entirely normal. Your assumption that the thoughts you're having aren't normal is the problem. The solution is to allow these thoughts to pass through your mind without engaging with them or trying to change, suppress, or hurry them along. Try to picture your thoughts like the ripples in a pool of water after you throw in a stone; eventually, the water becomes still again (as long as you don't throw in more stones). See Chapter 6 for more suggestions on managing your mind without interfering with it.

Being flexible and not trying too hard

If you have an obsessional problem, you're trying too hard at something. You may be trying too hard to get your home or desk looking just so. Or you may be trying to ensure that you or someone you feel responsible for is safe from harm or distress. Or perhaps you're inclined to follow moral or religious instruction to the letter rather than living within the spirit of these ideals.

Flexibility is one of the hallmarks of psychological health because it helps you adapt effectively to the real world. Consider the real-life consequences of holding standards or ideals too rigidly. Does refusing yourself the right to make errors really help you live the kind of life you want? Or does it just lead you to feel anxious about falling short of your ideals? Are the costs to yourself and others worth the benefits? If not, try to define how you'd behave if you were free from your obsessional problem, or take a leaf from someone else's book and try acting accordingly. Refer to Chapter 9 for more on doing a cost–benefit analysis.

Using external and practical criteria

A crucial difference between people with and without OCD is regarding the criteria they use to decide when to stop a particular behavior. People without obsessions tend to use external observations, or practical criteria, to evaluate situations and make decisions.

In contrast, people with OCD tend to use *internal criteria* — such as something feeling "right," "better," or "comfortable" — to make decisions. Here are two examples of internal criteria with their external alternatives:

>> A person with contamination OCD may wash their hands until they *feel* that their hands are clean enough. Someone without this problem may tend to stop washing when they can *see* their hands are clean or when they've been through a quick and convenient routine.

>> A person with OCD may lock, unlock, and relock the car door until they feel comfortable enough to trust that the door is actually locked. However, someone without OCD may just check the door handle once and be satisfied that the car is locked.

Strive to use normal criteria to decide when to stop an activity. Instead of stopping when you feel comfortable, force yourself to stop washing your hands or locking up your home or car *before* you feel comfortable. Making this change can reinforce the fact that your criteria for stopping rituals are the problem and prove to you that your discomfort, anxiety, and doubt can diminish spontaneously. Importantly, this technique can also show you that you *can* tolerate the discomfort of resisting your rituals, even if doing so is uncomfortable at first.

Allowing your mind and body to do their own things

Complete control of your thoughts and body is

>> **Impossible:** No one has it, not even highly trained doctors, athletes, monks, or psychologists.

>> **Counterproductive:** Attempting to completely control or censor your thoughts results in more of the thoughts and sensations you were trying to get rid of. You may even feel more out of control while trying to control the uncontrollable.

>> **Undesirable:** Being able to completely choose the thoughts that enter your mind effectively puts a stop to any originality and creative problem-solving. Being in control of your body would certainly result in your demise. After all, do you really know how to run a body?

Allowing your body and mind to go on autopilot is so much easier and more helpful than trying to control your thoughts and bodily sensations.

Normalizing physical sensations, emotions, and unpleasant thoughts

OCD can lead you to focus too much on your thoughts, emotions, and physical sensations. These problems also lead you to attach undue importance and meaning to your physical sensations, emotions, and upsetting thoughts.

>> OCD leads you to be guided too much by emotional distress. "If I feel anxious about a fire, checking that all the plug sockets are off is the right thing to do."

>> OCD also leads you to attach too much meaning to normal unpleasant thoughts that intrude into your mind. "Having a thought like that must mean something important. I have to stop those thoughts!"

>> OCD finally leads you to misunderstand physical normal sensations. "If I feel an urge to swerve my car into oncoming traffic, I must be at risk of doing just that."

REMEMBER

Your problem isn't the content of your thought, the feelings in your body, or the emotional distress you may experience, however unpleasant and unwelcome they may be. Your problem is *your belief* that these experiences are abnormal. People without OCD experience the same intrusive thoughts and urges that you do; they just dismiss them more easily. To help yourself overcome your obsessional problems, take the view that your thoughts, emotions, and physical sensations are *normal.* Conducting surveys (which we talk about in Chapter 5) is an excellent way of gathering evidence that many of the things you focus on and worry about are normal human experiences.

Facing Your Fears: Reducing (and Stopping) Rituals

In CBT, facing your fears and resisting the urge to carry out compulsions is called *exposure and response prevention.* This term has two important components:

>> **Exposure:** Deliberately facing up to the places, people, situations, substances, objects, thoughts, doubts, impulses, and images that trigger your feelings of anxiety and discomfort.

>> **Response prevention:** Reducing and stopping the rituals and any other safety precautions that you adopt.

To reduce or potentially stop your reliance on rituals, you must tackle your obsessions head-on. To accomplish this, you need to get better at tolerating doubt, allow thoughts and images to come and go from your mind, and be realistic about responsibility. And yes, you need to practice these skills.

You can make faster progress if you *deliberately* trigger off your upsetting thoughts and anxiety in a regular and consistent way. See Chapter 10 for more detail on designing an exposure program to combat your anxieties.

REMEMBER

Facing your fears when overcoming OCD is different from dealing with many other kinds of anxiety because the object of your fear may be more internal than external. For example, facing the mental image of pushing someone on to a train track is just as important as actually standing on the platform.

Putting up firm resistance

To overcome an obsessional problem, you need to develop a list of your main fears as well as your typical rituals and safety behaviors.

Keeping a daily record of the frequency of the rituals you want to reduce helps you track your progress and motivates you to keep reducing. You can record the frequency on your phone or go old school and buy a *tally counter* (a "clicker" that counts each time you press it) from an office supply store or online.

When you have your list, you need to systematically expose yourself to your main fears while simultaneously reducing and dropping your rituals and safety behaviors.

REMEMBER

Stopping your rituals only when the opportunity arises isn't sufficient to overcome your obsessions. You need to incorporate deliberate exposure to your fears to get the practice you need. In other words, seek out what you most typically avoid, and don't do what you typically would.

Delaying and modifying rituals

Delaying and modifying a ritual can also be a useful lead-up to dropping it entirely:

>> **Delaying rituals:** If you find stopping your rituals difficult, start by delaying them for a few minutes. Gradually build up the time delay until you can resist a ritual long enough for your anxiety to reduce of its own accord.

>> **Modifying rituals:** If you can't gear yourself up to stop your ritual entirely just yet, modify it. Instead of going for the full-blown version of a ritual, allow yourself to perform a shortened version. For example, if you normally vacuum every corner of a room, try making yourself stick to the areas you can see, without moving furniture or other objects.

REMEMBER

Overcoming OCD is supposed to be an uncomfortable experience. If you're working through the exercises in this chapter and not experiencing a temporary increase in your discomfort, either you're not exposing yourself sufficiently or you're not resisting your rituals sufficiently.

If you plan to stop a particular ritual but end up doing it anyway, *re-expose* yourself rather than letting your obsessional problem win. For example, if you have a fear of contamination, touch the floor to re-expose yourself after washing your hands.

WARNING

You may be tempted to err on the safe side and allow yourself to carry out more rituals or safety measures than the average person. Retaining avoidance and rituals can leave you prone to your obsessions returning. Keep working at your ritual reduction until your rituals are at least as low as those of the average person on the street. Think of rituals and avoidance as the roots of a weed you're trying to get rid of from your garden. If you don't get weeds up by the roots, they're sure to grow back.

Being Realistic About Responsibility

One of the hallmarks of OCD is a tendency to take too much responsibility. Individuals with OCD, for example, often take excessive responsibility for causing or preventing harm to themselves or others. A person with OCD may have an over-developed sense of responsibility for spotting potential dangers like a knife balancing precariously on the edge of a kitchen counter. This inflated sense of responsibility can drive the person to perform rituals and leave them feeling guilty if they don't.

Dividing up your responsibility pie

A helpful technique for developing a more realistic perception of your personal responsibility is to create a *responsibility pie chart,* as follows:

1. **Identify an event you fear being responsible for.**

   Examples include the house being burgled, causing harm, or offending someone without intending to.

2. **Write down the percentage level of responsibility you would feel for the event if it occurred.**

   You can have between 0 and 100 percent of the responsibility for an event occurring.

3. **List all the possible contributing factors to your feared event occurring, including yourself.**

4. **Create a responsibility pie chart.**

   Use a large empty circle to represent 100 percent, or all the responsibility for an event occurring. You can draw a circle yourself or use the circle provided in Figure 12-1.

   Proportionally divide the pie into wedges, based on how much responsibility you assign to each of the factors you list in Step 3. Be sure to put yourself in last.

5. **Rerate your estimation of your responsibility for your feared event.**

   Use the 0 to 100 percent scale described in Step 2.

   For example, Figure 12-2 shows the responsibility pie chart for Theresa, a mother with OCD who obsesses about harm coming to her children from poisonous substances. Initially, Theresa believes that she'd be completely to blame if any harm befell her children. However, after working through the responsibility pie chart activity, she's able to gain a more realistic perspective on her level of personal responsibility.

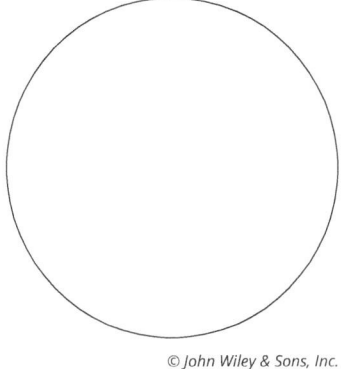

FIGURE 12-1:
The starting point for your responsibility pie chart.

© John Wiley & Sons, Inc.

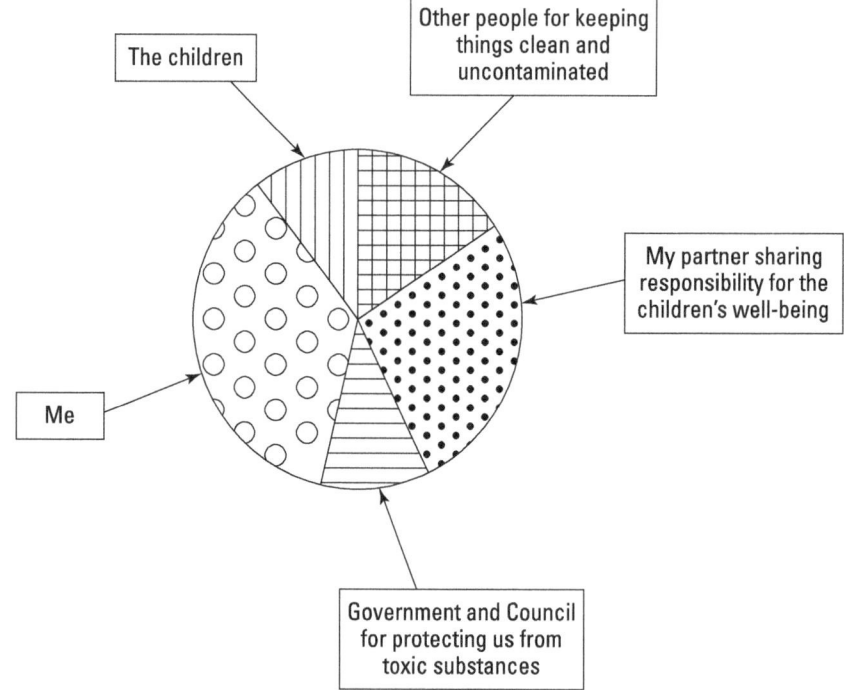

FIGURE 12-2:
Theresa's
responsibility
pie chart.

© John Wiley & Sons, Inc.

You can also use the responsibility pie chart with negative events that have actually happened and that you're blaming yourself for. These events might be job loss, a failed relationship, poor treatment from a loved one, or a friend's cancer diagnosis.

REMEMBER

The purpose of the responsibility pie chart is to help you see that you're not 100 percent responsible for an event happening. Many obsessional people give themselves more responsibility than is legitimate — or at least more than non-obsessional people do.

Taking *less responsibility* is something you steadily need to train your mind to do. Actually, you're retraining your mind to stop taking excessive responsibility.

Retraining your attention

If you think you're preoccupied with being responsible for harm coming to yourself or others *because you focus on it too much,* try to create a counterbalance by training your attention elsewhere. Chapter 6 gives you some more guidance.

SEEKING PROFESSIONAL HELP

Use the following checklist to determine whether an obsession or compulsion is normal or a problem for which you should seek professional assistance.

- **Your obsessional problems are impacting your physical health.** For example, you're not taking prescribed medication, attending medical appointments, or feeding and grooming yourself sufficiently.

- **Your obsessional problems are preventing you from leaving your home.** Sometimes people with severe OCD become housebound.

- **Your obsessional problems are having a serious impact on your social and occupational life.** For example, you're unable to continue working, you've lost a job, you're avoiding contact with friends, or your partner has left you.

- **Your obsessional problems are preventing you from caring adequately for your children.** This is a particularly painful point for many people with OCD. People with OCD typically take too much responsibility for the welfare of their loved ones. However, if you contemplate the needs of your children and decide *impartially* that your problems are stopping you from meeting those needs, get in touch with a professional.

- **You've given self-help an earnest try but are unable to overcome your problem.**

Your family doctor might be familiar with OCD, but you may be better off seeking out a specialist. Make an appointment with a psychiatrist for an assessment. If your problem is so severe that you're housebound, you may be able to get a home assessment via a community mental health outreach team. However, you may need to prepare yourself for going out of your safety zone and into a hospital or clinic.

Getting the best help for your obsessional problems isn't always straightforward, but don't give up. If you meet the criteria on the checklist in this sidebar, do seek help. Appendix A lists relevant organizations you can consider contacting for more information.

Chapter **13**

Building a Better Body Image and Beating Body Dysmorphic Disorder

There's more to life than being really, really ridiculously good looking, and I'm going to find out what it is.

— DEREK ZOOLANDER (PLAYED BY BEN STILLER IN *ZOOLANDER*)

Taking care of your physical health and appearance is both normal and healthy. Looking after yourself through regular exercise, good eating, and personal grooming is part and parcel of good mental health. However, many people place too much importance on being physically attractive and become overly afraid of being seen as ugly. Appearance can become an overriding preoccupation that leads you into emotional disturbance and low self-esteem and significantly interfere with your life.

Psychologists define the term *body image* as your internal sense of what you look like. In many cases, the ideas people hold about their appearance are roughly accurate; in others, they can be quite different from reality.

In this chapter we touch on some of the more severe and debilitating types of body image problems, help you determine if you have type this type of problem, and offer suggestions for treatment. The bulk of this chapter, however, deals with more commonly encountered body image problems. It introduces ways of thinking about your physical self and explains strategies for building a better body image.

First, let's define what we mean by healthy and unhealthy body image. Someone with a *healthy* body image may not necessarily love the way they look or even be above average in looks. Having a healthy body image is less about how attractive you are and more about keeping the value you place upon appearance in a healthy balance and avoiding becoming overly preoccupied. A healthy body image allows you to enjoy your life fully and be able to make the most of what nature gave you. People with *unhealthy* body images tend to desire looking radically different and imagine that they'd be far happier (or indeed only could be happy) if they were better looking.

You're certainly not the only person in the world who worries about physical appearance. Even people who are generally considered to be very attractive often are beset with body image problems. It just goes to show that your happiness with your appearance isn't inexorably linked to your objective attractiveness.

Making Friends with the Mirror

"Mirror, mirror on the wall, who's the fattest, ugliest, plainest, gawkiest, most freakish of them all?" (Delete as appropriate.) Does this refrain ring a familiar bell with you? Is your relationship with the mirror fraught with anxiety and horror? If so, join the club — it's a big one. Dissatisfaction with personal appearance is rife in the western world (and increasingly beyond). The severity of body image problems can vary from mild and irritating to severe and debilitating. At the mild end of the scale, you may just grumble about your looks but still be able to live an enjoyable life. If your body image problem is more extreme, however, it may lead to depression, poor self-esteem, social withdrawal, and complicated disorders like body dysmorphic disorder (BDD), anorexia, or bulimia.

REMEMBER

BDD is a disorder that involves extreme preoccupation with one or more physical features. The features the BDD sufferer regards as unacceptable and abnormal usually aren't that noticeable to other people. BDD sufferers often have compulsive behaviors such as masking physical areas of concern (through clothing and make-up) and checking in the mirror continually to ensure the perceived defect is still concealed (or hasn't worsened in some way). Both women and men can suffer from BDD.

A subdiagnosis of BDD called *muscle dysmorphia* occurs when an individual is pre-occupied with the idea that their body build is too small or insufficiently muscular. The media sometimes refer to this problem as *bigorexia*. Here you may excessively lift weights, be on a high protein diet, take supplements, or use steroids.

One of the keys to defeating BDD is to use the principles of *exposure and response-prevention* (ERP). This approach is the therapeutic use of facing your fears and stopping rituals and safety behaviors. We explore this treatment in more detail in Chapter 12's discussion on overcoming obsessions. Much of this chapter adds to these principles by helping you find ways of improving your perspective about your appearance and reducing the extent to which you've become preoccupied with your appearance.

Anorexia nervosa is an eating disorder characterized by severe fear of fatness, or indeed of being a normal healthy weight, coupled with intense efforts to lose weight. In most cases, the sufferer believes they look normal even though other people (including doctors and therapists) insist that they're underweight. Anorexia affects men and women alike, despite the misconception that it's a female illness. Typically, sufferers have elaborate rules and rituals about food that enable them to restrict calorie intake. Efforts to lose weight include severe restriction of food intake, excessive use of laxatives, overexercising, and vomiting after eating.

Bulimia nervosa is another eating disorder, but most sufferers are within a normal weight range. The disorder is characterized by periods of dieting punctuated by "binges." Typically, an individual consumes more than the recommended daily intake of calories in one binge-eating episode. Following a binge, the sufferer purges either through self-induced vomiting, use of laxatives, or both. Like anorexia, bulimia is often considered a "women only" problem; in reality, however, many boys and men develop bulimia too.

The following sections provide some questions to help you figure out whether body image is a problem for you.

Do I have BDD?

Do you think that you have a particular physical feature that's abnormal, defective, or ugly? This feature may be anywhere on your body. Remember that your perception of this feature is what counts here, even if others disagree with you about it. Consider your responses to these questions:

1. Has a close friend, family member, or health professional told you that your concerns about your feature(s) are groundless and there's nothing noticeably different or wrong about the way you look?

2. Do you continue to be distressed about and preoccupied with your feature(s) despite assurance from friends, family members, or doctors?

3. If you add up all the time you think about, worry about, or check your feature(s) of concern in one day, does it amount to one hour or more?

4. Do your specific worries about your physical feature(s) prevent you from socializing, working, or forming intimate relationships?

If you answer "yes" to any of these questions, you may have some degree of BDD. The good news is that CBT specific to BDD can help you. A professional psychiatric assessment may also be useful; discuss the issue with your doctor and ask for a referral. Even if you think your problems are at the mild end of the spectrum, we advise you to err on the side of caution and get a medical opinion anyway.

Do I have an eating disorder?

Extreme concerns about body image can be the result of eating disorders such as anorexia or bulimia. Answer these questions to ascertain your feelings in relation to food, weight gain or loss, and your self-image:

1. Are you fearful of gaining weight, staying at the same weight, or others thinking that you're fat?

2. Do you try to strictly monitor how much you eat (portion size), what you eat (food groups), or how many calories you consume each day?

3. Do you become distressed (depressed or agitated) if you eat more than you planned or consume a "forbidden" food?

4. Despite having lost weight, do you feel dissatisfied with your size and convinced that you must lose more?

5. Do you try to hide the fact that you're trying to lose weight from friends and family because they've expressed concern that you're underweight?

6. Do you induce vomiting, drink lots of water or diet soft drinks to fill yourself up, use laxatives, or exercise compulsively to lose more weight?

7. Are you preoccupied by food and your size? Do you find that they're almost always on your mind? (You may also have dreams about food and eating.)

8. Despite your best efforts, do you sometimes lose control and binge? A binge may be eating foods you typically avoid or consuming larger portions than you normally allow yourself. (You may feel intense guilt and regret afterward.)

9. Do you have certain rituals about eating, such as chewing a certain number of times, cutting up food into small pieces, consuming less than others you're eating with, eating at specific times, or wanting to eat in private?

10. Do you weigh yourself once a day or more? Check the prominence of your hip, joint, and shoulder bones daily? Test out your size in relation to certain articles of clothing?

If you answer "yes" to five or more of these questions, you may either be suffering from an eating disorder or at risk of developing one. Talk to your doctor and ask to be referred to a psychiatrist for an assessment. Medical units dedicated to treating eating disorders exist, and many CBT therapists will have specialist knowledge of this problem.

WARNING

If your perception of how you look is preventing you from going to work or school, socializing, and generally pursuing your goals (see Chapter 9 for more about goals), don't hesitate to seek professional help. Conditions like BDD and eating disorders tend to worsen over time if they're left untreated. We strongly advise you to pursue treatment as soon as possible. Chapter 23 has advice and information about getting professional help to deal with your problems.

REMEMBER

Many people make a full recovery from the body image disorders we discuss in this chapter. Doing so involves a lot of determination and work, but it can be done. Be optimistic and stubbornly stick to a recognized and effective form of treatment. (See Chapter 24 for pointers on where to seek help.)

Considering hypothetical cases

You may not have found the questions in the previous sections relevant to you but still recognize that your relationship with your physical self is less than ideal. Many of us have bouts of self-loathing regarding our appearance; these feelings may pass reasonably quickly or be indicative of more chronic dissatisfaction.

Have a gander at the following hypothetical examples:

> Jake is tall and slim. He was teased a lot during his school years and called "stretch" and "bean pole." Jake remains self-conscious about his height and build even today. He constantly compares himself to his friends at the gym who are more compact, muscular, and stocky. Jake has developed a habit of scrutinizing himself when he gets undressed in front of the mirror. Generally, he's uncomplimentary about what he sees: "What puny little shoulders I have! My stomach muscles are nonexistent. Why do I even bother working out? It clearly has no real effect."

Jake's habitual harsh self-criticism in front of the mirror isn't doing his overall self-esteem or body image any favors. But he's been doing it for so long that he doesn't realize how damaging this criticism is.

Savannah hates her face; she thinks that her nose is too prominent and that her eyes are too far apart. She takes no notice of her glossy hair and even teeth. In fact, she's so dissatisfied with her facial appearance that looking in the mirror is painful. Since adolescence, Savannah has avoided mirrors, spending as little time witnessing her own reflection as possible. She quickly does her hair and applies a modest amount of make-up each morning; then she avoids looking in the mirror for the rest of the day.

Savannah considers reflective surfaces to be her enemies. She completely discounts her best features and focuses instead on those she dislikes.

One of the key differences between people who have a healthy body image and those who have an unhealthy one is what they choose to focus on when they look at their reflection. People with poor body image typically home in on areas of dissatisfaction to the exclusion of other aspects of their looks. Those with a healthy body image are more likely to pay specific attention to areas and features that they consider to be their best points.

Both Jake and Savannah continually reinforce their negative body images through their use of mirrors. Jake uses the mirror too much to examine and berate his tall, slim shape. Savannah does the opposite; she hides away from the mirror because she fears confronting her "imperfect" face. If either of these two examples reminds you of your own relationship with the mirror, you may benefit from following the three simple rules of healthy mirror use:

1. **Observe yourself in the mirror, but suspend evaluation or judgment.**

Try not to entertain thoughts about yourself as either attractive or ugly. Just use the mirror to do whatever it is you need it for, such as fixing your hair or putting on make-up. This time should be quick and practical, not an examination.

2. **Regulate how much time you spend on average before the looking glass.**

If you stay in front of the mirror for too long, you may end up criticizing your appearance like Jake does. If you avoid the mirror like Savannah does, you may need to force yourself to observe your reflection more often.

3. **Resist selective scrutiny.**

Instead of focusing your attention on individual aspects of your appearance, try to view yourself as a whole. Again, be vigilant about suspending judgment. Simply look and see your whole physical self without positive or negative evaluation.

These rules are indeed simple — but they're difficult to stick to if you've been using the mirror to find fault with your appearance for years. Learning to appreciate your physical self instead of perpetually picking apart your looks takes determination and practice. Be stubborn and persist until you develop new healthy mirror habits.

REMEMBER

Use the mirror as a tool to check whether your hair is in place, to shave, and to determine whether you're suitably attired or if a bit of breakfast is lodged in your moustache. Don't use the mirror as a weapon to beat yourself up.

Taking Advertising and Media Messages with a Pinch of Salt

The advertising industry is guilty of promoting the over-valuation of physical attractiveness. Preying on the average person's physical insecurities is obviously in the best interest of the fashion industry (including producers of cosmetics, clothing, and personal hygiene products). Quite simply, it makes them money through product sales. Underlying many advertising messages is the subtext: "Buy our product, and you, too, can look this hot!" Bikini-clad women grace the covers of car and technological gadget magazines, while Adonis-like men are a regular feature on TV shows like *Love Island.* Spotting an obvious link between wearing a bikini and listening to an iPod isn't easy, but the message is roughly consistent: "These products are sexy; sexy people own them! Buy this and rub shoulders with the sexy people!" Or something along those lines.

Advertisements, magazines, films, and television programs frequently present a skewed representation of what the average person looks like or *ought* to look like. Models, for example, are typically unusually thin and tall. People on magazine covers and superstars of any ilk are photographed specifically to make them look their best. Photographs are often airbrushed to remove any imperfections. No doubt many actors, models, and celebrities are naturally good-looking people, but photography can make them look flawless. Most of us just don't look that special. Additionally, media coverage can make the most ordinary individual appear to be the height of physical perfection. Not all models, celebrities, or actors are superlatively good looking. We're simply encouraged to believe that they are. Many of the people in the center of media attention may possess powers of attraction that aren't anchored in their physical characteristics. Instead of accepting everything that the media encourages you to accept as true, try using your own judgment more often. Most of the world's population look pretty average.

Recognizing your own body image issues

You can run into body image trouble if you aspire to look like someone exceptionally physically beautiful from the cover of *Vogue* or *GQ* or if you compare yourself unfavorably to social media models and influencers on Instagram, YouTube, and so on. However, blaming poor body image on the media is much too simplistic. We know from research that appearance-related bullying or teasing can have a big impact. Similarly, experiences that make people feel "different," such as childhood abuse or problems like acne, can be significant risk factors.

Research also tells us that some people with appearance anxiety have an above average eye for art, design, and detail. This could be a phenomenal strength for a graphic designer or artist, for example, but it's worth being cautious about the extent to which that "eye" is trained on your appearance.

Persistent dissatisfaction with your looks will likely be maintained to your thinking and behavior. You may have unhealthy body image thinking and behavioral habits that you're only partially aware of. We'll try to highlight some examples next.

Unhealthy appearance-related thinking

Certain ways of thinking typically underpin an unhealthy body image:

>> **Making rigid demands and rules about the way other people must (or must not) judge your appearance:** "I couldn't stand it if someone thought I was plain or fat!" Fear of negative physical judgment isn't limited to members of the opposite sex (or the gender you're attracted to). Most people are also fearful of being judged as "ugly" by peers or those they have no romantic or sexual interest in. It may seem hard to believe, but there are worse things in the world than being judged as physically unattractive. Lasting attraction is based on much more than conventional beauty. Try to think of yourself as a whole person and not just a set of physical attributes.

>> **Linking your self-worth to your attractiveness:** If you have a poor body image, you may automatically assume that beautiful people are superior to you, have more rights, deserve special treatment, and lead charmed lives in general. You feel like the frog waiting for a kiss. We all have basic human worth regardless of how we look. You have a lot to contribute to this world besides being pleasing to the eye.

>> **Placing too much importance on physical appearance and underrating other characteristics that contribute to overall attractiveness, such as personality, values, and humor:** Beauty really is only skin deep. The people we find most attractive aren't necessarily supermodel material. Try to make a real effort to reduce the amount of time you spend thinking about, examining,

discussing, or researching appearance. Deliberately invest more time thinking about and engaging in all sorts of other activities. Your brain simply can't give you a body image that has your looks in a healthy perspective unless the importance you place on appearance is in proportion.

» **Overestimating the degree to which other people evaluate and even _notice_ your looks:** If you suffer from severely poor body image, you may assume that any person you catch glancing your way is thinking about how unfortunate looking you are. You may even assume that they won't want to know you based on your looks. People are often far less interested in criticizing your looks than you may assume. You may attract attention from others for any number of reasons or fall under their gaze simply because they're distracted and thinking about something else entirely. Try to bear in mind that your insecurity about your looks is unlikely to be terribly obvious (or interesting for that matter) to others.

» **Holding unrealistic expectations and standards for your own physical appearance:** There's a limit to the extent that you can improve or change your fundamental looks. If you constantly strive to look like a glamor model or a young film star, you may end up feeling chronically inadequate and dissatisfied in the looks department. Accepting your looks, and making the most of what you have, is far more productive than striving for unrealistic and unattainable ideals.

Unhealthy behaviors

Common behavioral characteristics associated with an unhealthy body image include the following:

» **Comparing your physical appearance to others on a regular basis:** You may not be aware of how much time you spend comparing yourself with others in terms of attractiveness. Doing so can become an insidious and pernicious habit. "Is my butt as shapely as hers?," "Do I look younger than that person?," "Am I as stylish as she is?" and so on and so on. Regardless of whether you make a positive self-comparison against another poor, unsuspecting individual, you're not doing your overall body image any good. Instead, you're perpetuating the potentially damaging idea that looks are all-important and feeding the fires of your preoccupation with external appearances.

TIP

Try doing the opposite for three weeks: observe others without judgment, and resist the urge to make personal comparisons. Then check out any positive benefits to your overall satisfaction with your own looks (there'll probably be a slight increase) and your degree of preoccupation with physical appearance generally (chances are it will have reduced appreciably).

>> **Overpreparing before going out in public:** Making sure that you look your best even to pop over to the corner store for a loaf of bread is a sure sign of poor body image (or overemphasis on the importance of physical attractiveness).

REMEMBER

You may truly believe that you look vastly different (better) when you're made-up, shaved, or groomed than you do fresh out of bed or the shower — in the raw — but you're probably wrong about that. The difference has much more to do with your internal perception of how you look than the external reality. You may *feel* like you look much more appetizing after completing your usual grooming regime, but if you did a survey of what others think you may well be surprised by how little difference they report.

>> **Dieting or exercising constantly to improve your looks:** A bit later in this chapter we discuss making positive changes to your lifestyle (and by association, your appearance) for positive reasons. Most of us could probably reap health benefits from improved eating habits and more regular physical exertion. Many people, however, are perpetually dieting and waiting to gain some muscle tone or shed some weight before they can consider themselves "worthwhile" or "attractive" individuals. Accepting yourself as you are right now, *while* acknowledging areas that leave room for improvement, allows you to make changes that promote health and happiness. Rather than striving to reach elusive physical ideals through fad diets, decide to make some long-term lifestyle changes.

>> **Attempting to hide away from scrutiny, even from lovers:** If you really suffer from body shame, you may avoid looking in the mirror (as discussed earlier in this chapter) and go to great lengths to prevent others from seeing your imperfections. You may be reluctant to wear a swimsuit or take off your shirt on a hot day at the beach. Perhaps you refuse to undress in front of your partner and insist on keeping the lights low when making love. Hiding away from the gaze of others (even those closest to you) may seem to make immediate sense — you feel less self-conscious. Ultimately, though, hiding away keeps you locked into a cycle of chronically poor body image.

If you really want to be more content with your physical appearance, you need to act in a way that reflects how you want to eventually feel. People who accept what they look like (flaws and all) generally don't wear cloaks to the beach or blindfold their lovers. The more you hide your body (or face) away, the more you perpetuate the belief that you actually have something unacceptable to hide.

>> **Seeking reassurance:** Asking people if they think you're fat, skinny, ugly, odd-looking, and so on can become a habit. You may feel better for a short time, but chances are your insecurities come to the fore again quickly. You

probably also dismiss reassurances and compliments because you think "people are just being polite." Reassurance-seeking can also take other forms, such as comparing yourself to people who you think look worse than you. Doing so is a short-lived solution to poor body image because it keeps you focused on physical appearance.

>> **Checking or examining your appearance in the mirror, in other reflective surfaces (such as your phone), by touch, or by taking selfies:** This habit is further practice in treating yourself like an aesthetic object — like you're a painting or sculpture to be examined and improved. You're not. You're a human being. Appearance-checking isn't what you're here for, and all this scrutinizing isn't a helpful use of your amazing (if complicated) brain.

>> **Being vigilant for people's negative judgment of your appearance:** The expression "if you go looking for trouble, you'll find it" is true. People with BDD are highly prone to misinterpreting neutral facial expressions as disapproving, so vigilance can be a significant problem. It can lead you to feel as though people share your overly critical views of your appearance, fueling your sense of shame and self-consciousness.

>> **Self-focused attention:** Monitoring how your appearance or body feels from the inside can work like using an inner magnifying glass. The more you tune in to a part of your body, the more unattractive or out of proportion it can feel. This picture then feeds back and informs the image you hold in your mind of how you feel you look. Try to avoid monitoring feelings of how you feel you look, such as *wobble watching* (where you tune in to areas of perceived fat), or monitoring the redness or feeling the size of a body part. Doing so fuels a distorted body image.

If you recognize any of these behaviors, you may well have body image issues. With determination, however, you can accept what you look like and recognize that your physical appearance doesn't define everything about you.

Accepting yourself

Instead of increasing your dissatisfaction with your appearance by engaging in the thinking and behaving outlined in the previous section, try practicing some self–acceptance. Accepting yourself as worthy *and* simultaneously striving to make improvements is entirely possible — whatever your natural physical appearance.

For example, consider Jake from earlier in the chapter. He can make a deliberate effort to improve his muscle tone but also consistently recognize that his natural shape is tall and slim — and that's okay. Rather than criticizing his shape all the time, he can help his body image by developing new attitudes toward himself. Realistically, Jake is unlikely to suddenly fall in love with his physique. However, he can change his relationship with his body over time by resisting his mirror rituals and sending accepting messages to himself, such as "I'd like to be more muscled, but I accept my natural shape" or "I'm not physically perfect, but the way I look is good enough." Jake can also help himself by dressing to suit his height and shape, working out but emphasizing fitness and strength rather than building visible muscles and refusing to compare his body with other guys at the gym who are naturally more stocky.

TIP

Accepting other people is the flipside to the coin of accepting yourself. You can eventually accept yourself as imperfect, fallible, physically flawed, and yet a worthy and valuable human being. Accepting yourself is easier to do (and maintain), however, if you also apply the same philosophy to everyone else. So don't allow yourself to be overly judgmental about other people's appearance. Accept others as they are, and work on taking the emphasis off physical beauty generally.

Seeing yourself as a whole person

Hey, sweetheart, you're not just a pretty face! A whole person exists inside that physical container known as your body. Your external presentation is just the conduit for all your internal attributes, feelings, ideas, and musings — that is, all your human facets. Look at Figures 13-1 and 13-2. Figure 13-1 represents the emphasis that many people with unhealthy body images assume others put on physical attractiveness in relation to other characteristics. You may also attach exaggerated importance to physical beauty. Figure 13-2 represents a more accurate split between looks and other important components of interpersonal attraction. The items included in this figure are merely *some* of the *many* idiosyncratic aspects that people tend to pay specific attention to when choosing friends or romantic partners. Sure, physical attraction plays a part, but that can grow (or indeed, wane) over time as you get to know one another. Looks are only one small and instantly obvious part of lasting affiliation between people.

Try this experiment to reinforce the idea that attractiveness isn't wholly dictated by actual physical beauty and that other virtues are of equal importance. On a piece of paper, list at least five people whom you really admire, find attractive, or enjoy being around but who aren't particularly/conventionally good looking. Draw on people you know personally and famous people. Next to their names, write down the main characteristic you associate with that person. Review your list from time to time, but especially when you catch yourself putting too much emphasis on physical appearance.

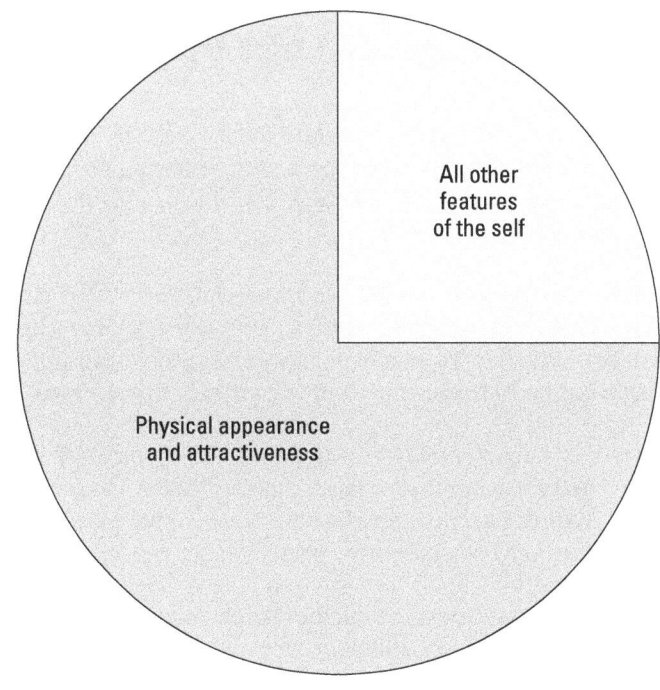

FIGURE 13-1:
The emphasis that people with unhealthy body image assume others put on physical attractiveness.

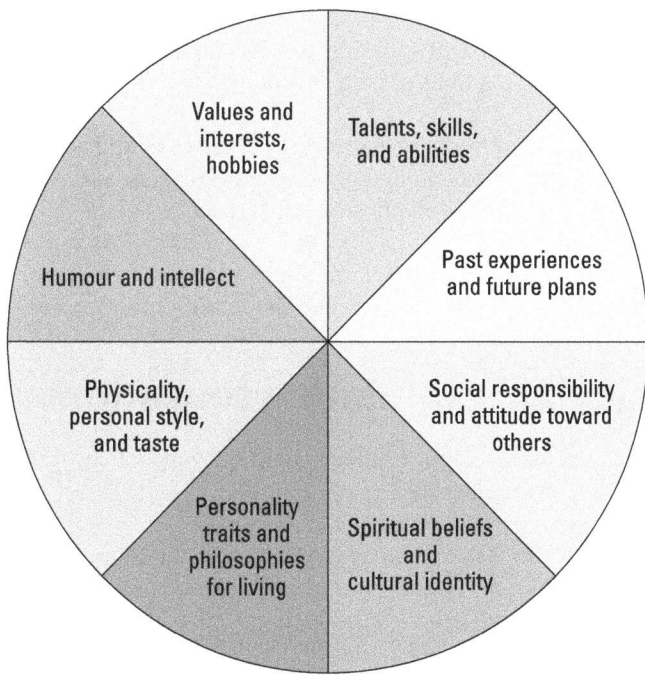

FIGURE 13-2:
A more accurate measure of the components of attractiveness.

Saluting Your Body for Services Rendered

Despite what society, the media, and the advertising industry may invite you to believe (or what you may have spent years believing on your own), there's more to you than meets the eye. Literally. Your face and body aren't merely for aesthetic purposes.

The eyes are described as windows to the soul. There's a reason for that. The look in your eyes, your facial expressions, and your body language convey countless messages. Whether we like it or not, other people can often read our feelings through our facial expressions and what they see in our eyes.

Your face is a highly mobile feature, especially if you allow it to be. You might be inclined to try to control your facial expressions for fear of looking weird or unattractive. Part of having a healthy body image involves allowing yourself to fully use your face and body to express yourself. They can tell myriad stories even if you say little or nothing at all. The way you hold yourself, position your body, and set your facial features conveys a plethora of messages to the casual or indeed studious observer. Your body and your face aren't simply features to be admired or rejected; they're vital and forceful means of communication. Communication is a hugely important and useful skill in all types of society. So whether you're a natural stunner, you're definitely (and inevitably) a natural communicator.

Spending so much time focusing on how you look that you neglect to fully recognize the other functions of your face and body fulfill isn't uncommon.

REMEMBER

We humans aren't here on earth just to look good and be sexually alluring. We're active, vibrant, ever-changing beings. We all have skills, purposes, values, and ideals that go far beyond physical appearance.

The following three sections highlight the other (frequently underappreciated) purposes of your physical body and the activities it allows you to enact and enjoy.

Enjoying scintillating sensations

Your five senses — sight, sound, smell, taste, and touch — allow you to take in the world and experience life.

Even when you lose one sense or are born without one, such as sight or hearing, your other senses typically compensate, which is pretty amazing. I spent a few years learning sign language, and it made me understand just how interesting our senses are. The experiences of deaf people are just as rich as those of hearing people. The visual concentration needed to communicate via sign language is extraordinary (less so if you're deaf, it turns out, because speaking and hearing are usually not options and hence not distractions). People who are deaf or blind are much more patient with the limitations of us sighted and hearing individuals than you may realize.

Your five senses are deserving of your appreciation and gratitude. Consider all they enable you to experience:

>> **Pain:** Okay, pain isn't something you may usually pause to appreciate, but it's a vital and inevitable part of the human experience. Physical and emotional pain puts you in touch with your humanity and can give you many opportunities to learn and grow. Consider the pain of heartbreak, grief, disappointment, a toothache, eating chilies, witnessing a traumatic event, hearing a loved one cry, seeing a bad film, doing something regrettable, giving birth, or falling off a skateboard. A wealth of experience is offered through pain.

>> **Pleasure:** Oh, yes. All five of your senses provide you with a host of pleasures. Pleasant smells, tastes, sights, sounds, and tactile sensations are associated with all manner of things, such as music, baking, making love, working hard, eating and drinking, creating art, being hugged, giving a hug — the list is endless.

Pain and pleasure often overlap to form a complete human experience. Some common examples include giving birth, running a marathon, completing a course of study, ending a relationship or beginning one, having an operation, doing physical therapy, moving to a new house, changing jobs, leaving home for the first time, and many, many more.

So other than simply being a creature of physical beauty (or not), you're also a creature of *experience*. To build a better understanding of yourself as a whole living person, you may need to think more about your senses and experiential existence and less about how hot you look in the buff.

Doing your daily duties

How often do you take time to consciously appreciate all that your body enables you to do? Like most of us, you may take your physical capabilities somewhat for granted. As we touched on in the previous section and do again in the nearby side-bar, people with physical disabilities or incapacities probably have a greater appreciation for all the human body can do than those of us who've never faced significant physical ability challenges. We could all probably benefit from being more attentive to the fact that our bodies serve so many vital functions. Again, above and beyond appearance, your body does a great deal for you every day:

>> **Job and career:** Your physical body allows you to pursue your career goals, earn a living, learn new skills, and adopt new knowledge.

>> **Housekeeping:** Being able to care for your environment, engage in home projects, drive a vehicle, do laundry, garden, take out the garbage, look after your children or other people in your family, shop, cook, dust, vacuum, iron, and everything else.

>> **Personal care:** Just being able to look after your own physical needs is something to be grateful for every day.

>> **Altruistic pursuits:** Taking care of others in need or helping a friend, family member, or neighbor is a selfless act that can make you feel good. Without your physical abilities, you'd be unable to behave in specific other-enhancing ways. People wouldn't benefit from your practical assistance, and you wouldn't be as readily able to reap personal benefits from doing so.

You don't need to be a model to be able to live a good and meaningful life. Your physical self (body and face) can bring you and others much joy and serve countless essential functions.

Here's another experiment in the interest of improving your body image and appreciating your whole self instead of simply focusing on your appearance. Spend a little time each day appreciating and being grateful for your physical abilities. You can put pen to paper and make a "gratitude list" that can help you value your physical self more readily.

Valuing your vehicle for experience

You may spend so much time lamenting over your appearance that you overlook the fact that without your physical shell (hypothetical warts and all) you'd be deprived of . . . *life*! I touch on this concept throughout this chapter, but at the risk of repetition (and it bears repeating), you *need* your physical body to be able to live your life. That's the long and the short of it. So if you believe that you'd rather be dead than alive in an average-looking or even less than average-looking physical vehicle, get some professional help. (See Chapter 24 for starters.) And give your head a serious shake.

Instead of thinking solely about how attractive you may or may not think you *look*, try giving some headspace to how you *live*. Your body is the vehicle through which you get to do the following:

- » **Form relationships:** Being in contact with others, be it superficially, more profoundly, or intimately, is part of your human experience — and is *not* exclusively dictated by your physical attractiveness.

- » **Feel emotions:** Feelings are fantastic. Positive ones tend to be more rewarding than negative ones, sure, but both are part and parcel of living a full and enriched life. (Consult Chapter 6 for more about emotions.)

- » **Make life choices:** You get to overcome adversity, choose your jobs and careers, build a family, live in line with your own personal standards and values (see Chapter 20), plus appreciate the world around you.

- » **Pursue interests:** You can't go on safari without being physically here on the earth, but you *can* do it even if you're blessed with a face made for radio. Going on safari, by the way, is merely an example. Even visiting an art gallery or a more commonplace interest-based activity is valid use of your fabulous, far-from-perfect form.

WARNING

Really good-looking people have human rights too! If you're able to see that you're obviously good looking or are told you're beautiful all the time, you probably are. Yet you're still allowed to feel insecure physically and doubt your powers of attraction. Sometimes the pressure of being considered unusually attractive can be problematic. You may feel that unless you stay looking good, your worth will evaporate. Or that you're only worthy, likable, and significant because you look good or that looks are all you have going for you.

None of these notions are true. Enjoy your good looks and use them to your advantage. But don't allow anyone to convince you that looks are all you have. You have the right to experience life and pursue your interests as much as anyone else. Beautiful people fall prey to unhealthy body image just as average and below-average-looking people do. So don't think you're excluded from the information offered in this chapter.

Choosing to Change for All the Right Reasons

Like many others battling with an unhealthy body image, you may make the following faulty conclusions about physical appearance:

Good looks = Worthwhile, lovable, successful person

Average/below average looks = Less worthwhile, unlovable, unsuccessful person

Several adjectives can be applied to that kind of conclusion, but two of the most fitting are "crazy" and "damaging." In short, it neither makes real sense nor does you any good.

Following are some examples of what we consider the wrong reasons to make physical changes (to your body and/or face):

>> Because you think that improving the way you look will make you a more worthwhile person

>> Because you think that improving your looks will make you a more likable and lovable person

>> To please a critical partner (who may be exacerbating your physical insecurity)

>> To try to overcome sexual/romantic jealousy

>> To win approval from people you believe you're fundamentally inferior to because of your looks

Now here are some potentially sound reasons for changing one or more aspects of your appearance (body or face):

>> To improve your health and fitness

>> To increase enjoyment

>> To improve your physical ability to perform specific activities and increase general mobility

>> To reduce physical pain

>> Out of a genuine desire to reduce self-consciousness and increase your social confidence

REMEMBER

Note the distinction between "confidence" and "worth." *Worth* is an overall value assigned to an object. For example, that diamond is worth almost $40,000. Because you're not an object, your human worth can't accurately be assessed like that of a jewel or car. Trying to judge your own (or another person's) overall worth is inappropriate, especially based on external packaging.

Confidence is more about your belief in your abilities. For example, you may have a solid sense of your own intrinsic worth but lack confidence as a cook, accountant, or public speaker. Social confidence often corresponds with a healthy body image, it's true. However, this doesn't mean that, to have a robust sense of your own worth or be socially confident, you have to be super good looking or believe that you are. Having a realistic view of your looks and believing that you're a worthwhile, likable individual is perfectly possible. Believing in your ability to draw people toward you based on your personality — and not just your appearance — usually amounts to social confidence.

Common targets for physical change and improvement often include these:

>> Hair styling and dying

>> Makeovers and cosmetic advice

>> Various detox treatments, such as colonic irrigation

>> Weight loss or gain regimes

>> Increased fitness and flexibility

>> Facial and bodily hair removal

>> Contact lenses to replace glasses or change eye color

>> Laser eye treatment

>> Dental work, including braces and teeth whitening

>> Skin treatments such as micro-derma abrasion, chemical peels, tattoo removals, and scar and birthmark reduction

>> Minor cosmetic operations like ear tucks, Botox, collagen implants, and mole removal

Less common and more complicated targets for physical change may include these:

>> Breast enlargement or reduction

>> Cleft lip restructuring

>> Nose reshaping and reconstruction

>> Hair replacement treatments

>> Major dental reconstruction

>> Stomach bands or stapling for weight loss

>> Major cosmetic surgery, including tummy tucks, facelifts, and skin grafting

These lists are by no means definitive, and many other forms of physical cosmetic treatment and surgical intervention exist. You can seek one of these (or similar) treatments provided you truly believe that doing so will help you accept yourself physically and build a healthy body image. But we strongly urge you to check and double-check your motivation before you embark on a treatment plan, however minor it may be.

WARNING

Don't take cosmetic surgery and other extreme ways of altering your appearance lightly. They can be risky and expensive. You need to accurately weigh your current dissatisfaction with your appearance against the risks inherent in cosmetic alteration. If you have any concerns (or people close to you do) that your desire for surgery is symptomatic of one of the disorders discussed in the beginning of this chapter, seek a professional psychiatric assessment before you go through with it. In individuals with BDD, surgery often produces the opposite of the desired effect. The sufferer is dissatisfied with the results, believing that they've made the problem worse. Or the focus of dissatisfaction is transferred to another aspect of their face or body. Many reputable cosmetic surgeons refuse treatment until they've ascertained that the patient isn't suffering from BDD or some other psychological disorder.

REMEMBER

Health and happiness show in your looks. Strong teeth, shining eyes, glossy hair, clear skin, and a wide smile are attractive features. Most of these are the by-products of overall good health and general contentment. So you can enhance your appearance by making improvements to your lifestyle and doing what you can to foster personal happiness (more on this in Chapter 21).

Maximizing enjoyment

Making physical changes (such as gaining or losing weight) to enjoy life more is a healthy motivation. Changes to body weight can increase energy and reduce pain in many instances, enabling you to take part in activities that may not have been possible before weight change. Improved physical fitness also can have a positive impact on sleep, digestion, concentration, circulation, and blood pressure and alleviate many other minor or major ailments.

Improving muscle tone can also help with back and joint pain and increase flexibility. So, by becoming fitter, you're likely to find new avenues for enjoyment, like walking, dancing, rock climbing, or picking up a new sport. You may even just be able to climb stairs without pain or breathlessness, thereby rendering daily life easier. Try to consider what additional benefits beyond looking better are likely to ensue from improved fitness.

Bringing out your best

You may decide to make changes to your appearance because you want to look your best. A subtle but important difference exists between being motivated to make physical changes to *increase your sense of worth* and simply *to optimize your appearance.* The former motivation suggests that you link your intrinsic human worth to outward appearance, which can compound low self-esteem and unhealthy relations with your body, as discussed earlier in this chapter. The latter motivation, however, implies that you value yourself generally and can consider improving your physical appearance as part of a self-care regime. To make this distinction clearer, look at the two examples of motivational attitudes offered here.

Jenny is in her late thirties and has started to go prematurely gray. Cheryl is roughly the same age as Jenny and is also going gray. Both women are of average good looks and are similarly built. Both women have black hair and the gray shows a lot, so they decide to have it dyed. Thus far, pretty much no difference exists between Jenny and Cheryl with regard to choosing to have their hair dyed. The hidden difference lies in their motivation.

Jenny thinks the following: "If I dye my hair it might make me look better, and other people will find me more attractive. I need other people's approval to feel okay about myself."

Cheryl thinks like this: "This gray is aging me, and I like to look my best. I'll have it dyed so that I can look my age again. I'll feel more positive about my appearance without the gray."

Jenny, unlike Cheryl, believes that she needs other people's approval of her looks to feel okay about herself and to feel like a worthwhile person. Cheryl, instead, focuses on her *own* satisfaction with her appearance and makes no connection between that and her overall sense of self-worth. Cheryl leaves other people's possible evaluations of her appearance out of the equation entirely.

Use this example to help you clearly assess your motivation for making even minor physical changes, such as changing your hair color or trying contact lenses. By all means have your hair dyed if you want to, but try to challenge unhealthy thinking like Jenny's in favor of adopting healthy thinking like Cheryl's. Make changes for the right reasons!

Being daring

Working out, having your teeth cleaned professionally, and being pampered with a facial or massage can help you feel more physically comfortable and confident. When you feel like you're looking your best, your physical confidence increases.

Sometimes making even small physical improvements can encourage you to be a bit more daring in your dress sense, activity choices, and self-expression in general. You may get a new hairstyle and suddenly feel confident enough to ask out that girl at the reception desk you've been noticing for the past few months. A little weight loss may spur you to wear a fitted dress and join the local salsa dancing class. Regular exercise might lead you to take part in coaching your child's football. You may feel more prepared to embark on new ventures once you've begun a physical improvement regime of some kind.

But bear in mind the basic principle of healthy body image:

> Improved appearance or fitness = Increased enjoyment and confidence

Not

> Improved appearance or fitness = Better, more worthwhile, and valuable human being

CHANGING WITH TIME

We all change physically, emotionally, and perhaps spiritually and philosophically as we grow older. Even if nothing exceptionally dramatic or notable happens to us, certain changes are inevitable. Our hair will gray; our facial features will adopt deep expressive wrinkles. Some of us actually improve physically with age — not to mention improving in personality-based ways, such as mellowing or becoming more accepting. But primarily, we just get older — and it shows.

Being able to acknowledge, adapt to, and accept the way your body's abilities and physical attributes change over time can help you maintain a healthy body image for life. Being older doesn't equate to being "uglier" or "less useful." It just means that you're naturally aging and your looks are changing. Your ability to climb up a mountain or dance the night away may diminish, but that's only natural and normal. Aging gracefully involves accepting the physical changes associated with getting older and adapting to new limitations while making the most of your capabilities. Many men and women come to terms with their changing appearances as they grow older and manage to maintain a healthy and robust body image. You can do the same if you apply a healthy attitude to growth, age, and change. As humans we're not stagnant. We evolve and develop over time. No one can be defined absolutely based on how they appear externally, however old they are.

So try to embrace rather than reject the ways in which your body and face change over time. Try to appreciate every smile line and worry wrinkle. They're the traces of a life fully lived.

Other events, such as accidents and illness, can also affect your appearance and physical abilities. Adjusting to drastic or unpredicted changes to your face and body can be difficult at any stage of life. Sometimes you may need some extra professional help. It can be inspiring to note that ordinary people do go on to lead satisfying lives even after serious accidents or illness.

Former model Katie Piper was a victim of an acid attack in 2008, which caused major damage to her face and blindness in one eye. Following a long and painful recovery, she started the Katie Piper Foundation to raise awareness of the plight of victims of burns and disfigurement injuries. She also published a book, took part in a documentary "Katie: My Beautiful Face," and was named winner of the Courage Award in 2010. She has since gone on to make several other public appearances.

The actor Christopher Reeve (1952–2004) is probably one of the best-known examples of famous people who've suffered this type of adversity. Reeve, famous for playing the role of Superman in a whole series of films, became a quadriplegic in 1995 after being thrown from his horse during a sporting competition. He then lobbied on behalf of people with spinal cord injuries and in support of human embryonic stem cell research.

Even if an accident or illness hasn't resulted in serious physical disability, comparatively minor issues, such as facial scarring or walking with a limp, can still be challenging. Adjusting to the loss of a limb, altered facial and bodily appearance due to an accident, loss of sight or hearing, and diminished mobility in response to disease can have a profound impact on your personal sense of identity and on your overall body image. Happily, many people adapt to these difficulties and lead full, enriched lives. If you've experienced any of the difficulties discussed here and feel you'd like some extra support, seek some professional and expert help (see Chapter 24).

Chapter **14**

Healing Health Anxiety

This chapter is about tackling fears or preoccupation with your health. Health anxiety, also known as *illness anxiety disorder* (IAD), refers to severe and persistent worries about health. It can relate to fear that you *are* ill or that you'll *become* ill. Previously, this condition was called *hypochondriasis*, but doctors have moved away from the diagnosis of hypochondriasis because the term *hypochondriac* has been misused over the years to describe someone who enjoys worrying about being ill. People with IAD don't enjoy the experience or faking symptoms for attention.

Illness anxiety can overlap with other problems, including the following:

>> Obsessive-compulsive disorder (OCD), such as fears of contamination

>> Generalized anxiety disorder (GAD), in which health can be part of a range of worries

>> Somatic symptom disorder (SSD), in which people become fearful of physical symptoms like pain or fatigue

In this chapter, we guide you toward identifying the processes that are maintaining illness anxiety and how you can overcome them.

Analyzing the Anatomy of Illness Anxiety

Illness anxiety consists of the following:

>> **You have a preoccupation with having or getting a serious illness.** When doctors use the term *preoccupation* in this context, they mean that your worry about your health is on your mind for more than an hour a day, but usually several hours.

>> **You have a high level of anxiety about health, and you're easily alarmed about your health.** You may have a sense that you have a particular vulnerability to an illness, focus on how awful a particular illness would be, or have an especially low estimation of how able you'd be to cope if you contracted your feared illness.

>> **You may repeatedly check your body for signs of illness.** Looking at (including taking photographs), touching, and tuning in to physical sensations are all common ways of checking.

>> **You may avoid triggers for your fears, such as certain people, places, films, TV shows, or news stories.**

>> **You may repeatedly seek reassurance about your health from doctors, specialists, other people, and the internet.**

REMEMBER

However, contrary to the stereotype, a significant number of people who have illness anxiety *don't* repeatedly seek medical reassurance from their doctors. In fact, you may find that you're inclined to avoid seeing your doctor for fear that they may deliver bad news or say something that triggers you to worry about your health.

REMEMBER

A diagnosis of illness anxiety disorder or health anxiety doesn't occur only in people who are well. If you have a medical condition or a high risk of developing a medical condition (for example, you have a strong family history of cancer), you may naturally feel some level of concern. But that concern crosses the threshold into IAD if the preoccupation is clearly excessive or disproportionate.

TIP

Monitor your illness anxiety for a week or two to get a clearer measure of the problem. For example, note how many times you check a part of your body or search the internet for more health-related information or how many hours you spend thinking about your health. Building a profile of your own avoidance and safety-seeking behavior helps you define the problem well, which is a crucial step toward the solution. Check out Chapter 8 for more on how your solutions can be the problem and how you can build a "vicious flower" of your illness anxiety.

Getting to Know Medically Unexplained Physical Sensations

One of the mistakes individuals prone to illness anxiety make is to assume that a healthy body is free from any uncomfortable or unwanted physical sensations. In fact, this idea is far from the truth. Here are some examples of common physical sensations that can occur without being a sign of a serious physical illness:

>> Abdominal pain

>> Diarrhea

>> Chest pain

>> Heart palpitations

>> Rapid breathing

>> Fatigue

>> Facial pain

>> Joint pain

>> Poor concentration

>> Muscle pain

>> Headache

>> Lump in throat

>> Wobbly legs

>> Ringing in ears

REMEMBER

We aren't saying that any physical symptoms you may have are all in your head or that the sensations in the preceding list are never a sign of ill health. We just want to point out that the human body is more than capable of producing a colorful variety of physical and mental sensations that are simply part of the normal range of sensations in your body.

If you suffer from illness anxiety, you're likely prone to catastrophically misinterpret sensations — to assume the worst. The trick, then, is to compensate for this tendency and bring your thinking into balance by more readily normalizing bodily sensations and assuming the best.

Try the following experiment to better understand the effect of your interpretation on your feelings about bodily sensations:

1. **Hold your hand out in front of you with your fingers raised.**

2. **When you notice your fingers tingling, ask yourself: What is the worst thing this feeling can mean?**

   When you thought this tingling may be something serious (for example, multiple sclerosis), how did that affect you? How did it make you feel? What did you do or want to do? What did you pay attention to?

Minimizing Your Fear of Missing an Important Symptom

At the core of illness-focused anxiety is the fear that if you stop being vigilant for your feared illness, you may miss a key symptom and live (or perhaps not live) to regret it. Fundamentally, this issue is an intolerance of uncertainty, and the solution is to increase your tolerance. The big question to ask yourself is whether remaining on red alert for a particular illness is really all that helpful.

TIP

Carry out a cool-headed cost-benefit analysis of trying to avoid missing an important symptom. If your illness anxiety were an insurance policy, would you be happy to pay the premium in terms of distress and impact on your life and the lives of those who care for you?

You may decide to take slightly more direct action against your fear of missing an indicator and ending up ill or dying. Chapter 10 has some guidance on deliberately confronting your fears to reduce them. In this case, writing out a vivid imagined account of your worst case coming true and rereading it for 20 minutes a day over a couple of weeks can be helpful — and challenging.

TIP

To manage your mind's tendency to jump to conclusions about your health and reduce habits like ove thinking, do the following: If you have a physical or mental sensation that triggers your illness anxiety, put a reminder in your diary (say, for a date about two weeks away) to come back to it. The benefit here is that you can decide to avoid preoccupation while assuaging your fear that you may be ignoring something important as a stepping-stone in recovery. Who knows? You may even avoid a needless test.

Feeling Secure in an Uncertain Body

For many individuals with illness anxiety, the core of the problem is a tendency to misinterpret normal bodily sensations as a sign of disease. Developing alternative, more helpful interpretations can be beneficial. One way to do so is to create a three-column chart like Table 14-1.

TABLE 14-1   **Finding Less Anxiety-Producing Interpretations of Bodily Sensations**

Bodily Sensation	Catastrophic Misinterpretation	Alternative Explanations
Sore patch on my mouth	I have mouth cancer.	A mouth ulcer, a burn from hot food, a scratch from food or your toothbrush, a sore from biting part of your mouth
Chest pain	I have a heart problem.	Tension in the muscles between your ribs caused by stress or anxiety
Feeling tired all the time	I have a cancer of the blood cells.	Fatigue caused by anxiety, low mood, restlessness, or poor sleep
Surroundings feel distant and unreal	I'm losing touch with reality. I'm going to develop schizophrenia.	Tiredness, anxiety-induced *de realization* (a natural protection against stressful events)
Tingling sensations in my hands	I have multiple sclerosis.	Too much oxygen in your blood caused by over-breathing when you're feeling anxious or stressed
Tender breasts	I have breast cancer.	Swelling and tenderness caused by hormonal changes in menstrual cycle, ill-fitting bra, accidental bruising, bruising caused by excessive checking
Joint pain	My bones are wearing out.	Normal joint stiffness caused by exercise or inactivity
Leg ache	I have motor neuron disease.	Muscle tension caused by stress or anxiety, strained muscle
Red marks on my skin	I have skin cancer.	A scratch, a bruise from having knocked against something, an insect bite
Stomach cramps	I have stomach cancer.	Gastric discomfort caused by more acid entering your stomach due to stress or anxiety, indigestion
Heart racing	My heart is overworking and will wear out.	Raised heart rate due to adrenalin increase caused by stress or anxiety, caffeine
Headache	I have a brain tumor.	Tension caused by stress or anxiety, too much caffeine, hangover, lack of sleep

Another strategy to practice generating alternative interpretations of bodily sensations is to make an interpretation pie chart.

1. **Identify your catastrophic interpretation of a bodily sensation.**

   For example, you may assume an unidentified lump always indicates cancer.

2. **Rate your strength of belief in that interpretation on a scale from 0 to 100.**

3. **List all possible causes of the bodily sensation, starting with your feared cause.**

4. **When the list is complete, draw a pie chart and divide it across all the possible causes.**

   Start at the bottom of the list. Adding your feared cause last, size each explanation according to your estimation of its likelihood of being the cause.

5. **Rerate your belief from Step 2. The hope is that you'll be able to hold in mind that there may be a range of possible explanations rather than just the one you fear. You might find an explanation for your sensation that is less threatening and more plausible. However, sometimes you won't, so don't forget that a big part of the solution to illness anxiety is to become more tolerant of uncertainty.**

You can use the pie chart for a current trigger and for past and possible future sensations.

To reduce your preoccupation with your health, tackle how much attention you place upon it. Take a look at Chapter 6 for more on the role of attention and how you can modify it. Combine redirecting your attention away from your health concerns with stopping your checking or reassurance strategies that inadvertently refocus your attention upon your health fears.

Acting Against Illness Anxiety

To truly break free from excessive anxiety about your health, you may need to act. A key target is reducing or stopping body-checking and self-monitoring. For many people, an equally important area to focus on is putting a stop to *cyberchondria* — researching feared illnesses on the internet. In both cases, the problem is that if you go looking for trouble, you'll find it. You risk overloading your mind with illness-related information and detecting bodily sensations and anomalies that you would otherwise ignore. Checking can have a significantly negative effect on your ability to tolerate doubt, boosting your anxiety and fueling your preoccupation. Avoiding certain words, TV shows, and even doctor's appointments is common in health anxiety and fuels your fear. All of this is a good reason to turn to Chapter 8 and focus carefully on how your solutions to your illness anxiety may be making things much worse, and then start to turn your anxiety on its head.

TIP

Because health anxiety shares many features with OCD (it's technically an OCD-related disorder), like avoidance, checking, reassurance seeking, and fear, reading Chapter 12 on OCD can strengthen your understanding of the problem and how to overcome it.

Chapter **15**

Sleeping Soundly

Sleep is often something people struggle with when they're going through periods of stress or are suffering from psychological problems like depression or anxiety. Short-term sleep disturbance can be uncomfortable and lead to poor concentration, irritability, and emotional sensitivity. It can also make it harder to get through the day. Happily, most sleep problems are temporary and resolve on their own, especially after stressful periods have passed or depression has lifted. Sometimes unsatisfactory sleep can be secondary to another emotional problem. It may even be quite persistent.

CBT can help you with simple strategies that have been proven to work for most people. In this chapter, we help you identify some common factors that can get in the way of a good night's sleep and what you can do about them.

REMEMBER

Your body needs sleep to function just like it needs food and air. Your body is designed to sleep when it needs to and, given the opportunity, will take sleep — even when you may be trying to stay awake. Remembering this simple truth can help you let your body fall asleep by not letting your worry about a poor night's sleep block a natural process.

Assessing Your Sleep Situation

The average adult sleeps between seven and nine hours each night. Some people need slightly more or less sleep than average, but few people can sustain less than six hours of sleep for long periods without noticing negative effects. The term *insomnia* means a consistent disruption to normal sleep patterns that includes one or more of the following:

>> Difficulty nodding off to sleep (tossing and turning, not being able to shut off your thoughts, or finding it hard to get comfortable)

>> Frequent waking after you're asleep (glancing at the clock for a few seconds or feeling fully awake and finding getting back to sleep difficult)

>> Early waking (usually about one to two hours before the alarm is set to go off)

>> Nonrestorative sleep (feeling tired no matter what kind of night you had or how many hours you slept)

For a formal diagnosis of insomnia, you need to consistently have had these sleep problems three nights out of seven for at least three months.

TIP

Knowing for sure just how much you're sleeping can be tricky. When you're tired, your memory is poor, and the nights seem to merge into one miserable mass. Keeping a diary of your sleep for two weeks can be useful for establishing a sleep baseline. You can find an app for your phone to track your wake-sleep pattern and provide an overview of hours slept per night. Wearable fitness trackers can sync with your phone and do the diary work for you.

WARNING

It's important to take a balanced view on sleep-tracking. Monitoring your sleep can help you work out what your current sleep pattern looks like. It's also useful to intermittently check progress when you're on a sleep improvement regime, but dwelling on the results of your diary can lead to worry and frustration about sleep and become part of your sleep problem.

Eliminating Unhelpful Sleep Expectations

During the day and while you try to fall asleep, you may well have thoughts like "I'll never be able to get to sleep" or "I'm in for another night of waking up every two hours." Understandably, you may have these expectations if your sleep has been disturbed for some time, but such thinking is likely to perpetuate your sleep disturbance. Be aware of your worrying thoughts about sleep problems, such as

"I'll never be able to cope on such little sleep," or "I've got to get some sleep tonight."

We talk about the thought–feeling link in Chapter 4, and it applies here as well. How you think about sleep can really affect how well you sleep. Bad thinking can lead to bad sleeping in a few ways, some of which are illustrated in this section.

For one, you may fall into the mind trap of thinking you need more sleep than you actually do, especially if you've had some sleeping problems.

> Ishtar has been sleeping poorly for several months. Using the techniques found in this chapter, she begins to get better-quality sleep. However, because she's felt tired for so long, she decides she must need more hours of sleep than the average person. So she goes to bed an hour earlier at night and stays in bed two hours longer on weekends than her wife.
>
> This routine strains their relationship, and when they sit down together and look at the number of hours Ishtar typically spends in bed versus the time she's actually asleep (12 hours in bed and only 7.5 hours sleeping), Ishtar realizes that her expectation of needing 10 to 12 hours of sleep is erroneous.

You may also start to predict how awful you'll feel or perform the next day if sleep eludes you. The more pressure you put on yourself to sleep, the more elusive sweet slumber becomes.

> Ezra values giving his best at work. Poor sleep has made reaching his ideal of peak performance harder. Every weeknight he gets into bed thinking, "I've *got* to get to sleep within the half hour!" Thirty minutes tick past on the clock, and Ezra thinks, "This is terrible! I'll be exhausted and of no use. I'm going to drop the ball and let my team down. Being tired at work is the worst!" Ezra tries harder and harder to bully himself to sleep.
>
> Finally he seeks help. His CBT therapist encourages him to think more along the line of "If I don't sleep, I'll be tired, but that's more uncomfortable and inconvenient than it is the *worst*. I can talk to my teammates and let them keep the balls in the air for a while."

REMEMBER

Trying to force yourself to go to sleep is rarely successful, and doing so contradicts the principle of allowing yourself to *rest and relax* because you're making an *effort* to sleep.

Protracted problems sleeping can cause you to make negative associations with going to bed. You may be fully expecting to be awake all night or to have a fitful sleep with anxiety dreams. If you find yourself putting off bedtime for fear of what thoughts and feelings await you, you probably have a nasty case of *bed-dread.*

Jolene went through a break-up six months ago. Since then her sleep has been pretty hit-and-miss. Sometimes she stays in bed all day trying unsuccessfully to sleep away her sadness. When she does go to bed at a normal time, her sadness and fear about the future seem to engulf her, and she often has unpleasant dreams. Her mood has started to lift, but her association with bed and feeling bad has led to bed-dread.

Jolene has an amazing, supportive best friend who tells her to stop expecting *bedtime* to be *dread-time.* Now Jolene goes to bed thinking, "If I can't get off to sleep straightaway, I can simply let my body relax and rest. I can choose to think of pleasant things. Dreams are only sleeping thoughts, and they can't hurt me."

TIP

Although it may sound like a tall order, try to take the attitude that you can cope with very little, or poor-quality, sleep. You'll be far less afraid of not sleeping, which is helpful because worry is hardly conducive to sleep. Also, answer your sleep expectations by briefly telling yourself that you don't know for sure how you may sleep tonight and that you're just going to see how it goes.

Getting into a Clean Sleep Routine

You've probably heard the term *sleep hygiene,* which refers to establishing healthy bedtime routines and behaviors. Leading health organizations in Europe and North America recognize the guidelines we offer in this section.

What you do, eat, and drink during the day affects how well you sleep at night. You may not need to be as strict with your routine after your sleep has returned to normal as you do when you're still getting back on track, although anyone can benefit from sticking to a clean slumber routine. This section provides tips that can improve your chances of greeting the Sandman.

Tiring yourself out

Few things ensure a deep sleep more than being physically tired. People who work in jobs that involve a lot of manual labor often report predictably restorative sleep. If that's not an option for you, get some exercise. We can't overstate the benefits of regular exercise. It's good for your mood, your body, and your sleeping.

You can do vigorous exercise during the day or even first thing in the morning to get your *endorphins* (the feel-good chemicals in your brain) charging. If you want to exercise in the evenings to help you wind down and destress, keep it gentle and not too close to your bedtime. Strolls, an easy workout at the gym, or a leisurely bike ride are ideal choices. Exercising outdoors increases the sleep-inducing effect.

You can make minor changes to your daily routine to increase the amount of exercise you get. It may seem insignificant, but taking the stairs rather than the elevator, walking to places nearby and leaving the car parked, and walking briskly can get your heart rate up.

Establishing a consistent sleep window

Climbing out of bed at the same time every day can help you get your sleeping back on track. Experts recommend these steps:

1. **Start with a six-hour sleep window.**

   Decide what time you want to get up each day; this point sets up your sleep window. So if you want to get up at 7 a.m., go to bed at 1 a.m. Even if you take some time to fall asleep or wake up during the night, pull yourself out of bed at 7 a.m.

2. **Continue following the schedule you set in Step 1 for two weeks.**

   Over the next fortnight, your sleep quality should improve, and you'll start to fall asleep more quickly after you're in bed. Even though you're only asleep for six hours, the sleep will be more restorative.

3. **Over the following week to ten days, bring your bedtime forward by 30 minutes every couple of days until you're sleeping seven to eight hours each night.**

   In this example, you end up going to bed around 11 p.m. for your 7 a.m. wake-up time.

The idea is to stay roughly in sync with the sun rising and setting to fit the brain that nature gave you. Your routine needs to stay the same on the weekends. Don't vary by more than half an hour, or you risk pushing your sleep pattern out of routine and worsening your sleep quality.

The following sections clue you in to a couple of pitfalls that come with setting up a sleep routine.

Navigate napping

Catnapping may be tempting, but it can interfere with your ability to get a good night's sleep. Opinions vary a bit on napping, and when your sleep pattern is in good shape, you might find that up to half an hour's nap can be restorative. However, when you're trying to get your sleep routine in shape, restricting your sleep quantity can help your sleep quality in the long run, as paradoxical as that may sound.

If you know that you get the urge for a siesta around the same time every day, make plans to be out of the house at that time. Make yourself busy to keep yourself awake.

Tossing out tossing and turning

Avoid lying in bed awake. If you find dropping off to sleep difficult, or you wake in the middle of the night and can't get back to sleep easily, don't lie in bed tossing and turning for longer than ten minutes. Get out of bed and do something until you feel ready for sleep. Ideally, that would be something boring like sorting laundry, reading a book on a subject you find dull, or drinking something warm and low in caffeine, such as milk or cocoa. Try to stay awake until your eyelids start to feel heavy.

If you do decide to stay in bed, focus on resting and being detached from your thoughts rather than trying to sleep.

Slowing down on stimulation

Avoid caffeinated drinks from mid to late afternoon onward. Caffeine can stay in your system for a long time. We're not just talking about tea and coffee; many soft drinks, chocolate (although not so much), and energy drinks contain caffeine. Even some herbal teas contain stimulants, such as matte and guarana, so check labels. As for alcohol, your best bet is to avoid it altogether until your sleep is sorted out. Alcohol has an initial sedation effect, but it soon rebounds and can lead to early waking.

You should also avoid stimulating activities while in bed, including eating and reading gripping page-turners. The idea is to help your fatigued mind build helpful, sleep-inducing associations with your boudoir. Restrict your device use to listening to soothing music or tranquilizing podcasts, and avoid watching programs or working, gaming, and so on. Bottom line: The only activities you really should do in bed are sleeping and getting ready to sleep (and, of course, sex).

Set any device you're using to turn off within about 30 minutes, maximum. Soothing background sounds can help your mind turn off, but also try falling asleep in silence. If you read in bed, choose something easy, and observe the same 30-minute time limit.

Building a better bedtime routine

Going through the same pre-bedtime procedures each night can help your mind realize that you're getting near to shutdown time. Your routine may include having a warm bath, putting on your favorite pajamas, doing gentle stretches, cuddling with your pet, or having a warm drink. Sometimes having a light, easily digestible snack before bedtime can prevent sleep disturbance associated with going to bed hungry. Whatever works for you, try to keep it consistent every night. Aim to start your winding-down rituals about 45 minutes before your bedtime — and put that phone down!

Relaxing your muscles

Your muscles as well as your mind need to relax if you're going to depart for Snoozeville. You can systematically relax your muscle groups in a variety of ways; looking for a simple step-by-step guide online is worthwhile. One way is to gently squeeze and release your muscles starting from your feet and moving up the body. Doing a bit of muscle relaxation on a comfortable chair is better than doing it lying in bed. If you're experiencing muscle tension, consider booking a professional massage.

Limiting the (blue) light

One of the enemies of sleep in this modern age is the blue light from screens and certain light bulbs. It tricks your brain into thinking it's daytime and inhibits the switching-on of your natural sleep cycle. Many phones and tablets now have a night mode that limits the blue light output. Some people also find using yellow-tinted glasses beneficial; they're inexpensive and help screen out blue light. Another good rule is to avoid screens in bed. (Head to the earlier section "Slowing down on stimulation" for more information on activities to avoid in bed.)

Limiting your screen time throughout the day — and in particular prior to bedtime — can greatly aid restful sleep. Our copyeditor made a point of turning off her screens an hour before bed and was rewarded with improved sleep.

Making your bedroom better for sound sleep

Take care to make your bed and bedroom a relaxing, soothing place to be. Buy yourself nice bed linens, have low lighting options, remove clutter from the room, hang some relaxing pictures on the walls, and adjust the temperature so it feels just right. Also check the age of your bedding; have you had your mattress so long that it's sagging in places it shouldn't be? Have your pillows lost their plump? Has your quilt quit? If so, replace them!

Smells can carry strong associations, so consider putting out a few candles, using a pleasant fabric softener on your bed linens, or getting a special-purpose pillow spray. Just a soothing smell on your bedding can be enough for you to associate your bed with sleeping.

Making friends with not being able to get to sleep

Bear with us. We haven't lost the plot. We know sleep is important and that being low on sleep can be uncomfortable. However, as with so many aspects of the way our mind and bodies work, too much pressure can backfire. We all have difficulty sleeping at times, but becoming anxious and irritated about it can make things worse. In fact, being anxious about not getting enough sleep can be the root of sleep trouble.

TIP

Put "rest" on the menu of useful nocturnal activities to do in bed. By avoiding being black-or-white about sleep — "I must get eight hours of sleep or I'll feel awful," you'll be making a good input into your sleep quality. Resting may not be as restorative as sleeping, but it can be pretty good. Practicing light relaxation or mindfulness can help. Think of it as a stepping stone to sleeping well. The key is to set the right conditions for sleep so that your mind and body can accept it when they're ready.

Chapter **16**

Overcoming Low Self-Esteem and Accepting Yourself

D isturbing feelings, such as depression, anxiety, shame, guilt, anger, envy, and jealousy, are often rooted in low self-opinion. If you're prone to experiencing these feelings, you may well have a problem with your self-esteem. You may assume that you're only as worthwhile as your achievements, online presence, love life, social status, attractiveness, or financial prowess. If you link your worth to these temporary conditions and for some reason they diminish, your self-esteem can plummet too. Alternatively, you may take a long-standing dim view of yourself. However favorable the conditions mentioned, your self-esteem may be chronically low. Whatever the case, you can follow the philosophy of self-acceptance that we outline in this chapter, which can significantly improve the attitude you hold toward yourself.

Identifying Issues of Self-Esteem

Implicit in the concept of self-esteem is the notion of *estimating*, or rating and measuring, your worth. If you have high self-esteem, your measure of your value or worth is high. Conversely, if you have low self-esteem, your estimate of your value is low.

Condemning yourself globally is a form of overgeneralizing, known as *labeling* or *self-downing*. (We talk about overgeneralization in more detail in Chapter 2.) This thinking error creates low self-esteem. Labeling yourself makes you feel worse and can lead to counterproductive actions, such as avoidance, isolation, rituals, procrastination, and perfectionism (which we talk about in Chapters 8, 12, and 13), to name but a few.

Examples of labeling or self-downing include statements such as the following:

I'm disgusting	I'm a failure	I'm stupid
I'm inferior	I'm useless	I'm boring
I'm inadequate	I'm not good enough	I'm bad
I'm unlovable	I'm worthless	I'm defective
I'm incompetent	I don't matter	I'm pathetic
I'm weak	I'm no good	I'm a loser

When you measure your worth based on one or more external factors, you're likely to go up and down like a yo-yo in both mood and self-concept because life is changeable.

Developing Self-Acceptance

One approach to tackling your low self-esteem is to boost the estimate you have of your worth. The underlying problem, however, remains; and like an investment, your self-esteem can go down as well as up.

Self-acceptance is an alternative to boosting self-esteem and tackles the problem by removing self-rating. If you don't have a sturdy belief that your value is *intrinsic*, or built-in, you may have difficulty concluding that you have any worth at all when things go wrong for you.

REMEMBER

Unconditional self-acceptance means untangling your self-worth from external measures or ratings of your value as a person. Eventually, you can become less likely to consider yourself defective or inadequate based on failures or disapproval because you view yourself as a *fallible human being*, whose worth remains more or less constant.

Self-acceptance involves making the following assertions:

>> As a human being, you're a unique, multifaceted individual.

>> You're ever-changing and developing.

>> You may be able, to some degree, to measure specific aspects of yourself (such as how tall you are), but you'll never manage to rate every facet of yourself because you're too complex and continuously changing.

>> Humans, by their nature, are fallible and imperfect.

>> By extension, because you're a complex, unique, ever-changing individual, you can't legitimately be rated or measured as a whole person.

The following are the principles of self-acceptance. Read them, reread them, think them over, and put them into practice in your daily life to significantly enhance your self-acceptance. The principles are good sense, but we're leaving it up to you to decide how "common" this kind of sense is. The principles are derived from the rational (self-helping) thinking methods developed by Albert Ellis and Windy Dryden.

Understanding that you have worth because you're human

Albert Ellis, founder of rational emotive behavior therapy, one of the earliest approaches to CBT, states that all human beings have extrinsic value to others and intrinsic value to themselves. But we humans gamely confuse the two and classify ourselves as "worthy" or "good" based on assumed value to others. We humans too easily allow our self-worth to be contingent upon the opinions and value judgments of others. Many cognitive behavior therapists (and indeed other kinds of psychotherapists) hold the implicit value of a human being at the very heart of their perspective.

Imagine how much easier your life would be, and how much more stable your self-esteem would be, if you realized that you have worth as a person *independently* of how much other people value you. You can appreciate being liked, admired, or respected without feeling a dire necessity to prompt these responses, or living in fear of losing them. You can consider yourself to be a valuable human while accepting that not everyone you meet must hold you in high regard for this to be true.

Appreciating that you're too complex to globally measure or rate

You may mistakenly define your whole worth — or even your entire self — based on your individual parts. Doing so is pointless because humans are ever-changing, dynamic, fallible, and complex creatures.

Humans have the capacity to work on correcting less desirable behaviors and maximizing more desirable behaviors. You have the distinctive ability to strive for self-improvement, to maximize your potential, and to learn from your own and others' histories, mistakes, and accomplishments. In short, you have the capacity to develop the ability to accept yourself as you are, while still endeavoring to improve yourself if you so choose.

Consider the following experiment. Imagine that you have a bowl of fresh, hand-picked fruit, beautiful in almost every respect. Now imagine that one of the apples in the fruit bowl is bruised. Do you consider the whole bowl of fruit to be worthless? Of course not. It's a beautiful bowl of fruit, with a single bruised apple. Avoid overgeneralizing by seeing that your imperfections are simply *facets* of yourself and don't define the whole of you.

Letting go of labeling

Self-acceptance means deciding to resist labeling yourself at all and rather to entertain the idea that ratings are inappropriate to the human condition. For example,

>> You lied to a friend once. Does that make you a liar forever and for all time?

>> You used to eat meat but then you decided to go vegetarian. Are you still a meat eater because you once ate meat?

>> You failed at one or more tasks that were important to you. Can you legitimately conclude that you're an utter failure?

>> By the same token, if you succeeded at one important task, are you now a success at everything you do?

As you can see by reviewing these examples, basing your self-esteem on one incident, one action, or one experience is a gross overgeneralization.

Believing you're more than the sum of your parts

Take a look at Figure 16-1. The big *I* is composed of dozens of little *i*'s. So, what's the point of the figure? When you evaluate yourself *totally* based on one characteristic, thought, action, or intention, you're making the thinking error that a single part (the little *i*) equals the whole (the big *I*).

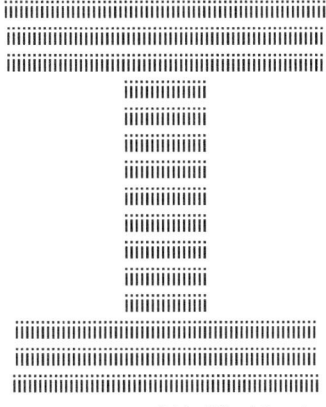

FIGURE 16-1:
Which do you see first: the big *I* or all the little *i*'s?

Along similar lines, consider a finely woven tapestry made up of countless variations of texture, color, and pattern. Within this tapestry, you may find one or more flaws, where the colors fail to meet or the patterns are slightly out of sync. The flaws in the tiny details don't cancel out the beauty or value of the overall piece. And what about the *Venus de Milo*? Over the years, she's lost a limb or two, but the officials at the Louvre don't say, "Um, sorry, she's flawed; put her in the bin!" The fact that the statue is damaged doesn't diminish or define its overall worth. The statue is valued *as it is,* and the absence of arms doesn't negate the impact it has on our understanding of the evolution of art.

TIP

If your child, sibling, or nephew failed a spelling test, would you judge them a total loser? Would you encourage them to think of themselves as a global failure, based entirely on one test? If not, why are you doing this to yourself?

Start acting in accordance with the belief that your parts don't define your wholeness. If you truly believe this idea, what do you do when you fail at doing something, behave badly or wickedly, or notice that you have a physical imperfection or character flaw? How do you expect to feel when endorsing this belief?

Here's another experiment you can try. Take a pack of self-adhesive notes and a large, flat surface. A wall or a door works well, or try a friend if they have a few spare minutes. Write down on one of the notes a characteristic that you, as a whole person, possess; then stick the note on the wall, door, or your friend. Keep doing this, writing down all the aspects of yourself you can think of until you run out of characteristics or sticky notes. Now step back and admire the illustration of your complexity as a human being. Appreciate the fact that your individual characteristics make up your whole and don't singly define you.

Acknowledging your ever-changing nature

As a human being, your nature is to be an ever-changing person. Even if you measure all your personal characteristics today and come up with a global rating for yourself, it'll be wrong tomorrow. Why? Because each day you change a little, age slightly, and gather a few new experiences.

Consider yourself a work-in-progress and try holding a *flexible* attitude toward yourself. Every skill you acquire or interest you develop effectively produces a change within you. Every hardship you weather, every joyous event that visits you, and every mundane occurrence you endure cause you to develop, adapt, and grow.

Ellis theorizes that your essential value or worth can't be measured accurately because your *being* includes your *becoming*. Ellis suggests that each human is a process with an ever-changing present and future. Hence, you can't conclusively evaluate yourself while you're still living and developing.

Accepting your fallible nature

Sorry if we're the ones to break it to you, but human beings are flawed and imperfect. You may be a pretty impressive product of evolution, but essentially you're just a powerful animal on the planet. Even if you believe you're the creation of a divine entity, do you really think the design brief was perfection? Maybe being complex, different, and with a built-in tendency to make mistakes is all part of the plan. When people say "You're only human," they have a point: Never can you be flawless or stop making mistakes. Neither can anyone else. It's just how we're built.

During the process of accepting yourself, you may experience sadness, disappointment, or remorse for your blunders. These healthy negative emotions may be uncomfortable, but usually they can lead to self-helping, corrective, and "adaptive" behaviors. Self-condemnation or self-depreciation, on the other hand, are likely to lead to far more intense, unhealthy negative emotions, such as depression, hurt, guilt, and shame. So, you're more likely to adopt self-defeating, "maladaptive" behaviors, such as avoidance or giving up.

FORGIVING FLAWS IN YOURSELF AND OTHERS

Interestingly, you may overlook some imperfections in yourself while condemning the same shortcomings in others, or vice versa. To some degree, this relates to what you consider important, your flexibility, and your level of self-acceptance. Consider the following scenarios:

- Julian works in a computer shop. Whenever he's about to close a sale, he gets excited and trips over some of his words. He feels a bit foolish about this, although none of his customers has ever mentioned it.

- Margarita has a poor sense of direction. Sometimes she forgets which way is left and which is right. When she's driving, she has difficulty following directions and frequently finds herself lost.

- Carlos is a good student but has difficulty in exam situations. He studies earnestly but, come the day of the test, he forgets what he's read and performs poorly.

You can't always change things about yourself. Sometimes you can improve a bit, but sometimes you can't change at all. If you're a fully developed adult and five feet tall, you're unlikely to be able to make yourself grow to six feet through sheer determination. The trick is to begin to recognize where you can make changes and where you can't. Living happily is about accepting your limitations without putting yourself down for them and capitalizing on your strengths. So, taking the same three examples,

- Julian may be able to make himself less anxious about a potential sale; therefore, he may speak more coherently. By accepting that he mangles his words sometimes but not condemning himself for it, he may make headway toward overcoming this aspect of his behavior.

- Margarita may simply be someone who's not particularly good at navigation. She may improve with practice, but she may also do well to accept that she's the person who turns up late for parties two streets away from her home.

- Carlos can look at his studying habits and see whether he can study more effectively. However, he may simply be someone who does better on practical assignments rather than tests.

(continued)

(continued)

Overall, Julian, Margarita, and Carlos can choose to accept themselves as fallible human beings and work to improve in the areas described, while also accepting their personal limitations. They can choose to embrace their inherent fallibility as part of the experience of being a human and understand that their "less good" traits are part of their individual composition as much as their "good" traits.

Alternatively, they can choose to evaluate themselves based on their "less good" traits and judge themselves as worthless, or less than worthy. But where, oh where, do you go from there?

Valuing your uniqueness

Who else do you know who's exactly — and yes, we do mean *exactly* — like you? The correct answer is no one because the human cloning thing hasn't really taken off yet. So you are, in fact, quite unique — just like everyone else.

REMEMBER

You alone are the possessor of your own idiosyncrasies. So learn to laugh it up because the mistakes and foot-in-mouth moments will just keep on coming, whether you like them or not.

Taking yourself overly seriously isn't a successful path to obtaining good mental health (which we talk about in Chapter 25). Your individual human fallibility can be both amusing and illuminating. Think about comedy shows and films. Much of what makes these programs funny is the way the characters behave, the mistakes they make, their social blunders, their physicality, their personal peculiarities, and so on. When you laugh at these characters, you aren't being malicious — you just recognize echoes of yourself and of the entire human experience in them. Furthermore, you're unlikely to put down these characters based on their errors. Give yourself a similar benefit of the doubt. Accepting the existence of personal shortcomings can help you understand your own limitations and identify areas that you may wish to target for change.

For example, as your authors, we have a couple of our own quirks that we try to accept, and even celebrate, as unique. Rob has no sense of direction, which can leave him lost in an empty parking lot for hours; believe us when we say that no map or GPS helps. Sometimes we wonder if he even knows where he lives. Rhena has her own special pronunciation for many words. (That's to say, she gets them wrong.) These are only two of our personal foibles that we're prepared to commit to print!

WHY SELF-ACCEPTANCE BELIEFS WORK

At first glance, self-acceptance and self-acceptance beliefs may seem like a tall order or "not what people think." However, incorporating self-accepting beliefs into your life can really make a difference, and we recommend it for the following reasons:

- **Self-acceptance beliefs are helpful.** You're inspired to correct your poor behavior or address your shortcomings because you give yourself permission to be flawed. You allow yourself a margin for error. When problems occur or you behave poorly, you can experience appropriate and proportionate negative emotions and then move on. People are generally more effective problem-solvers when they're not severely emotionally distressed.

- **Self-acceptance beliefs are consistent with reality.** Do you know anyone who's entirely flawless? If you have only conditional self-acceptance, you're subscribing to a belief that you cease to be acceptable, or worthwhile, when you fall short of those conditions or ideals. Basically, you're telling yourself that you must succeed at any given task. Because you can (and do) both fail and succeed, the evidence suggests that your demand to always succeed is erroneous.

- **Self-acceptance beliefs are logical.** Just because you *prefer* to behave in a certain way doesn't mean that you *must*. Nor does your failing to act in that manner logically render you a failure in all respects. Rather, this "failure" supports the premise that you're a fallible human capable of behaving in differing ways at various times. To broaden the point, this "failure" highlights your humanness and your inherent capacity to do both "well" and "less well."

You're unique because no one is a facsimile of you. At the same time, you're *not* special or unique because *everyone* is an individual and, hence, not replicable. Your uniqueness means that you're *different* from all others and, paradoxically, that you're the *same* as all others.

Using self-acceptance to aid self-improvement

As we touch upon in the nearby sidebar "Forgiving Flaws in Yourself and Others," self-acceptance can lead to healthy and *appropriate* negative emotional responses to adverse experiences. This type of emotional response tends to lead to functional or *adaptive* behaviors. Self-denigration, on the other hand, leads to unhealthy, *inappropriate* emotional responses, which in turn tend to produce unhelpful or *destructive* behaviors. Look at the following situation.

Wendy's been a full-time mom for the past ten years. Before she had her children, she worked as a legal secretary. Now that her children are older, she wants to return to work. Wendy attends a job interview. During the interview, she becomes nervous and is unable to answer some of the questions adequately. She notices that she's becoming flustered and hot. It also becomes clear to her that secretarial work has evolved in the past ten years, and she lacks the IT skills necessary for the post. Unfortunately, she doesn't get the job.

Now consider two different responses to the interview:

Response A: Wendy leaves the interview, ruminating on her poor performance all the way home. "I looked like such an idiot," she tells herself. "They must have seen me as a real amateur, blushing and stuttering like that. I'm such a failure. Who'd want to hire someone as subpar as me? I don't know what made me think I'd be able to get into work again anyway. I'm clearly not up to standard at all." Wendy feels depressed and hopeless. She mopes around the house and continues to think about what a failure she is. She feels so ashamed about failing the interview that she avoids talking about it to her friends, thus denying herself the opportunity to receive feedback, which may be useful or help her feel more balanced. Wendy stops looking at job alerts on her phone.

Response B: Wendy leaves the interview and thinks, "I really didn't present myself very well in there. I wish I hadn't been so obviously nervous. Clearly, I need to get some IT skills before I'm likely to get a job offer." Wendy feels disappointed about not getting the job, but she doesn't conclude that failing one important task makes her a failure. She feels regretful, but not ashamed, about her performance and talks to a few friends about it. Her friends give her some encouragement. Wendy then enrolls in an IT course at her local college. She continues to look at employment websites and job alerts.

In Response B, Wendy is understandably disappointed with how the interview turned out. She's able to recognize her skills deficit. Because she accepts herself with this specific deficit, she takes concrete steps toward improving her skills base.

In Response A, Wendy isn't thinking about how to do better at the next interview. She's thinking about how she'd like to crawl under the carpet and spend the rest of her days there. It's a bit of an extreme reaction considering the circumstances, but Wendy isn't considering the circumstances. She's decided that messing up an interview equals total failure, and she's feeling far too depressed and ashamed to start problem-solving.

REMEMBER

Generally, your failures and errors aren't as important or calamitous as you think they are. Most of the time, your failures mean a lot more to you than they do to others.

Understanding that acceptance doesn't mean giving up

We don't suggest that Wendy must resign herself to a life of unemployment simply because she's been somewhat left behind by technological advancements. Why should she? Clearly, she can do things to ensure that she stands a good chance of getting back into the job market.

In her case, self-acceptance means that she can view herself as worthwhile, while getting on with self-improvement in specific areas of her life. By contrast, if she refuses to accept herself and puts herself down, she's far more likely to resign — perhaps even condemn — herself to her current state of unemployment.

TIP

Resignation requires little or no effort, but self-acceptance can involve a lot of personal effort.

>> **High frustration tolerance** (HFT) is the ability to tolerate discomfort and hard work in the short term, en route to achieving an identified long-term goal. In Response B in the job interview example, Wendy accepts herself and holds an HFT attitude. She's prepared to do the work necessary to reach her goal of getting a job.

>> **Low frustration tolerance** (LFT) is unwillingness to tolerate short-term pain for long-term gain. An LFT attitude is present in statements such as "It's too difficult to change — this is just the way I am" and "I may as well just give up." Resignation and LFT go hand in hand. In Response A, Wendy refuses to accept herself in view of her recent experience and resigns herself to unemployment.

REMEMBER

Resignation may seem like an easier option than self-acceptance because it means you have to do less. However, people tend to feel miserable when they resign and condemn themselves, refusing to put effort into improving their situation.

Being Inspired to Change

You may think that self-acceptance is all fine and well when talking about human error, social gaffes, and minor character flaws, but the dice are more loaded when you've transgressed your personal moral code.

If you've behaved in an antisocial, illegal, or immoral manner, you may have more difficulty accepting yourself. But you can! Accepting yourself doesn't mean accepting the negative behavior and continuing to do it. On the contrary, accepting yourself involves recognizing that you, an acceptable human being, have engaged in a poor, or unacceptable, behavior. Accepting yourself makes you more likely to learn from your mistakes and act more constructively, which is in both your interest and the interest of those around you.

Consider the following two scenarios:

>> Malcolm has an anger problem. He puts unreasonable demands on his wife and children to never get on his nerves. He has a bad day at work and comes home to find no dinner on the table and his two young children playing noisily in the sitting room. Malcolm shouts at his wife and slaps her. He calls his children names and hits them. His family is afraid and upset. This happens on a regular basis.

>> Fiona works in a shoe shop. She's been stealing money from the till to buy alcohol and codeine-based painkillers. Usually, she takes the tablets through-out the day and drinks heavily in the evenings until she passes out. Lately, she's called in sick to work more often because she has terrible hangovers and feels depressed. Fiona often calls herself a "useless drunk" and "a low-life thief" and then drinks more to stop herself from thinking this way. She works hard to hide her drinking and stealing and feels ashamed of herself most of the time.

Are Malcolm and Fiona bad people, or are they just currently exhibiting bad behaviors? If you condemn Malcolm or Fiona — or, indeed, yourself — as a "bad person" based on bad behavior, you're missing the point that a person is more complex than a single act.

To overcome destructive or socially unacceptable behaviors, you need to do the following:

>> **Take personal responsibility for your bad behavior.** Rather than deciding you're just a bad person who has no control or responsibility for your actions, accept that you're doing bad things.

In the previous example, Malcolm's doing bad things when he takes out his anger on his family. But if he decides that he's a bad person overall, he relinquishes his responsibility to change. Basically, he's saying, "I beat my family because I'm a bad person and therefore I can't change." He's also more likely to attribute his violence to external factors rather than to his own unreasonable demands: "They know what I'm like and they should damn well stay out of my way when I come home from work."

>> **Identify clearly what you're doing that's wrong or unacceptable.** Be specific when pinpointing bad behaviors.

For example, Fiona has two definite serious problems or "bad" behaviors. First, she has an addiction; second, she's stealing to support that addiction. Fiona's shame and self-condemnation are likely going to get in the way of her overcoming her problems. She can't put in the hard work needed to recover from her addiction (which includes seeking professional help) if she can't accept herself as worth the effort.

To move on in life in a way that contributes to the kind of world you'd like to live in, assume personal responsibility and keep working on your self-acceptance.

Actioning Self-Acceptance

Just like virtually all skills worth acquiring, you're going to have to work hard and practice to achieve successful self-acceptance skills. This section focuses on ways to start integrating self-acceptance into your daily life.

Self-talking your way to self-acceptance

What's in a name? Rather a lot, actually. As we discuss in Chapters 4 and 10, most people largely feel the way they think. In other words, the meanings you assign to events have a great deal to do with how you feel about those events.

Similarly, meaning is attached to the names you call yourself. If you use abusive, harshly critical, or profane terminology to give utterance to your behaviors or traits, you're heading toward emotional disturbance.

The notion that you may start to believe something if you tell it to yourself enough times is partly true. Fortunately, you can choose what messages you give yourself and choose how you think and feel about yourself.

TIP

How you talk to yourself affects immediately, or obliquely, your sense of self. Try the following self-talk strategies to make the best impact on yourself:

>> **Desist with global labels.** Humans often call themselves losers, idiots, failures, stupid, or unlovable because of certain events or actions they've been involved in or done. You may use even worse language on yourself in the privacy of your own head. Why? Because you're caving in to the temptation to rate your entire selfhood on the evidence of one or more isolated incidents.

>> **Be specific with your self-assessments.** Before you classify yourself as a failure, ask yourself the following questions: "In what specific way have I

failed?" "In what specific way have I acted stupidly?" It's far less easy to fall into global self-rating when you force yourself to be specific.

>> **Say what you mean and mean what you say.** You may be saying to yourself right now, "Oh, but I don't *mean* it when I call myself those bad names." No? Then don't say them! Get into the practice of using language that describes accurately your behavior and is in keeping with self-acceptance beliefs. Instead of muttering, "I'm such an idiot for missing that deadline," try saying, "Missing that deadline was a bad move. I'm disappointed about it."

REMEMBER

Resisting self-abusive language cuts two ways. This chapter focuses on self-acceptance, but much of the advice applies to acceptance of others, too. Generally, people are nicer and more forgiving to their friends than they are to themselves. But people are still capable of damning others and calling them ugly names. Start exercising a different type of consistency. Stop name-calling. Period. When you put a halt on name-calling, you can feel less intense anger and hurt when others behave poorly, which helps to reinforce your self-acceptance beliefs. If you're practicing not globally rating others, you're minimizing the tendency to globally rate yourself.

Following the best friend argument

Out of habit, most humans employ double standards: You judge your friends by an entirely different, often more accepting, standard than you use on yourself.

Try to take the same attitude of acceptance toward yourself that you take toward your friends and family. Consider the following:

>> **Act like your best friend by judging your behavior but not judging yourself.** Eustace has been having difficulties in his marriage. He has been staying out late and drinking with his friends before going home and being verbally abusive to his wife. His best friend, Lucian, has highlighted Eustace's poor behavior in their conversations, but he's maintained an understanding attitude toward his friend's unhappiness. Lucian isn't about to define Eustace as a complete pig on the strength of his recent, excessive drinking and arguments with his wife.

>> **Accept your failings as you would those of a dear friend.** Laura just failed her driving test for the fourth time and feels down about it. Her best friend, Maggie, tells her to try again and be less hard on herself. Maggie wants Laura to take the driving test again. She doesn't view Laura as a total failure based simply on her difficulty in passing a test. Even if Laura never drives, Maggie will likely remain her friend because of other things she likes and appreciates about Laura.

>> **View your behavior within the context of your circumstances, and above all, be compassionate.** Rivka had an abortion following a short affair. She feels guilty and can't imagine putting the event behind her. Rivka's close friend, Carla, reminds her of the unfortunate circumstances she found herself in at the time and tells her that she's still someone that Carla likes and respects. Carla can see that Rivka has made a difficult decision. She compassionately considers that Rivka has acted out of a degree of desperation. Rivka may have been unlucky, or a bit careless, with respect to birth control, but Carla doesn't judge her based on the abortion.

Ask yourself whether the punishment fits the crime. Are you being fair to yourself? What punishment would you dole out to your best friend for the same behavior? Be aware that you may be making yourself feel extremely guilty, or ashamed, inappropriately. If you wouldn't like to see anyone else feeling such extreme emotions in response to the same transgression you've committed, you're applying a double standard that's loaded against you.

REMEMBER

Are you created so differently that you must subscribe to an exceptional code of conduct? (Consider this an inverted inferiority complex.) Having some exceptional code of conduct implies that you, and you alone, are somehow designed exclusively to transcend the ubiquitous human essence of fallibility. However, you're human. You don't fail any more extravagantly than any of your peers, nor do you succeed more dramatically than they do. If you're going to exercise compassion toward your friends' failures and wobbles, you need to consistently apply the same rules of compassion and understanding to yourself.

Dealing with doubts and reservations

Many people feel that, by accepting themselves, they're simply letting themselves off the hook. But self-acceptance is about taking personal responsibility for your less good traits, actions, and habits. Self-acceptance is about targeting areas that you both *can* and *wish to* change and then taking the appropriate steps toward change. Self-acceptance isn't saying, "Hey, I'm human and fallible! Therefore, I just am the way I am and I don't need to think about changing anything."

REMEMBER

You are, at baseline, worthy and acceptable, but some of your behaviors and attitudes may be simultaneously unacceptable.

Another common fear is that by accepting yourself, you're condoning undesirable aspects of yourself: "Hey, I'm an acceptable human being; therefore, all I think and do is acceptable." Not so.

Work on accepting your overall self based on your intrinsic human fallibility, and be prepared to judge *specific* aspects of yourself. You can both condone your personhood and condemn, or reject, certain things that you do.

Selecting the Self-Help Journey to Self-Acceptance

A common reason for people persistently putting themselves down is that they hope to become better by calling attention to their mistakes, flaws, and failings. Unfortunately, this process frequently includes feeling depressed or anxious, which may well already be underpinned by low self-esteem.

Trying to solve an emotional problem at the same time as calling yourself useless, worthless, and pathetic is much like trying to mend a broken leg while hitting yourself with crutches. Your actions are likely to make both jobs much harder. Self-esteem is such an important issue for so many people that we've written an entire book on the subject: *Boosting Self-Esteem for Dummies* (Wiley).

REMEMBER

Accepting yourself has two interesting implications for overcoming emotional problems and personal development. First, you're equal in worth to other human beings just as you are, which reduces emotional pain. Second, because you're not distracted by beating yourself up, you can focus better on coping with adversity, reducing disturbance, and self-improvement.

IMPERFECT SELF-ACCEPTANCE

Because you're a fallible human being, you won't be perfect at self-acceptance either. You'll probably slip into putting yourself down from time to time, as everyone does — us included. The aim is to accept yourself more often and more quickly, if you notice that you're putting yourself down. Such acceptance gets easier and more consistent with practice.

Broadly speaking, you may be using one of two common strategies to manage low self-esteem: avoiding doing things or doing things excessively. For example, a person who believes they're worthless unless they're liked by everybody may try extra hard to avoid rejection or to win people's approval, while a person who regards themselves as a "failure" may try to avoid situations in which they might fail. Look at Chapter 26 for more on self-esteem strategies that can backfire.

Chapter **17**

Cooling Down Your Anger

Anger's a pretty common emotion that all of us feel to some extent now and then. However, anger is also increasingly recognized as an important emotional problem. Anger, especially when it leads to aggression, can be detrimental to relationships, health, and self-esteem.

In the bad old days of psychological treatment for anger, people were encouraged simply to "get it out," often by beating pillows to vent their fury. The result? Just like anything you practice, these people got better at being angry. The notion that expressing your rage can "get it out of your system" is something of a myth. More often, you wind yourself up further, generating even more anger. A better solution is to come to grips with managing your angry feelings responsibly and to master skills that can help you feel less angry, less often.

CBT offers clear and effective management of anger by tackling the thinking that underpins your anger and helping you express it in a healthy manner. This chapter focuses on CBT techniques that can help you deal directly with your feelings of anger.

Discerning the Difference Between Healthy and Unhealthy Anger

Essentially, two different types of anger exist: healthy and unhealthy:

>> **Healthy anger is helpful annoyance and irritation.** This is the kind of anger that spurs you on to assert your rights and stand up for yourself when it's important and healthy that you do so.

>> **Unhealthy anger is unhelpful rage and hate.** This type of anger leads you to behave aggressively or violently even in response to mild or unimportant provocation. Unhealthy anger can also mean you bottle things up and vent your anger indirectly (sometimes called *passive aggression*) or take it out on innocent parties.

All emotions have *themes* — that is, sets of circumstances or triggers from which they arise. (We explain this a bit more in Chapter 7.) Themes for anger include someone breaking one of your personal rules or threatening your self-esteem through word or deed. Another anger theme is frustration: when someone or something gets in the way of you reaching a goal.

The triggers for healthy and unhealthy anger are the same, but the behavioral responses they typically produce are very different. Both anger types are also associated with different ways of thinking and attention focus.

Key characteristics of unhealthy anger

Unhealthy anger is far more likely than healthy anger to cause fractures in your personal relationships, create trouble in your career, or land you in prison. You're also likely to feel more physically and emotionally uncomfortable when you're unhealthily angry.

Several ways of thinking typically underpin unhealthy anger:

>> Making rigid demands and rules about the way other people must or must not behave

>> Insisting that other people don't offend, disrespect, insult, or ridicule you or your opinions

>> Demanding that life conditions and other people don't get in the way of you getting what you want

>> Overestimating the degree to which people deliberately act in undesirable ways toward you

>> Assuming automatically that you're right and the other person's wrong

>> Refusing to consider another person's point of view and to accept others' right to hold a different point of view

Common behavioral characteristics associated with unhealthy anger include the following:

>> Attacking or wanting to attack another person physically or verbally

>> Attacking another person in an indirect — also known as *passive-aggressive* — way, such as by trying to make someone else's job difficult

>> Taking out your anger on innocent parties, such as another person, an animal, or an object

>> Plotting revenge

>> Holding a grudge

>> Attempting to turn others against the person you believe has behaved undesirably

>> Sulking

>> Looking for evidence that someone has acted with malicious intent

>> Searching for signs of an offense being repeated

>> Being over-vigilant for people breaking your personal rules or acting disrespectfully toward you

Common physical signs of unhealthy anger include the following:

>> Clenched fists

>> Muscular tension, especially in the neck and shoulder muscles

>> Clenched jaw

>> Trembling or shaking

>> Raised heart rate

>> Feeling hot

TIP

For many people, anger can come on hot and fast. Familiarizing yourself with your own early warning signs of anger can help you intervene earlier.

Hallmarks of healthy anger or annoyance

In general, people experience healthy anger as intense but not overwhelming. You can feel intensely angry in a healthy way without experiencing a loss of control. Healthy anger doesn't lead you to behave in antisocial, violent, or intimidating ways.

In addition, healthy anger is typically underpinned by the following ways of thinking:

» Holding strong preferences rather than rigid demands about how people should act

» Having flexibility in the rules you expect people to abide by

» Strongly preferring that others don't insult or ridicule you

» Desiring that other people and life conditions don't get in the way of you getting what you want

» Thinking realistically about whether other people have deliberately acted undesirably toward you

» Considering that both you *and* the other person may be right *and* wrong to a degree

» Trying to see the other person's point of view and recognizing others' right to disagree with you

Behavioral characteristics typical of healthy anger include these:

» Asserting yourself with the other person

» Staying in the situation with the intent of resolving any disagreement

» Requesting that the other person modify their behavior — and respecting their right to refuse to do so

» Looking for evidence that the other person may not have behaved with malicious intent

» Being able to forgive and forget

Assembling Attitudes That Underpin Healthy Anger

If you're serious about overcoming your unhealthy anger, you have to take a long, hard look at some of the attitudes you hold. This involves honestly looking at the way you believe that other people and the world at large *must* treat you. You may hold some common toxic beliefs that frequently lead to unhealthy anger in people. Some of these toxic thoughts include the following:

>> "No one must ever treat me poorly or disrespectfully."

>> "The world must not be unjust or unfair — *especially* not to me!"

>> "I must get what I want when I want it, and nothing should get in my way."

>> "I must never be led to feeling guilty, inadequate, embarrassed, or ashamed by other people or life events."

>> "No one and nothing must ever expose my weaknesses or errors."

Having looked long and hard at your attitudes, you need to make your toxic attitudes more helpful and realistic. (See Chapter 4 for more on tackling toxic thoughts in general.) Once again, positive emotional change comes from changing the way you think about yourself, other people, and the world in general. If you want to be emotionally healthy and high-functioning, you need to start developing flexible, tolerant, and accepting attitudes. High-functioning individuals experience fewer disturbing emotional responses, are able to enjoy life, and bounce back fairly readily from everyday hassles and annoyances. It's all in the way you look at life and the kind of attitude you take toward life's ups and downs (particularly regarding anger).

REMEMBER

We can explain the types of attitude that are likely to help you overcome unhealthy anger. However, you must decide to agree with these attitudes and ultimately act in accordance with them if you want to see a change in the anger you experience.

The following sections describe the healthy attitudes you need to take to overcome your unhealthy anger.

Putting up with other people

Other people exist in the same universe as you. Sometimes this can be a rather pleasant state of affairs, but on occasions you may find that these other people are a damnable inconvenience. Whether you like it or not, other people can exist, do exist, and will continue to exist in your universe for the foreseeable future.

Accepting that these other people have as much right as you to inhabit the planet just makes sense. And while cohabitating, you may as well accept the reality that sometimes other people may get on your nerves. Because you're not in charge of the universe, you'd better accept that other people are allowed to act according to their own rules and values. They're not obliged to subscribe to yours.

You've probably noticed that humans come in a variety of shapes, sizes, and colors. And not all people share the same religion, culture, political opinions, moral codes, or rules of social conduct. Now, without going into a long-winded speech about the value of diversity, accepting individual difference is terribly important. Acknowledging that other people have the right to their own ideas about how to live their lives — even when you flatly disagree with their ideas — can save you a lot of emotional upset. People will continue to exercise these rights, whatever your opinion.

Accepting others can save you a world of unhealthy anger. Consider this: Every morning Jill and Tim travel to work together by bus. Every time she boards the bus, Jill says a pleasant "Good morning!" to the driver, who ignores her completely. One day, Tim asks Jill why she persists in greeting the driver even though he never acknowledges her. Jill says, "Because I choose to behave in line with my standard of politeness rather than respond to his standard of rudeness."

Jill's high tolerance to rudeness from the bus driver means that she can avoid making herself unhealthily angry. She does this by

>> Accepting that the driver has the right to be rude. No law exists against responding (or not) to another person's greeting.

>> Not taking the driver's rudeness too personally. The driver doesn't know Jill, so it's highly unlikely that he's actually "out to get her" specifically. He's probably foul-tempered to many people in addition to Jill.

>> Exercising her right to behave according to her own standard of politeness, even in the face of another person's rudeness. Although the bus driver is rude to Jill, she chooses not to respond in the same way. She can carry on being a generally polite person even in the face of another person's rudeness if she so chooses.

Forming flexible preferences

Wanting others to treat you well and with respect makes sense. Similarly, you probably want other people to do their jobs well and to help you get what you want. You're likely to want life to roll your way and for world events to gel with your personal plans.

However, expecting and demanding these conditions to be met all the time doesn't make sense.

REMEMBER

Keeping your attitudes flexible and based on preferences, rather than demands or expectations, can preserve your anger in the healthy camp. Rigid and demanding attitudes can land you in unhealthy, destructive anger, time and time again.

Consider the relationship of Ade and Franco. Ade holds rigid beliefs about other people showing him respect and courtesy. Franco holds the same principal attitudes, but flexibly. Ade and Franco go for lunch together and sit near a table of young men, who drink a bit too much and end up talking very loudly and rudely. Franco and Ade can't hear each other, and their lunch is being ruined by the behavior of these young men. Franco suggests that he and Ade move to another table, where they won't be disturbed by the men's antisocial behavior. Ade, however, gets up and shouts at the men, ending up in a brawl outside the cafe. He's lucky not to be hurt more seriously than he is.

Ade's rigid attitudes about the situation are

"How dare these idiots treat me this way"?

"I won't tolerate being disrespected like this."

"I've got to show these idiots who's boss."

Franco's more flexible attitudes about the situation are

"These guys are behaving like idiots."

"These guys are really annoying me with their disrespectful behavior."

"I don't want to put up with this, so I think I'll get away from these guys."

Flexible preferences for things like respect allow for the possibility of you being treated disrespectfully. Rigid demands don't allow for the possibility of life and other people treating you in ways that you think they shouldn't. Inevitably, you'll end up feeling outraged if you always demand that others behave in a specific way. People behave according to how *they* want to behave, not how *you* want them to behave.

Accepting other people as fallible human beings

When you angrily condemn another person as "useless," "no good," or "idiotic," you make a gross overgeneralization. The other person isn't a complete idiot just because they're acting idiotically; they surely act in different ways in other situations, just like you do.

The critical point here is also a practical point: Putting down other people makes respecting others difficult. You need to sustain a level of respect for others to be able to consider behaviors objectively and act appropriately assertive.

The alternative to putting down others is to accept them as fallible human beings (FHBs) who may act in objectionable ways to you. When you consider others as FHBs, you can appropriately condemn the behavior but not the person. This acceptance is critical in helping you keep a level head and master your angry feelings.

TIP

Accepting other people is the other side of the coin to accepting yourself. You can simultaneously accept yourself because you're applying the same essential philosophy of acceptance to everyone.

Accepting yourself

Sometimes people default to unhealthy anger because they have a fragile sense of their own worth. If someone treats you poorly, insults you, or seems to hold a negative opinion of you, you may be reminded of how low an opinion you have of yourself. To protect your self-worth, you may attack the other person. Think of the rationale as "If I can put you down, then I can avoid putting myself down."

By believing that you're an unrateable, complex, ever-changing, fallible human, you may see that you can never be less worthwhile, even when people treat you poorly. In Chapter 16, we offer more guidance on self-acceptance.

Developing high frustration tolerance

Frustration occurs most often when something or someone gets in the way of you achieving your specific goals and aims. The more important your goal is to you, the more angry or annoyed you're likely to feel when something blocks your attempts to reach that goal.

People who frequently experience unhealthy anger tend to have a low tolerance for frustration. Their low threshold for tolerating hassle, mishaps, or obstruction from life and others is echoed in statements like these:

"I can't stand it!"

"It's intolerable!"

"I just can't take it anymore!"

Increasing your tolerance for frustration helps you experience appropriate levels of healthy annoyance in response to goal obstruction. Having a *high frustration tolerance* (HFT) makes you more effective at solving problems. Your anger doesn't get in the way of you seeing possible solutions to everyday hassles and setbacks. High frustration tolerance is present in statements such as these:

"This is an uncomfortable situation, but I can stand the discomfort."

"This event is hard to bear, but I can bear it. Some difficult things are worth tolerating."

"Even if I *feel* like I can't take it anymore, chances are that I can."

To increase your tolerance for frustration, ask yourself these kinds of questions when life pulls a fast one on you:

"Is this situation really terrible, or is it just highly inconvenient?"

"Is it true that I can't stand this situation, or is it more true that I don't like this situation?"

"Is this situation truly unbearable, or is it really just difficult to bear?"

Being less extreme in your judgment of negative events can help you have less extreme emotional responses, such as unhealthy anger.

REMEMBER

Most of what you think is intolerable isn't as bad as it seems. Many things are difficult to tolerate but are tolerable, hard to bear but bearable, or unpleasant and inconvenient — but you *can* stand them!

To underscore the point, imagine getting stuck in traffic on your way to the airport and then missing your flight. Deeply annoying! However, you getting angry and screaming at the traffic isn't going to make the cars move any faster. Of course, becoming healthily annoyed about the traffic doesn't change the situation either. But your healthy anger is less likely to cause you such extreme discomfort and is more likely to help you create a contingency plan. Rather than using up your energy swearing and bashing your phone against the dashboard, you can focus your efforts on trying to get yourself bumped to the next available flight.

DOING YOUR ABCs

Practice writing down your unhealthy angry thoughts on paper and replacing them with healthier thoughts. Refer to Chapter 4 to see how to use an ABC form to tackle toxic thoughts and replace them with realistic renderings, pertinent preferences, additional acceptances, self-acceptance, and high frustration tolerance.

Pondering the pros and cons of your temper

Believing that you're right to be angry and steadfastly sticking to this perception is one of the more common obstacles to conquering unhealthy anger.

REMEMBER

You certainly have the right to feel angry. You may even *be* right to be angry, in the sense of objecting to something you object to. However, you may feel better and behave more constructively if you have healthy anger rather than unhealthy anger.

To commit more fully to changing your anger, review the costs and benefits of your current anger and of a healthier alternative. Refer to Chapter 9 for some pointers on completing a cost-benefit analysis, which can help you facilitate this change.

Imparting Your Indignation in a Healthy Way

Expressing your feelings readily when they occur can be a good antidote to bouts of unhealthy anger. On the other hand, bottling up your feelings can mean that you allow your emotions to fester until they bubble up to the surface and you explode.

People who talk openly and appropriately about their emotional responses to events are less prone to unhealthy feelings like anger and depression. The following sections offer tips and techniques to improve your communication skills and to deal with dissatisfaction in a healthy manner.

Asserting yourself effectively

Assertion involves standing up for yourself, voicing your opinions and feelings, and firmly ensuring that your basic rights are considered. Assertion differs from aggression in that it doesn't involve violence, intimidation, or disregard for the rights of others.

Using assertion rather than aggression is more effective in getting you what you want. When you're being assertive, you're still in control of your behavior, but when you're unhealthily enraged, much of your behavior is impulsive. People with unhealthy anger frequently regret their fury-fueled actions once the red mist has cleared.

REMEMBER

People are likely to respond to your wishes when you're being assertive simply because you're making yourself clear, not because they're afraid of your anger.

Often, your aggression is about winning an argument and getting the other person to back down and agree that you're right. Assertion isn't about winning per se. Rather, assertion is about getting your point across but not insisting that the other person agrees with you or backs down.

TIP

If you tend to get angry and become verbally or physically aggressive quickly, give yourself time out and go and count to ten (or as high as you need to feel calmer). You can then consider more useful perspectives and behavioral steps. Removing yourself from an inflammatory situation is often a sensible first step in adopting healthy assertion.

Assertion is a skill you can practice. Many people with anger problems benefit from breaking down assertion into the following steps:

>> **Get the other person's attention.** For example, if you want to make a complaint in a store, wait until you have the store manager's attention rather than shouting at them when they're busy with another task. Likewise, if you want to talk to your partner about a specific issue, ask for some of their time.

>> **Be in the right place.** The best time to assert yourself may depend on where you are when you're irked. If your boss makes a comment that undermines you during a board meeting, you're probably best to bring it up with them a bit later in less public surroundings.

>> **Be clear in your head about what you want to say.** If you're new to assertion but more familiar with the shouting and screaming thing, give yourself time to really think about the message you want to get across.

>> **Stick to your point and be respectful.** Don't resort to name-calling or hurling insults.

>> **Take responsibility for your feelings of annoyance.** Don't blame the other person for *making* you feel angry. Use statements like, "I feel angry when you turn up an hour late for our appointments," or "I felt let down and angry that you didn't invite me to your wedding reception."

WARNING

Assertion doesn't always work. Simply because you make the superlative effort to stop yelling your lungs out and to stop battering other people about the head doesn't mean that you're always going to get what you want. In fact, some people may even meet your assertion with their own aggression. So strive to maintain your healthy anger and to behave assertively, even when other people don't. Remind yourself that other people have the right to choose to behave badly and that you have the right to remove yourself from them rather than responding in kind.

Before you assert yourself, decide whether the situation's really worth your time and energy. Ask yourself whether the problem merits you being assertive. Is the issue more trouble than it's worth? If you're a former unhealthy anger junkie, you're probably not used to just letting things go. You can practice deciding when asserting yourself is in your best interests and when you're wiser to simply not respond at all.

Coping with criticism

Criticism isn't always intended to anger or undermine the receiver. Well-delivered specific criticism can provide useful information and need not cause offense. Most people like to hear positive feedback; it's the negative stuff that really gets under the skin.

People who demand perfection from themselves, or expect approval from significant others, can often take criticism badly. They tend to take criticism overly seriously and personally. They often assume that any form of negative comment means that they're less than worthy. If you're this sort of person, a comment from your boss such as "I'm not entirely happy with this report you've written" is translated in your head as something like this:

> My boss thinks my report is horrible. = All my reports are horrible. = I'm horrible at my job. = I'm worthless.

You may even become unhealthily angry to defend your self-worth and launch a counteroffensive on the person you feel has attacked you.

REMEMBER

You can take the sting out of criticism by keeping these points in mind:

>> Criticism can help you improve your work performance and your relationships.

>> You can assess criticism, decide how much of it you agree with, and reject the rest.

>> Criticism is something everyone experiences from time to time. You can't reasonably expect to avoid it forever.

If someone criticizes you in a global way — for example, your sister calls you an incompetent loser — try asking her to be more specific: "In what specific ways am I an incompetent loser?" Asking questions can make the criticism more useful to you. Or, if the person can't be more specific, your question can disarm her. The following section discusses disarming in greater detail.

Using the disarming technique

Okay, not all the criticism that you get is well intended. Sometimes another person may bombard you with a load of negative remarks or insults. What are your options? You *can* get unhealthily angry and shout at or otherwise attack your antagonist. Or you can keep your annoyance in the healthy camp and try nondefensively disarming your critic. The disarming technique works on the following principles:

>> Look for a grain of truth in what the other person is saying and agree with them on that specific point.

>> Show your critic some empathy.

>> Ask your critic for more information about their point of criticism.

>> Express your own point of view as "I feel" statements.

For example, Heidi's friend criticizes her for being late to meet her for coffee. She says angrily, "You're always late, Heidi. You're just so disorganized!" Heidi would usually be defensive and hostile about criticism, resulting in many past arguments. Instead, this time Heidi uses the disarming technique and replies, "You're right! I'm not the most organized person in the world" (partial agreement). "Are you feeling really annoyed"? (empathy/asking for more information). This takes the heat from her friend's anger, who then goes on to say how frustrated she's feeling in general.

Using the disarming technique, you come out on top by keeping your cool. You also gain the satisfaction of having managed a critical comment well. Who knows — you may even *improve* your relationship with your critic.

Acting Assertively in the Workplace

Keeping your cool at work is an important issue for many people. After all, you spend a lot of your waking hours at work, and you probably need a regular income. Sometimes unhealthy anger can lead to unnecessary work life strife or even put your job in jeopardy.

Maintaining good relationships with your colleagues and managers can make working life a lot more pleasant. Work environments are often a trouble spot for people with a history of unhealthy anger. If you think about it, work typically involves encountering criticism, dealing with authority, coping with stressful deadlines, living up to achievement expectations, and collaborating with others on projects. If you have fragile self-esteem or a fundamental intolerance of other people's poor behavior, you'll potentially be going off like a firecracker.

The same attitudes and strategies associated with healthy anger (previously outlined in this chapter) apply to the workplace. However, we offer you some additional specific pointers to help you remain healthily assertive while you work:

>> **Desire, but don't demand, success.** Success in your job is an understandable goal to have. (See Chapter 9 for more on goals and goal-setting.) However, when you strive for a degree of professional success but resist insisting that you *have to get it,* you can safeguard your mental health and avoid unhealthy anger. Unfortunately, success is never guaranteed, even with hard work and dedication. Keep your high standards by all means, but be sure to build in a margin for error and failures.

>> **Set realistic performance standards.** Yes, aiming high is fine, but you also need to allow for the possibility of failing to meet those standards from time to time. Being a humble human equipped with mere human ability and stamina may mean that you sometimes fall short of your professional performance standards.

>> **Be a team player.** No person's an island. At work, try to share the load with your colleagues when appropriate. Working with others is a skill that may take practice to develop. You might not agree with everything fellow team members suggest or with the way they do things. But if you avoid working with others for these reasons, you deprive yourself of the chance to grow. Developing confidence in your ability to disagree with others respectfully and offer your own ideas politely will make you less prone to bouts of unhealthy anger.

>> **Make allowances for other people's personal interaction style.** Simply because you're working hard to overcome unhealthy anger doesn't mean that all your coworkers are doing the same, unfortunately. Some people will be rude. Sometimes your supervisor may speak to you in a less than courteous manner. Rather than letting other people's rudeness throw you into a rage or eat you up inside, stick to your own standards of courteous communication. You don't have to condone poor behavior from others, but you do need to remember that how they behave is their choice. Resist sinking to the same level and instead rise above it.

>> **Differentiate between professional and personal comments.** When someone at work makes a negative comment about an aspect of your performance, they don't necessarily mean anything unpleasant about you as a *person.* Even if the comment is tactlessly delivered, you have a choice about whether or not to feel personally attacked. Try to differentiate clearly between remarks about your work-related performance and those about your character. This may help to diffuse a situation because you're not misinterpreting other people's intentions as deliberately malicious.

TIP

If someone at work does level a personal criticism at you, think first and respond later. The other person is probably behaving unprofessionally, and you don't have to respond in kind. Give yourself time to cool down before taking any action.

>> **Strike a work–life balance.** Sometimes tempers fray in the workplace because people are overworked. They may be pressured into putting in long hours, for example. If you have your own business, you may find it difficult to justify taking much time off. Striking a balance between working life and home life is important. Not making time for yourself outside of work can leave you burnt out and short of patience. Build in time to recharge your batteries and enjoy yourself.

REMEMBER

You're a person *first* and an employee *second* (or even third, fourth, or fifth, depending on your personal priorities). Over identifying with your work role can make it harder to keep your perspective and your cool when things go awry. No matter how important your work role is to you, bear in mind that you're a whole person. There's more to you than what you do for a living.

Putting your point across positively

Despite your newly cultivated Zen-like ability to take work disagreements in stride, sometimes you *do* need to address issues. Try using the tips in the following sections to eliminate unnecessary strife and ensure that you stay in the healthy anger camp — no matter what!

Assessing what you aim to achieve

Before a confrontation, however minor, decide what you aim to achieve. Whether this means requesting a pay rise, time off or more resources, or an explanation of some kind, assess precisely what you hope to achieve. You stand a better chance of clear, calm communication and getting what you want when you're clear in advance about *what* that is. Also think of acceptable compromises to your ultimate aim before initiating discussion with the other person. In your attempts to rid yourself of unhealthy anger, forewarned is forearmed.

Taking time to think

Give yourself time to think of how best to get your point across. Consider the appropriate time and place. Clearly decide on what it is you want to communicate in advance. Write some bullet points on paper to refer to if you think that'll help you stay focused. In some circumstances, it pays to prepare yourself for a negative response and devise ways of dealing with it. Having some ideas about how you'll respond to not getting your way or being misunderstood can help you stick to assertion rather than falling into old aggressive patterns.

Leaving well enough alone

At work, as in other areas of your life, there comes a point when further discussion just isn't likely to pay off. In work situations, an endgame exists that you just need to accept. For example, no funding may be available to meet certain requests, deadlines may be immoveable, working hours non negotiable, and so on. If you continue to push the point with your bosses or coworkers, you may create extra stress for yourself or rupture your working relationships.

Promoting a professional image

Behaving professionally can help eliminate confrontation at work and increase your overall confidence. People who take a professional attitude toward work, whatever their occupation, are more likely to remain calm in crisis. They also remember to deal with anger-triggering situations assertively and without flying off the handle. Here are some basic rules of communication that facilitate smooth running in the workplace:

>> Keep your head up and maintain good posture.

>> Make good eye contact with fellow workers and managers.

>> Speak clearly and audibly, and take your time.

>> Ask questions directly, and request support in a straightforward manner when you need it.

>> Sit centrally in meetings rather than on the fringes.

>> Strike a balance between offering your own ideas and opinions and listening attentively to the ideas and opinions of others.

Remaining professional

You can also improve your chances of remaining in control of your feelings at work by adhering to the principles of professional conduct. Bear these tips in mind:

>> **Be punctual.** Being consistently late is irksome for your boss and those who rely on you being around to do their own jobs. You probably don't like others being late, so try to practice what you preach.

>> **Be prepared.** Ensure that you have everything you need to do your job and have put in any preparation needed for certain projects.

>> **Dress accordingly.** Wearing the attire expected of you in the workplace contributes to creating a professional environment.

>> **Be polite.** Treat others as you'd like to be treated. Be consistently courteous with your coworkers even if you arrive in a bad mood. People feel secure around people who are predictably polite.

>> **Keep home and work life separate.** You're only human, so you're likely to be affected by home troubles when you're at work occasionally. But airing your "dirty laundry" at work is likely to bring you other difficulties that you don't need. You're paid to do your job, and that's what your boss and clients will tend to expect of you. If personal problems are clouding your ability to work effectively, consider time off or speak about the situation to the relevant person at work.

Dealing with Difficulties in Overcoming Anger

Even if you know that your anger responses are causing you problems in your life, you may still be reluctant to let go of your anger. Sometimes, people are reluctant to break free from unhealthy anger and related behaviors because they can't see an alternative, and they think that they may end up being passive or getting walked over instead.

However, if you develop your assertion skills, you may be more inclined to let go of your anger. Assertive people understand that unhealthy anger isn't necessary to look after your well-being. That said, here are some common obstacles to getting rid of unhealthy anger and some suggestions to help you take on healthy anger instead:

>> **You lack empathy and understanding of the impact your unhealthy anger responses have on those near to you.** When you're not angry, ask your loved ones how they feel about your anger. Try to remember times when you've been on the receiving end of aggressive or intimidating behavior and how it affected you. Use feedback about your anger and your own experiences of aggression from others to help you change how you express feelings of annoyance in the future.

>> **Letting go of your anger means that you're weak.** You may consider yourself an angry person, and you may like it that way. You may think that if you don't continue to be angry, other people may discover that you're weak, a pushover, or someone they can mess with. Work to realize that people who are assertive — firm but fair — tend to earn respect. You don't need to be angry to be strong.

>> **You think that your unhealthy anger helps you control other people and encourages them to respect you.** If you're aggressive, people who are important in your life, such as your children or your partner, may go out of their way to avoid incurring your wrath. Don't mistake fear and dislike for respect. You may control the people in your life by your anger, but their compliance is likely borne of fear and loathing, not from genuine regard for you. When you behave respectfully and assertively, people are likely to respond out of a genuine regard for your feelings rather than out of fear.

>> **Your unhealthy anger makes you feel powerful.** Although some people find the intensity of their unhealthy anger uncomfortable and even scary, others feel invigorated by the rush of their fury. Unhealthy anger is based on putting down another person. Unhealthy anger often means that you're stepping on another person's rights or abusing or intimidating somebody else. If you enjoy these aspects of your anger, you probably hold a low opinion of yourself generally. Look for other ways to experience your personal power without undermining those around you.

>> **Your anger is self-righteous.** You may be clinging stubbornly to your anger because you think it's justified. You may be refusing to admit that you could be wrong or that the other person could be right. Rarely are confrontations as cut and dried as one party being utterly in the right and the other utterly in the wrong. Remind yourself that being wrong is okay. It isn't a sign of weakness or inferiority. Allow yourself to admit that you may be wrong and that the other person may have a good point.

Feeling a bit skeptical? Test your predictions about adopting healthy anger and behaving in an assertive rather than an aggressive manner. You can use the blank behavioral experiment sheet in Chapter 5. (Chapter 5 has more help on conducting behavioral experiments.)

BODY BENEFITS FOR BRIDLING YOUR ANGER

Being angry, especially feeling frequently hostile toward other people and the world, is bad for you. Scientific research shows an association between hostility and raised blood pressure, which can lead to heart problems. Take the pressure off your mind, your interactions with other people, and your heart by controlling — rather than being controlled by — your anger.

Chapter **18**

Strengthening Your Social Confidence

D o you often find yourself worrying about social interactions? Do you frequently avoid social gatherings because you're scared of being judged or embarrassed? If so, you're not alone! Social anxiety (also commonly called social phobia) is incredibly common, and the good news is that CBT can help you conquer those fears. As with so many common emotional problems, once you understand better how the problem works, the solution will become much clearer.

Understanding Social Anxiety

Social anxiety is more than just shyness. It's an intense and persistent fear of social situations that significantly affects daily life. Common features include:

>> Excessive fear of social events, such as going to a party, having a conversation, and meeting unfamiliar people

>> Anxiety about being observed, such as eating or drinking in a group or public situation

>> Anxiety about performing in front of other people, including giving a presentation or making a speech

>> Fear of being negatively judged by the way you act or what you say

>> Fear of being humiliated or embarrassed

>> Feeling excessively self-conscious

>> Physical signs like blushing, sweating, and trembling

>> Avoiding social interactions or enduring them with significant distress

>> Using safety-seeking behaviors within social situations

>> Planning and mentally reviewing your social interactions

Common social confidence–sapping cognitions

As we've seen throughout this book, your feelings affect your thoughts. Cast your mind back to a good example of feeling anxious in a social or performance situation and ask yourself, "What was going through my mind?" There's a good chance that your thoughts bear some resemblance to these examples:

>> I might shake (or turn red or look sweaty), and people will think I'm weird for seeming nervous.

>> I'll say something stupid or inappropriate. People will think I'm an idiot, and I'll be horribly embarrassed.

>> Everybody is looking at me and noticing (and judging me for) any sign of anxiety.

>> I'm just bound to say the wrong thing sooner or later.

>> I have nothing interesting to say; I must seem desperately boring.

>> If I'm not confident, I can't possibly be good company.

>> The fact that I'm anxious in front of a crowd means I'm an impostor and people will see it.

>> I'm fundamentally just different from most other people and unlikable.

>> Other people will always find something not to like about me. It's just a matter of time.

>> Being relaxed and at ease in a social situation is something other people can do, but I can't.

You can use the ABC form from Chapter 4 as a starting point to help you tackle any anxiety-creating thoughts you've identified.

REMEMBER

Social anxiety is certainly an anxiety problem, but it's also a problem of shame and embarrassment. In fact, one way of understanding it is as a great fear of embarrassment. When we feel ashamed or embarrassed, we tend to imagine people will forever remember our faux pas. But over estimating this threat is part of anxiety. You can help cool down your fear by remembering that even if you do screw up, people will soon stop thinking about it.

Spotting social situation safety-seeking behaviors

Understanding your safety-seeking behaviors and then breaking free from them is the key to a lifetime of much improved social confidence. Safety-seeking behaviors can be fairly obvious (to you, at least), like avoiding certain kinds of social situations, or drinking alcohol to calm your nerves. Others can be more subtle, such as being too quick to agree with people or rehearsing conversations. Whatever the case may be for you, rest assured that you're in good company. Social and performance anxiety is incredibly common and can be significantly improved. Fear of being embarrassed truly is nothing to be embarrassed about.

Following are some examples of common safety-seeking behaviors in social anxiety:

>> Avoiding social or performance situations

>> Arriving late, leaving early

>> Staying on the edges of social situations, avoiding eye contact, or limiting social interactions

>> Taking on roles in social situations to limit social interaction

>> Seeking to please others to an excessive degree

>> Wearing "neutral clothes" to avoid attention

>> Choosing clothes that will cover up whether you're sweating

>> Mentally rehearsing sentences, talking fast

>> Trying to keep the focus of conversation on other people

>> Excessively monitoring your behavior to try to avoid negative judgment

>> Monitoring your body closely for any signs that you might appear anxious, such as blushing, feeling hot, sweating, shaking, or voice trembling

>> Using alcohol or drugs to cope or hide your anxiety

>> Using a phone or other objects to avoid direct interaction

>> Spending excessive time preparing for social or performance situations

>> Depending on another person to make introductions and small talk

Take a little time to understand your own patterns of avoidance and other safety-seeking behaviors. Review Chapter 8 on understanding how your solutions to your fear of negative evaluation have become the problem by increasing your self-consciousness and maintaining your anxiety.

Paying particular attention to your attention

One of the more important mechanisms that collapses social confidence is feeling self-conscious. Self-consciousness can make us feel awkward, interrupt our natural flow, and increase the likelihood that our minds will jump to the conclusion that other people are thinking negatively about us. Unsurprisingly, self-consciousness is driven by self-focused attention, which is a key reason to really, er, focus on it as you stand up to social anxiety.

Self-focused attention will also mean you're more likely to notice any physical anxiety responses. If you fear blushing, sweating, or trembling in social situations, it's easy to see why this can backfire in a big way. So again, while you're doing your detective work on what's keeping your social anxiety going, try to notice how much of your attention is on yourself in a social situation and how much is on the world around you. If it's more than 50 percent on yourself, you have an important target for change.

Again, look at Chapter 6 for a reminder on the role of attention and some key strategies for taking more control of it. We'll also look at this a little more deeply next.

REMEMBER

Social anxiety can significantly overlap with other problems, such as panic disorder and body dysmorphic disorder (BDD), so if you're concerned about this, consider seeking further advice from your doctor or a suitably qualified mental health professional.

Constructing Your Social Confidence

The following are some key principles for breaking free from social and performance anxiety (see Table 18-1 below). As with so many fears, the starting point is to counteract your patterns of avoidance and to drop your safety-seeking behaviors. It can be helpful to head to Chapter 8 to help work through them. Below is a table for you to use to start your plan.

Facing your feared social or performance situations without safety-seeking behaviors

TIP

After you've confronted your fear, rate the *actual* level of anxiety or discomfort you experienced. In the case of social or performance anxiety, it's particularly important to note whether you used any safety-seeking behaviors during your exposure session, so keep a note of those.

Side-stepping self-consciousness

Feeling self-conscious and awkward in a social or performance situation isn't only extremely unpleasant, it can make you perform more poorly, be less comfortable, and be less able to engage with people because your mind is overloaded. To help with this, practice training your attention in the ways we describe in Chapter 6.

When you're in a social situation or standing ready to give a talk, switch the focus of your attention. Interrogate the room. Try to tune in to the things you see, hear, feel, and smell to "hook" your attention externally. It takes a bit of practice, but it will hugely reduce your self-consciousness and improve your confidence. It's a great one for a behavioral experiment. See Chapter 5 for more on experiments.

TABLE 18-1 **Exposure to Feared/Avoided Social Situations**

Feared or Avoided Trigger	Anticipated Anxiety or Self-Consciousness 0–10	Actual Anxiety or Self-Consciousness 0–10

Give your attention a head start by focusing externally before you enter the situation. Even as you walk toward the bar or lecture theatre, pay attention to the ground beneath your feet, what you can see and hear around you. Doing so will help you hit the ground running with your attention in the right place.

Taking your thoughts and images with a pinch of salt

One of the features of social and performance anxiety is that not only do you generate anxiety-producing thoughts, you're also likely to generate an image of yourself within the situation. This is a key part of what Professor Adrian Wells calls "processing yourself as a social object."

It's important to take this with a pinch of salt because it's unlikely to be accurate if you're in an anxious state. You might see a trembling, red-faced wreck in your mind's eye, but outwardly, people will see something far less troubling. Your self-focused attention and safety behaviors will distort this image, so until you have those sorted, consider that your impression of how you feel you look is much worse than the reality.

Setting aside safety-seeking behaviors

Alongside facing your feared situations and refocusing your attention, it's essential to drop your safety behaviors. They maintain your anxiety, increase your self-focus, give you brain fog, and even interfere with your ability to converse naturally. Get that list, and work to eliminate them. Really consider, "If I were truly more comfortable and free from excessive anxiety in social or performance situations, how do I think I'd act differently?"

So face those fears, drop those safety-seeking behaviors, externalize the focus of your attention, and practice, practice, practice. Your more confident future-self will be forever grateful.

4

Looking Backward and Moving Forward

Chapter **19**

Taking a Fresh Look at Your Past

Your past experiences have affected how you think and function now. Sometimes you may endure bad experiences and be able to make some good things happen from them. At other times, you may be wounded by unpleasant events and carry that injury with you into your present and future.

This chapter encourages you to examine openly whether your past experiences have led you to develop core beliefs that may be causing your current emotional difficulties.

People are sometimes surprised to find out that CBT considers the past an important aspect of understanding one's problems. Unlike traditional Freudian psychoanalysis, which focuses intensively on childhood relationships and experiences, CBT specifically investigates past experiences to see how these early events may still be affecting people in their present lives.

Exploring How Your Past Can Influence Your Present

We don't know what your childhood and early adulthood were like, but many people share relatively common past experiences. The following examples highlight various aspects of past experiences that may resonate with your life history. Rather than focusing on the differences between these examples and your own experiences, use the examples to identify similar things that have happened in your own life.

>> Sybil grew up with parents who fought a lot. She learned to be quiet and to keep out of the way so that her parents' anger wouldn't be directed at her. She always tried to be a good girl and no trouble to anyone.

>> Rashid had critical parents. The demands Rashid's parents made of him to be a "high achiever" made it clear to him that he would get their love and approval only when he did well in sports and at school.

>> Beth had a violent father who would frequently beat her and other family members when he was in a bad mood. At other times, her father was very loving and funny. Beth could never predict accurately what mood her father would be in when he came through the front door.

>> Milo's relationships have never lasted for very long. Most of the women he's dated have been unfaithful to him. Milo's partners often complain that he's too insecure and suspicious of their friendships with members of the opposite sex.

>> Mahesh lost his oldest son and the family business in a fire five years ago. His wife has been depressed since the fire, and their marriage seems to be falling apart. Recently, his teenage daughter has been in trouble with the police. No one seems to offer Mahesh support. He feels dogged by bad luck.

Many other different kinds of difficult experiences can contribute to the development of negative core beliefs:

>> Death of loved ones

>> Growing up with neglectful, critical, or abusive parents or siblings

>> Divorce

>> Being bullied at school or via social media

>> Experiences of racism and discrimination

>> Having to seek asylum in a foreign country

>> Being abandoned by a parent or significant other

>> Undergoing a trauma, such as rape, life-threatening illness, accidents, or witnessing violent attacks on other people

These are just some examples of the types of events that can have a profound effect on mental health generally. Negative events that contribute to the way you think about yourself, other people, and the world often occur in childhood or early adult life. However, events occurring at any stage of your life can have a significant impact on the way you think about the world.

Understanding Core Beliefs

REMEMBER

Your *core beliefs* are ideas or philosophies that you hold strongly and deeply. You usually develop these ideas in childhood or early in adult life. Core beliefs aren't always negative. Good experiences of life and of other people generally lead to the development of healthy ideas about yourself, other people, and the world. In this chapter we deal with negative core beliefs because these are the types of beliefs that cause people's emotional problems.

Sometimes the negative core beliefs that are formed during childhood are reinforced by later experiences, which seem to confirm their validity.

For example, one of Beth's core beliefs is "I'm bad." She developed this belief to make sense of her father beating her for no real or obvious reason. Later, Beth had a few experiences of being punished unreasonably by teachers at school, which reinforced her belief in her "badness."

Core beliefs are characteristically global and absolute, like Beth's "I'm bad" one. People hold core beliefs to be 100 percent true under all conditions. You often form your core beliefs when you're a child to help you make sense of your childhood experiences; consequently, you may never evaluate whether your core beliefs are the best way to make sense of your adult experiences. As an adult, you may continue to act, think, and feel as though the core beliefs of your childhood are still 100 percent true.

Your core beliefs are called *core* because they're your deeply held ideas, and they're at the center of your belief system. Core beliefs give rise to rules, demands, or assumptions, which in turn produce *automatic thoughts*, which are thoughts that just pop into your head when you're confronted with a situation. You can think of these three layers of beliefs as a dartboard, with core beliefs as the bull's-eye. Figure 19-1 shows the interrelationship between the three layers and the assumptions and automatic thoughts that surround Beth's core belief that she's bad.

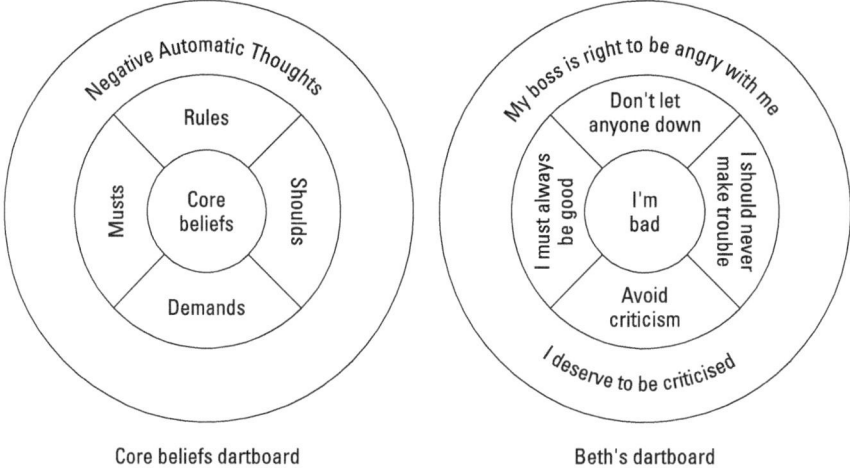

FIGURE 19-1:
The core beliefs dartboard and Beth's dartboard, showing the three layers of beliefs.

Core beliefs dartboard

Beth's dartboard

© *John Wiley & Sons, Inc.*

TIP

Another way of describing a core belief is as a lens or filter, through which you interpret all the information you receive from other people and the world around you.

Introducing the three camps of core beliefs

Core beliefs fall into three main camps: beliefs about yourself, beliefs about others, and beliefs about the world.

Beliefs about yourself

Unhelpful negative core beliefs about yourself often have their roots in damaging early experiences. Being bullied or ostracized at school, or experiencing neglect, abuse, or harsh criticism from caregivers, teachers, or siblings, can inform the way in which you understand yourself.

For example, Beth's experiences of physical abuse led her to form the core belief "I'm bad."

Beliefs about other people

Negative core beliefs about others often develop because of traumatic incidents involving other people. A traumatic incident can mean personal harm inflicted on you by another person or witnessing harm being done to others. Negative core beliefs can also develop from repeated negative experiences with other people, such as teachers and parents.

For example, because Beth's father was violent and abusive toward her but also could be funny when he wanted to be, she developed a core belief that "people are dangerous and unpredictable."

Beliefs about the world

People who've experienced trauma, lived with severe deprivation, or survived in harmful, insecure, unpredictable environments are prone to forming negative core beliefs about life and the world.

Beth holds a core belief — "the world is full of bad things" — which she developed because of her early home situation and events at school later on.

Sometimes core beliefs from all three camps are taught to you explicitly as a child. Your parents or caregivers may have given you *their* core beliefs. For example, you may have been taught that "life's cruel and unfair," "people are selfish," or "you'll never amount to anything; our kind never do" before you had any experiences that led you to form such a belief yourself. Sometimes people will tell us unhelpful things with the best of intentions — trying to spare us pain and disappointment. Sometimes it's just intentional cruelty. The point is that now's a time to look at what you've come to believe and consider whether it's 100 percent true 100 percent of the time.

Seeing how your core beliefs interact

Identifying core beliefs about yourself can help you understand why you keep having the same problems. However, if you can also get to know your fundamental beliefs about other people and the world, you can build a fuller picture of why some situations distress you. For example, Beth may find being yelled at by her boss depressing because it fits with her core belief "I'm bad," but the experience also seems to confirm her belief that people are unpredictable and aggressive.

Like many people, you may hold core beliefs that you're unlovable, unworthy, or inadequate; these beliefs are about your basic worth, goodness, or value. Or perhaps you hold beliefs about your capability to look after yourself or to cope with adversity; these beliefs are about how helpless or powerful you are in relation to other people and the world.

Mahesh, for example, may believe "I'm helpless" because he's experienced tragedy and a lot of bad luck. He may also hold beliefs that "the world is against me" and "other people are uncaring." Looking at these three beliefs together, you can see why Mahesh feels depressed.

Detecting Your Core Beliefs

Because core beliefs are held deeply, you may not think of them or "hear" them as clear statements in your head. You're probably much more aware of your negative automatic thoughts or your rules than you are of your core beliefs. (See Figure 19-1 earlier in the chapter.)

The following sections show you some methods you can use to really get to the root of your belief system.

Following a downward arrow

One technique to help you pinpoint your problematic core beliefs is the *downward arrow* method, which involves identifying a situation that causes you to have an unhealthy negative emotion, such as depression or guilt. (For more on healthy and unhealthy negative emotions, check out Chapter 7.)

After you've identified a situation that brings up negative emotions, ask yourself what the situation means or says about you. Your first answer is probably your *negative automatic thought* (NAT). Keep asking yourself what your previous answer means or says about you until you reach a global, absolute statement, such as "other people are dangerous" or "I'm bad" in Beth's case.

For example, when Rashid uses the downward arrow method to work out why he feels so ashamed about failing a university entrance exam, he has this negative automatic thought:

> NAT: "I won't get into any of the good universities."
>
> *What does this NAT mean about me?*
>
> "I've disappointed my parents again."
>
> *What does disappointing my parents mean about me?*
>
> "When I try to make my parents proud, I fail."
>
> *What does failing mean about me?*
>
> "I'm a failure." (Rashid's core belief)

TIP

You can use the same downward arrow technique to get to your core beliefs about other people and the world. Just keep asking yourself what your NAT means about others or the world. Ultimately, you can end up with a conclusive statement that's your core belief. The following is an example of how to do this, using the situation of being made redundant:

> NAT: "None of my friends has been made redundant; why has this happened to me?"
>
> *What does this mean about the world?*
>
> "Hard work and dedication don't pay off."
>
> *What does this mean about the world?*
>
> "The world is unfair and cruel." (Core belief)

Picking up clues from your dreaming and screaming

Imagine your worst nightmare. What dream scenarios wake you up screaming? Somewhere in these terrifying scenarios may be one or more of your core beliefs. Some examples of core beliefs that can show themselves in dreams and nightmares include the following:

» Trembling and forgetting your words while speaking publicly

» Being rejected by your partner for another person

» Being criticized in front of work colleagues

» Getting lost in a foreign country

» Hurting someone's feelings

» Doing something thoughtless and being confronted about it

» Letting down someone who's important in your life

» Being controlled by another person

» Being at someone else's mercy

REMEMBER

Look for the similarities between your nightmare scenarios and situations that upset you in real life. Ask yourself what a dreaded dream situation may mean about yourself, about other people, or about the world. Keep considering what each of your answers means about yourself, others, or the world until you reach a core belief.

Tracking themes

Another way of journeying to the core of your core beliefs is looking for themes in your automatic thoughts. A good way of doing this is by reviewing your completed ABC forms, which we describe in Chapter 4.

For example, if you find that you often have thoughts related to failure, getting things wrong, or being less capable than other people, you may have a core belief of "I'm inadequate" or "I'm incompetent."

Filling in the blanks

Another method of eliciting your core beliefs is simply filling in the blanks. Take a piece of paper, write the following, and fill in the blanks:

I am _____

Other people are _____

The world is _____

This method requires you to take almost a wild guess about what your core beliefs are. Ultimately, you're in a better position than anyone else to take a guess, so the exercise is worth a shot.

TIP

You can review written work that you've done, which is a good technique for discovering your core beliefs. Going over what you've recorded again enables you to refine, tweak, or alter your beliefs. Be sure to use language that represents how you truly speak to yourself. Core beliefs are idiosyncratic. However you choose to articulate them is entirely up to you. The same is true of the healthy alternative beliefs you develop. (See the "Developing Alternatives to Your Core Beliefs" section later in this chapter.)

Understanding the Impact of Core Beliefs

Core beliefs are your fundamental and enduring ways of perceiving and making sense of yourself, the world, and other people. Your core beliefs have been around since early in your life. They're typically so ingrained and unconscious that you're probably unaware of their impact on your emotions and behaviors.

Spotting when you're acting according to old rules and beliefs

People tend to behave according to the beliefs they hold about themselves, others, and the world. To evaluate whether your core beliefs are unhealthy, you need to pay attention to your corresponding behaviors. Unhealthy core beliefs typically lead to problematic behaviors.

For example, Milo believes that he's unlovable and that other people can't be trusted. Therefore, he tends to be passive with his girlfriends, to seek reassurance that they're not about to leave him, and to become suspicious and jealous of their interactions with other men. Often, Milo's girlfriends get fed up with his jealousy and insecurity and end the relationship.

Because Milo operates according to his core belief about being unlovable, he behaves in ways that tend to drive his partners away from him. Milo doesn't yet see that his core belief, and corresponding insecurity, is what causes problems in his relationships. Instead, he views each time a partner leaves him for someone else as further evidence that his core belief of "I'm unlovable" is true.

Sybil believes that she mustn't draw attention to herself because one of her core beliefs is "other people are aggressive." Therefore, she's quiet in social situations and reluctant to assert herself. Her avoidant, self-effacing behavior means that she doesn't often get what she wants, which feeds her core belief of "I'm unimportant."

Sybil acts in accordance with her core belief that other people are aggressive and likely to turn on her and, subsequently, deprives herself of the opportunity to see that this isn't always going to happen. If Sybil and Milo identify their negative core beliefs, they can begin to develop healthier new beliefs and behaviors that can yield better results. We look more closely at how to develop new, more positive core beliefs later in this chapter.

Understanding that unhealthy core beliefs make you prejudiced

When you begin to examine your core beliefs, it may seem to you that everything in your life is conspiring to make your unhealthy core belief ring true. More than likely, your core belief is leading you to take a prejudiced view of all your experiences. Unhealthy beliefs, such as "I'm unlovable" and "other people are dangerous," distort the way in which you process information. Negative information that supports your unhealthy belief is let in. Positive information that contradicts the negative stuff is either rejected or twisted to mean something negative in keeping with your unhealthy belief.

The prejudice model in Figure 19-2 shows you how your unhealthy core beliefs can reject positive events that may contradict them. At the same time, your core beliefs can collect negative events that may support their validity. Your unhealthy core beliefs can also lead you to distort positive events into negative ones so that they continue to make your beliefs seem true.

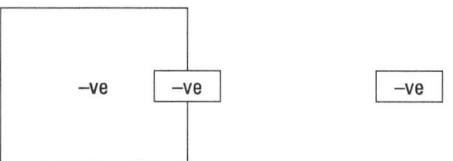

Negative information fits in with negative belief

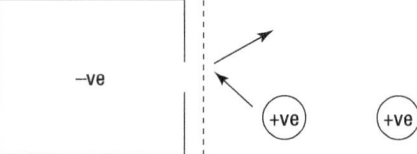

Positive information ignored or dismissed

© John Wiley & Sons, Inc.

FIGURE 19-2: The prejudice model illustrates how you sometimes distort positive information to fit in with your negative core beliefs.

Positive information distorted to fit in with negative belief

For example, here's how Beth's core belief "I'm bad" causes her to prejudice her experiences:

>> **Negative experience:** Beth's boss is angry about a missed deadline, affirming her belief that "I'm bad."

>> **Positive experience:** Beth's boss is happy about the quality of her report, which Beth distorts as "he's happy about this report only because all my other work is such rubbish," further affirming her belief that "I'm bad."

Beth also ignores smaller *positive* events that don't support her belief that she's bad, such as these:

» People seem to like her at work.

» Coworkers tell her that she's conscientious at work.

» Her friends text her and invite her out.

However, Beth is quick to take notice of smaller *negative* events that seem to match her belief that she's bad:

» Someone pushes her rudely on a busy train.

» Her boyfriend shouts at her during an argument.

» A work colleague doesn't smile at her when she enters the office.

Beth's core belief of "I'm bad" acts as a filter through which all her experiences are interpreted. It basically stops her from reevaluating herself as anything other than bad; it makes her prejudiced against herself. This is why identifying negative core beliefs and targeting them for change is so important.

Formulating Your Beliefs

When you've identified your core beliefs using the techniques outlined in the previous sections, you can use the form in Figure 19-3 to formulate your beliefs and rules. Filling out this form gives you an "at a glance" reference of what your negative core beliefs are and how they lead you to act in unhelpful ways. The form is a handy reminder of the beliefs you need to target for change and why.

Follow these steps to fill out the form:

1. **Relevant Early/Past Experiences: In this box, write down any significant past events that you think may have contributed to the development of your specific negative core beliefs.**

   For example, Beth records

   • Father was physically abusive and had unpredictable mood swings.

   • Father told me that I was bad.

   • I received severe and unreasonable punishment from teachers.

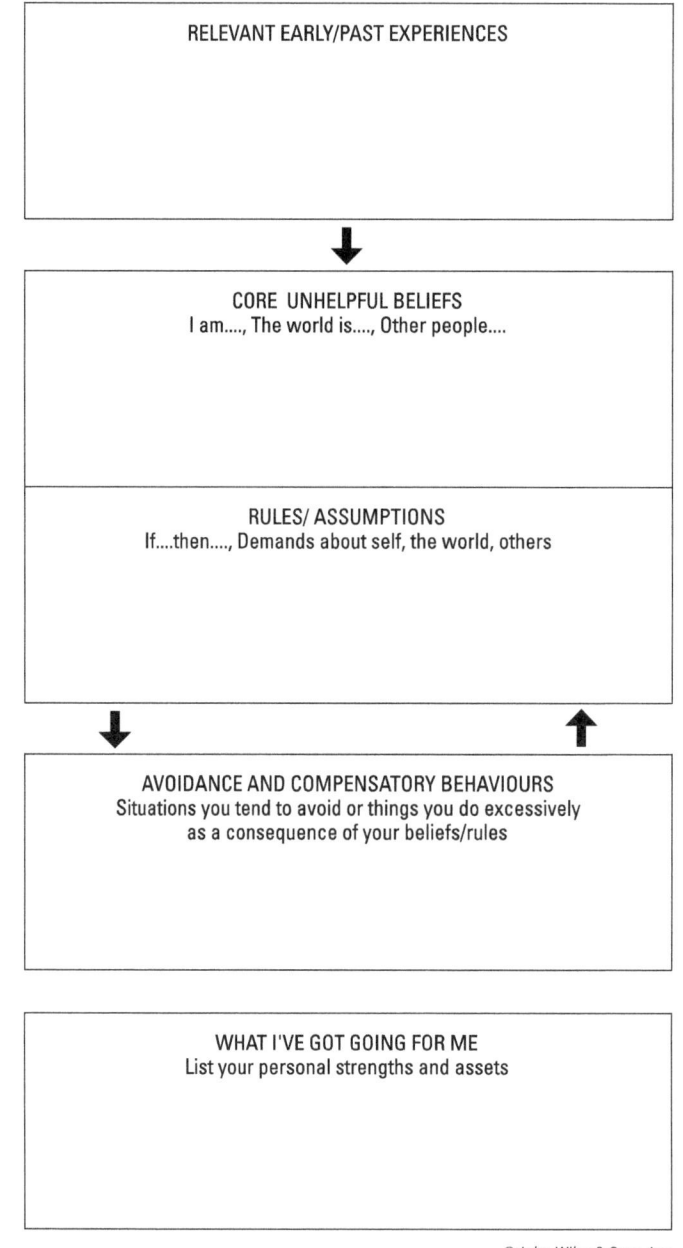

FORMULATION OF MY BELIEFS AND RULES

RELEVANT EARLY/PAST EXPERIENCES

CORE UNHELPFUL BELIEFS
I am...., The world is...., Other people....

RULES/ ASSUMPTIONS
If....then...., Demands about self, the world, others

AVOIDANCE AND COMPENSATORY BEHAVIOURS
Situations you tend to avoid or things you do excessively
as a consequence of your beliefs/rules

WHAT I'VE GOT GOING FOR ME
List your personal strengths and assets

FIGURE 19-3:
Formulating your
beliefs with the
help of this form.

© John Wiley & Sons, Inc.

2. **Core "Unconditional" Unhelpful Beliefs: Write your identified core beliefs about yourself, other people, and the world in this box.**

Beth records her beliefs like this:

- I am bad.
- Other people are unpredictable and dangerous.
- The world is full of bad things.

The word *unconditional* is used on this form to remind you that core beliefs are those beliefs that you hold to be 100 percent true, 100 percent of the time, and under any conditions.

3. **Rules/Assumptions: In this box write down the rules or demands you place on yourself, other people, and the world *because of* your core negative beliefs.**

Beth writes the following:

- I must be "good" at all times (demand on self).
- *If* I am criticized *then* it means that I'm a bad person (conditional rule).
- Other people must not find fault with me or think badly of me (demand on others).
- The world must not conspire to remind me of how bad I am by throwing negative experiences my way (demand on the world).

4. **Avoidance and Compensatory Behaviors: Use this box to record how you try to avoid triggering your negative core beliefs, or unhelpful things you do to try to cope with your negative core beliefs when they're triggered.**

Beth records

- Being a perfectionist at work to avoid any criticism
- Avoiding confrontation and thereby not asserting myself at work or with friends
- Over-apologizing when I'm criticized or make a small mistake
- Always assuming that other people's opinions are "right" and that my own opinions are "wrong"
- Being timid in social situations to avoid being noticed
- Not trusting others and assuming that they're ultimately going to hurt me somehow

5. **What I've got going for me: Write down positive things about yourself that fly in the face of your negative core beliefs.**

Beth writes

- My work colleagues seem to like me.

- I'm very conscientious at work. My boss and colleagues have commented on it.

- I have some good friends who are trustworthy.

- There have been some good things that have happened to me, such as finishing college and getting a good job.

- I'm generally hardworking and honest.

- I care about other people's feelings and opinions.

Information you write down in this box is important because it can help you develop more balanced and helpful alternative core beliefs. (We explain more about how to construct healthy core beliefs in the following sections.)

Limiting the Damage: Being Aware of Core Beliefs

To reduce the negative impact of your unhelpful core beliefs, try to get better at spotting the beliefs being activated. Step back and consider a more unbiased explanation for events rather than getting swept along by the beliefs.

TIP

One way of improving your awareness of your core beliefs is to develop a *core belief flashcard.* This written-out statement includes the following:

>> What your core belief is

>> How your core belief affects the way you interpret events

>> How you tend to act when the core belief is triggered

>> What a more unbiased interpretation of events is likely to be

>> What alternative behavior may be more productive

For example, Sybil wrote the following core belief flashcard:

> When my core belief of "I'm unimportant" is triggered, I'm probably taking something too personally or concluding that I'm being ignored, which makes me want to withdraw. Instead, I can remember that most people don't mean to ignore me and I'm just as important as others. Then I can stay engaged in the social situation.

Carry your flashcard around with you and review it often — even several times a day. Use your flashcard when you notice that your core belief has *been* triggered or just before you enter a situation where you know that your old core belief is *likely* to be triggered.

Developing Alternatives to Your Core Beliefs

When you've put your finger on your core beliefs and identified those that are negative and unhealthy, you're able to develop healthier alternative beliefs.

Your new core belief doesn't need to be the extreme opposite of your old belief. Changing an extreme belief such as "I'm unlovable" to "I'm lovable" may be too difficult when you're just starting out. Instead, give yourself some compassion and realize that simply by beginning to understand that an unhealthy core belief is not 100 percent true all the time is enough. Here are some examples:

>> Beth's alternative to her unhealthy belief "I'm bad" is "there are good things about me."

>> Rashid replaces his unhealthy belief "I'm a failure" with "I succeed at some things."

>> Mahesh chooses the alternative "good things do happen in the world" to replace his old belief "the world's against me."

>> Sybil replaces her belief "other people are aggressive" with the healthier belief "many people can be kind."

>> Milo substitutes his old core belief "I'm unlovable" with the more accurate belief "some people do like me, I am lovable at least to some degree."

Generating alternatives for your unhealthy and absolute core beliefs isn't about positive thinking or platitudes, but it is about generating less absolute, more accurate, more realistic opinions about yourself, other people, and the world around you.

Revisiting history

Many people can look back over their lives and get a fairly clear picture of where their core beliefs have come from. Sometimes, though, the source of core beliefs isn't so clear.

Although most core beliefs arise from your early experiences, you can still form deep, entrenched ideas about yourself, life, and other people when you're older. For example, Mahesh develops his core beliefs about the world being against him following a string of bad luck and tragic events during his adult years.

Revisit your history with a view to coming up with some reasons behind the ways that you think and behave in the present. Be compassionate with yourself, but recognize that you're the only one who can retrain your brain into updated and healthier ways of understanding your experiences.

Replacing old meanings with new ones

You gave meaning to the experiences that you had earlier in life. As an adult, you're in the fortunate position of being able to reassess those meanings of certain events and to assign more sophisticated meanings where appropriate.

For example, Beth forms the belief "I'm bad" based on the information she had when her father was abusing her. She was young and worked on various assumptions, including the following:

>> Daddy tells me that I've been bad, and this must be true.

>> You get punished when you're bad.

>> I must've done something bad to deserve this treatment.

Now that she's no longer a child and recognizes that she has this core belief, Beth can choose to look at her father's abuse and assign different meanings to his treatment of her:

>> My father had an anger problem that had nothing to do with me.

>> No child should be punished so severely, no matter how disobedient they've been.

>> My father was wrong to beat me, and I didn't deserve to be beaten.

>> My father did a bad thing by beating me and his bad behavior doesn't mean that I am bad.

Use the three-column old meaning/new meaning worksheet in Appendix B to review past events that contributed to the development of your core beliefs and reinterpret them now as an older, wiser person.

The sheet has three headings. Fill them in as follows:

1. **In the first column, "Event," record what actually happened.**

2. **Under "Old Meaning" in the second column, record what you believe the event means about you.**

   This is your unhealthy core belief.

3. **Under "New Meaning" in the third column, record a healthier and more accurate meaning for the event.**

   This is the new belief that you want to strengthen.

Table 19-1 shows an example of Beth's worksheet.

TABLE 19-1   ## Beth's Old Meaning–New Meaning Worksheet

Event	Old Meaning	New Meaning
My dad yelling, telling me I was bad when I was little.	I must be bad for him to say this so often.	I was much too young and afraid to be "bad." My father's anger was the problem.

Incorporating new beliefs into your life

Constructing newer, healthier, more accurate core beliefs is one thing, but beginning to live by them is another. Before your new beliefs are really stuck in your head and heart, you need to act *as if* they're already there. For Beth, this may mean forcing herself to face up to criticism from her boss and making appropriate adjustments to her work without berating herself. In short, she needs to act *as if* she truly believes that there are good things about herself, even in the face of negative feedback. She needs to operate under the assumption that her boss's anger is a reasonable (or possibly an unreasonable) response to an aspect of her work, rather than proof of her intrinsic badness.

In Chapter 20, we suggest several techniques for strengthening new alternative beliefs.

Starting from scratch

We won't tell you that changing your core beliefs is easy because that simply isn't true. In fact, erasing your old belief systems is so difficult that we think the best way of dealing with them is to make alternative healthy beliefs stronger so that they can do battle with your unhealthy beliefs.

Think of your old beliefs as well-trodden paths through an overgrown field. You can walk quickly and easily down these paths, as they've been worn down from years of use. Developing new, alternative beliefs is like making new paths through the field. At first, the new paths are awkward and uncomfortable to walk on because you need to break down the undergrowth.

You may be tempted to walk along the old paths because they're easier and more well-known, but with practice, your new paths can become familiar and natural to walk along. Similarly, with regular practice, thinking and acting along the lines of your alternative beliefs can become stronger and more automatic, even when the going gets tough!

Thinking about what you'd teach a child

When you're challenging your negative core beliefs, try to think about what you'd tell a child. Act as your own parent by reinstructing yourself to endorse healthy ways of viewing others, yourself, and the world.

Ask yourself what types of belief you'd teach a child. Would you encourage the child to grab hold of the negative core beliefs that you may hold about yourself, or would you want them to think of themselves in a more positive and accepting way? Would you wish for the child to think of other people as evil, untrustworthy, dangerous, and more powerful than they are? Or would you rather the child had a more balanced view of people, such as variable but basically okay, generally trustworthy, and reliable? Would you want the child to believe that they can stand up for themselves?

Considering what you'd want a friend to believe

When challenging your core beliefs, think about having a friend like Mahesh, Beth, Rashid, Milo, or Sybil. What advice would you give them? Would you say "Yes, Rashid, you're a failure," "I agree, Mahesh — life's against you," "Beth, you're bad," and "Sybil, no one ever thought you were important anyway"?

SHAPING YOUR WORLD

When you start to adopt healthy core beliefs, it can feel as if you're going against the grain because, in fact, that's what you're trying to do. Your old, negative core beliefs are familiar, deeply entrenched, and "feel" like they must be true. New, healthy beliefs can feel false and unnatural at first. Remind yourself that just because you've believed something for a long time doesn't make it true. People believed the earth was flat for years, but that old belief doesn't change the fact that the world is round.

Some things are true, regardless of whether you believe them. Likewise, other things will never be true, no matter how fervently you believe them.

Or would you be quietly horrified to spout these unhealthy and damaging beliefs? We assume the latter.

If you wouldn't want your dear friends to believe such things, why believe them yourself? Talk to yourself like you would to your best friend when your negative core beliefs are activated.

Chapter **20**

Moving New Beliefs from Your Head to Your Heart

After you've identified your unhelpful patterns of thinking and developed more helpful attitudes, you need to reinforce your new thoughts and beliefs. The process of reinforcing new beliefs is like trying to give up a bad habit and develop a good one in its place. You need to work at making your new, healthy ways of thinking second nature at the same time as eroding your old ways of thinking. This chapter describes some simple exercises to help you develop and nurture your new beliefs.

Fundamentally, integrating your new beliefs with your daily mindset, emotions, and actions is *the* critical process in CBT. A parrot can repeat rational philosophies, but it doesn't understand or believe what it's saying. The real work in CBT is turning intellectual understanding into something you know in your gut to be true.

Defining the Beliefs You Want to Strengthen

Many people who work at changing their attitudes and beliefs complain: "I know what I *should* think, but I don't believe it!" When you begin to adopt a new way of thinking, you may *know* that something makes sense, but you may not *feel* that the new belief is true.

When you're in a state of *cognitive dissonance,* you know that your old way of thinking isn't 100 percent right, but you aren't yet convinced of the alternative. Being in a state of cognitive dissonance can be uncomfortable because things don't feel quite right. However, this feeling is a good sign that things are changing.

In CBT, we often call this disconnection between understanding and truly believing the *head-to-heart problem.* Basically, you know that an argument is true in your head, but you don't feel it in your heart. For example, if you've spent many years believing that you're less worthy than others or that you need the approval of others to approve of yourself, you may have great difficulty *internalizing* (believing in your gut and heart) an alternative belief. You may find the idea that you have as much basic human worth as the next person, or that approval from others is a bonus but not a necessity, difficult to buy.

Your alternative beliefs are likely to be about three key areas:

>> Yourself

>> Other people

>> The world

Alternative beliefs may take the following formats:

>> A *flexible preference* instead of a rigid demand or rule, such as "I'd very much prefer to be loved by my parents, but sadly there's no reason they absolutely *have* to love me. Their degree of love is by no means a measure of how loveable I really am."

>> An *alternative assumption,* which is basically an if/then statement, such as "*If* I don't get an A on my test, *then* that proves I'm fallible like everyone else, not that I'm a failure. I can still move on in my academic career."

>> A *global belief,* which expresses a positive healthy general truth, such as "I'm basically okay" rather than "I'm worthless," or "The world's a place with some safe and some dangerous parts" instead of "The world's a dangerous place."

When you do experience the head-to-heart problem, we recommend acting *as if* you really do hold the new belief to be true. We explain how to do this in the following section.

REMEMBER

One of your main aims in CBT, after you've developed a more helpful alternative belief, is to increase how strongly you endorse your new belief or raise your *strength of conviction* (SOC). You can rate how much you believe in an alternative healthy philosophy on a 0–100 percentage scale, 0 representing a total lack of conviction and 100 representing an absolute conviction.

Acting "As If" You Already Believe

You don't need to believe your new philosophy entirely to begin changing your behavior. Starting out, it's enough to know in your head that your new belief makes sense and then act according to your new belief or philosophy. If you consistently do the acting-as-if technique, which we explain here, your conviction in your new way of thinking is likely to grow over time. This version of "fake it 'til you make it" can be an incredibly powerful tool in strengthening your new, more helpful belief.

You can use the acting-as-if technique to consolidate any new way of thinking, in pretty much any situation. Ask yourself the following questions:

>> How would I behave if I truly considered my new belief to be true?

>> How would I overcome situational challenges to my new belief if I truly considered it to be true and helpful?

>> What sort of behavior would I expect to see in other people who truly endorse this new belief?

You can make a list of your answers to these questions and refer to it before, after, and even during an experience of using the acting-as-if technique. For example, if you're dealing with social anxiety and trying to come to grips with self-acceptance beliefs, use the acting-as-if techniques that follow, and ask yourself similar kinds of questions, such as these:

>> **Act consistently with the new belief:** If I truly believed that I was as worthy as anyone else, how would I behave in a social situation?

Be specific about how you'd enter a room, the conversation you may initiate, and what your body language would be like.

>> **Troubleshoot for challenges to your new belief:** If I truly believed that I was as worthy as anyone else, how would I react to any social hiccups?

Again, be specific about how you may handle lulls in conversation and moments of social awkwardness.

>> **Observe other people:** Does anyone else in the social situation seem to be acting as if they truly endorse the belief that I'm trying to adopt?

If so, note how the person acts and how they handle awkward silences and normal breaks in conversation. Imitate their behavior.

When you act in accordance with a new way of thinking or a specific belief, you reinforce the truth of that belief. The more you experience a belief *in action*, the more you can appreciate its beneficial effects on your emotions. In essence, you're rewiring your brain to think in a more helpful and realistic way. Give this technique a try, even if you think that it's wishful thinking or seems silly. Actions do speak louder than words. So if a new belief makes sense to you, follow it up with action.

Building a Portfolio of Arguments

When an old belief rears its ugly head, try to have on hand some strong arguments to support your new belief. Your old beliefs or thinking habits have probably been with you a long time, and they can be tough to shift. You can expect to argue with yourself about the truth and benefit of your new thinking several times before the new stuff will truly replace the old.

Your portfolio of arguments can consist of a collection of several arguments against your old way of thinking and several arguments in support of your new way of thinking. You can refer to your portfolio anytime that you feel conviction in your new belief is beginning to wane. Get yourself a small notebook or use your phone to record your portfolio of arguments. The following sections help to guide you toward developing sound rationales in support of helpful beliefs and in contradiction of unhelpful beliefs.

Generating arguments against an unhelpful belief

To successfully combat unhealthy beliefs, try the following exercise. At the top of a sheet of paper, write down an old, unhelpful belief you want to weaken. For example, you may write, "I have to get approval from significant others, such as my boss. Without approval, I'm worthless." Then consider the following questions to highlight the unhelpful nature of your belief:

>> **Is the belief untrue or inconsistent with reality?** Try to find evidence that your belief isn't factually accurate (or at least not 100 percent accurate for 100 percent of the time). For example, you don't *have* to get approval from your boss. The universe permits otherwise, and you can survive without such approval. Furthermore, you can't be defined as worthless on the strength of this experience because you're much too complex to be defined by one person's opinion.

REMEMBER

Considering why a certain belief is *understandable* can help you explain why you hold a particular belief to be true. For example, "It's understandable that I think I'm stupid because my father often told me I was when I was young, but that was really due to his impatience and his own difficult childhood. So it follows that I believe myself to be stupid because of my childhood experiences and not because there's any real truth in the idea that I am. Therefore, the belief that I'm stupid is consistent with my upbringing but inconsistent with reality."

>> **Is the belief rigid?** Consider whether your belief is flexible enough to allow you to adapt to reality. For example, the idea that you *must* get approval or that you *need* approval to think well of yourself is overly rigid. It's entirely possible that you'll fail to get approval from significant others at some stage in your life. Unless you have a flexible belief about getting approval, you're destined to think badly of yourself whenever approval isn't forthcoming. Replace the word *must* with *prefer* in this instance, and turn your demand for approval into a flexible preference for approval.

>> **Is the belief extreme?** Consider whether your unhelpful belief is extreme. For example, equating being disregarded by one person with worthlessness is an extreme conclusion. It's rather like concluding that being late for one appointment means that you'll always be late for every appointment you have for the rest of your life. The conclusion that you draw from one or more experiences is far too extreme to accurately reflect reality.

>> **Is the belief illogical?** Consider whether your belief actually makes sense. You may want approval from your boss, but logically they don't *have* to approve of you. Not getting approval from someone significant doesn't logically lead to you being less worthy. Rather, not getting approval shows that you've failed to get approval on this occasion, from this specific person.

>> **Is the belief unhelpful?** Consider how your belief may or may not be helping you. For example, if you worry about whether your boss approves of you, you'll probably be anxious at work much of the time. You may feel depressed if your boss treats you with indifference or visibly disapproves of your work.

You're less likely to say no to unreasonable requests or to put your opinions forward. You may be less effective at work because you're so focused on making a good impression. You may even assume that your boss is disapproving of you when that isn't the case. So is believing that you absolutely must have your boss's approval helpful? Clearly not! Just because you only get a few "likes" on a recent post, does that mean everyone else hated it? Is believing you're only likable if you get a lot of online "likes" a good way to judge your worth? Or is it a stone-cold crazy idea?

TIP

Running through the preceding list of questions is an exercise that involves putting pen to paper, thumb to screen, or fingertips to keyboard. Try to pick out your unhelpful beliefs and to formulate helpful alternatives, and then generate as many watertight arguments against your old belief and in support of your new belief as you can. Try to fill up one side of a sheet of paper for each belief you target.

TIP

You can include in your portfolio evidence gathered from other CBT techniques you use to tackle your problems, such as ABC forms (Chapter 4) and behavioral experiments (Chapter 5). You can use any positive results observed from living according to new healthy beliefs as arguments to support the truth and benefits of these new beliefs.

Generating arguments to support your helpful alternative belief

The guidelines for generating sound arguments to support alternative, more helpful ways of thinking about yourself, other people, and the world are similar to those suggested in the preceding section, "Generating arguments against an unhelpful belief."

On a sheet of paper, write down a helpful alternative belief that you want to use to replace a negative, unhealthy view you hold. For example, a helpful alternative belief regarding approval at work may be "I want approval from significant others, such as my boss, but I don't *need* it. If I don't get approval, I still have worth as a person."

Next, develop arguments to support your alternative belief. Ask yourself the following questions to ensure that your helpful alternative belief is strong and effective:

>> **Is the belief true and consistent with reality?** For example, you can really want approval and fail to get it sometimes. Just because you want something

very much doesn't mean you'll get it. Lots of people don't get approval from their bosses, but that doesn't mean they're lesser people.

>> **Is the belief flexible?** Consider whether your belief allows you to adapt to reality. For example, the idea that you *prefer* to get approval but that it isn't a dire necessity for either survival or self-esteem allows for the possibility of not getting approval from time to time. You don't have to form any extreme conclusions about your overall worth in the face of occasions of disapproval.

>> **Is the belief balanced?** Consider whether your helpful belief is balanced and non-extreme. For example, "Not being liked by my boss is unfortunate, but it's not proof of whether I'm worthwhile as a person." This balanced and flexible belief recognizes that disapproval from your boss is undesirable and may mean that you need to reassess your work performance. However, this recognition doesn't hurl you into depression based on the unbalanced belief that you're unworthy for failing to please your boss on this occasion.

>> **Is the belief logical and sensible?** Show how your alternative belief follows logically from the facts, or from your preferences. It follows logically that your boss's disapproval about one aspect of your work is undesirable and may mean that you need to work harder or differently. It doesn't follow logically that because of your boss's disapproval you're an overall bad or worthless person.

>> **Is the belief helpful?** When you accept that you want approval from your boss but that you don't *have* to get it, you can be less anxious about the possibility of incurring your boss's disapproval or failing to make a particular impression. You also stand a better chance of making a good impression at work when you prefer, but are not desperate for, approval. You can be more focused on the job that you're doing and less preoccupied by what your boss may be thinking about you. Plus, you can more accurately assess whether your boss's expectations are realistic and fair.

Here's another fun exercise to try. Imagine you're about to go into court to present to the jury arguments in defense of your new belief. Develop as many good arguments that support your new belief as you can. Most people find that listing lots of ways in which the new belief is helpful makes the most impact. Try to generate enough arguments to fill one side of a sheet of paper for each belief.

TIP

Review your rational portfolio regularly, not just when your unhealthy belief is triggered. Doing so helps you reaffirm your commitment to thinking in healthy ways.

Understanding That Practice Makes Imperfect

Despite your best efforts, you may continue to think in rigid and extreme ways and experience unhealthy emotions from time to time. Why? Well, oh yes, we say it again: You're only human.

Practicing your new, healthy ways of thinking and putting them to regular use minimizes your chances of relapse. However, you're never going to become a perfectly healthy thinker. Humans seem to have a tendency to develop thinking errors, and you need a high degree of diligence to resist unhelpful and unhealthy thinking.

TIP

Be wary of having a perfectionist attitude about your thinking. You're setting yourself up to fail if you expect that you can always be healthy in thought, emotion, and behavior. Give yourself permission to make mistakes with your new thinking, and use any setbacks as opportunities to discover more about your beliefs.

Dealing with your doubts and reservations

You must give full range to your skepticism when you're changing your beliefs. If you try to sweep your doubts under the rug, those doubts can re-emerge when you least expect it — usually when you're in a stressful situation. Consider Sylvester's experience:

> Sylvester, or Sly for short, believes that other people must like him and goes out of his way to put people at ease in social situations. Sly takes great care to never hurt anyone's feelings and puts pressure on himself to be a good host. Not surprisingly, Sly's often worn out by his efforts. Because Sly's work involves managing other staff, he also feels anxious much of the time. Sly worries about confrontation and what his staff members think of him when he corrects them.

> After having some CBT, Sly concludes that his beliefs need to change if he's ever going to overcome his anxiety and feelings of panic at work. Sly formulates a healthy alternative belief: "I want to be liked by others, but I don't always *have* to be liked. Being disliked is tolerable and doesn't mean I'm an unlikable person."

> Sly can see how this new belief makes good sense and can help him feel less anxious about confronting staff members or being not-so-super-entertaining in social situations. But deep inside, Sly feels stirrings of doubt. Still, Sly denies his reservations about the new belief and ignores niggling uncertainty. One day, when

Sly's confronting a staff member about persistent lateness, his underlying doubts rear up. Sly resorts to his old belief because he hasn't dealt with his doubts effectively. Sly ends up letting his worker off the hook and feeling angry with himself for not dealing with the matter properly.

Had Sly faced up to his misgivings about allowing himself to be disliked, he may have given himself a chance to resolve his feeling. Sly may then have been more prepared to deal with the stressful situation without resorting to his old belief and avoidant behavior.

Zigging and zagging through the zigzag technique

Use the zigzag technique to strengthen your belief in a new, healthy alternative belief or attitude. The zigzag technique involves playing devil's advocate with yourself. The more you argue the case in favor of a healthy belief and challenge your own attacks on it, the more deeply you can come to believe in it. Figure 20-1 shows a completed zigzag form based on Sly's example.

You can find a blank zigzag form in Appendix B. To go through the zigzag technique, do the following steps:

1. Write down in the top-left box of the zigzag form a belief that you want to strengthen.

On the form, rate how strongly you endorse this belief, from 0 to 100 percent conviction.

WARNING

Be sure that the belief is consistent with reality or true, logical, and helpful to you. See the "Generating arguments to support your helpful alternative belief" section earlier in this chapter for more on testing your healthy belief.

2. In the next box down, write your doubts, reservations, or challenges about the healthy belief.

Really let yourself attack the belief, using all the unhealthy arguments that come to mind.

3. In the next box, dispute your attack and redefend the healthy belief.

Focus on defending the healthy belief. Don't become sidetracked by any points raised in your attack from Step 2.

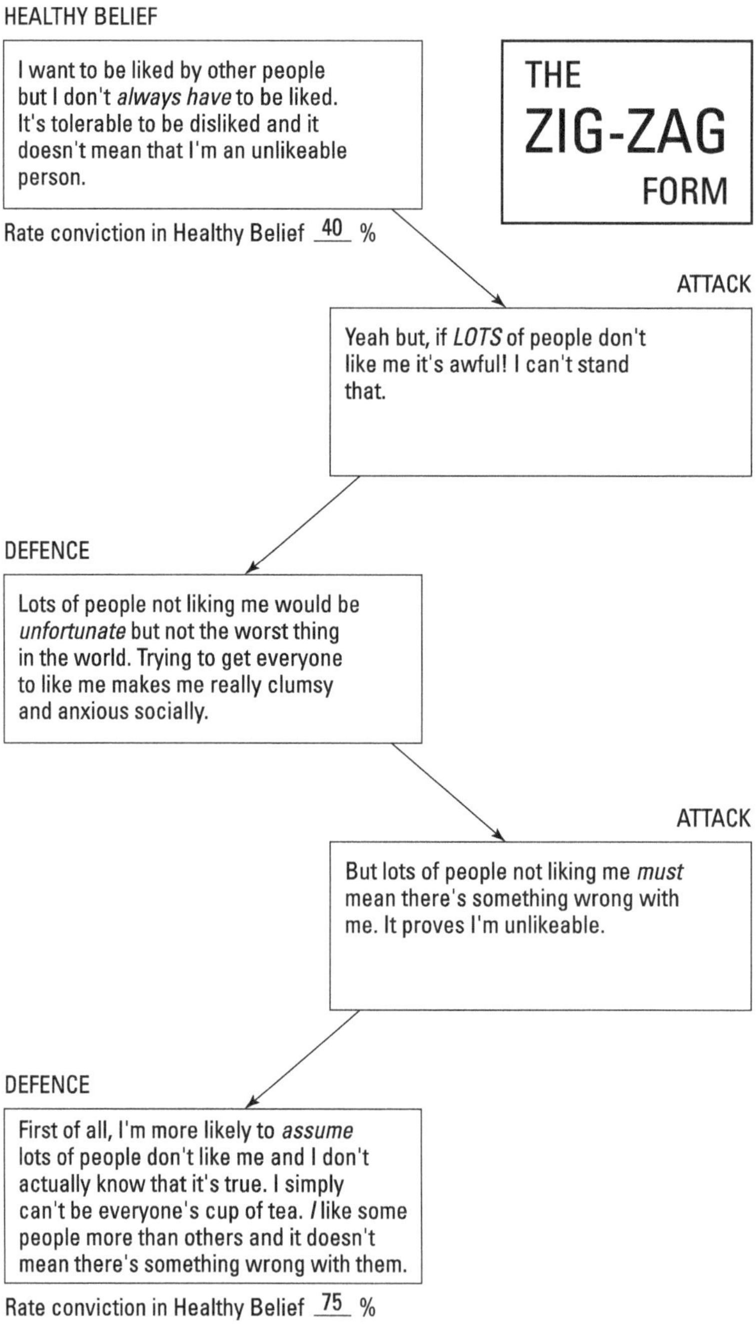

HEALTHY BELIEF

I want to be liked by other people but I don't *always have* to be liked. It's tolerable to be disliked and it doesn't mean that I'm an unlikeable person.

Rate conviction in Healthy Belief __40__ %

THE ZIG-ZAG FORM

ATTACK

Yeah but, if *LOTS* of people don't like me it's awful! I can't stand that.

DEFENCE

Lots of people not liking me would be *unfortunate* but not the worst thing in the world. Trying to get everyone to like me makes me really clumsy and anxious socially.

ATTACK

But lots of people not liking me *must* mean there's something wrong with me. It proves I'm unlikeable.

DEFENCE

First of all, I'm more likely to *assume* lots of people don't like me and I don't actually know that it's true. I simply can't be everyone's cup of tea. *I* like some people more than others and it doesn't mean there's something wrong with them.

Rate conviction in Healthy Belief __75__ %

FIGURE 20-1: Sly's completed zigzag form.

© *John Wiley & Sons, Inc.*

4. **Repeat Steps 2 and 3 until you exhaust all your attacks on the healthy belief.**

   Be sure to use up all your doubts and reservations about choosing to really go for the new, healthy alternative way of thinking. Use as many forms as you need, and be sure to stop on a defense of the belief you want to establish rather than on an attack.

5. **Rerate, from 0 to 100 percent, how strongly you endorse the healthy belief after going through all your doubts.**

TIP

If your conviction in the healthy belief hasn't increased or has increased only slightly, revisit the previous instructions on how to use the zigzag form. Or, if you have a CBT therapist, discuss the form with them and see whether they can spot where you zigged when you should have zagged.

Putting your new beliefs to the test

Doing pen-and-paper exercises is great. They really can help you move your new beliefs from your head to your heart.

However, the best way to make your new ways of thinking more automatic is to put them to the test. Putting them to the test means going into familiar situations where your old attitudes are typically triggered and acting according to your new way of thinking.

So our friend Sly from earlier in the chapter may choose to do the following to test his new beliefs:

>> Sly confronts his staff member about her lateness in a forthright manner. Sly bears the discomfort of upsetting her and remembers that being disliked by one worker doesn't prove that he's an unlikable person.

>> Sly throws a party and resists the urge to make himself busy entertaining everyone and playing the host with the most. Instead, he relaxes and makes conversation in an easy manner.

>> Sly works less hard in work and social situations at putting everyone at ease and trying to be super-likable mister nice guy.

TIP

If you're really serious about making your new beliefs stick, you can seek out situations in which to test them. On top of using your new beliefs and their knock-on new behaviors in everyday situations, try setting difficult tests for yourself. Sit down and think about it: If you were still operating under your old beliefs, what situations would really panic you? Go there. Doing so will "up the ante" regarding endorsing your new beliefs.

Coping with everyday situations, such as Sly's previous example, is useful, and it's often enough to move your new belief from your head to your heart. But if you really want to put your new beliefs under strain, with a view to making them even stronger, put yourself into out-of-the-ordinary situations. For example, try deliberately doing something ridiculous in public or being purposefully abrupt and aloof. See if you can remain resolute in your new belief such as "disapproval does not mean unworthiness" in the face of your most feared outcomes. We think you can! This is a tried and tested CBT tool for overcoming all sorts of problems, such as social anxiety. (Refer to Chapter 16 for more guidance on developing *self-acceptance* and Chapter 24 for more on devising *shame attacking* exercises.)

Here are some tests that Sly (or we could now call him "Braveheart") may set up for himself:

>> Go into shops and deliberately be impolite by not saying "thank you" and not smiling at the manager. This test requires Sly to bear the discomfort of possibly leaving the manager unhappy after making a poor impression.

>> Say good morning to staff without smiling and allow them to form the impression that he's "in a bad mood."

>> Mope about, deliberately trying to look moody and aloof in a social setting.

>> Make a complaint about faulty goods he's purchased from a local shop where the staff know him.

>> Bump into someone on the bus or train and fail to apologize.

You may think that Sly's setting himself up to be utterly friendless because of this wretched belief change lark. On the contrary. Sly has friends. He still has a reputation of being a generally kind and affable guy. What Sly doesn't have now is a debilitating belief that he has to please all the people all the time. Rather, Sly can come to truly believe that he can tolerate the discomfort of upsetting people occasionally and that being disliked by one or more people is part of being human. That's life. That's the way it goes sometimes. Sly can believe in his heart that he's a fallible human just like everyone else, that he's capable of being liked and disliked, but basically he's okay. And after he's learned that important lesson, Sly can go back to being a nice but not a "trying-too-hard-nice" guy.

Nurturing Your New Beliefs

As you continue to live with your alternative helpful beliefs, gather evidence that supports your new beliefs. Becoming more aware of evidence from yourself, other people, and the world around you that supports your new, more helpful way of thinking is one of the keys to strengthening your beliefs and keeping them strong.

TIP

A *positive data log* is a record of evidence you collect that shows the benefits of holding your new belief. The positive data log helps you overcome the biased, prejudiced way in which you keep unhelpful beliefs well-fed, by soaking up evidence that fits with them, and discounting or distorting evidence that doesn't fit. Using a positive data log boosts the available data that fits your new belief and helps you retrain yourself to take in the positive.

Your positive data log is simply a record of positive results arising from acting in accordance with a healthy new belief and evidence that contradicts your old, unhealthy belief. You can use any type of notebook or even your phone to record your evidence. Follow these steps:

1. **Write your new belief at the top of a page or note.**

2. **Record evidence that your new belief is helpful to you; include changes in your emotions and behavior.**

3. **Record positive reactions that you get from others when you act in accordance with new beliefs.**

4. **Record any experiences that contradict your old belief.**

   Be specific and include even the smallest details that encourage you to doubt your old way of thinking. For example, even a newspaper vendor making small talk when you buy your paper can be used as evidence against a belief that you're unlikable.

5. **Make sure that you record every bit of information in support of your new belief and in contradiction to your old belief.**

   Fill up the whole notebook or file if you can.

TIP

If you still have trouble believing that an old, unhelpful belief is true, start by collecting evidence daily that your old belief isn't 100 percent true, 100 percent of the time. Collecting this sort of evidence can help you steadily erode how true the belief seems.

In your positive data log, you can list the benefits of operating under your new belief, including all the ways in which your fears about doing so have been disproved.

For example, Sly might record the following observations:

>> His staff still seem to generally like being managed by him, even though he challenges them when needed.

>> Being less gregarious at parties doesn't stop others from having a good time or from engaging with him.

>> His anxiety and panic about the possibility of being disliked have reduced in response to his belief change.

Your positive data log can not only remind you of the good results you've reaped from changing your unhealthy beliefs to healthy ones but also help you be compassionate with yourself when you relapse to your unhealthy beliefs and corresponding behaviors. Use your positive data log to chart your progress so that when you *do* fall back you can assure yourself that your setback need to be only temporary. After all, practice makes imperfect.

TIP

Many people add to their positive data log for months or even years. Keeping the log provides them with a useful antidote to the natural tendency to be overly self-critical.

Be sure to refer to your positive data log often — even daily or several times each day — when you're bedding down new beliefs. Keep it in your desk, on your phone, in a notebook in your bag, or wherever you're most likely to be able to access it during the day. As a rule, you can't look at your positive data log too often!

Chapter **21**

Heading for a Healthier and Happier Life

The way that you think influences the way that you feel and behave. How you behave also influences the way you end up feeling and thinking . . . and 'round and 'round the cycle goes.

So, how you *live* from day to day affects your overall mood. In this chapter, we look at what makes a lifestyle *healthy*. Developing a healthy lifestyle can contribute enormously to keeping you in tip-top physical and psychological condition.

We use the term *healthy* to mean looking after your physical self, which includes exercise, adequate sleep, sex, nutritious food, and a pleasant living environment. Psychological health is about doing things that give you a sense of enjoyment and achievement, holding helpful and balanced attitudes toward life, and building satisfying relationships.

Being in tip-top psychological and emotional health also involves revisiting your values. Taking a thorough look at what's most important to you, and making time in your busy schedule to reflect your values through regular action, greatly contributes to an overall sense of well-being.

TIP

Make looking after yourself a priority rather than an afterthought. An ounce of prevention really is worth a pound of cure. Remember, you have more to offer to others when you keep yourself in good physical and psychological shape.

Planning to Prevent Relapse

Once you start to recover from your problems, your next step is to devise a plan to prevent a resurgence of symptoms to ensure that you don't suffer a relapse. A *relapse* means that you return to your unhealthy original state of mind and poor mood. An important part of your relapse-prevention plan is nurturing yourself and guarding against falling back into old, unhelpful lifestyle habits, such as working too late, eating unhealthily, drinking too much caffeine and alcohol, and isolating yourself. Chapter 23 deals with relapse prevention in depth. The following sections in this chapter provide pointers on how you can make your life fuller and how to take better care of yourself.

Filling in the Gaps

When you start to recover from certain types of emotional problems, such as depression, anxiety, and obsessions, you may find that you have a considerable amount of spare time available to you, which previously your symptoms occupied. Indeed, you may be astounded to find out just how much energy, attention, and time common psychological difficulties can consume.

Finding constructive and enjoyable things to do to fill in the gaps where your symptoms once were is important. Keeping yourself busy with pursuits that are meaningful to you (and reflect your core values and priorities) gives you a sense of well-being and leaves less opportunity for your symptoms to re-emerge.

Choosing absorbing activities

Activities that you used to enjoy may take a back seat while you wrestle with your problems. However, you can rediscover them and even try new activities. The following pointers can help you generate ideas about what activities and hobbies you can begin building into your life:

>> List things you used to do and would like to start doing again.

>> Make a separate list of new activities you'd like to try.

» Try to create a balance between activities that do and don't involve physical exercise.

» Include everyday activities like cooking, reading, DIY, and keeping up social contacts. It's easy to neglect these activities when you're overwhelmed by symptoms.

» Choose to focus on around five activities to revive or pursue, depending on how full your life is with work and family commitments.

In case you're still at a loss as to what you want to do, here are some ideas, but remember that this list is by no means exhaustive:

» Antiques	» Golf
» Art appreciation	» Interior decorating
» Astronomy	» Kickboxing
» Baking	» Languages
» Chess	» Painting
» Dance	» Pets
» Drama	» Quizzes
» Dressmaking	» Tennis
» Enameling	» Traveling
» Fishing	» Volunteering
» Football	» Wine tasting
» Gardening	» Writing

TIP

Pets are great companions. The right one can make an excellent companion and give you an unavoidable reason to get up in the morning. Rhena now has three new little dogs, three cats, and a small colony of giant rabbits. But pets also require considerable work and commitment. Before you decide to get a pet, research the best pet for your living environment, work routine, and financial situation. Otherwise, you may find yourself lumbered with an animal that's far more maintenance than you initially expected.

TIP

Don't just think about it. Decide *when* you're going to begin doing your chosen activities. If you don't give yourself a concrete start date, forgetting about things or putting them off can be all too easy.

Matchmaking your pursuits

You know yourself better than anyone else, so you're the best person to judge which hobbies can bring you the most satisfaction. Try to match your recreational pursuits to your character. If you know that you love details, you may enjoy needlework or making jewelry. High-energy sports may appeal to you if you've always been good at physical activities and like adrenalin rushes. Conversely, if you've never been very musical, taking up an instrument may not be the best choice for you.

TIP

We recommend that you stretch yourself by trying things you haven't done before. Who knows — you may end up really liking the new activities. However, if you choose pursuits that are too far removed from your fundamental personality or natural abilities, you might lose heart and abandon them.

Putting personal pampering into practice

Oh, the joys of a good massage, a hot foamy bath, or a trip to the opera. (Okay, we understand that not everyone feels the same about opera.) You can't overcome your problems without a significant degree of personal effort. Congratulate yourself for your hard work, and treat yourself to a few nice things.

REMEMBER

Take care of yourself on a day-to-day basis, and look out for when you deserve special treats. Friday nights are good times to indulge in something pleasurable after a long week at work.

Your treats don't have to be expensive. Arranging cut flowers in a vase, making your living space smell nice, playing pleasant music, and watching a favorite film or television program, for example, are free or inexpensive.

Consider pampering yourself as part of your *relapse-prevention plan*. (See Chapter 23 for more on relapse prevention.) Even using nice bath oils or eating a special meal once a week can remind you to value yourself and to treat yourself with loving care.

Overhauling Your Lifestyle

We suggest that you take a close look at the way you currently live and determine the things that are good for you and the ones that aren't. Be sure to consider the following key areas:

>> **Regular and healthy eating:** The principle is relatively simple: Have three meals and a couple of healthy snacks a day, with plenty of fruit, vegetables, and wholegrain foods. Minimize your consumption of sugar and simple carbohydrates, like white bread, and don't overdo saturated fat. Have what you like in moderation. If you think you need help with healthy eating, talk to your doctor, who can refer you to a dietician.

TIP

Try keeping a record of everything you eat for a week. Identify where you can make positive changes toward eating more regularly and more healthily. If you find that your actions don't match your good intentions, use the Tic-Toc technique (which we discuss in Chapter 22) to tackle the thoughts and attitudes that can get in the way of healthy eating.

>> **Regular exercise:** Ample evidence suggests that exercise is beneficial for both your mental and your physical health. Aim for at least three sessions of physical exercise, lasting 20 to 30 minutes each, per week. (Five sessions is ideal, but you may need to build up to that.) Consult your doctor if you haven't exercised regularly for a while. You can get great exercise from simple changes like walking more and doing some gardening or home projects.

>> **Leisure pursuits:** Include activities that bring you pleasure or satisfaction and aren't attached to your job or home life. Remind yourself of what you used to do and of what you've been meaning to do when choosing activities and hobbies.

>> **Social contact:** Introduce yourself to new people or reinvigorate your existing relationships. Sometimes relationships suffer because of psychological illness. See the "Getting intimate" section later in this chapter that talks about intimacy and communication.

>> **Vitally absorbing interests:** Get involved with causes you feel are important, such as recycling, environmental action, LGBTQ and diversity action, a cause that reflects your spiritual or cultural identity, wildlife pursuits, or animal rights campaigns. Even small, everyday actions like smiling at a store owner, holding the door for a stranger, forgiving an indiscretion, picking up a bit of litter, or spending time with an older person can help you recognize that you're contributing to the kind of world you'd like to live in.

>> **Resource management:** This catch-all may involve drawing up a budget, getting an accountant, developing a system to deal with your household bills efficiently, renegotiating your working hours, earmarking time for relaxation, arranging some babysitting, or hiring a housekeeper.

Ideally, you can create a nice balance between the aspects of your life so that none is neglected.

REMEMBER

Everyone needs delineated time for the replenishment of psychological and physical energy *as well* as for getting things done. Be aware of both; you can't have one without the other.

TIP

Look at the things you do on a daily or weekly basis and decide what you're doing too much of, such as drinking, surfing social media, working late, or eating fast food. Try to replace some of these activities with others that you're doing too little of, such as exercising, spending time with your family, cooking healthy meals, or studying.

Breaking free from addictive behavior

Often people start "self-medicating" an underlying mental health problem, such as anxiety or depression, with alcohol or drugs or through behaviors like gambling. Substance use and engaging in compulsive behaviors (shopping, gambling, gaming, pornography, sex, endless scrolling on your phone, and so on) can take the edge off emotional pain in the immediate and short term. However, in the long term these strategies typically cause more problems than they solve.

Part of developing a healthier lifestyle, for many people, involves mastering an addictive behavior. When you first give up any sort of addiction, you get cravings. Sometimes you may find them annoying but easy to shrug off, and other times they may feel like a monster devouring you. To increase your chances of remaining in control, you need to plan for what to do for those intense cravings. Follow these tips to help you ride them out:

>> **Know your triggers.** Certain advertisements, environments, and even people can trigger your urge to engage in behaviors that you're trying to stop or reduce. Negative feelings and events can also make it hard to resist. Write down a list of triggers, when you know you're most at risk, and plan what to do instead. (See the next point.)

>> **Do something else.** One of the best ways to get through a period of craving is to take your mind off it. Although it's easier said than done, you *can* distract yourself. Make a phone call, do a crossword puzzle, wash the dog, go for a run.

>> **Be grateful.** Since most people engage in addictive behavior to forget woes and dissatisfactions, gratitude for what you have can be a great relapse deterrent. Focus on the positive stuff in your life and how you can capitalize on it.

Here's an experiment you can try. Get out that pen and paper or your phone again and list at least 50 things you're grateful for, however small they may be. (Yes, we said 50. You can find them if you look hard enough.) Review this list when you find yourself sinking into self-pity and hopelessness.

>> **Gird your loins.** Yes, cravings truly do suck. But lots of things in life are painful, and you cope with many of them every day. Be compassionate with yourself but also firm. You're big enough to take the pain without welching on your commitment to yourself.

The more often you experience cravings and yet resist using, the more your confidence in your ability to resist old and unhelpful coping strategies will grow. You can start to pride yourself on having a high threshold for discomfort and give yourself well-deserved credit for your successes.

Cravings are normal. Giving up an addiction without experiencing cravings would be decidedly odd. Accept your cravings, and don't mistakenly decide that they mean that you're destined to lose the battle. Cravings are *not* a sign of weakness; rather, they show that you're struggling forward.

Extending the time between urge and action

An old overcoming addiction adage says, "Put at least half an hour between yourself and your money." If your addiction requires cash to be realized, make it harder for yourself to relapse by keeping yourself in self-imposed penury. If you need to go to the ATM before you can buy alcohol or drugs, you have more time to talk yourself out of relapsing. Get rid of your credit cards so you can't gamble online. Delete addiction-related numbers and apps from your phone. Treat yourself like someone who can't be trusted to spend your money responsibly. In short, patronize yourself. You won't have to do this forever, but in early recovery, making relapse as difficult as possible is sound sense.

Dealing with deprivation

When life deals you a particularly cruel hand and you're struggling with uncomfortable emotions, being deprived of your substance or distraction of choice can seem a hard loss indeed. You may find yourself hankering for the supposedly "good old days" when you could lose yourself in a haze of alcohol, drugs, gambling, or whatever. Getting used to dealing constructively with stress and negative emotions takes time. Be patient but firm with yourself. If you give in at the first sniff of discomfort, you're unlikely to successfully kick the habit. It would be great if life just cut you some slack and gave you an easy ride during your early recovery, but life doesn't play fair all the time. We use the acronym HARD LOSS to highlight some of the more common emotions and conditions that can pose a challenge to recovery.

>> **H: Hurt.** Feelings of hurt often lead to a sense of victimization and a desire to use. You may also feel a thirst for revenge: "I'll relapse and show them just what they've done to me!" The person you're really causing suffering to is yourself. No one likes feeling hurt, but remind yourself that you have personal responsibility for dealing with your feelings constructively.

>> **A: Anger.** As with hurt, the desire to reach for the bottle, pills, or computer can be extreme when you're in a rage. Remember that your uncomfortable feelings will subside on their own. Instead of picking up your addictive substance, do some vigorous exercise or remove yourself from the situation until you feel calmer.

>> **R: Reward.** "I've been good all week and I deserve a reward." Don't mislabel a relapse as a "reward" drink or hit. Find other ways to treat yourself after a hard week at work or for completing a job. Plan ahead. Make yourself a nice meal or go out to a movie.

>> **D: Depression.** People often want to drink or use drugs to escape the pain of depression and temporarily relieve sleep problems associated with depression. If you think you're depressed, look at the strategies we outline in Chapter 11 and seek professional help.

>> **L: Loneliness.** Feeling lonely can be a relapse risk. Especially during the early stages of recovery, scheduling in social activities and renewing friendships is important. Keep yourself in regular contact with friends, and get out of the house at least a few evenings per week. Remind yourself that feeling lonely is uncomfortable and unpleasant, but it won't kill you. So you don't need to resort to your addiction as a means of escape.

>> **O: Overwhelmed.** When you're trying to maintain new healthy habits, you need to be realistic and careful about how much stress you can manage. You'll increase your ability to cope with stress *without* risk of relapse with practice. In the initial stages of recovery, however, trying to reduce your everyday stresses is prudent. Again, forward planning can help with keeping life demands under some degree of control.

>> **S: Stagnant.** Oh, the curse of boredom. Letting yourself stagnate and get well and truly bored is a serious risk to your newfound sobriety. Keep your schedule varied and interesting to reduce your risk of turning to your addiction for entertainment.

>> **S: Self-pity.** "Poor little me; how I suffer!" Get a grip. We all suffer, struggle, and feel the pain of this mortal coil. Don't allow your addictive urges to convince you that you need to use because you're specially challenged. You're not. Recognize your personal difficulties and accept your problematic circumstances, both past and present. But saddle up and get back on the horse. Take courage and rise to meet your own personal challenges.

Walking the walk

The best-laid plans are apt to go astray.

You're serious about making positive changes to your lifestyle; however, just thinking about it and setting out plans isn't enough — although it's a great first step. The next step is to *do it!* Actions speak louder than words, so act on your intentions sooner rather than later.

Keeping your body moving

We can't emphasize enough the multiple benefits of regular exercise. Exercise is good for you in so many ways. If you don't believe us, try it. Exercise a few times each week and see if you don't end up feeling better. We defy you to contradict us.

You can exercise in ways that don't involve going to the gym. Gardening, walking, cycling, dancing, and housework all give your body a workout. Find out which activities suit your interests, schedule, and current level of fitness — *and do them!*

WARNING

Be careful that you're exercising for the right reasons, such as to enjoy yourself, de-stress, and keep physically and mentally healthy. Check that you're not exercising obsessively. The following are unhealthy motivations for exercising:

>> **To keep your weight lower than is medically recommended:** People who suffer from eating disorders often exercise fanatically.

>> **To improve your looks:** People with body dysmorphic disorder (BDD) or eating disorders sometimes use exercise to compensate for imagined defects in their physical appearance. (Chapter 13 has more about these psychological problems.)

>> **To punish yourself:** People with feelings of shame and low self-worth may exercise to excess as a means of self-harming.

TIP

Ask your physician to work out your *body mass index,* or BMI, which gives you a weight range that is normal for your age and height.

Using your head

Perhaps your emotional problems get in the way of your work, skills development, or study. Maybe your difficulties interfere with you making progress in your career or changing jobs. After all, many people with psychological problems also experience work and education difficulties.

Start to set goals for how you'd like your work or personal development to progress. Build a realistic plan of action for reaching your professional, developmental, or educational goals by following these steps:

1. **Start your plan by considering where you'd like to be and what you need to do in terms of study and training to get there.**

2. **Break your goal down into smaller, bite-sized chunks.**

   You may need to gather references, build a portfolio, write a CV, or apply for a loan or grant to fund your studies.

3. **Investigate facilities for learning.**

   Use the internet to look for specific courses, contact universities and colleges for a prospectus, see a careers advisor, or consult a recruitment agency.

4. **Build your study or training plan into your life with a view to keeping a balance between study, work, social, and leisure activities.**

5. **Set a realistic time frame to achieve your goal.**

   Pushing yourself to get there too fast is likely to cause you stress, impair your enjoyment of the journey to your goal, or even lead you to abandon your goal altogether.

TIP

Go out and learn just for the sake of it. Developing a new skill or exploring a new subject area can be highly rewarding for you, whether the studying is applicable directly to your work or not. Adult education classes and intensive workshops can be a great way to explore new topics and for you to meet new people, which can be beneficial if your social life has suffered during your illness.

Getting involved

Think about the kind of world you want to live in and how you can contribute toward creating it. You can get involved with anti-litter campaigns, local building-restoration projects, charities, or whatever you feel is important. You can usually choose how much time to devote to these pursuits.

Becoming spiritual

Sometimes people with specific disorders, such as obsessive-compulsive disorder (OCD) or extreme guilt, can find that their religion or spiritual beliefs get mixed up with their problems. Re-establishing a healthy understanding of your faith can be an important aspect of your recovery. Resuming your usual manner of worship — be it meditation, attending Mass, or going to a synagogue or temple — can help you reintegrate with your religious beliefs or your community. You might also find that discussing your recent problems with a religious leader or a member of your congregation is helpful.

Talking the talk

Emotional problems can have a detrimental effect on your personal relationships. Sometimes your symptoms can be so all-consuming that you have little space to show interest in what others around you are feeling and doing. Therefore, you may need to rebuild your existing relationships when you feel better.

When your symptoms subside, you may want to give more of your attention to the other people in your life. This may involve playing with your kids, talking to your partner about how your problems have affected your relationship (without blaming yourself or them, of course), or renewing contact with friends and extended family.

People in your life are likely to be aware of how troubled you've been, and they may notice recent positive changes in you. Let them talk about the changes they've noticed within you. Listening to other people's experiences of your problems can reinforce the idea that the other people in your life care about you. Improving your relationships and simply spending time in the company of other people can help you keep your symptoms at bay. You can also involve others in your relapse-prevention plan, if appropriate.

A supportive relationship with a significant other can help you stay healthy. This relationship doesn't need to be a romantic one. Platonic relationships are important as well. Research has shown that having a network of social contacts, as well as having someone you're able to confide in, reduces your emotional problems in general.

TIP

It's never too late for you to make friends. Even if your problems have led you to isolate yourself, now's the time to go out and meet people. Be patient, and give yourself the time and opportunity to start forming good relationships. Go to where the people are! Join some clubs or classes.

SIX STEPS FOR TALKING AND LISTENING

Good relationships are sustained by thoughtfulness, effort, and time. Many of the changes in your relationships may occur naturally because, as you become less preoccupied with your problems, you're more able to focus on the world around you.

Effective communication is the cornerstone of good relationships. Bear in mind that you can communicate not only with what you say but how you listen. Your body language can also convey a message to others. Things like eye contact and physical contact are also means of getting a message across. A simple hug can mean a lot.

(continued)

(continued)

Try the following six steps to improve your communication skills:

1. **When you have something important to discuss with someone, find a mutually suitable time to do so.**

   Make sure that you both have ample time to talk and listen to each other.

2. **Use "I feel" statements, such as "*I feel* disappointed that you came home late," rather than blaming language, such as "*You* made me so angry."**

3. **If you want to give negative feedback to someone about their behavior, keep it clear, brief, and specific.**

   Remember to also give positive feedback about the behavior you want to reinforce; for example, thank your partner for texting to say they'll be late.

4. **After you've given positive or negative feedback, ask the person how they feel and what they think about what you've said.**

5. **Don't fall into the trap of thinking that a right or true way of doing things exists.**

   Accept that different people value different things. Seek compromises when appropriate. Listen to the other person's point of view.

6. **Be prepared to accept negative feedback and criticism from others.**

   Look for points that you agree with in what the other person is saying. Give the other person a chance to air their views before you get defensive or counteractive. Give yourself time to assess the feedback you receive.

Getting intimate

Your specific problems may lead you to avoid intimate relationships with other people. You may have been too preoccupied by your problems to be able to form or maintain intimate relationships. If you want to be close to others, you have to let others into your life. Allowing yourself to trust others enough to share at least some of your personal history can make you feel closer to your listeners. Intimacy is a give-and-take affair — ideally, the balance is roughly equal.

If you think you're incapable of getting truly close to someone else, you're probably wrong. Give other people — and yourself — a chance to be honest with each other. Reciprocally enhancing relationships usually evolve naturally, but you need to be open to the possibilities of intimate relationships for this evolution to happen. Sometimes people can take you by surprise, and before you know it, you're friends!

Sex and other animals

Your interest in sex, regardless of your age or gender, may diminish because of your emotional disturbance. Many people dealing with emotional problems can lose interest in sex. When you begin to feel better, getting your sex life back on track may take some time.

Sex drive is a bit like appetite: You don't always realize you're hungry until you start eating.

Sometimes couples stop having sex regularly but don't ever discuss the change. Often, both partners get into a routine of not being sexually intimate and try to ignore the problem. Some are too shy to talk about sex or feel guilty for having lost interest in it. Additionally, many are too embarrassed to discuss their loss of sex drive with their doctor or even their friends.

Taking the plunge and talking about changes in your sex drive with your therapist or doctor can be worthwhile. Your therapist or doctor may offer you useful suggestions and may even tell you that certain medications you've been taking may contribute to your decreased interest in sex.

REMEMBER

Loss of interest in sexual activities is a normal side effect of certain experiences. Many psychological disorders, such as depression, post-traumatic stress disorder, obsessional problems, health anxiety, postnatal depression, and low self-esteem can impact your ability to feel aroused. Bereavement, physical illness, and stress can also put your sexual desires on the backburner. Fortunately, decreased libido is often temporary.

Talking about sex

"Birds do it, bees do it, even educated fleas do it," but sometimes the issue of sex is like an elephant in a tutu doing the dance of the seven veils in the middle of your bedroom. Both you and your partner can end up studiously ignoring its presence, even though it's right there, begging for your attention.

If you can't bring yourself to broach the topic of sex with your partner as you begin to recover, you can do a few things to rekindle the flames of desire. Try some of the following:

>> **Resume non sexual physical contact.** Hold hands, stroke your partner's arm or back as you chat, sit closer to each other on the sofa, and reintroduce cuddling. Nonsexual contact can help you get comfortable with touching one another again and set the scene for a revival of more intimate contact.

>> **Kiss.** If you've gotten into the habit of a quick kiss on the cheek as you leave the house, aim for the mouth instead. Kissing is a powerful form of communication. It also can be highly sensual and enjoyable.

>> **Create opportunities.** Getting into bed at the same time, before you're both bone tired, and then snuggling up can create a nonthreatening reintroduction to sexual relations.

>> **Take the pressure off.** If you tell yourself that you have to get aroused or you have to have sex tonight, you can work yourself into such a state that all spontaneity is quashed. Try to take the attitude that if it happens, it happens.

>> **Give yourself a chance to get in the mood.** You don't have to feel very aroused to start getting intimate. Sometimes you may need to have a lot of low-level sexual contact like stroking, petting, and kissing before you're ready to go further. Be patient with yourself, and try to talk to your partner about how you're feeling. Sometimes just talking about sex is enough to relax you to let nature take its course.

>> **Take the onus off orgasm.** Any sexual or close physical contact can be fulfilling. You may not be able to achieve orgasm for some time. Instead, enjoy foreplay as you may have done in the early stages of your relationship. For example, kissing is a powerful form of expression. You can really get your sex life back on track — and possibly make it better than it was before — if you give a lot of attention to the preliminaries.

Whatever turns you on is worth exploring further. Talk to your partner. You may be able to find things that can help you both get more in the mood for lovemaking. Try to be open-minded about your sex life. Just be careful to set your own personal boundaries about what turns you on and what has the opposite effect.

REMEMBER

Sometimes couples find that sex is just less important to both parties than it once was. This conclusion can be a welcome and mutual understanding to reach and can create space for other ways of expressing love and care. The key is to communicate. Don't make assumptions without talking first.

Living in Line with Your Values

Most people enjoy life most when they consistently act in accordance with their personal values. People we see in CBT treatment typically report better mood, improved self-opinion, and a general sense of well-being and of "being true to themselves" — once they've identified and started to act in line with their individual value systems.

By *values*, we mean the things in life that are most important to you: your personal ethics, morals, philosophies, ideals, standards, and principles. Sometimes, however, your depression, anxiety, poor self-esteem, and other types of emotional problem can relegate your interests and values to the sidelines. Now is the time to rediscover and honor them, in the interest of your continued mental health and happiness.

Because all people are unique, you won't always share the same values. That said, however, people with similar values are generally attracted to one another and end up in the same places. You may find like-minded people at workshops, rallies, charitable events, courses, and so on. Taking a closer look at your personal values can potentially enrich your social life.

Getting back in touch with your core values can be difficult if your mind has been clouded with anxieties and dark thoughts for some time. Be patient with yourself and permit yourself time to rediscover what you're all about.

Use the items in this list to help you pinpoint your personal principles:

>> Work and career

>> Study and skills-based training

>> Community involvement

>> Neighborhood enhancement projects

>> Cultural pursuits and identity

>> Religion and spirituality

>> Sports and other active hobbies

>> Nature, animal welfare, wildlife, and the environment

>> Friendships and friendship groups (book clubs, social clubs, and so on)

>> Family and home life

>> Causes and charities

>> Politics

>> Travel

>> Overall social responsibility

>> Art, music, and theater (either observing or participating)

>> Reading for pleasure

>> Cooking

>> Doing crafts like woodwork, knitting, or pottery

>> Upholding standards for social conduct, such as being polite, friendly, and assisting others

This list merely outlines some common areas of value-based activity. Don't be restricted by it. Be creative, thinking both big and small. Anything you do in honor of your values, minor or major, is valid and beneficial to you and those around you.

For example, one of our colleagues has a strict rule of conduct that she leaves a public toilet in the state she'd like to find it, which is often a grim task. Another mutual friend values the services of his local rubbish collectors very highly. He habitually thanks them heartily and tips them when appropriate.

You may find defining your personal values easier if you reflect on the values of a person you respect and admire. Try following these steps:

1. **Think of someone that you either know very well or you know a lot about and record their name on a sheet of paper.**

2. **Make a list of the values they seem to hold, have openly talked about, or demonstrate through their actions.**

   Chances are you'll realize that you share some basic values with this person.

3. **Make specific notes about the things your admired person does that support and reflect their personal and your shared values.**

4. **Make plans to follow this person's example!**

   Write down things you can do and when you can realistically do them. Use the blank form in Table 21-2, later in this chapter, to help you organize your thoughts. Don't forget the tiny, everyday things that can really have a positive impact on yourself and others.

WARNING

The purpose of this experiment is to help you remember and recognize what's most important to *you*. Nobody has a monopoly on values, so sharing them is a natural and normal part of life. Just beware of unwittingly adopting other people's values because self-doubt tells you that your own views and opinions can't be trusted. Allow others to inspire you, but make up your own mind about your values.

Reflecting your values through action

Identifying your values can be easier said than done. But you can help yourself become more value aware by asking yourself some basic questions. Consider the following example.

Callum has battled with social anxiety for the past five years. (For more on this, see Chapter 10.) Though always a sensitive and shy child, Callum's anxiety about what others may think of him came to a head during late adolescence. Adolescence is a common time for people to develop social anxiety. Callum has spent so many years worrying, striving to impress his peers, guessing, and trying to influence other people's opinions of him that he's largely forgotten what he thinks about things *himself.*

Like many people struggling with poor self-esteem and extreme fear of being judged negatively by others, Callum consistently held beliefs like "others know better than me" and "my opinions don't carry much weight." As a result of this way of thinking, Callum's values, interests, and opinions have been seriously neglected. Happily, he successfully used CBT to get himself out of the trap of social anxiety.

Callum asked himself some of these questions to get reacquainted with his forgotten values, opinions, and interests:

>> What were my earlier interests before social anxiety overtook my thinking?

I used to be interested in mechanics and vintage cars. I also used to really enjoy sci-fi films and novels. I still have an interest in these two areas today.

>> If I put the opinions of others aside, what are some of my personal principles and mottos?

I believe in living in a socially responsible manner that adds to the community around me.

I believe in "working to live" rather than "living to work."

I believe in supporting the rights of less privileged, vulnerable groups such as the elderly, people with disabilities, those living in poverty, and animals.

>> What pursuits do I get passionate about?

Supporting charities that aim to improve the lives of children and the elderly.

Being a responsible pet owner.

Supporting sustainable farming and reducing CO_2 emissions. Traveling and enjoying nature. Reading and learning for pleasure.

Being consistently polite and friendly to other people.

TIP

Whether social anxiety, general poor self-esteem, depression, or some other problem has overshadowed your values, you can apply the same questions Callum used to yourself.

Once you've identified your core values, honoring them through deliberate and persistent action makes sense. Doing so is likely to improve your overall enjoyment and give you a sense of living your life well. To turn your good intentions into actions, make a plan.

Callum made plans to live more consistently with his values. He identified several actions that reflect his principles and interests and scheduled in clear times for carrying them out, as shown in Table 21-1.

TABLE 21-1   ## Callum's Value-Based Behaviors Form

Value	Related Activity	Frequency
Working to live	Booking regular time off	Booking vacation times at the start of each year
Responsible pet ownership	Taking my dog for a long walk	Thrice weekly
Supporting vulnerable groups	Donating to charities	Monthly
Reducing CO_2 emissions	Walking to work	Daily
Being polite to others	Saying "thank you," smiling at those I meet	Daily
Reading and learning for pleasure	Reading novels	Twice weekly

Use the blank form provided in Table 21-2 to schedule your own value-based behaviors.

TABLE 21-2   ## My Value-Based Behaviors Form

Value	Related Activity	Frequency

REMEMBER

Wanting to be accepted and feel part of a larger social group is human nature. However, bear in mind that, while the thoughts and views of people around you are important, they aren't more important than your own. Nor is it necessary to base your self-image solely on the way others seem to think about you. You can reject other people's judgments of you entirely or in part, or you can accept them if you think they're accurate. At the end of the day, you know yourself better than anyone else does.

Staying focused on what's most important

Unearthing your basic broad values can help you remember what things in your life are most important to you on a day-to-day basis. Sometimes the pressures of modern living can skew your idea of what matters. For example, being at a work meeting may seem more important than attending your nephew's school play. However, later, when he's excitedly telling you how he remembered all his lines, you may regret having put work demands first.

You can't always do what's fundamentally most important to you without incurring unwanted consequences, of course. However, if you scrutinize things more closely, you'll probably find opportunities to honor the important things in life rather than blindly responding to external pressures from work and other places.

Reshuffling priorities

Knowing your personal values well also helps you prioritize daily duties more effectively. In general, your priorities will be compatible with and mirror your intrinsic value system.

TIP

Review your work in the previous sections of this chapter and make a numbered list of your personal priorities. Keep your list handy and refer to it regularly as a reminder of how you ideally want to live your life.

REMEMBER

Priorities shift and shuffle according to what's going on in your life. For example, putting work first (for a time) if you need extra money to pay off debts is normal and constructive. Or you may carve out extra time for your elderly relative during his convalescence from an operation. Remind yourself, however, that changes in your fundamental priorities are usually temporary; reshuffle them once a crisis has passed.

Chapter **22**

Overcoming Obstacles to Progress

H uman beings have a keen way of blocking their own progress and sabotaging their own goals. Maybe you obstruct your progress without even being aware that you're doing it. Or perhaps you're conscious that you're sabotaging yourself with faulty thinking. Whatever the case, this chapter explores common obstacles that get in the way of positive change and suggests tips for overcoming blocks to progress.

Tackling Emotions That Get in the Way of Change

As if having an emotional problem isn't enough, you may be giving yourself an extra helping of discomfort and distress because of the meanings you attach to your original problems. Some of the feelings that you may experience about your primary emotional problems, such as shame, fear, guilt, or even pride, can *interfere with your progress.*

Shifting shame

When people feel ashamed of their problems, they usually believe that their symptoms are a sign that they're weak, flawed, or defective. If you feel ashamed, you're less likely to seek help because you worry that other people may judge you harshly for having a psychological problem or perhaps may think you're silly for having other types of problems. You may worry that anyone you tell about your problem will be horrified by your thoughts or actions and will reject you. If you suffer from obsessive-compulsive disorder (OCD), which is typified by unpleasant and unwelcome thoughts or images, you may worry that other people won't understand you. People with OCD frequently assume that no one else in the world experiences the kind of upsetting thoughts that they do. In fact, everyone has intrusive and upsetting thoughts from time to time. In Chapter 12, we talk about the intrusive thoughts that are common in OCD.

You may be too ashamed to even admit to yourself that you have a problem. Blaming the problem on external events or other people is often a result of shame. Shame is corrosive to change because it can

>> Make you isolate yourself, which can lower your mood even further.

>> Lead you to deny the problem. And you can't work on problem-solving if you're unwilling to acknowledge that the problem exists in the first place.

>> Result in your blaming other people and events for your problems, robbing you of your personal power for change.

>> Make you overestimate your symptoms as "abnormal," "weird," or "unacceptable."

>> Lead you to overestimate the harsh degree by which others judge you for having the problem.

>> Stop you from seeking out more information that can help you realize that your problem isn't so unusual.

>> Prevent you from getting appropriate psychological help or the right medication.

TIP

Fight back against shame by refusing to hide your problems from yourself. Seek out information to make your experiences seem more normal. Practice self-acceptance beliefs like the ones we outline in Chapter 15. Take responsibility for overcoming your emotional problems, but resist blaming yourself for your symptoms.

Getting rid of guilt

Guilt is an unhealthy negative emotion that's particularly notorious for blocking positive change. You may be telling yourself guilt-provoking things like the following:

>> "I'm causing my family a lot of bother through my problems."

>> "Other people in the world are so much worse off than me. I've no right to feel depressed."

>> "I should be more productive. Instead, I'm just a waste of space."

Guilt sabotages your chances of taking positive action. Guilty thoughts, such as the preceding examples, can lead you to put yourself down further, thereby making yourself more depressed. Your depression leads you to see the future as hopeless and saps your motivation. (Have a peek at Chapter 7 for more information about unhealthy negative emotions and how they work against you.)

Even if the thoughts that are making you feel guilty about your depression, anxiety, or other emotional problem hold some truth, try to accept yourself as someone who's *unwell.* When you're suffering from a mental health problem, it impedes your ability to function just like a physical illness can. For example, your diminished ability to be productive is a side effect of depression, not an indication that you're a lazy or selfish person.

Shame and guilt grow in the dark. Hiding your problems, and your feelings *about* your problems, from other people tends to make things worse over time. Talking about your anxiety, obsessions, depression, addiction, or other problems gives you the chance to share your fears and discomfort with someone else, who may be far more understanding than you imagine.

Putting aside pride

Having too much pride can get in the way of your progress. Sometimes pride is a sort of compensatory strategy for feelings of shame. Your pride may protect you from the shame that you think you'd experience if you were to accept that the methods you've used thus far to overcome your problems have been less than ideal. The following are common pride-based attitudes that may be stopping you from making positive changes:

>> **"It's absurd to say that I can help myself — if I could make myself better, I'd have done it ages ago"!** Actually, people rarely know how best to help themselves out of emotional problems. Often, you need to read some

self-help books (like this one!) or have techniques explained to you before you really understand how to implement specific techniques and why these methods work.

>> **"I'm an intelligent person, and I should be able to work out this stuff on my own"!** Maybe you *can* work out how to help yourself overcome emotional problems without any help whatsoever. But remember: Even the most intelligent people need to see specialists for advice from time to time. For example, you may be bright, but you still need to take your car to a mechanic to be fixed.

>> **"I like to think of myself as strong. Admitting to having these problems shows me up as weak."** Getting a bout of flu or having epilepsy doesn't make you a weak person — and neither does a bout of depression or anxiety. For example, refusing to seek medical treatment for an infected wound is foolish, not an example of strength.

TIP

Swallow your pride and be ready to seek advice and help. Recognizing and accepting that you have a problem and that you need to get guidance on how to deal with it shows strength, not weakness.

Seeking support

After you begin to get over your shame, guilt, and pride, you can start to look for help in earnest. The help you seek may take the form of reading a self-help book like this one, approaching a therapist, talking things over with a friend (who could even support you using this book), or looking through some online resources. Some people find that self-help techniques are enough. But if you think you need more support, be sure to get help sooner rather than later. Putting off seeking professional help when you need it only prolongs your discomfort. Don't wait to take positive action until your problem has advanced to the stage where your relationships, employment situation, or daily functioning are suffering. (In Chapter 24 we explain how to seek professional help.) Many people also find it helpful to share their plan to change with someone they can trust. If you need something a little more private, keeping a personal journal on the emotional experience of growth and change can be surprisingly helpful and even help you cope with the stress and strain of the work.

Trying a little tenderness

Shame and guilt involve kicking yourself — and really putting the boot in — when you're already feeling down. You wouldn't kick some else to get them back on their feet, so don't do that to yourself either.

BOOK NOW TO AVOID DISAPPOINTMENT

Many people with emotional problems wait months or even years before sharing them with anyone else. For example, people with OCD put up with their symptoms for an average of ten years before they seek professional help. They may even keep their problems secret from their friends and family. People with depression and other anxiety problems can also wait for months or years before talking about their problems with another person.

The most common reason for keeping problems under wraps is shame. Thinking that you need to keep problems a secret is quite tragic because you end up suffering in silence needlessly. You can refer to the list of professional resources we supply in Appendix A. Exploring your options *now* can assure you that your symptoms are common and that you have nothing to be ashamed of. Get yourself on the road to recovery so you can begin reclaiming enjoyment from life.

You haven't *chosen* your problems, although you may accept that you're stuck in a pattern that's making your problems worse. Take other contributing factors into account when you think about how your problems may have started.

You can take responsibility for overcoming your emotional disturbances and be compassionate with yourself in the process. Being kind to yourself when you're working hard to get better makes sense, particularly if you consider that a lot of the work involves making yourself uncomfortable in the short term. Surely you deserve to give yourself a little encouragement during exposures and behavioral experiments rather than piling on the self-criticism.

TIP

Try being your own best friend instead of your own worst critic for a while, and see whether this helps you make some positive strides. (Look at Chapter 16 for more tips on how to treat yourself with compassion.)

Adopting Positive Principles That Promote Progress

Some of the attitudes you hold probably aren't going to do you any favors as you try to overcome your emotional problems. Fortunately, you can swap your unhelpful attitudes for alternative beliefs that can give you a leg-up on the ladder to better emotional health.

Understanding that simple doesn't mean easy

Most of the steps to overcoming psychological problems with CBT are relatively simple. CBT isn't rocket science — in fact, many of the principles and recommendations may seem like common sense. CBT may be sense, but it ain't that common. If it was, fewer people would be suffering with emotional problems.

Even if CBT is as simple as ABC, the actual application of CBT principles is far from easy. Using CBT to help yourself requires a lot of personal effort, diligence, repetition, and determination.

REMEMBER

Because CBT seems so simple, some people get frustrated when they discover that they're not getting well fast or easily enough for their liking. If you want to make CBT work for *you*, take the attitude that getting better doesn't have to be easy. Your health is worth working for.

Being optimistic about getting better

One of the biggest blocks preventing you from getting better is refusing to believe that change is possible. Be on the lookout for negative predictions that you may be making about your ability to get better. Challenge any thoughts you have that resemble the following:

>> "Other people get better, but they're not as messed up as I am."

>> "I'll never change. I've been like this for too long."

>> "This CBT stuff will never work for someone as useless as me."

If these thoughts sound familiar, check out the "Trying a little tenderness" section earlier in this chapter, which covers how to be a little kinder to yourself, as well as Chapter 16 on training your mind to be more compassionate. Would you encourage a friend to believe such thoughts, or would you urge her to challenge her thinking? Try to give yourself the kind of good advice that you'd give another person with your type of problem.

Look for evidence that you *can* make changes. Remind yourself of other things you've done in the past that were difficult and required effort to overcome. If you don't give a new treatment method a fair shot, how can you possibly *know* it can't work? If it works for others, you stand a good chance of benefiting from it too. Disobey those self-defeating thoughts and give it a try.

WARNING

Don't fall into the trap of deciding that your problems are so special and unusual that you can't be helped by conventional methods like CBT. Sometimes people can be quite defensive about their emotional problems because they believe that they're part of what makes them unique. You'll still be a unique person when you've recovered from your problems. You'll just be happier. Clinging to the idea that no one can possibly understand or assist you can become a self-fulfilling prophecy. You may hold rigidly to the idea of being a hopeless case because it protects you from getting your hopes up and being disappointed. Take the risk of possible disappointment for the chance of success.

Staying focused on your goals

If you want to continue making healthy progress, occasionally you need to renew your commitment to your goals. You may find that you stop dead in your tracks because you've forgotten what the point is. Or perhaps you find yourself feeling ambivalent about getting over your problems. After all, staying anxious, depressed, or angry may seem easier than changing.

Remind yourself regularly of your goals and the benefits of striving to achieve these goals. You can use the cost-benefit analysis (CBA) form to reaffirm the benefits of making goal-directed changes. In Chapter 9, we describe the CBA form and give you some more information about setting goals. Turn to Appendix B for a blank version of the CBA form.

TIP

Always try to set goals that are within your grasp. You can establish shorter-term goals along the way. Starting small and manageable allows you to move onto more daunting steps with new confidence in your ability to cope. For example, if your goal is to move from being largely housebound to being able to travel freely, set a goal of being able to go to a particular shop to buy something specific. You can then concentrate on the steps needed to reach that smaller goal before moving on to tackle larger goals.

Persevering and repeating

We often hear people say that they tried a technique or experiment once but that it didn't make them feel better. Trying something once is rarely enough. When you work at changing ingrained patterns of thinking and behaving, you're likely to have to try out new alternatives many times before you appreciate any beneficial change. You need to give yourself plenty of opportunity to get used to the new thought or behavior. Also, you can expect new ways of thinking and behaving to feel unnatural at first.

Think of your core beliefs and old ways of behaving as automatic responses, just like using your right hand to apply your lipstick. If you injure your right arm badly, you'll have to use your left hand to apply your makeup for a while. Imagine that your new healthy beliefs and behaviors are represented by your left hand. Each time you go to use your new beliefs, they feel awkward and don't seem to work very well. Every morning when you reach for your lipstick with your broken right arm, you'll have to remind yourself to struggle with using your left arm instead. You'll find it difficult to make a good outline of your lips and on some occasions look almost clown-like. However, over time you'll get better at using your left hand to apply make-up, until one day your automatic response will be to reach for the lipstick with your left hand. After your right arm is healed, you'll still be able to put on your lipstick and do other tasks left-handed. The difference with belief change is that you need not go back to the old way after the new way is familiar.

People retrain themselves into using new patterns of behavior all the time. Think about those who give up smoking or change their diets. Our injured-arm example is but one illustration of the type of life changes that people, just like you, make to improve their lives and adjust to circumstances beyond their control. Belief change can be almost as difficult as learning to live without a functioning limb, but you can do it if you decide to do it.

TIP

Changing your diet and even altering your route to work are other examples of behavioral retraining. You can retrain your thinking as well as your behavior; perseverance and repetition apply to both. Behavior and thought are closely linked, as we discuss in Chapter 4.

Tackling Task-Interfering Thoughts

The *TIC-TOC* technique is a simple yet effective way of unblocking obstacles to change. The technique gives you a helping hand toward achieving your goals.

TICs are *task-interfering cognitions,* the thoughts, attitudes, and beliefs that get in the way of your progress. You need to respond with *TOCs — task-orienting cognitions,* which are constructive alternatives to TICs. The list of unhelpful attitudes (sand traps) in the nearby sidebar is helpful for getting some ideas about task-interfering cognitions.

Fill out the TIC-TOC sheet by following these steps:

1. **Identify the goal or task you want to focus on.**

2. **In the left column (TICs), list your thoughts, attitudes, and beliefs that get in the way of you achieving your aim.**

3. **In the right column (TOCs), put responses to each of your TICs that will help you achieve your goal or task.**

You can find a blank TIC-TOC form in Appendix B. Use it whenever you notice that you're not pursuing a goal or carrying out a self-helping task. Table 22-1 is an example of a TIC-TOC sheet.

TABLE 22-1   Example of a TIC-TOC Sheet

Goal or task Task-Interfering Cognitions (TICs)	Setting time aside and filling out my university application forms Task-Orienting Cognitions (TOCs)
1. If I start I'll get too stressed.	1. Doing this is a hassle, but if I take it one step at a time I'll cope.
2. It's too complicated; I'm bound to get it wrong.	2. If I read the guide carefully, I'll probably do a good enough job.
3. I'm bound to be rejected.	3. I've got a good chance, and I'll really regret it if I miss the deadline.
4. There's no point in trying; I always end up putting it off.	4. I have put it off, but it's not inevitable that I'll keep doing so, especially if I start now!

SIDESTEPPING SAND TRAPS

Along the path to better mental health, you're sure to encounter obstacles. The following are popular reasons for abandoning your goals or not getting started with pursuing goals in the first place:

- **Fearing change:** Despite feeling miserable, you may be afraid of what'll happen if you take steps to change. You may have been depressed or anxious for so long that you can't really imagine doing anything else. Perhaps some of the people in your life are helping you to live with your problems, and you fear that by getting better you may lose those people. However, getting yourself well gives you a chance to build more fulfilling relationships and to develop your independence.

- **Having low-frustration tolerance:** When the going gets tough, the tough go home to bed, right? No! You may be tempted to go to bed, but you just wake up every morning with the same old problems. The only way to increase your tolerance to frustration in all its forms is to grit your teeth and stick with it. However uncomfortable you may be while working on changing yourself, the effort is almost certainly a lot less painful than staying unwell for the rest of your life.

(continued)

(continued)

- **Being passive:** Maybe if you wait long enough someone else will get better for you. Perhaps a miracle will happen to change your life, or a magic button will appear for you to push. Presto, and you're fixed! Maybe, but don't hold your breath waiting. Take responsibility for doing the work needed to feel better.

- **Having a fear of being bossed around:** Some people have a strong sense of autonomy, and they can be sensitive to other people trying to influence or coerce them. If you're one of these people, you may think that your therapist or somebody close to you is trying to take over when they suggest you try new strategies. Try to be open-minded to what professionals and people who care about you suggest. Deciding to give someone else's ideas a try is up to you. No one else can really control you or your decisions.

- **Being fatalistic:** Perhaps your motto is "This is the way I am and how I'm destined to be for all time." Being convinced that your moods are governed by forces beyond your control, such as chemicals, hormones, biology, the past, fate, or God, means that you're prone to surrender yourself to your symptoms. Why not put your theories to the test by making a real effort to rewrite your supposed destiny? You never know: Your original assumptions may be wrong!

- **Love is the drug that I'm thinking of . . .** You may be convinced that love is the only true path to happiness. You may be unable to imagine that you can have a satisfying life by learning to cope with your problems on your own. You may think that you'll remain unhappy and emotionally disturbed until your special someone rides in on a steed to rescue you from this crazy mixed-up world. Love is a real bonus to human existence, make no mistake. However, the healthiest relationships are those where both parties are self-sufficient and enjoy the companionship of one another without being overly dependent.

- **Waiting to feel motivated:** A lot of people make the mistake of waiting to feel like doing something before they get started. The problem with waiting for inspiration, or motivation, is that you may hang about for far too long. Often, action precedes and begets motivation. When overcoming emotional disturbance, you often need to do an experiment (check out Chapter 5), or you can stick to an activity schedule (in Chapter 11), even when doing so is the last thing that you feel like doing. Positive action is the best remedy for overcoming the feelings of lethargy and hopelessness.

Chapter **23**

Psychological Gardening: Maintaining Your CBT Gains

L ooking after the positive changes you've made is a major part of helping you stay emotionally healthy. You can nurture your belief and behavior changes every day. The process is a bit like tending a plant to keep it thriving. The more care you take of yourself both generally and specifically — for example, by practicing your new ways of thinking and acting — the more you reduce the chances of returning to your old problematic ways.

This chapter offers practical tips and advice to help you prevent relapses and effectively manage setbacks if they do occur.

Knowing Your Weeds from Your Flowers

Think of your life as a garden. Unhealthy, rigid ways of thinking and correspond-ing behaviors like avoidance, rituals, safety strategies, perfectionism, and trying too hard to please are the weeds in your garden. The flowers consist of your healthy, flexible thinking, such as accepting yourself and others, accepting uncertainty and allowing yourself to be fallible, and your healthy behaviors, such as assertion, communication, problem-solving, and facing your fears.

No garden's ever totally weed-free. Planting desirable plants isn't enough. You need to continuously water and feed the flowers and uproot the weeds to keep your garden thriving. If you tend your garden regularly, the weeds don't get a chance to take hold because there you are with your trowel, digging 'em out at the first sign of sprouting. Depending on the virulence of your weeds, you may need to use some metaphorical weed killer from time to time in the form of appropriately prescribed medication.

After you've identified your unhealthy behaviors and thinking tendencies and bedded down some healthy alternatives, you can keep a better lookout for emerging weeds and monitor the health of your flowers.

To differentiate your weeds from your flowers, ask yourself the following questions:

>> **What areas do I most need to keep working at to maintain my gains?** The areas you identify are those where weeds are most likely to first take root.

>> **What CBT strategies aid me most in overcoming my emotional problems?** Think about the new attitudes you've adopted toward yourself, the world, and other people. These areas are your tender, new flowers. Their delicate shoots need your attention.

>> **What are the most useful techniques that I've applied to overcoming my emotional problems?** Think about the new ways of behaving that you've adopted (daffodils) and the old ways of behaving that you've dropped (bindweed). Stick to your new, healthy behaviors, and be vigilant against slipping back into your former unhealthy patterns of behavior. Use an activity schedule to help you carry out beneficial routines and behaviors. (Jump to Chapter 11 for more about activity scheduling.)

TIP

Write down the answers to the preceding questions so that you can look at them often to remind yourself of where to put in the hoe.

Working on Weeds

This section deals with weed-related topics and offers you some suggestions on how to stop them from taking over your garden, anticipating where they're likely to grow, and managing those that keep coming back.

Nipping weeds in the bud

Out of the corner of your eye, you see a weed sticking up its insidious little head. You may be tempted to ignore it. Maybe it'll go away or wither and die on its own. Unfortunately, weeds seldom eliminate themselves. Rather, they tend to spread and smother your burgeoning bluebells. Assume that any weed you identify needs savage and prompt killing.

A common reason for ignoring resurging problems is shame. If you feel ashamed that your problems are recurring, you may try to deny it and avoid seeking help from professionals or support from friends or family. You may be less likely to make a personal effort to whack down the problems the way you did the first time.

REMEMBER

Setbacks are a normal part of development. Human beings have emotional and psychological problems just as readily as physical problems. You don't have to be ashamed of your psychological problems any more than you should be ashamed of an allergy or a heart condition.

Another common reason for people ignoring the reappearance of psychological problems is *catastrophizing,* or assuming the worst. (Head to Chapter 2 for more info on thinking errors.) Many people jump to the conclusion that a setback equals a return to square one, but this certainly doesn't have to be the case. You can take the view that a problem you conquered once is at a fundamental disadvantage when it tries to take hold again. This is because you know your enemy. Use what you already know about recognizing and arresting your old thinking and behavior to help you pluck that weed before it gets too far above the ground.

Some emotional and psychological problems are more tenacious than others. Examples are bipolar disorder, obsessive-compulsive disorder (OCD), and eating disorders. Just because a problem's tenacious doesn't mean that it has to take over your life or even cause you too much interference. However, you can expect to meet tenacious problems again. Keep up with treatment strategies even when your original problems are no longer in evidence; doing so will help prevent a relapse.

For example, if you have a history of depression, you may notice that weeds are popping up when you do some of the following:

>> Begin to think in a pessimistic way about your future and your ability to cope with daily hassles.

>> Ruminate on past failures and on how poor your mood is.

>> Lose interest in seeing your family and friends.

>> Have difficulty getting out of bed in the morning and want to sleep more during the day instead of doing chores or exercising.

If you spot these stinging nettles making their way into your otherwise floral existence, try some of these techniques:

>> Challenge your pessimistic thinking bias and remind yourself that your thoughts aren't accurate descriptions of reality but symptoms of your depression. (See Chapter 2 for more on thinking errors.)

>> Interrupt the rumination process by using task-concentration and mindfulness techniques. (We explain these in Chapter 6.)

>> Continue to meet with family and friends, despite your decreased interest, because doing so makes you feel better rather than worse.

>> Force yourself out of bed in the morning and keep an activity schedule. (Read Chapter 13 for more on activity schedules.)

Whatever your specific problems, follow the preceding example: Write down your descriptions of anticipated weeds and some specific weed-killing solutions to have on hand.

Don't ignore signs that your problems are trying to take root. Be vigilant. But also be confident in your ability to use the strategies that worked before and in your ability to use them time and again, whenever you need to.

Spotting where weeds may grow

To prevent relapse, become aware of where your weeds are most likely to shoot up.

Most people, regardless of their specific psychological problems, find themselves most vulnerable to setbacks when they're run down or under stress. If you're overtired and under a lot of environmental stress, such as dealing with work deadlines, financial worries, bereavement, or family/relationship difficulties, you tend to be more prone to physical maladies, such as colds, flu, and episodes of eczema. Psychological problems are no different from physical ones in this regard: They get you when you're depleted and at a low ebb.

You may notice that some problems, like OCD, anxiety, and depression, are more evident when you're recovering from a physical illness. Recognizing this common human experience can help you combat any shame that you may feel and decatastrophize a return of your symptoms.

Compile a list of situations and environmental factors that are likely to give your weeds scope to take on triffid-like power (a triffid is a fictional plant that could become gigantic). For example, you may be able to pinpoint environment triggers for your depression, such as the following:

>> Seasonal change, especially during autumn, when the days get shorter and the weather becomes colder. This trigger may be especially relevant to specific climates.

>> Sleep deprivation, due to work commitments, young children, illness, or any other reason.

>> Lack of exercise and physical activity.

>> Day-to-day hassles piling up at once, such as the furnace breaking down in the same week that the washing machine explodes and a few extra bills arrive.

>> Reduced opportunity for positive social interaction with friends and family.

You can also identify interpersonal triggers for your depression, such as the following:

>> Tired and irritable partner.

>> Disagreements with your partner, children, parents, or extended family.

>> Critical or demanding boss.

>> Disagreeable work conditions.

Compile a list of high-risk situations for yourself, including situations that are most likely to fire up your unhealthy core beliefs (we explain core beliefs in Chapter 18) and situations that put you under strain. Creating such a list helps you have a clear idea of when you're most vulnerable to relapse and identify which psychological soil is the most fertile for weed growth.

Dealing with recurrent weeds

Some weeds just seem to keep coming back. You may think you're rid of them, only to open your garden door to a scene from *Little Shop of Horrors.* ("Feed me, Seymour!")

Some unhealthy beliefs are harder to erode than others. *Core beliefs* (refer to Chapter 19) are those that typically you've held to be true for a very long time — most of your life even. These beliefs will keep trying to take root and may be particularly resistant to your attempts to kill them. Certain unhealthy behaviors, such as addictions and rituals associated with body dysmorphic disorder (BDD; see Chapter 13) or OCD (Chapter 12), for example, can be very stubborn.

The best way to deal with these recurrent weeds is to not become complacent. Keep reinforcing your alternative beliefs. Keep up with activities that fill the gaps left by your addictions or preoccupation with your appearance. Keep doing exposure and response-prevention activities (refer to Chapter 12) to combat your OCD. Trust that over time and with persistence, your new ways of thinking and acting will get stronger.

Are you unwittingly feeding your weeds? Avoidance is a major weed fertilizer. You may have developed a healthy belief, such as "I want to be liked by people, but I don't have to be. Not being liked by some people doesn't mean that I'm unlikable." And yet, if you still avoid social situations, self-expression, and confrontation, you're giving your old belief that "Everyone must like me, or it means that I'm an unlikable person"! the opportunity to germinate.

TIP

Check out your reasons for avoiding certain situations and experiences. Are you not going to a party because you don't want to, or because you want to avoid the possibility of others judging you negatively in some way? Are you not visiting a farm because it doesn't interest you, or because you want to avoid contamination from pesticides?

When you spot a recurrent, mulish weed in your garden, dig it out from the root. You can kill off weeds entirely by getting the roots, *and* the shoots, out of the soil. Try not to make half-hearted efforts at challenging your faulty thinking; use a systemic weed killer. Dispute your thinking errors (Chapter 2) and push yourself back into challenging situations using your healthy coping strategies (we cover thinking errors in Chapter 2, and we talk about coping strategies in Chapters 4 and 8).

TECHNICAL STUFF

We're sure you realize this weed killer thing is an extended metaphor, but rest assured that we do care about the environment!

Tending Your Flowers

Knowing when you're most prone to the symptoms of your original problems resprouting is one thing. But knowing how to troubleshoot problems and prevent weeds from growing back is another thing altogether.

REMEMBER

The techniques, behavioral exercises, and experiments that helped you overcome your problems in the first place will probably work again. So, go back to basics. Keep challenging your negative thinking and thinking errors. Keep exposing yourself to your feared situations. If your life is in turmoil due to inevitable things like moving, work difficulties, or ill health, try to keep to your normal routine as much as possible while also nurturing yourself through a hard time.

Above all, even when things are going well, water your peonies! *Psychological watering* involves keeping up with your new ways of thinking and behaving by giving yourself plenty of opportunity to consistently practice and test your new ways of living. As we mentioned in Chapter 21, healthy, alternative beliefs take time to become habitual. Be patient with yourself, and keep doing healthy things, even when you're symptom-free.

Developing a plan for times of crisis is another good idea. Here are some examples of what you may want to include in your plan to overcome a possible relapse:

» Consider seeing your general practitioner or psychiatrist to determine whether you need to go on medication for a while.

» Talk about your feelings to someone you trust. Pick a person you can rely on to be supportive. Seek the help of a professional if talking to a friend or family member isn't enough.

» Review your efforts from previous CBT work and reuse the exercises that were most effective.

» Keep your lifestyle healthy and active.

Planting new varieties

Digging out a weed (unhealthy belief and behavior) is important, but you also need to plant a flower (healthy belief and behavior) in its place. For example, if you notice that an old belief like "I have to get my boss's approval; otherwise, it proves that I'm unworthy" is resurging, dispute the belief with arguments about the logic, helpfulness, and truth of the belief. (Chapter 19 has more about disputing unhealthy beliefs.)

You also need to plant a healthy belief, such as "I want my boss's approval, but I don't have to get approval to be a worthwhile person." You can strengthen the new belief by gathering arguments for the logic, helpfulness, and truth of the alternative healthy belief.

To strengthen new beliefs and behaviors further, you can devise situations that you know are likely to trigger your old unhealthy beliefs and work at endorsing and acting according to your new beliefs instead. For example, deliberately seek your boss's feedback on a piece of work that you know isn't your best. Resist your old behaviors that arise from the unhealthy belief that "I must get my boss's approval," such as over-apologizing or making excuses. Instead, accept yourself for producing a less good piece of work and take note of constructive criticism. (Refer to Chapter 16 for more about self-acceptance, and head to Chapter 20 for more techniques to strengthen new beliefs.)

You can dig out unhealthy behavioral weeds and plant behavioral flowers in their place. For example, you may note that you drink more alcohol in the evenings as your mood lowers with the shortening days. You know that the onset of winter gets you down because you spend more time in the house. You can make the choice to stop drinking more than one glass of wine in the evening and start going to a local dance class or some other activity instead. You can also make a list of activities to do indoors that will keep you occupied during the winter evenings.

REMEMBER

Plant flowers in place of weeds, and tend those flowers to keep them hardy. Your weeds will have greater difficulty growing again where healthy flowers are thriving. Continued healthy thinking and behavior create an excellent psychological ground cover.

A HAPPY GARDENER'S CHECKLIST

Here are some points to help you prevent and overcome relapse. Use this checklist to stop your daisies from getting drowned by dandelions.

- **Stay calm.** Remember that setbacks are normal. Everyone has ups and downs.

- **Use your setbacks.** Your setbacks can show you the things that make you feel worse as well as what you can do to improve your situation. Look for preventive measures that you may have used to get better but that you may have let slide when your symptoms reduced.

- **Identify triggers.** A setback can give you extra information about your vulnerable areas. Use this information to plan how to deal with predictable setbacks in the future.

- **Use what you've learned from CBT.** Sometimes you think that a setback means that you're never going to get fully well or that CBT hasn't worked for you. But if the stuff you did worked once, then chances are the same stuff can work again. Stick with it; you have nothing to lose by trying.

- **Put things into perspective.** Unfortunately, the more you've improved your emotional health, the worse black patches will seem in contrast. Review your improvement and try to see this contrast in a positive way as evidence of how far you've come.

- **Be compassionate with yourself.** People often get down on themselves about setbacks. Take appropriate responsibility, but be self-compassionate. You can help yourself get back on track by seeing a setback as a problem to overcome rather than a stick with which to beat yourself.

- **Remember your gains.** Nothing can take your gains away from you. Even if your gains seem to have vanished temporarily, you can find them again. You can take action to make this happen more quickly.

- **Face your fears.** Don't let yourself avoid whatever triggered your setback. You can devise further exposure exercises (refer to Chapters 9 and 14) to help you deal with the trigger more effectively the next time it happens.

- **Set realistic goals.** Occasionally, you may experience a setback because you plant more than you can pick. Keep your goals challenging but not overwhelming. (Eyeball Chapter 9.) Break bigger goals into smaller, mini-goals.

- **Hang on!** Even if you can't get over a setback immediately, don't give up hope. With time and effort, you can overcome the setback. Don't hesitate to get appropriate support from friends and professionals if you think you need to. Remind yourself of times in the past when you felt as despairing and hopeless as you might now. You got out of the slump then. Use the same strategies now.

Happy gardening!

Being a compassionate gardener

What do you do if one of your precious plants isn't doing so well? If you notice that you have blight on your prize rose, do you deprive it of food and water, or do you try to treat the disease? It's better not to abuse or neglect the plants in your garden for failing to thrive because, if you do, they may only wilt further. You probably don't blame the plant for ill health, so why should you blame yourself when you relapse?

Yes, take responsibility for anything that you may be doing that's self-defeating. And yes, accept responsibility for taking charge of your thinking, and ultimately, for engineering your own recovery. But also take a compassionate view of yourself and your problems. Some of your unhealthy tendencies may have taken root partly due to childhood and early adulthood experiences. Others may have some biological underpinnings. Some of your problems may have arisen from a trauma. You're not alone in having emotional problems. You're part of the human race, and you shouldn't expect more of yourself than you do of others with regard to staying emotionally healthy.

If you take a responsible, compassionate view of setbacks, you'll be more able to help yourself get well again.

HOW DOES YOUR GARDEN GROW?

Research shows that CBT has a better relapse-prevention rate than medication on its own or other types of therapy. This difference may be because CBT encourages you to become your own therapist. Doing behavioral and written exercises does seem to help people stay well, and for longer. Try to continue to be an active gardener throughout your life. Left to their own devices, most gardens become overrun with weeds. Think of maintaining the health of your psychological garden as an ongoing project.

TIP

You've heard that you should talk to your plants to make them grow. Well, it may sound a bit daft, but maybe there's something to that. Try imagining yourself as a little pot plant on your kitchen windowsill. Talk to yourself encouragingly and lovingly when you notice your leaves drooping. Give yourself the types of messages that nurture rather than deplete you.

Chapter **24**

Working with the Professionals

C BT has gained popularity in recent years, due in part to research showing that it's an effective treatment for many common psychological problems. CBT is increasingly becoming the treatment of choice for most mental health conditions. Doctors and psychiatrists are referring more people for CBT therapy than ever before. More government funding is being allocated to train people in the health services to use CBT techniques. These days, you can access CBT treatment in books, remotely via the internet, in groups, and in one-on-one sessions. (Appendix A lists websites and organizations that you may want to contact.) This chapter helps you determine how to seek further help, how to select a CBT therapist, and how to get the most from your treatment.

Procuring Professional Help

The information in this book may be all you need to overcome your emotional problems. Or, you may consider checking out some of the other self-help books or other resources we recommend in Appendix A, which can give more guidance on specific problems.

Alongside self-help, you may decide that you want or need additional assistance from a qualified therapist. If you have problems that are severe or difficult to overcome, your doctor may prescribe medication or refer you to a psychiatrist for a more specialized assessment of your difficulties. Psychiatrists can usually refer you to a CBT psychotherapist who's qualified to treat your specific problems. Your doctor may also be able to suggest a therapist, whether or not you've also been referred to a psychiatrist.

REMEMBER

Self-help approaches, such as books like this one, have the advantage of costing little, being readily available — even in the middle of the night and during holidays — and providing enduring advice for years to come. Perhaps most importantly, when you use a self-help book, you know that the person who's making the changes in your life is *you.* A good self-help book can be invaluable, even if you're also seeking professional help. In fact, most CBT therapists recommend a book or two during treatment. Your therapist may collaborate with you, using a book of your choice as a resource. Alternatively, ask your therapist whether they have any suggestions for material you can read to help you get the most from your treatment.

Ask yourself the following questions to determine whether now is the right time to look for professional help:

>> **How severe are your current problems?** For example, if you have severe depression or if you feel like you just can't do it on your own, seeking expert help is strongly recommended, as you may be too ill to benefit fully from self-help techniques. By *severe*, we mean that your problem is interfering significantly with your relationships, ability to work, or carry on with normal daily activities. If you've experienced uninterrupted symptoms for more than two months, or if you notice that your symptoms are worsening or coming back more often, you should really seek professional help.

>> **Have you tried self-help approaches in a consistent and systematic manner for at least two (but ideally six) weeks?** If you feel you're making some progress on your problems, you may not need to work with a professional at this time. However, if you're not satisfied with your rate of progress and still feel bad much of the time, then structured therapy sessions may help you.

>> **Do your problems interfere with your ability to concentrate and utilize self-help material?** If so, a therapist may well be able to help you digest information and techniques at a pace you can manage.

>> **Do you see the sense in self-help principles but struggle to apply them to your own life?** Most therapists are much more experienced than you in applying psychological principles to specific types of problems. They can

suggest more ways to help you move forward and guide you on how best to use the therapeutic techniques described in self-help books.

>> **Have you reached a plateau or obstacle in your self-help program that you can't overcome on your own?** By working with a trained and experienced therapist, you may develop the ability to overcome barriers and jump-start your treatment. A therapist can often suggest ideas that you may not have tried, which can motivate you to get your treatment moving again.

>> **Are you ready to share your problems with someone and team up with them on achieving shared goals for therapy?** Therapy is a team effort. Therapists don't "fix" you. Your treatment still needs lots of input from you.

Thinking about the right therapy for you

REMEMBER

Doctors and psychologists often recommend CBT because research evidence supports its effectiveness. (Refer to Chapter 1.) Specifically,

>> CBT is an active problem-solving approach that helps you develop skills and enables you ultimately to become your own therapist.

>> CBT focuses on the present and how your past has influenced your present-day difficulties, whereas many other therapies focus intensively and almost solely on your past. In CBT, exploring your childhood experiences helps you and your therapist understand how you may have developed specific beliefs and ways of behaving. However, the focus is on your *current* problems and the ways in which your thinking and acting perpetuate your problems.

>> CBT emphasizes a collaborative relationship in therapy. CBT therapists can help you build skills, and they're likely to expect you to carry out assignments between sessions.

>> CBT is a transparent approach to helping you overcome your difficulties. Your therapist will explain their rationale for suggesting a behavioral strategy or a thinking technique.

WARNING

As with any form of therapy, be sure to research the treatment before you commit to it. Also make sure you find a fully accredited and qualified practitioner.

In addition to CBT, you may come across dozens more therapeutic approaches when you investigate your treatment options. Some of the more common psychotherapies practiced today include these:

>> **Transactional analysis:** Focuses on the internal relationship between the parent, adult, and childlike aspects of human personalities.

>> **Person-centered therapy:** Emphasizes the therapist displaying warmth, empathy, and genuineness toward the client, but without directing the client.

>> **Psychodynamic therapy:** Focuses on the client expressing feelings derived from early experiences, as these feelings arise during the ongoing relationship between client and therapist.

>> **Systemic therapy:** Commonly used with families and couples, this emphasizes the idea that emotional problems are the product of a dysfunctional system, such as a family or relationship.

>> **Interpersonal therapy (IPT):** Focuses on changes in life roles, grief, and disputes with significant others. IPT is another proven treatment for depression and some eating disorders.

Meeting the experts

Lots of mental health professionals can provide general counseling and support. If you specifically want CBT, don't hesitate to say so. Many psychiatrists, psychologists, and nurses have had some training in CBT, but check out the extent of their training and experience. Ideally, choose someone who's had specialist training in CBT. *Specialist training* means that the therapist has obtained a postgraduate degree or master's qualification in CBT from a university or recognized training institute.

REMEMBER

Specialist CBT training typically takes a minimum of two academic years of study. People trained through "fast-track" government initiatives have limitations to their experience and theoretical knowledge. They have some useful CBT techniques to offer but may lack the depth of disorder-specific knowledge, training, and expert supervision required to make them competent to treat more severe and complicated problems.

You can ask your therapist to tell you where and when they studied, and if you're skeptical, you can verify this information with the relevant educational bodies. Some therapists have their certificates, which outline their qualifications, on display. If you're referred to a therapist by a psychiatrist, the psychiatrist may be able to give you more details about your therapist's credentials or to verify the information that a therapist gives you.

WARNING

Anyone can call themselves a counselor or a psychotherapist, regardless of whether they have professional training. A therapist with a recognized professional qualification won't be offended if you ask about their relevant training. You have every right to satisfy your desire to know about your therapist's background and training because this is *your* treatment. If you know that you want CBT as part of your treatment, you must ask about the CBT specifics of your therapist's training and experience.

In case you're a bit flummoxed by the range of different professionals offering help, here's a little breakdown of them:

- » *Psychiatrists* are medical doctors who specialize in psychological problems. They can prescribe medication and typically are more knowledgeable than family doctors about the drugs used to treat psychiatric illness. Not all psychiatrists are trained in CBT, although many can refer you to a CBT therapist whom they're familiar with.

- » *Clinical psychologists* have usually studied a broad range of therapies and have basic training in how to apply therapeutic principles to specific problems. Many can offer CBT but may not have specialist training.

- » *Counseling psychologists* have been trained in basic counseling and different types of psychotherapy. Like clinical psychologists, most counseling psychologists have no specialist training in CBT, but they may offer it as part of the techniques they use.

- » *Nurse therapists* are originally trained in psychiatric nursing. They have a more in-depth understanding of psychological processes and disorders than general nurses. Psychiatric nurses may have undergone further training to specialize in CBT.

- » *Counselors* are usually trained in listening and helping skills. They may hold a certificate in basic counseling or be more specialized in certain problem areas, such as addiction. They don't always have a psychology degree or in-depth knowledge of psychological problems. Often, counselors won't be specialized in a specific psychotherapeutic orientation like CBT.

- » *Psychotherapists* normally specialize in a specific school of therapy, such as psychodynamic, CBT, or person-centered therapy. The level of training and experience, however, can vary widely.

REMEMBER

You have the right to ask your therapist or other mental health professional how much experience they have using CBT and to what level they've trained. You can also ask them how much experience they have dealing with your specific problems, such as depression, panic disorder, or obsessive-compulsive disorder (OCD). If you're not satisfied with the answers you receive, take the matter further. In most cases, you can request a referral to another therapist through either your family doctor or your psychiatrist. You can also consult the BACBP (and international equivalent) directories. (See Appendix A.)

TIP

You can also ask your CBT therapist how often they receive clinical supervision. This monthly mandatory requirement for all accredited therapists involves both discussing cases and playing actual sessions — with client consent — to a more experienced and more highly qualified CBT therapist, who ideally holds an additional specific CBT supervision qualification. This practice ensures that your therapist is providing competent treatment and upholding professional and ethical standards in their practice.

Tracking Down the Right CBT Therapist for You

After you've decided to search specifically for a therapist with CBT training, you may have a bewildering number of questions to ask both yourself and potential therapists. This section poses, and helps you begin to answer, these questions.

Asking yourself the right questions

Sifting through directories of CBT therapists can be quite daunting. You may feel like there's a lot you want to find out about but aren't sure exactly how to ask for the information.

To locate and select the best CBT therapist for you, consider the following questions:

>> **Where can I find a CBT-trained therapist?** Begin by asking for recommendations from your doctor, psychiatrist, or friends. Many practitioners are listed in online directories, although you may need to contact them to find out more about their backgrounds. *Accredited therapists* have reached a recognized level of training and experience. In the United Kingdom, therapists are accredited by the BABCP or the UKCP (or both). In the United States, therapists are licensed by the state in which they practice.

>> **How much can I afford to pay?** Your doctor is your best first port of call if you're not able to afford private treatment. You do have a right to appropriate treatment through the NHS. If your doctor recommends you for CBT, then technically the NHS needs to provide it for you. If you've done some background research on your specific problems and have articles outlining CBT as the recommended treatment, you can show these to your doctor and request a referral.

But bear in mind that the NHS has limited resources. Check out how long you need to wait for NHS treatment in the United Kingdom. Putting your name on a waiting list sooner rather than later is a good plan if resources are overstretched in your area.

Fees for private CBT vary from practitioner to practitioner, depending on location, training, and experience. In general, the more experienced and highly trained the therapist, the higher the fees. But shopping around can save you money. Some practitioners have a limited number of lower-fee sessions for people on low incomes. Sometimes trainee and newly qualified CBT therapists offer a reduced rate. Many trainees are competent and provide good-quality service. However, before beginning therapy with a trainee, find out who provides their training and who monitors their clinical supervision. Then you know who to talk to if you have concerns or complaints about the treatment your trainee therapist provides.

» **Would I prefer a male or female practitioner?** When you're selecting a therapist, try to be open-minded about their gender. However, some people, perhaps because they have issues with sexual abuse or relationships, may prefer either a male or a female therapist. If you feel the gender of your therapist impairs your ability to discuss your problems openly, raise your concerns with them or your doctor, who should then refer you to another therapist.

You may also wish to have therapy with someone who's from the same cultural background as you are. Ask your doctor if they can recommend a local service that may be able to offer culturally specific counseling.

» **Does the therapist have the appropriate background or training?** NHS professionals are trained to use CBT techniques that work for mild depression and anxiety. If you have a specific problem, such as panic attacks, addiction, or OCD, it's best for you to look for a therapist with experience in treating your specific disorder. If you find a practitioner you like but who lacks the experience in your disorder, ask whether they're willing to seek expert supervision and training about your problem. If not, find another therapist. To make this a little more complicated, there are several "types" of therapy that can usually be found under the CBT umbrella. Here are some key examples:

- Cognitive Therapy
- Behavior Therapy (including Exposure and Exposure and Response Prevention)
- Rational Emotive Behavior Therapy (REBT)
- Acceptance and Commitment Therapy (ACT)
- Compassion-Focused Therapy
- Dialectical Behavior Therapy (DBT)
- Meta-Cognitive Therapy

- Mindfulness-Based Cognitive Therapy (MBCT)
- Schema-Focused Therapy
- Functional Analytic Psychotherapy (FAP)

We don't want to make the process of choosing a therapist more difficult here, but it's worth noting that not all CBT practitioners employ the same principles and techniques. CBT has long had the tradition of incorporating a range of techniques "so long as they work," and practitioners will often add to their skills over the years. It's entirely reasonable to ask if there are schools of thought that particularly influence your therapist in the way they plan to work with you so that you can make a more informed choice.

>> **How many sessions do I need?** Estimating the number of therapy sessions you may need is difficult. In general, CBT is briefer than psychoanalysis or psychodynamic therapy, which typically involves two sessions per week for a year or more, whatever your disorder. CBT estimates the number of sessions you need based on the nature of your specific diagnosis. We suggest initially agreeing to six sessions and then reviewing the treatment progress with your therapist. Your therapist will be in a better position after six sessions to judge how many more you need. You can also air any concerns, doubts, or reservations you may have at the six-week review.

A common estimate for CBT is between 13 and 20 sessions. You'll normally start off with weekly sessions and build in bigger gaps as you progress. However, for complex and longstanding problems, CBT can last two years or more, occasionally with more than one session per week. Ask your therapist to give you a rough idea of how many sessions they believe you need after their initial assessment of your problems.

Your therapist should also regularly review your treatment with you, which may give you a clearer sense of how many more sessions you need.

Ultimately, you — not your therapist — decide how long to stick with CBT treatment. If you want to stop or take a break, that's your choice.

REMEMBER

>> **Can I take along my copy of *CBT For Dummies* or another self-help book?** As we mention earlier, CBT therapists often suggest self-help material and can usually help you work through a self-help book. If you've been using a book that you find useful, take it along to your first session. Your therapist may already be familiar with the resource; if not, they may be prepared to read through it.

Speaking to the specialists

Make the most of your initial phone or email contact with possible therapists by asking whatever questions are on your mind. You may also receive an assessment form via email to complete before you meet for the first time. This document gives the therapist an overview of your problem and can save time in assessment. Once you make an assessment appointment with a therapist, you may want to list a few things that you want to discuss during your first meeting.

TIP

The following questions are reasonable to ask after you identify a potential therapist:

>> How much do you charge [if the therapist is a private practitioner]?

>> How long are your sessions?

>> Do you charge a cancellation fee?

>> Do you have any experience treating my particular kind of problems?

>> Are sessions booked in a fixed time slot each week, or can they vary?

>> Where do you practice? Do you have a waiting room?

>> Can I record our sessions?

If you're comfortable with the answers you receive from your potential therapist, seek out answers to the following more detailed questions during your first meeting:

>> Can you explain your theory about what's maintaining my problems?

>> What sort of things do you think I need to do to overcome my problems?

>> How many sessions do you estimate that I need?

>> What do you expect of me in therapy, and what can I expect from you?

>> Can you recommend any reading or self-help materials to me?

FIGHTING YOUR FEARS ABOUT SEEKING SPECIALIST HELP

We often comment to each other about how strange our jobs are. We like what we do very much, but the reality is that for most people therapy is an unfamiliar experience. Most people don't sit in front of a stranger and tell them about personal problems. Being apprehensive about starting therapy is entirely natural, and you may have some common worries about seeking help, such as the following:

- **What if working with a professional doesn't help me?** Treatment may not have an immediate effect. However, if you're committed to getting better, the treatment

(continued)

(continued)

will probably have at least some benefit. Proceeding down the professional path may seem like a big risk, but you're very likely to be glad you took it.

- **What if talking about my problems makes them worse?** Good therapy, or the right medication, rarely worsens problems. Sometimes you may feel a temporary increase in discomfort while on the road to long-term recovery. Change by its very nature means stepping out of your comfort zone. However, if you're finding therapy too overwhelming, one of the key benefits of working with a professional can be them helping you with this problem. They might offer more support, or they might help you find more manageable steps.

- **What if I'm too embarrassed to tell my therapist what's really bothering me?** Tell your therapist if you're feeling embarrassed or ashamed. They may well be able to put your mind at rest by explaining that many of your feelings, thoughts, and experiences are normal. You don't have to divulge all to your therapist straightaway (although doing so may be the most efficient route), and you can take some time to build trust between the two of you.

- **What if my therapist thinks I'm crazy and wants to keep me in the hospital?** Your therapist or psychiatrist isn't going to think that you're crazy or judge you negatively for being disturbed. Therapists frequently see patients with your type of problems. People are assessed to be hospitalized against their will only in extreme circumstances. If you're a danger to yourself or to others, if you're actively suicidal, or if you're neglecting yourself severely, you may be detained in the hospital, but this would be to keep you safe, not to punish you. Home treatment teams may also exist in your area.

- **What if my therapist passes on my private information to social services or my employer?** The information that you share with any mental health professional is confidential and won't be given to family members or employers without your explicit (usually written) consent. An exception to this is when clear risks to yourself or others — including children — are identified.

  Only in extreme and relatively rare circumstances do therapists ask social services to assess the impact of a mental health problem on a patient's family or children. In all but the most extreme circumstances, your therapist can tell you of their intention to involve outside agencies.

If you have any of these worries, voice them with your doctor or therapist. Worrying is normal, and any mental health professional with even the smallest amount of therapy experience can be sensitive to your concerns and discomfort. If they're not sensitive to your needs, consider seeking help from somebody else.

Making the Most of CBT

So what can you expect from your CBT therapist? As a rule, a lot! Most likely, you'll end up feeling that you're working hard both during and between sessions.

Discussing issues during sessions

When you meet with your CBT therapist, expect extensive two-way discussion, as well as some challenging questions from them. Topics for collaboration may include the following:

>> **Treatment goals:** CBT is goal-focused. Your therapist is likely to ask you about your therapeutic goals early in treatment. If your goals aren't realistic, your therapist will discuss modifying them with you.

>> **Specific problems, causes, and solutions:** A skilled CBT therapist can share their ideas about what's perpetuating your problems and invite you to work with them on what can help you in the long run. You can also expect your therapist to agree *with you* to a treatment strategy, which is likely to include homework assignments.

REMEMBER

Although you may, on occasion, feel awkward with your therapist, they're speaking from a place of sound, clinical experience and know that some behavioral exercises, although they can be uncomfortable for you in the short term, can get you better in the long term.

Expect your sessions to be focused. Your therapist may interrupt and refocus you if you stray off course and don't address the actual issues that brought you to treatment. Additionally, a good CBT therapist may pull you up if you avoid working on your problem areas.

Your CBT therapist is a human just like you. Your therapist shouldn't give the impression that they consider themselves above you or fundamentally different from you simply because you're the patient and they're the professional. Most skilled CBT therapists acknowledge that they're the experts on CBT, and possibly on particular psychological problems, but that *you* know yourself best. Therefore, they may ask you a lot of questions about your experiences, thoughts, and feelings rather than telling you what you experience, think, and feel.

Just as you can expect your CBT therapist to be open and honest during sessions, you can get even more from your sessions by being open about your doubts and reservations. Although doubt is wholly natural, be prepared to reconsider your reluctant feelings about change.

Even if you know intellectually that a new way of thinking or acting is better, you may still have a gut reservation. For example, we often see clients who realize that their rigid expectations of themselves are leading to extreme stress but still fear that they may perform badly if they give them up. In these cases, we often must help people see that being more flexible doesn't mean dropping their ideal standards. You can still strive for your personal best without demanding excellence.

Being active between sessions

CBT is in part educational, so your therapist may use a whiteboard, pen and paper, and various printed forms in your treatment. At some stage, your therapist may give you an ABC form or a thought record sheet (which we explain in Chapter 4).

Some of your homework will be written and some will be behavioral. Whatever form it takes, however, you can expect your therapist to give you a solid rationale for any intervention they use or homework they suggest. Your therapist is also likely to give you handouts and reading materials or recommend online resources.

TIP

Being ready to engage actively in therapy is a major key to your success, so if you're asked to do an exposure assignment or behavioral experiment that you don't feel ready to take on, say so, and suggest an alternative. You may want to address any ambivalence about therapy using a cost-benefit analysis. Weigh the costs and benefits of carrying on as you are versus trying out new ways of thinking and behaving.

To make your CBT experience successful, do your homework. We find that whether a client completes therapy assignments or not is the single best predictor of success. CBT involves retraining your attention, changing your behavioral patterns, and adopting new ways of thinking. Breaking old patterns and replacing them with new ones takes practice and repetition.

REMEMBER

Consider therapy as a temporary experiment. Give your therapist's advice a shot and see what happens. You can always return to your old ways or try out a new strategy if you think your therapy isn't working.

HALLMARKS OF A GOOD CBT THERAPIST

CBT practitioners exhibit some fairly predictable behaviors in session. You can use the following list of attitudes, actions, and interactions to help you determine whether you're actually receiving CBT treatment and to assess the standard of your therapy. In general, good CBT therapists

- Help you define problems and ask about your goals and expectations for therapy.

- Explain a bit about CBT at your first meeting and invite you to ask questions.

- Use scales and measures to record things like your levels of depression or anxiety and help monitor your progress.

- Evaluate your problems based on the CBT model and explain this process to you so that you can do it yourself in the future.

- Ask questions to elicit your thoughts and help you evaluate them.

- Are active in sessions, educating you about CBT and its perspective on your problems, asking questions, writing things down, and suggesting ways to try to improve your problems.

- Develop therapy homework exercises with you to be carried out between sessions.

- Review your homework. If you haven't done it, a thorough therapist can discuss the obstacles that stopped you from doing so.

- Regularly review your progress and reassess your goals with you.

- Invite feedback about therapy generally and openly listen to any constructive criticism you give.

- Invite you to voice any doubts, reservations, and fears you have about aspects of your CBT.

- Challenge your unhelpful beliefs and behaviors and help you do the same on your own.

- Encourage you to be independent and to take personal responsibility for your mental health.

- Answer most of your questions and tell you why if they don't or can't answer others.

- Refer you to another professional if you require additional or alternative help.

(continued)

(continued)

- Receive regular clinical supervision (in which they have their work listened to or have discussions with other therapists) to improve their practice. Don't be afraid to ask about this. It's important!

Okay, so this list is rather long, but we recommend consulting it if you have any doubts about your CBT therapist. Don't hesitate to take this list to your therapist and ask them to clarify their position on any or all these points. Even though you may be seeing an experienced or qualified CBT practitioner, attitudes and styles of therapeutic delivery can vary dramatically. Like many therapists, we're always pleased when clients suggest ways in which we can make sessions more helpful.

5 The Part of Tens

Chapter **25**

Ten Healthy Philosophies for Living

A s we discuss many times in this book, the attitudes you hold about your-self, other people, and the world greatly affect your ability to respond suc-cessfully to negative life events. Even in the absence of unusual or difficult circumstances, your core philosophies influence your overall experience of life. People who hold flexible and healthy philosophies are generally less prone to emotional disturbances, such as anxiety and depression, and are more readily able to solve problems.

This chapter offers ten healthy philosophical standpoints that are good for your psychological health. Read them, reread them, think them through, and test them out for yourself.

Assuming Emotional Responsibility: Owning the Way You Feel

Bad or unfortunate things, such as splitting up from a partner, losing a job, or having a car accident, can happen to anyone. You may reasonably have negative feelings in response to such events. Experiencing extreme sadness or annoyance in the face of misfortune is wholly understandable.

In some instances, bad things occur through no fault of your own. In other cases, you may have some personal responsibility. We don't suggest that you blame yourself for every bad thing that comes your way. However, try to assess a given situation and determine whether you have any *legitimate responsibility* for its development and look for a resolution.

Even if you're not personally responsible for a negative event, you can still take responsibility for your emotional and behavioral responses to the event. For example, after a period of appropriate sadness and readjustment following a relationship breakdown, many people move forward with their lives and begin to let go of the past. Others may continue to nurse their hurt feelings and nurture ongoing resentment that prevents them from moving on. The element of choice here is undeniable.

People who deny their part in creating their own emotional problems in the face of negative events don't recognize how their thoughts and actions can make a bad situation worse. They hand over their personal power to make things better by waiting passively for someone or something to step into the breach.

When you hold an attitude of personal responsibility for your feelings and actions, you're more able to find creative solutions, and your belief in your ability to cope with adversity is heightened. You empower yourself by focusing on your capacity to influence the way you feel even if you can't control events.

On a cheerier note, when good things happen, you can also assess the extent to which they're a result of your own efforts — and then give yourself credit where due. You can appreciate good fortune without sabotaging your positive feelings with worries that your luck may run out.

Thinking Flexibly

Making demands and commands — thinking in terms of "must," "should," and "have to" — about yourself, other people, and the world around you is a fundamental problem because it limits your ability to adapt to reality. The human capacity to adapt creatively to what's going on is one of the hallmarks of the species' success. However, humans are fallible, and the world continues to be an imperfect place. Insisting "It shouldn't be this way!" can leave you irate, depressed, or anxious and much less able to focus on how to cope with and adapt to reality.

TIP

Consider animals that manage to adapt and cope with ever-changing and challenging environments, like the urban fox. Try to adapt and solve problems instead of wasting time banging your head against a solid wall. Be like a fox and find a way around it.

REMEMBER

Although circumstances could well be desirable, preferable, and even better if the situation were different, they don't *have* to be a particular way. Accepting reality and striving to improve it where wise and achievable can help you save your energy for creative thought and action. See Chapter 2 for more on demands and Chapter 16 for more on developing realistic attitudes toward yourself.

Valuing Your Individuality

You can express your individuality in many ways, such as in your dress sense, musical tastes, hobbies, political opinions, and choice of career. Yet perhaps you're hesitant to express your individuality openly because you fear the reaction of others. People who develop the ability to value their idiosyncrasies and to express them respectfully tend to be well-adjusted and content. Accepting that you're an individual and have the right to live your life, just as other people have the right to live theirs, is a pretty good recipe for happiness.

As social animals, humans like to feel part of a group or social structure, and they tend to be happier when interacting meaningfully with others. However, the ability to go against group mentality when it's at odds with your own personal views or values is a tremendous skill. You can be both socially integrated and true to your values by accepting yourself as an individual and by being a selective nonconformist. Check out Chapter 16 for more on accepting yourself.

Accepting That Life Can Be Unfair

Sometimes, life's just plain unfair. People treat you unjustly, and nothing is done to reset the balance. Bad things happen to the nicest of people, and people who don't seem to have done a deserving thing in their lives get a winning ticket. On top of being unfair, life is unpredictable and uncertain a great deal of the time. And really, that's just the way life is.

What can you do? You can whine and moan and make yourself thoroughly miserable about the lamentable state of the world. Or you can accept things and get on with the business of living. No matter how much you insist that the world should be fair and you should be given certainty about how things are going to pan out, you ain't going to get it.

Life's unfair to pretty much everyone from time to time, which means that perhaps things aren't as desperately unfair as you thought. If you can accept the cold, hard reality of injustice and uncertainty, you're far more likely to be able to bounce back when life slaps you in the face with a wet fish. You're also likely to be less anxious about making decisions and taking risks. You can still strive to play fair yourself, but if you accept that unfairness exists, you may be less outraged and less horrified if and when justice simply doesn't prevail.

Understanding That Approval from Others Isn't Necessary

Receiving approval from someone important to you is nice. Getting a bit of praise from a boss or a friend can feel good. But if you believe that you *need* the approval of significant others or, indeed, everyone you meet, then you probably spend a lot of time feeling unhappy and unsure of yourself. Many people get depressed because they believe they're only as good as the opinions others hold of them. These people don't feel good about themselves unless they receive positive feedback or reassurance from others.

TIP

Accept yourself, independent of overt approval from other people in your life. Having a *preference* for being liked, appreciated, and approved of by others — but not believing that you *need* approval — means that your self-opinion can be stable and you can weather disapproval. You may still behave in ways that are more likely to generate approval than disapproval, but you can also assert yourself without fear. You can consider praise and compliments a bonus rather than something you must cling to and work super-hard to maintain.

If you hold the belief that you *need* rather than *desire* approval, you may pay emotionally for it somewhere along the line. You're likely to feel anxious about whether approval's forthcoming — and when you get approval you may worry about losing it. If you fail to get obvious approval or — horror of all horrors — someone criticizes you, you're likely to put yourself down and make yourself depressed. Refer to Chapter 10 for more on combating anxiety, and Chapter 11 for tackling depression.

REMEMBER

You can't please all the people all the time, and if that's what you try to do, you're almost certainly going to be overly passive. If you can take the view that disapproval isn't the end of the world, intolerable, and an indication that you're less than worthy, you can enjoy approval when you get it and still accept yourself when you don't.

Realizing Love Is Desirable, Not Essential

Some people would rather be in any relationship — even an unsatisfying or abusive one — than in no relationship at all. This need may stem from a belief that they can't cope with feelings of loneliness or get through life in general if they're alone. Other people consider themselves worthy or lovable only when they're reassured by being in a relationship.

Romantic relationships can enhance your enjoyment of life, but they're not essential for you to enjoy life. Holding this attitude can help you feel good about yourself when you're not part of a couple and may lead you to make more discerning partner choices in the future since you'll choose, rather than be compelled, to be with someone. Believing that your basic lovability is relatively constant, regardless of whether a significant other actively loves you, can help you feel secure *within* a relationship and secure within yourself *outside* of a relationship.

People who strongly prefer having a partner and yet believe that they can survive a break-up or periods of being single tend to experience little romantic jealousy. Jealousy can be a big obstacle to relationship satisfaction. Jealous people tend to believe that they *must* keep their partner and end up focusing on signs (real or imagined) of infidelity or waning interest rather than on the pleasure of the relationship. Jealousy's turned many a relationship sour. A jealous partner can end up alienating the other person through constant reassurance-seeking or suspicious monitoring, leaving both parties feeling that mutual trust doesn't exist between them.

Preferring instead of *demanding* to have a relationship helps you to retain your independence and individuality. Then when you *are* in a relationship, you're less likely to fall into the trap of trying to be the perfect partner — which means you can continue to attend to your own interests while being able to negotiate compromises when appropriate. You'll also be able to call a halt to destructive relationships when evidence suggests that there's no way forward.

Tolerating Short-Term Discomfort

Healthy, robust, and successful people are often able to tolerate temporary discomfort in the pursuit of longer-term goals. They practice self-denial and delay gratification when doing so is in their long-term interests. These people are the ones who eat healthily, exercise regularly, save money, are romantically faithful, study effectively, and so on. We're not saying that distress doesn't matter or that we don't wish you a life free from experiences that cause pain and suffering. This whole book is aimed at reducing their suffering. However, a growing body of research shows that the way we tolerate discomfort predicts a huge range of self-helping behaviors.

REMEMBER

You can experience intense pleasure in the present and the future, but often some degree of pain and effort *today* are necessary to win you greater pleasure *tomorrow*. This will be true for many of the achievements you've already made in life. Putting up with temporary discomfort is also going to be crucial in *reducing* painful feelings of anxiety and depression. See Chapters 10 and 11 for more on overcoming these problems. The good news is that there's also evidence from research that embracing discomfort is something we can get better at with practice and may be a whole lot more useful than us wishing we had more willpower.

Enacting Enlightened Self-Interest

Enlightened self-interest is about putting yourself first most of the time and one, two, or a small handful of selected others a very close second. Enlightened self-interest is about looking after your own needs and interests while also being mindful of the needs of your loved ones and others living on the planet.

So why put yourself first? When you reach a certain age, you need to look after yourself because nobody else is going to do it for you. If you can keep yourself healthy and content, you're better able to turn your attention to caring for the people in your life that you love.

Many people make the mistake of always suppressing their own needs and end up tired, unhappy, or ill. People may think they're doing the right thing by putting others first all the time, but in fact they're leaving themselves with very little to give.

Of course, you'll experience times when putting someone else's needs before your own and making personal sacrifices is a good choice. For example, parents frequently put the welfare of their children before their own. But you must make space for your own pursuits too.

If you're starting to get concerned that "self-interest" translates to "selfish beast," stop! To clarify, self-interest involves taking responsibility for looking after yourself because you understand that you're worth taking care of. Self-interest means being able to care for others deeply. When you're self-interested, you're able to meet your own needs and take a keen interest in the welfare of other people in the world around you. You can also determine when you're going to put yourself *second* for a period because someone else's need is greater than your own — which is where the "enlightened" part comes into play.

Selfishness is not — we stress, *not!* — the same animal as self-interest. Ultimately, selfish people put their own wants and needs first *to the exclusion and detriment of other people.* Selfishness is much less about taking responsibility for looking after yourself and much more about demanding that you get what you want, when you want, and to hell with everybody else. The two concepts are very different, so don't be scared. Head to Chapter 21 for more on building a lifestyle that promotes taking care of yourself.

Pursuing Interests and Acting Consistently with Your Values

Evidence indicates that people are happier and healthier if they pursue interests and hobbies. Have you let your life become dominated by work or chores at home, and do you spend your evenings sitting in front of the television as a means of recharging? If your answer to this question is "Yes!", then you're in extremely good, but not optimally healthy, company.

One of the arts of maximizing your happiness is pursuing personally meaningful goals, such as furthering your education, participating in sports and exercise, developing skills, improving relationships, getting involved in your community, or acting in ways that contribute to the sort of world you'd like to live in, such as by doing some volunteer work. Try to structure your life to ensure that you have some time for personally meaningful pursuits. Check that the things you do in life reflect what you believe is important.

As far as we can tell, life isn't a dress rehearsal. Will you really look back and regret missing a bit of time on social media because you dragged yourself away from a screen to spend time on a hobby, to exercise, to enjoy a night out with your friends, or to participate in some charity work?

People today spend a lot more time on virtual relationships than previous generations could've even imagined possible. While a lot of good comes from the ease of communication that technology provides, old-fashioned face-to-face contact has unparalleled benefits.

Tolerating Uncertainty

This topic has become an important focus in recent years. Healthy and productive people tend to be prepared to tolerate a degree of risk and uncertainty. Demanding certainty and guarantees in an uncertain world is a sure-fire recipe for worry and inactivity (not to mention disappointment). Safety (or more accurately, the *illusion* of complete safety) comes at a cost: fewer rewards, less excitement, and fewer new experiences.

The fact that you don't know what the future holds is grounds for calculated risks and experiments, not avoidance, reassurance-seeking, or excessive safety precautions. You can make educated decisions and take calculated risks, but if you accept that 100 percent certainty is exceptionally rare (and, in fact, unnecessary), you can reduce undue anxiety and worry. Risk is inherent to existence. You know that you're mortal and therefore destined to die one day but, to remain sane, you keep that knowledge on the outer track of your daily consciousness. You live in an uncertain world every single day of your life. Embrace it, enjoy it, and relegate it to your peripheral vision.

Chapter **26**

Ten Common Self-Esteem Boosters to Avoid

The way you run your mind is in large part down to behaviors that were either rewarded or punished as you grew and developed. Not only were you not given a user's manual to the human mind when you were "delivered" to the world, nobody else got one either. It's hardly surprising that we humans sometimes fall into suboptimal traps. You may be trying to manage your low self-esteem in ways that are counterproductive, particularly in the long term. This chapter highlights ten techniques that don't boost your self-esteem effectively.

"Why focus on where I'm going wrong?" you may ask. Well, using the strategies we describe in this chapter to boost your self-esteem is like trying to dig your way out of a hole. Your first step is to realize you're digging yourself deeper, so put down that shovel! Only when you stop digging can you begin to look for other ways to get out of the hole. Fortunately, we include several self-esteem ladders within this book to help you find your way out.

The following ten points describe counterproductive strategies for boosting your self-esteem. We explain why they don't work and suggest more constructive ways of increasing your sense of self-worth.

Putting Others Down

If you measure your self-esteem by comparing yourself with other people and tend to regard yourself as inferior, you may try to boost your worth by putting down other people, whether in your mind, by moaning about them to others, or by criticizing them directly.

By trying to put others into a position of inferiority, you may manage to persuade yourself temporarily that you're in a position of superiority — "better than they are." But it's not true, and you don't change the underlying problem: your attitude toward yourself. Putting down others is tiring not only for you but also for other people, and doing so doesn't elicit warm responses from others.

Instead, try respecting your own uniqueness and that of others. The human race refers to a species, not a competition. Focus on following your own values and pursuing your own goals. Pay more attention to your own strengths rather than others' weaknesses.

REMEMBER

If you think of yourself as inferior, reevaluating your attitude toward the person in the mirror is more effective than trying to pull down someone else's self-esteem. Respecting others and valuing their human frailty can also help you be self-compassionate. (See Chapter 18 for more on compassionate mind training.)

Thinking You're Special or Superior

You may have superior, equal, or inferior traits compared with other people, but the idea that you're either an inferior or a superior person is an overgeneralization. No one is superior or inferior to everyone else in every way. We all have different strengths and weaknesses.

Some people can only feel good about themselves when they convince themselves that they're "the best." Many people with this tendency try to demonstrate their superiority by showing off their physical or psychological strength. For example, you may feel driven to impress people with your wit, intellect, or other talent. Unfortunately, these solutions are only temporary ones to your underlying feelings of inferiority, which should be your real target for change. At worst, your attempts at superiority serve only to alienate other people and mask your true strengths.

TIP

Trying to replace a sense of worthlessness with a feeling of specialness is another common self-defeating technique that ultimately maintains low self-esteem. Look out for times when you tell yourself "If I'm not different, I'm nothing" or "Being average or normal is like not existing."

The problem here is that, as far as the universe is concerned, you're not special. No one is. Or everyone is. You may be unique, but so is everyone else; it becomes a circular argument. In fact, you may well try so hard to avoid the "horror" of mediocrity that you end up living an unhappy and unfulfilled life. This tendency largely stems from an extreme form of all-or-nothing thinking (which we cover in Chapter 2) and the mistaken idea that you need to reduce low self-esteem by wildly overcompensating.

TIP

Rather than trying to assert that you're special or better, focus your attention in a more constructive direction. Challenge the idea that you need to be special to feel okay about yourself. Accept yourself as a normal, ordinary, worthwhile individual, just like everyone else.

Trying to Get Everyone to Like You

Substituting your dislike of yourself by trying to win the approval of others is a recipe for anxiety. You can end up feeling anxious about not achieving your goal of being liked by someone or a group. If you do achieve your goal and win approval, you're likely to become anxious about losing your prize.

The real pity is that your imagined need for approval may not help you give off the attractive, self-assured air you'd so dearly like. Believing that you need to be liked to like yourself can leave you in a desperate position. Allowing people to walk all over you to win their approval has a pretty negative impact on your self-esteem for fairly obvious reasons.

People who like themselves tend to focus on finding people that they like and forging mutually rewarding relationships. In other words, people with solid self-esteem focus on liking others rather than on trying desperately to be liked *by* others.

TIP

Rather than attempting to win approval, strive for respect. If you respect yourself, you give off an air of being comfortable in your own skin. People with true self-respect are often those who are most respected by others. You don't have to be a slave to this principle, but seeking respect can help you assert yourself more readily.

Placing Yourself Above Criticism

Placing yourself above criticism is a classic tactic if you believe that being criticized reveals you to be inadequate, useless, or a failure. Perfectionism, covering up your weaknesses, and defensiveness are the inevitable result. You try to be flawless so that other people can't criticize you. However, you end up being unduly harsh with yourself for your shortcomings and errors. You may even believe that you can knock yourself into shape by criticizing yourself, unwittingly lowering your self-image further.

Instead, try to accept your human fallibility without condemning yourself. Mistakes and flaws are an unavoidable aspect of being human, no matter how hard you try to change things. Don't be ashamed of your shortcomings. Everyone else has flaws too. Do you think people will really lose respect for you if they find out you're only human? They probably won't. Chances are, they'll be relieved and feel more able to relax in your company. Their respect for you may even grow because they can accept you, warts and all.

Reveal an imperfection and check out the response you get. Try accepting yourself nondefensively in the face of criticism. If someone criticizes you, try asking them for more information. Most people find owning up to their human fallibility a far more productive strategy than striving to be perfect.

REMEMBER

Choosing perfection as your goal is setting yourself up to fail because no one is capable of being perfect. The more you fail to reach your unrealistic goal, the more you put yourself down. Don't be tempted to try harder to be perfect. Instead, try harder to accept your imperfection.

Avoiding Failure, Disapproval, Rejection, and Other Animals

You may find that you avoid situations, places, or people that trigger your tendency to put yourself down. This approach is very much a way of papering over the cracks. Your underlying attitude toward yourself remains the problem. By avoiding potential failure, you don't change your attitude; you simply postpone setting off your insecurity for a while.

TIP

A long-lasting, elegant solution to overcoming poor self-esteem is for you to uncover, examine, and change any unhelpful attitudes you may have developed toward yourself. Then you can deliberately seek out the things you've been avoiding, while practicing your new self-accepting attitude. (Head to Chapter 16 for more.)

Avoiding Your Emotions

You may try to block out certain emotions because you regard them as a sign of weakness. Although you may try to persuade yourself that you're strong because you can control your emotions, your relationships and psychological health are likely to suffer.

Having a wide range of emotions is part of what makes you human. Try as you might, avoiding these emotions is difficult — and unhealthy. You may end up feeling isolated, cold, and aloof in your relationships, which can rob you of much richer and more satisfying experiences. Begin to accept your feelings and recognize that this acceptance shows courage, not weakness.

REMEMBER

Experiencing strong negative emotions can be a natural response to adversity, a part of the healing process, and a sign of strength in facing up to difficulties.

Attempting to Feel More Significant by Controlling Others

If you try to control others, the underlying assumption is that you need to prove your significance by influencing other people. The problem is that without this proof, you're (in your eyes) insignificant.

Perhaps you immediately offer unsolicited advice or try to convert others to a favorite cause to prove that you're a person of influence. Unfortunately, your lack of respect for others' thoughts, feelings, and behaviors may actually be a turn-off to those other people.

Compulsively trying to influence or affect people shows you have a lack of control. You also reinforce a negative self-image by acting as if you must prove something to be worthwhile or significant.

Imagine how you'd interact with people if you didn't have the need to prove your power or influence. You can use this imagining exercise as a guide to new, healthier behavior.

Over-Defending Your Self-Worth

We don't advocate you being a doormat, but the healthy alternative to being passive is to stay calm in the face of minor slights. Constantly defending your self-worth can lead to verbal or physical aggression (Chapter 17). Besides, if you're confident in your self-worth, do you really need to guard it so carefully? Insisting that others must show you respect at all times leads to unhealthy anger. Your compulsive outrage at being disrespected can simply drive you to take people to task for minor assaults on your fragile self-esteem.

Respect yourself regardless of whether other people treat you respectfully. Self-respect affords you the ability to assert yourself appropriately when it's worth doing so.

Confusing Taking Personal Responsibility with Taking the Blame

Blaming your problems on your past, genetics, hormones, brain chemistry, or other people has the distinct advantage of temporarily alleviating any sense that you're stupid, pathetic, or less worthwhile. This blame system stems from the mistaken idea that if you take an appropriate degree of responsibility for your emotional problems, it means that you're to blame for those problems. But protecting your self-esteem by blaming something or someone else typically backfires, which makes real change more difficult because you attribute your problems to factors outside of your control.

Half of the people in the Western world experience some kind of significant emotional problem during their lives. So having an emotional problem simply means you're human.

TIP

Use your understanding of your past and your makeup to develop a compassionate, sympathetic perspective toward your current difficulties. Take some personal responsibility for keeping your problems going. Recognizing how you may be making your problems worse gives you the power to make changes for the better.

Unhelpful ideas about how to feel good about yourself can stem from childhood messages. Teachers or parents may have told you one or more of the following:

>> Be the best.

>> Never admit that you're wrong.

>> Our family is better than other families.

>> Failure isn't an option.

>> Boys don't cry.

Such messages may have been offered to you as words of wisdom, but as an adult you can reevaluate their truth and helpfulness. You can decide to dump them in favor of updated, self-acceptance, and other acceptance beliefs. Many of the mottos you may have grown up with are gender biased and have a "girls are like this and boys are like that" message. When you notice them, take a psychological stand against them.

Mistakenly Believing That Self-Esteem Is the Road to Happiness

If you ask the average person on the street which aspect of thinking is most likely to increase happiness or emotional well-being, they're very likely to put improved self-esteem. This is a commonly held view, and with social media allowing unqualified "influencers" to have at least as loud a voice as any science-informed expert, there has never been an echo chamber for nonsense like it. You're reading this book, so we're, in a sense, "preaching to the choir." But just to reinforce the point, there's a lot more to mental health than that.

At the core of CBT theory are three fundamental views that are hugely important: your beliefs about self, others, and the world. If you only move one of those in a healthier direction, you'll be missing a great deal. Moreover, CBT holds that our beliefs are fed by our thinking biases and our behaviors. Further, we're social animals, so focusing on our self-esteem at the expense of improving our relationships with others is missing out on one of the most important sources of mental well-being. Self-sacrifice in and putting others' needs ahead of your own, in good measure, is often more likely to give you lasting mental health and happiness than taking care of your ego.

TIP

Break free from the self-esteem trap by taking a more sophisticated view. Consider compassion (for others and yourself), building balanced and healthier beliefs about other people and the world you live in, taking real care of your body and your environment, following your values, tolerating distress, keeping a healthy range of activities, and deepening your connection with others as items on your menu of options to help yourself truly feel good.

Chapter **27**

Ten Mythical Monsters of Mental Health

Throughout this book, we've aimed to convey that psychological problems are no more mysterious than physical ones. In the recent past (and even today), people often viewed mental health problems as a sign of intrinsic character flaws. If your body has a problem, that's understandable, but if your mind has a problem, then something must be wrong with you. Not true. Mental health problems don't happen because you're weak or crazy. Mind and body aren't separate entities; you're no more to blame for psychological problems than for physical problems. The points in this chapter highlight and bust many myths surrounding mental health. Some contradict one another, yet people often find that they hold more than one conflicting negative idea at the same time.

Psychological Problems Mean You're Weak

When you're depressed or suffering from anxiety or panic (to name but a few), you're in a diminished state. You're ill or you're in a weakened state. Would you consider yourself weak for having a bout of the flu or epilepsy? Probably (and hopefully) not. Weakened through illness doesn't mean weak overall.

Similarly, mental strength doesn't equal mental health. Many resilient people who pride themselves as "copers" find periods of poor mental health particularly hard to accept. Even people with jobs that require tremendous mental fortitude, such as parents, teachers, nurses, surgeons, firemen, paramedics, the military, performers, and athletes, can and do suffer periods of mental illness. So if someone tells you that they've never had psychological problems in their life, it doesn't mean that they're stronger than you; it means that they're either extraordinarily fortunate or lying.

I Should Be Able to Get Better on My Own

Should you, though? This monster myth dances a damaging duo with the one in the preceding section. Shame about mental ill health leads to secrecy and tends to keep people suffering in silence for a long time. We may be writing a self-help book, but that's only one way to get better. (See Chapter 24 for more about getting additional professional support.)

REMEMBER

Mental health professionals exist because everyone needs help to overcome problems; you can't always do it by yourself. Suffering needlessly has no virtue, so get help sooner rather than later.

Mental Health Is an Either/Or Issue

Like your physical body, your mind is ever vulnerable to injury or illness. A bad episode in your life, such as a trauma, can leave you psychologically injured, and you need proper care to repair. Protracted periods of stress can wear you down and leave you open to a nasty bout of depression. Even if you suffer from a chronic mental health disorder like bipolar disorder, you're not *always* mentally unwell. With the appropriate medication and treatment, you can lead a stable life much the same as someone suffering from epilepsy or diabetes. Therefore, nobody is ever either completely mentally well or unwell; everyone experiences both in a lifetime.

You Get Better All at Once

Just like getting physically fitter and more flexible, recovery from depression or anxiety takes time. Everyone's journey is different; how quickly and consistently you start to improve depends on a host of factors, including the severity of your illness to start with. Be patient with yourself, and don't give up if you have a setback. Setbacks are a normal part of recovery, and you often can learn from them. If you really want to know what predicts a good outcome in CBT, it's getting started!

Pacing yourself — being realistic about goals — is important. A good CBT therapist motivates you and reins you in if you're expecting too much of yourself. Even after you're beginning to see the light flickering at the end of the proverbial tunnel, remember that you're convalescing. Keep treating yourself compassionately and be aware of your limitations until you're well and truly back on your feet.

The Drugs Don't Work; They Just Make You Worse

Many people recover from common mental health problems without needing psychiatric medication. Some need medication for only a short period of time, perhaps to aid sleep, alleviate anxiety symptoms, or readjust depleted levels of serotonin via an antidepressant. Most of the psychiatric medications your doctor might prescribe have relatively minor side effects and aren't dependency-forming or addictive.

REMEMBER

Doctors should be mindful of limiting the number of prescriptions given, do standard medication reviews, and inform you of any potential side effects so you know what to expect. Your doctor should also consult you about stopping medications and give you a gradual reduction regime to curtail any possible withdrawal effects. The majority of individuals we treat have no major difficulties going on or coming off medication.

WARNING

While lessons continue to be learned, a lot of scaremongering goes on out there about everyday psychiatric medications. Psychiatric problems have long been an easy target for controversy and extreme opinion. If you go online to research a drug, stick to reputable websites and avoid opinion-based anecdotal forums. Research into the efficacy and safety of drugs can be confusing and misleadingly represented in the media, so be skeptical about what you hear.

For many people, the drugs do work; for others, medication isn't something they can afford to do without. Conditions like bipolar, forms of psychosis, and severe OCD or BDD require carefully considered medications or combinations of medications to be successfully managed. Speak to a registered psychologist or psychiatrist if you're in need of a professional opinion.

Certain Types of Psychological Disorders Are Glamorous

Here's one of the contradictions we talked about earlier in the chapter. On the one hand, people tend to view psychological illness as shameful, while on the other they romanticize some forms of disturbance. Have you ever heard someone describe themselves as "a little OCD" because they like a tidy house or are very organized? Or perhaps you know of someone who describes themselves as having a "phobia" of something that they really just dislike.

Trivializing or romanticizing any type of mental health problem this way minimizes the profound suffering these disorders can cause. Of course, people use psychological terms in a colloquial sense and mean no harm by it. But for someone with true OCD that impacts their ability to work and maintain relationships, a flippant comment can be hard to swallow. Then you have the articles in the news about online sites that seem to promote or glamorize self-harm and eating disorders.

REMEMBER

Serious misrepresentations and misunderstandings of mental health problems among individuals are floating around online, in film, on TV, and even among well-meaning health workers who may lack specific psychiatric training. Mental illness is no laughing matter, and it's not stylish to deliberately adopt or mimic selected symptoms. Some social media sites are attempting to limit profiles that promote self-harm or eating disorders, but it's still a work in progress.

Mental Illness Is Unpreventable; It's Just Bad Luck

You can do a lot to keep your mind fit and well. Just as you watch your diet and exercise regularly to keep your body performing well, you can do a lot to keep your mind healthy. Happily, a lot of what you do to keep physically healthy also helps to keep you on an even psychological keel. Good food, a varied lifestyle of work and play, plenty of rest and restorative sleep, as well as connected relationships play important parts in your overall well-being.

Many of the tips and strategies in this book are useful not just to pull yourself out of a slump but to keep you running at optimal levels. You may not be able to prevent every physical or mental illness through conscientious care of your mind/body "machine"; indeed, that would be impossible. But you can look after yourself during hard times, seek professional help at the first hint of relapse (if you've had psychological difficulties in the past), and embrace the types of healthy mental attitudes peppered throughout this book.

Everyone Can Tell When a Person Has a Mental Illness

Actually, it's almost impossible to tell just by looking whether a person is depressed or anxious, has OCD or PTSD, or suffers panic attacks. Even psychosis isn't immediately obvious and requires professional assessment. When people experience panic attacks in public, others often come to their aid thinking a physical explanation is to blame. Your best friend may not have a clue about how depressed you're feeling. That's why asking people in your life for support rather than hiding away because you feel vulnerable and exposed is important.

REMEMBER

Sharing your emotional and psychological problems for the first time can be difficult, but if you don't, others who care about you may never guess. Your doctor may give you some measures to fill out that can help identify anxiety and low mood. But even a doctor needs you to give them basic information about how you're feeling. Don't wait for help to come; wave a metaphorical distress flag that others can't miss.

Having a Mental Illness Means You're Dangerous

Very few individuals with severe and complex psychological disorders are ever a danger to others. Films hugely misrepresent mental disorders because it makes for good viewing; accuracy isn't often the filmmakers' main concern. You don't go from having intrusive OCD thoughts or images to becoming a serial killer. Nor will your anxiety mount and mount until your mind eventually breaks and you're no longer in control of your actions or are left a quivering wreck forever.

The common psychological disorders in this book don't change your value system or alter your moral compass. You're not a risk to others just because you're feeling bad. Yes, people sometimes engage in self-harm, misjudge risks, or have thoughts of suicide when experiencing poor mental health. It's important to tell someone close to you, your therapist, your doctor, and any other professional involved in your care if you're self-harming or feel the urge to do so.

If you're having thoughts of ending your life, seek support immediately, especially if you've developed a plan.

We advise behaving with an abundance of caution where any risk is concerned. That said, having dark thoughts about the point of life and the future is common when you're depressed or battling with another type of disorder. People often have suicidal thoughts and images that they worry they may impulsively act upon. Having thoughts about dying or death doesn't mean you're intent on suicide. However, it does mean you're feeling really awful.

Seeking Help Will Hurt My Future Prospects

If you get a formal diagnosis, it does go on your medical record, as does any medication you're prescribed. You'll be in good company, however, with the many thousands of others with some mental health issue on their records. Records are there to make sure you get the best treatment possible if you change doctors or must go into the hospital. The records' intended purpose is to be helpful, not to act as ammunition against you in the future. Most employers never see your full medical records. Also, the days of discrimination based on a history of psychological problems are over. Unfair treatment because of mental illness — past or present — is illegal. Know your rights; many charitable organizations offer legal advice, and some lawyers specialize in mental health cases. We've worked with many patients, and we can't recall any situation where seeking help caused a great impact on their lives. However, the previously untreated problem had all too often had a profound effect.

Appendix **A**

Recommended Resources

n this appendix we list some CBT and CBT-related resources to complement the information in this book. Some of the resources we've included will relate to self-help and others to CBT and psychology more generally.

Books

Numerous self-help resources, books, and professional manuals on CBT are available. We've tried to choose resources that reflect the diversity of CBT as an approach and that can add to your armory of knowledge and skills in tackling disturbing emotions or behaviors. We've also included some resources that aren't strictly CBT but contain useful information that will complement your self-help. The books included in this chapter are all ones that we know very well ourselves and have used successfully with our clients over the years (some we have written!). The list is not exhaustive, but these suggestions can point you in the right direction when it comes to investigating helpful, sound CBT literature.

>> *Cognitive Behavioral Therapy Workbook For Dummies* (Wiley): This book makes an excellent companion to the one you're currently reading. It includes lots of extra practical exercises to help you put core CBT skills into practice.

It can be used for independent self-help or in conjunction with a CBT therapist. Written by Rhena Branch and Rob Willson, this book is a valuable resource both for anyone seeking help overcoming their problems and for trainee CBT therapists alike.

>> *Boosting Self-Esteem For Dummies* **(Wiley):** No, the title isn't intended to be ironic! This *For Dummies* book (also by Branch and Willson) is another excellent companion to the one you're reading, if we do say so ourselves! It focuses on helping the reader to understand the underpinnings of poor self-esteem and the ways in which it is maintained. In it we also offer clear CBT-based strategies to improve your relationship with yourself (and others). This is a very useful and informative book for those many people in the world who struggle daily with feelings of low self-worth.

>> *Cognitive Therapy and the Emotional Disorders* **(Penguin Psychology):** *Cognitive Therapy and the Emotional Disorders* by Aaron T. Beck, the founder of cognitive therapy's original text on his research-based approach to emotional problems. Beck's contribution to the field of CBT has been phenomenal, not least because of the emphasis placed on scientifically evaluating CBT treatments. This is a historic book, and a good introduction to the fundamentals of CBT.

>> **The** *Overcoming . . .* **series (Robinson Press):** The *Overcoming . . .* books are an excellent series that attends to specific kinds of problems. These books are usually written by experts in their fields and are frequently recommended by professional therapists. The series includes *Overcoming Childhood Trauma* by Helen Kennerly; *Overcoming Depression* by Paul Gilbert; *Overcoming Obsessive Compulsive Disorder* by David Veale and Rob Willson; *Overcoming Health Anxiety* by Rob Willson and David Veale; *Overcoming Body Image Problems and BDD* by Rob Willson and David Veale; *Overcoming Social Anxiety and Shyness* by Gillian Buttler; *Overcoming Traumatic Stress* by Claudia Herbert and Ann Wetmore; and *Overcoming Mood Swings* (bipolar affective disorder) by Jan Scott.

>> *Overcoming Anger* **(Sheldon Press):** Windy Dryden, author of *Overcoming Anger,* has written or edited more than 150 books in the areas of counseling and psychotherapy. In a clear and forceful style, Windy shows how people create their anger with their attitudes and beliefs. He goes on to show how thinking rationally helps overcome unhealthy anger and communication with others. This Sheldon series also includes several other self-help books written by Windy Dryden focused on overcoming common emotional disorders such as hurt, envy, and shame.

>> *Reason and Emotion in Psychotherapy* **(Birch Lane Press):** Dr Albert Ellis, the author of *Reason and Emotion in Psychotherapy: A Comprehensive Method for Treating Human Disturbances, Revised and Updated*, is the true founding father of cognitive behavioral approaches to therapy. The rational emotive behavior therapy approach, described in this extensive volume, was the first fully

developed cognitive behavioral theory and treatment, dating back to the mid-1950s. This version of Ellis's seminal text gives an insight into the philosophy underpinning the approach and Ellis's phenomenal mind. Anyone interested in how reason and philosophy can be applied to reduce human suffering would do well to read this book.

>> *Cognitive Behavior Therapy: Basics and Beyond* **(The Guilford Press):** Judith S. Beck is the daughter of Aaron T. Beck. Now in its second edition, this book is regarded by many as the go-to introductory text for people seeking professional training in CBT.

>> *Oxford Guide to Behavioral Experiments in Cognitive Therapy:* James Bennett-Levy and colleagues edited this comprehensive text on the principles and applications of behavioral experiments.

>> *Compendium of CBT Treatment for Anxiety and Depressive Disorders* **(Cambridge University Press):** This is a comprehensive treatment manual covering a variety of mental health disorders (edited by Rhena Branch and Gillian Todd). It includes the latest research and CBT treatment protocols and guidelines written by well-known experts in each area. This book is useful for both CBT practitioners and students in the field.

Websites

Following are some reputable websites providing guidance on CBT strategies, assessment questionnaires for specific disorders, and other useful information.

>> **Nice Guidelines (`www.nice.org.uk/guidance`):** This website provides details of recommended treatment guidelines in the United Kingdom for a range of mental health problems.

>> **Professor David Veale (`www.veale.co.uk/`):** Professor David Veale is a consultant psychiatrist at Maudley NHS Trust and the Priory North London. He specializes in obsessive-compulsive disorder (OCD), body dysmorphic disorder (BDD), illness anxiety disorder (IAD) and specific phobia of vomiting (emetophobia). This website contains useful articles and a range of measurement tools and self-report measures for these disorders.

>> **MCT Institute (`https://mct-institute.co.uk/`):** Developed by Adrian Wells, this website provides details of developments in the field of *metacognitive therapy* (MCT), which deals with what you think about your thoughts. It contains a range of measures that some clinicians may find helpful relating to attention focus and attentional training techniques.

>> *Association for Behavioral and Cognitive Therapies* (`www.abct.org`): This America-based CBT organization provides information about CBT, conferences, continuing education, and an online directory of CBT therapists.

>> **British Association for Behavioral and Cognitive Psychotherapies (BABCP;** `www.babcp.com`**):** The BABCP website contains details of conferences and training courses in CBT. It also contains a list of BABCP-accredited CBT therapists within the United Kingdom, known as the CBT register. (You can access the register directly at `www.cbtregisteruk.com`.)

>> **Oxford Cognitive Therapy Centre (OCTC;** `www.OCTC.co.uk`**):** This page contains useful information about training courses and continued professional development (CPD) events in the United Kingdom.

>> **Anxiety and Depression Association of America (ADAA;** `www.ADAA.org`**).**

>> **Aaron T. Beck, founder of cognitive therapy** (`www.beckinstitute.org`**).**

>> **Albert Ellis** (`https://albertellis.org/`): Ellis was the founder of rational emotive behavior therapy (REBT), which is the practice of confronting your unhelpful beliefs and substituting better ones.

Videos

Following are sources of videos related to CBT:

>> **Judith S. Beck: "What is CBT?"** — a brief walkthrough of CBT from one of the key figures. `https://www.youtube.com/watch?v=I1maA5nToYM`.

>> **NHS Every Mind Matters: Self-help CBT video guides** (short, practical clips on reframing thoughts, facing fears, problem-solving, etc.) `https://www.nhs.uk/every-mind-matters/mental-wellbeing-tips/self-help-cbt-techniques/`.

>> **BABCPtv** (`https://www.youtube.com/@BABCPtv`) has a range of videos and conference presentations for those looking for a deeper dive into the world of CBT via video.

Appendix B

Forms

In this appendix you will find blank forms that you can photocopy and fill in, using the instructions provided here and within specific chapters.

The "Old Meaning–New Meaning" Sheet

The sheet has the three headings. Fill them in as follows:

1. **In the first column, "Event," record what actually happened.**

2. **Under "Old Meaning" in the second column, record what you believe the event means about you.**

   This is your unhealthy core belief.

3. **In the "New Meaning" third column, record a healthier and more accurate meaning for the event.**

   This is the new belief that you want to strengthen.

Head to Chapter 19 for a worked example of the sheet and for more about reviewing past events.

Event	Old Meaning	New Meaning

The Cost–Benefit Analysis Form

Carry out a *cost–benefit analysis* (CBA) to examine the pros and cons of something that can help galvanize your commitment to change. You can use a CBA to examine the advantages and disadvantages of a number of things, such as the following:

>> **Behaviors:** How helpful is this action to you? Does it bring short-term or long-term benefits?

>> **Emotions:** How helpful is this feeling? For example, does feeling guilty or angry really help you?

>> **Thoughts, attitudes, or beliefs:** Where does thinking this way get you? How does this belief help you?

>> **Options for solving a practical problem:** How can this solution work out? Is this really the best possible answer to the problem?

Evaluate the pros and cons:

>> In the short term

>> In the long term

>> For yourself

>> For other people

Try to write CBA statements in pairs, particularly when you're considering changing the way you feel, act, or think. What are the *advantages* of feeling anxiety? And the *disadvantages?* Write down pairs of statements for what you feel, do or think *currently,* and for other, healthier alternatives. Head to Chapter 8 for worked examples of the form.

Costs and benefits of:	
Costs (Disadvantages)	**Benefits (Advantages)**

The "TIC-TOC" Sheet

TICs are *task-interfering cognitions*, the thoughts, attitudes, and beliefs that get in the way of your progress. You need to respond with *TOCs* – *task-orienting cognitions*, which are constructive alternatives to TICs.

Fill out the TIC-TOC sheet by following these steps:

1. Identify the goal or task you want to focus on.
2. In the left column (TICs), list your thoughts, attitudes, and beliefs that get in the way of you achieving your aim.
3. In the right column (TOCs) put responses to each of your TICs that will help you achieve your goal or task.

Head to Chapter 22 for more on the TIC–TOC sheet.

Goal or task:	
Task-Interfering Cognitions (TICs)	**Task-Orienting Cognitions (TOCs)**

The Zigzag Form

Use the zigzag to help you really challenge those unhelpful thoughts! Similarly to the TIC-TOC sheet, this method will help you zig and zag your way out of unhelpful thinking habits.

1. Write down in the top left-hand box of the zigzag form a belief that you want to strengthen.

2. In the next box down, write your doubts, reservations, or challenges about the healthy belief.

3. In the next box, dispute your attack and redefend the healthy belief.

4. Repeat Steps 2 and 3 until you exhaust all your attacks on the healthy belief.

5. Re-rate, from 0 to 100 percent, how strongly you endorse the healthy belief after going through all your doubts.

Refer to Chapter 20 for more information about the zigzag form.

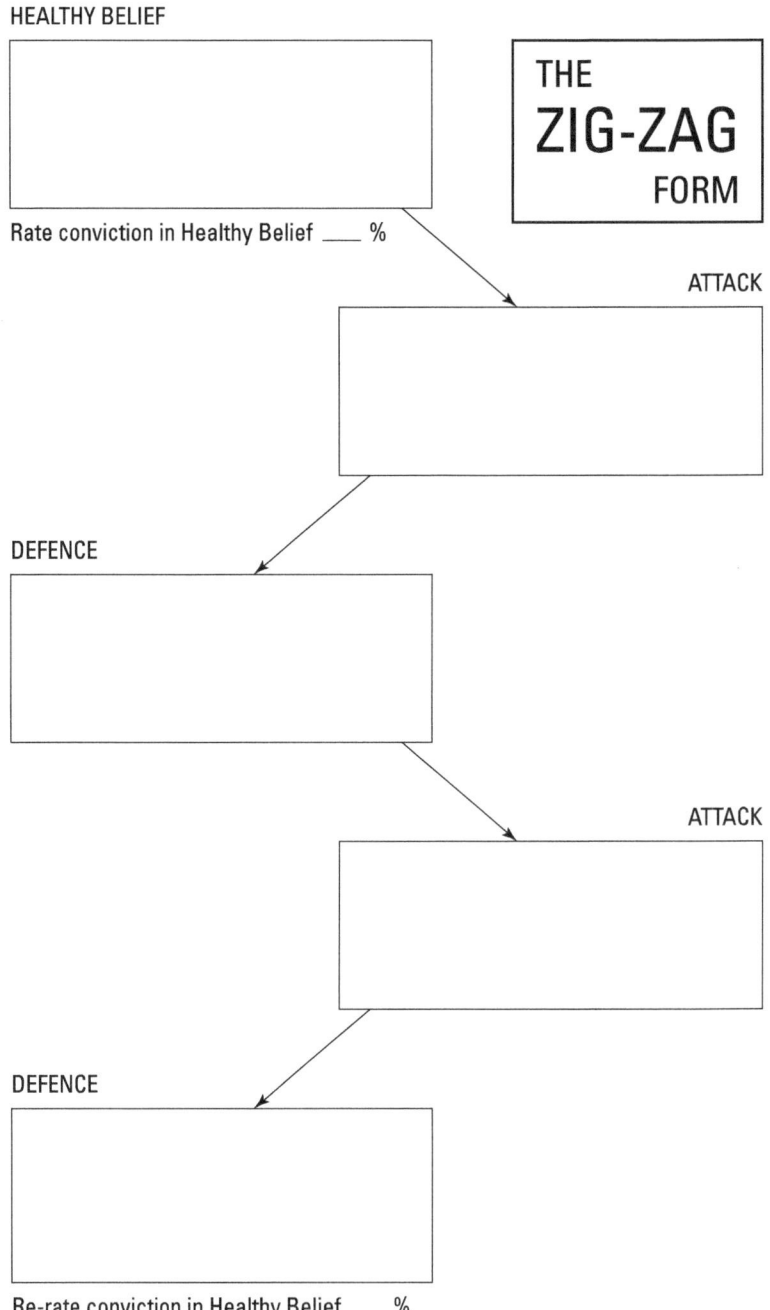

HEALTHY BELIEF

Rate conviction in Healthy Belief ____ %

THE
ZIG-ZAG
FORM

ATTACK

DEFENCE

ATTACK

DEFENCE

Re-rate conviction in Healthy Belief ____ %

The Vicious Flower

Use the vicious flower to help you see how things that may help you feel better in the short term actually maintain your problems in the long term.

1. In the Trigger box, write down the trigger that makes you feel anxious or upset.

2. In the central circle, write down the key thoughts and meanings you attach to the trigger.

3. In the flower petals, write down the emotions, behaviors, and sensations you experience when your uncomfortable feeling is triggered; in the top petal, write down what you tend to focus on.

Chapter 8 has loads more about the vicious flower exercise, and a filled-in example.

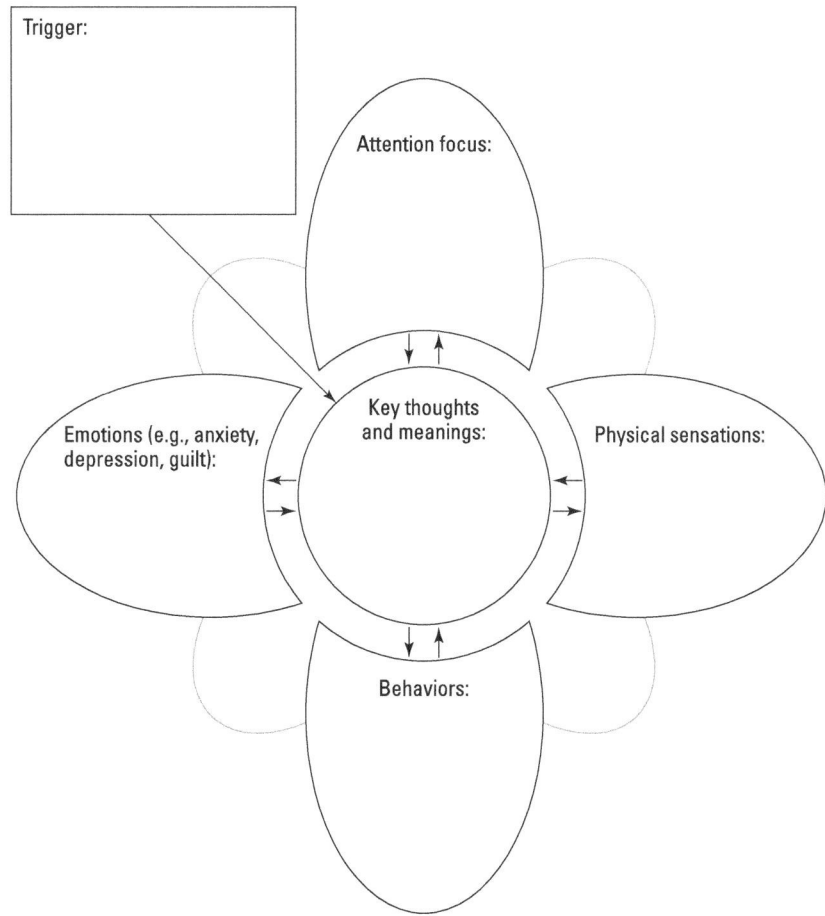

The Task-Concentration Sheet

Head to Chapter 6 for more about the task-concentration exercise, and a filled-in example.

Situation	Attention	Excercise	Feeling	Results
Who were you with? Where were you? What were you doing?	Record your focus of attention. Note what you focused on most. 1. Self % 2. Task % 3. Environment and other people % (Total = 100%)	Use task concentration to direct your attention outward. Remember to focus on your task or environment. Note what you did.	Record how you felt.	Record anything you learned from the excercise. Note how the situation turned out, changes in your anxiety level and your ability to complete the task.

The ABC Form I

This form helps you to make sense of how your thoughts, feelings, and behaviors interact, a core principle of CBT.

1. **In the "Consequences" box, point 1, write down the emotion you're feeling.**
2. **In the "Consequences" box, point 2, write down how you acted.**
3. **In the "Activating Event" box, write down what triggered your feelings.**
4. **In the "Beliefs" box, write down your thoughts, attitudes, and beliefs.**
5. **In the "Thinking Error" box, consider what your thinking errors may be.**

Refer to Chapter 4 for more detailed instructions on filling out the first ABC form.

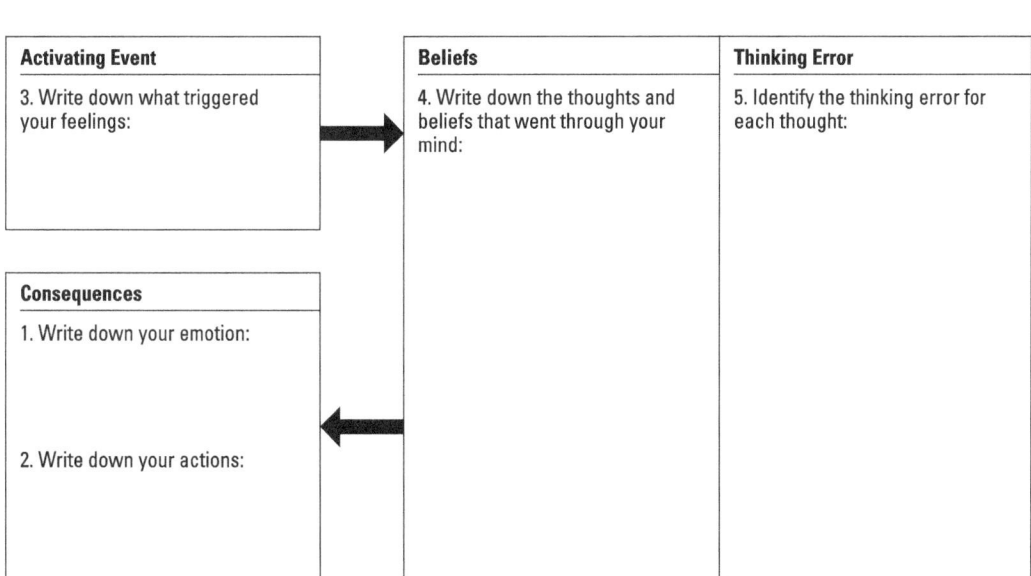

The "ABC" Form #I

Date _____

Activating Event	Beliefs	Thinking Error
3. Write down what triggered your feelings:	4. Write down the thoughts and beliefs that went through your mind:	5. Identify the thinking error for each thought:

Consequences
1. Write down your emotion:
2. Write down your actions:

The ABC Form II

Follow the guidance at the bottom of the form and head to Chapter 4 for more detailed instructions on filling in the second ABC form.

Date _____

The "ABC" Form #II

Activating Event (Trigger).	**B**eliefs, thoughts, and attitudes about **A**.	**C**onsequences of A+B on your emotions and behaviors.	**D**ispute (question and examine) **B** and generate alternatives. The questions at the bottom of the form will help you with this.	**E**ffect of alternative thoughts and beliefs (**D**).
2. Briefly write down what triggered your emotions. (e.g. event, situation, sensation, memory, image)	3. Write down what went through your mind, or what **A** *meant* to you. **B**'s can be about you, others, the world, the past, or the future.	1. Write down what emotion you felt and how you acted when you felt this emotion.	4. Write an alternative for each **B**, using supporting arguments and evidence.	5. Write down how you feel and wish to act as consequence of your alternatives at **D**.
		Emotions e.g: Depression, guilt, hurt, anger, shame, jealousy, envy, anxiety. Rate intensity 0–100.		**Emotions** Re-rate 0–100. List any healthy alternative emotion e.g. Sadness, regret, concern.
		Behavior e.g. Avoidance, withdrawing, escape, using alcohol or drugs, seeking reassurance, procrastination.		**Alternative Behavior or Experiment** e.g. Facing situation, increased activity, assertion.

Disputing (Questioning and Examining) and Generating Alternative Thoughts, Attitudes, and Beliefs: 1. Identify your 'thinking errors' at **B** (e.g. Mind Reading, Catastrophising, Labelling, Demands, etc.). Write them next to the appropriate 'B'. 2. Examine whether the evidence at hand supports that your thought at **B** is 100% true. Consider whether someone whose opinions you respect would totally agree with your conclusions. 3. Evaluate the helpfulness of each **B**. Write down what you think might be a more helpful, balanced and flexible way of looking at **A**. Consider what you would advise a friend to think, what a role model of yours might think, or how you might look at **A** if you were feeling OK. 4. Add evidence and arguments that support your alternative thoughts, attitudes and beliefs. Write as if you were trying to persuade someone you cared about.

Index

graded practice (task concentration exercise), 82–83

guilt
    about depression, 113, 158
    action tendencies, 109–110
    attention focus, 110–111
    demand-based thinking, 107
    as obstacle to progress, 327
    themes linked with, 106–107

H

haemophobia, 153

HARD LOSS
    anger, 312
    depression, 312
    hurt, 311
    loneliness, 312
    overwhelmed, 312
    reward, 312
    self-pity, 312
    stagnant, 312

head-to-heart problem, 292–293

health. *See also* exercise
    anger, effect on, 262
    friendships and, 315
    intimate relationships and, 316–318
    overview, 305–306
    personal care, 308
    relapse, preventing, 306
    sexuality, 317–318
    spare time, activities for, 306–308
    spirituality, 314

health anxiety/illness anxiety disorder, 43

healthy emotions
    action tendencies, 109–110
    attention focus, 110–111
    checklist for assessing, 113
    comparing to unhealthy, 96–104
    naming emotions, 94–95
    physical sensations, 111–112
    preference-based thinking, 108
    themes, 106–107
    thinking what to feel, 96
    unhealthy positive emotions, 113

helplessness, 45

high frustration tolerance (HFT), 39, 239, 252–253

hobbies, 306–307, 367

hopelessness, 45, 158

human being, valuing worth as, 231–232

hurt, 311
    synonyms for, 95

hypomania, 169

I

icons, inspiring, 135

ignoring resurging problems, avoiding, 337

illness, physical changes due to, 211

illness anxiety disorder (IAD), 70
    acting against, 218–219
    characteristics of, 214
    disorders associated with, 213
    experiment for, 216
    fear of missing symptoms, minimising, 216
    interpreting physical sensations, 217–218
    overview, 174, 213
    physical sensations unrelated to illness, 215–216

imperfect self-acceptance, 244

inactivity, depression and, 157, 161–162

inconsiderate behavior, 13

individuality, valuing, 363

influencing others, 124, 373–374

insomnia, 222

inspiration
    for change, 134–135
    for self-acceptance, 239–240

interactions between core beliefs, 275–276

internal criteria, 180–181

internalising alternative beliefs, 292–293

interpersonal therapy (IPT), 348

interpersonal triggers, 339

intrinsic value, 231

intrusive thoughts
    thought suppression, 127–128
    tolerating, 88–90, 179–180

IPT. *See* interpersonal therapy (IPT)

isolating and mood-depressing behaviors, 15

J

jealousy
    effect on relationships, 365
    intolerance of uncertainty, 121–124
    need for control, 120–121
    synonyms for, 95

About the Authors

Rob Willson, PhD, is a cognitive behavior therapist, with a special interest in OCD, BDD, and Illness anxiety disorder. He has worked in the field for 30 years. Rob currently divides the majority of his work time between seeing patients, supervising, writing, and teaching. He is the chair of Body Dysmorphic Disorder (BDD) Foundation, the world's first charity exclusively devoted to BDD. Before building his own practice, Rob spent 12 years working at the Priory Hospital North London where he was a therapist and therapy services manager. He also trained and supervised numerous CBT therapists over a seven-year period working at Goldsmiths College, University of London. Rob has written several CBT-based books and is passionate about disseminating CBT principles through self-help.

Rhena Branch BSc, MSc, Dip CBT, is a BABCP-accredited CBT therapist and holds a post-graduate clinical supervision qualification. Rhena has recently left her London practice to relocate to Norfolk. She now runs a private practice in Norwich. Rhena lectured and supervised, alongside Prof. Windy Dryden, on the MSc course in CBT/REBT at Goldsmith's College, University of London, for 14 years. She also lectured and supervised on the post-graduate CBT diploma at Anglia Ruskin University for three years. Rhena is currently an Associate Tutor in the psychology department at the University of East Anglia. She has written several books on CBT in addition to her *For Dummies* publications.

Dedication

From Rob: For my parents.

From Rhena: For Felix and Atticus as always.

Authors' Acknowledgments

From Rob: It is humbling to be asked to update a 4th edition of this book. I want to thank the team at Wiley, especially Thomas and Tracy, for helping to bring this edition into being. I'd also like to thank Katie for her technical edits.

From Rhena: It's greatly rewarding and exciting that this book continues to be helpful to our readers. As it enters the 4th edition, I am thankful for the team at Wiley for their support. In particular, Thomas and Tracy, you have both been great to work with.

I would like to extend my sincere gratitude to Windy Dryden for his guidance, inspiration, and generosity over the years.

Thank you to Rob for his input.

From both of us: Many researchers, fellow therapists, and authors have influenced our understanding and practice of CBT over the years and therefore the content in this book. Founding fathers, Albert Ellis and Aaron T. Beck, of course merit special mention. Others include (in no specific order): Ray DiGiuseppe, Mary-Anne Layden, Jacqueline Persons, David A. Clarke, Adrian Wells, Stanley Rachman, Paul Salkovskis, Christine Padesky, Michael Neenan, David Veale, David M. Clark, David Burns, Kevin Gournay, and many more.

Special thanks go to Windy Dryden for his extensive writings and for teaching us both so much.

Finally, a genuine thank you to all our clients (past and present) for allowing us to get to know you and learn from you.

Publisher's Acknowledgments

Acquisitions Editor: Tracy Boggier

Project Editor: Thomas Hill

Copy Editor: Karen Gill

Technical Editor: Katie D'Ath

Managing Editor: Murari Mukundan

Production Editor: Magesh Elangovan

Cover Image: © Marina Denisenko/Getty Images